THE LAST CARD

INSIDE GEORGE W. BUSH'S DECISION TO SURGE IN IRAQ

EDITED BY
TIMOTHY ANDREWS SAYLE,
JEFFREY A. ENGEL,
HAL BRANDS,
AND WILLIAM INBODEN

CORNELL UNIVERSITY PRESS

Ithaca and London

Copyright © 2019 by Cornell University

All rights reserved. Except for brief quotations in a review, this book, or parts thereof, must not be reproduced in any form without permission in writing from the publisher. For information, address Cornell University Press, Sage House, 512 East State Street, Ithaca, New York 14850. Visit our website at cornellpress.cornell.edu.

First published 2019 by Cornell University Press

Printed in the United States of America

Library of Congress Cataloging-in-Publication Data

Names: Sayle, Timothy A., editor. | Engel, Jeffrey A.,
    editor. | Brands, Hal, 1983– editor. | Inboden, William,
    1972– editor.
Title: The last card : inside George W. Bush's decision
    to surge in Iraq / edited by Timothy Andrews Sayle,
    Jeffrey A. Engel, Hal Brands, and William Inboden.
Description: Ithaca [New York] : Cornell University Press,
    2019. | Includes bibliographical references and index.
Identifiers: LCCN 2019009158 (print) | LCCN 2019009537
    (ebook) | ISBN 9781501715198 (e-book epub/mobi) |
    ISBN 9781501715204 (e-book pdf) | ISBN 9781501715181 |
    ISBN 9781501715181? (hardcover ;?alk. paper)
Subjects: LCSH: Iraq War, 2003–2011—Decision making. |
    Iraq War, 2003–2011—Campaigns. | Counterinsurgency—
    Iraq—History. | Military planning—United States. |
    United States—Military policy—Decision making. |
    Iraq—Politics and government—2003–
Classification: LCC DS79.76 (ebook) | LCC DS79.76 .L37
    2019 (print) | DDC 956.7044/34—dc23
LC record available at https://lccn.loc.gov/2019009158

Contents

Editorial Note vii

Introduction: The American Occupation
of Iraq by 2006 and the Search for a
New Strategy Timothy Andrews Sayle
and Hal Brands   1

Part 1

1. America's War in Iraq: 2003–2005   25

2. This Strategy Is Not Working: January–
   June 2006   46

3. Together Forward? June–August 2006   74

4. Silos and Stovepipes: September–
   October 2006   89

5. Setting the Stage: Early November 2006   113

6. A Sweeping Internal Review: Mid–Late
   November 2006   130

7. Choosing to Surge: December 2006   153

8. What Kind of Surge? Late December
   2006–January 2007   182

Part 2

9. How the "Surge" Came to Be Stephen
   Hadley, Meghan O'Sullivan,
   and Peter Feaver   207

10. Iraq, Vietnam, and the Meaning
    of Victory Andrew Preston   239

11. Decisions and Politics Robert Jervis   260

12. Blood, Treasure, and Time:
Strategy-Making for the Surge
Richard K. Betts   277

13. Strategy and the Surge Joshua Rovner   296

14. Civil-Military Relations and the 2006
Iraq Surge Kori Schake   314

15. The Bush Administration's Decision
to Surge in Iraq: A Long and
Winding Road Richard H. Immerman   328

16. The President as Policy Entrepreneur:
George W. Bush and the 2006 Iraq
Strategy Review Colin Dueck   344

Appendix A. Cast of Characters   *361*

Appendix B. Time Line   *363*

Notes   *367*

Acknowledgments   *394*

Contributors   *395*

Index   *397*

Editorial Note

This is a work of oral history, allowing the participants in a historic event an opportunity to tell their story, and recast their memories, in their own words. It is also a work of analysis, putting those memories to the test. The eight narrative chapters in part 1 have been crafted from the transcripts of twenty-eight interviews conducted between March 2015 and September 2016. (Individual interview dates can be found in appendix A.)

Textual accuracy has been one of our central goals. For the sake of clarity, however, we have made emendations, corrections, and annotations, eliminating some stock words, phrases, and quirks of speech, such as "you know." We have also on occasion eliminated false starts and corrections and necessarily imposed sentence and paragraph structure on the spoken language. Natural breaks made by the speakers have been signified by the em dash (—). We have used ellipses (. . .) to inform of the removal of text within a paragraph. For the sake of clarity and readability, the editors have not signified textual breaks between paragraphs. Text may have been eliminated between paragraphs, or paragraphs reordered if a speaker returned, later in the interview, to provide context to an earlier thought.

These changes are made for reading clarity, but without loss of accuracy. Full transcripts, and more importantly video, of nearly every interview are concurrently available for public scrutiny on our associated website, at https://www.smu.edu/CPH/. To allow readers to identify the relevant passages and quotations in either the transcript or the video of the interview, citations to the oral histories use minute markers instead of page numbers. Minute markers in the notes indicate the last minute marker in the transcript or the video before the quotation or paraphrased remark. The entire project is a memory archive; this book is an attempt to impose order on views from partners—and sometimes competitors—in one of the most critical strategic decision-making processes in recent American history. We therefore encourage considering the following pages as an appetizer for those scholars, students, and citizens who yearn to draw a fuller conclusion of their own.

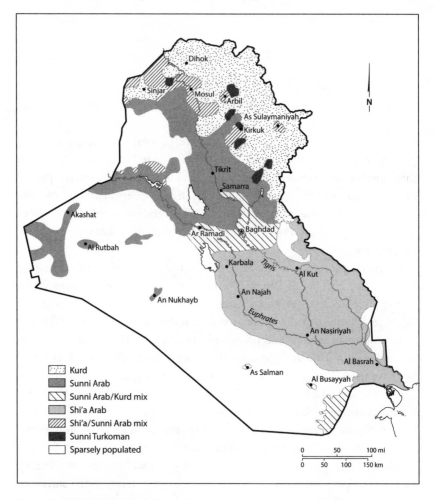

FIGURE 1.   Ethnic distribution in Iraq

Source: Adapted from "Ethnic Distribution in Iraq," in US Government Accountability Office, "Stabilizing Iraq: An Assessment of the Security Situation," no. GAO-06-1094T (September 11, 2006), p. 13, https://www.gao.gov/products/GAO-06-1094T.

Introduction

The American Occupation of Iraq by 2006 and the Search for a New Strategy

TIMOTHY ANDREWS SAYLE AND HAL BRANDS

"It is clear we need to change our strategy in Iraq." President George W. Bush's announcement, beamed to the nation from the White House library on January 10, 2007, was the first public announcement of what would come to be known as "the surge." On his command, more American troops would go to a country embroiled in war since 2003, in hope of finally quelling incessant, and increasing, violence. It was a desperate attempt to bring order to chaos, and to salvage his administration's signature foreign policy achievement: the ouster of Iraq's tyrannical despot, Saddam Hussein, nearly four years before. Unlike in 2003, however, when Bush ordered troops into harm's way, this time there was no similar confidence or seeming guarantee of success. In 2003, the American-led coalition against Saddam expected to win. This time, they weren't sure.

The speech and the change in policy it announced were hardly the work of spontaneous initiative, but instead marked the end of a long and secretive process designed to determine whether and how to change the course of a failing war in Iraq. The president's decision had not been easy. In fact, it had been resisted by most of his advisors, including many of his top military commanders, who feared greater loss of lives and treasure, and ultimately defeat. That was a sentiment Bush shared as well. "The president's job is to decide if we want to win or not," Bush said nearly a decade later when recalling that moment and the difficult months that led to it. "And if the strategy is not winning, then the president's job is to demand another strategy."

Iraq stood on the precipice of civil war as 2007 began, but it was hardly certain that more American troops and a new strategy could improve conditions on the ground. Many advisors feared that putting more US forces in Iraq would not turn the war around and would instead weaken American positions elsewhere around the globe while straining the US military to the breaking point. Bush and his top aides thus recognized that the surge constituted a major strategic gamble, as well as their final chance to restore a floundering US project in Iraq. As the president later told interviewers for this book, "I knew that this was our best shot, only shot."[1]

Prior to Bush's speech, the American strategy in Iraq had assumed that political progress would lead to improved security. It had emphasized fostering a democratic political process while training Iraqi security forces to enable the progressive withdrawal of US troops. As the development of pluralistic processes and institutions drew Iraqis into democratic politics, the logic behind this strategy ran, the appeal of insurgent and sectarian violence would wane; "As Iraqis stand up," Bush said in June 2005, "we will stand down."

By some measures this strategy had appeared to be working up until early 2006, but every success proved transitory, and enduring stability was elusive. Iraqis had elected a transitional National Assembly in January 2005, approved a new constitution, and in December 2005 voted in a parliamentary election. The maturing political process had seemed to some observers to validate the American strategy in Iraq. But in the months after the parliamentary election, political progress stalled while violence rocketed upward.

Throughout 2006, Bush received mixed assessments from his advisors in Washington, from the uniformed military leadership in the Pentagon, and from his military commander and ambassador in Iraq. Some argued that the American strategy was succeeding. Others warned that Iraq was near—if not already in—civil war, and that the US project in that country was careening toward irretrievable failure. In Baghdad, especially, Sunni extremists and Shia militias were killing civilians of the opposite sect, provoking more and bloodier retaliatory attacks. Iraq was trapped in what Bush called a "vicious cycle of sectarian violence."

The president's speech on January 10, 2007, announced a new strategy based on security leading to political progress. The new goal was to "put down" the interethnic killing by providing security for the civilian population, particularly in and around Baghdad and in Anbar Province in western Iraq. These improvements in security would then create space for political progress, the White House's strategy proposed, as Iraqis could then resolve their differences with ballots instead of bullets.

The new emphasis on security required more troops: five more brigades of US forces, totaling over thirty thousand servicemen and women.[2] For a military—and an American populace—already strained by five years of constant war since the terrorist attacks of September 2001, and worn down by growing casualty lists in particular, this was a daunting development. More troops deployed among the population would likely result in more deaths and injuries, at least in the short term. A surge in military force would also have to be paired with more effective efforts from, and reconciliation among, Iraqis if it were to succeed. This new strategy, the increase in American troops for Iraq, and the installation of a new "country team"—that is, a new field commander and a new ambassador in Iraq—have come to be known as "the surge." Bush ordered the surge of forces to Iraq because he wanted to win the war, but also because he believed the nation could not bear the costs of losing. As he later urged his interviewers, "You've got to ask the question, what caused me to want to win?" His answer was that he "understood the stakes"—he understood that US failure in Iraq would have profound and far-reaching geopolitical consequences—and that he "believed we could win." "I believed we could win because we're a superior military," Bush recalled, "but I also believed we could win because we have a superior philosophy to those we're fighting."[3] Freedom and democracy, he had long argued, held universal appeal, and would prevail if given enough time to incubate and grow.

Bush also viewed the struggle in Iraq within the broader context of American goals, and its grand strategy, since 9/11. That strategy, the president recounted in his interview, "spoke to an ideology of marginalizing the thugs—that in order to have a peaceful world, there has to be an ideology that takes root, and it would not take root without US influence." Finally, and as Bush acknowledged, there was a deeply personal component to his quest to find a path to victory in Iraq that meant keeping faith with the military and the families of the fallen. "I could not stand the thought of allowing somebody who sacrificed to just wither on the battlefield. . . . I couldn't stand the thought of making decisions that enabled defeat. How could I look at a mother and say your son—what your son did ended up being useless. And so behind the thought was, failure was not an option for me."[4]

The president's remarks provide a window onto his thinking on one of the most consequential decisions of his presidency. It was, indeed, arguably the most difficult decision he faced in office, more so even than his initial decision to invade Iraq in 2003. Military strategists predicted victory then, but offered no sense of similar confidence when evaluating the surge's likelihood of success. But Bush's remarks only hint at a much more complex process and rationale that informed the making of the surge. So how and why did the president decide that a new strategy was necessary for Iraq, and why did he choose the surge? This book seeks to answer those questions by drawing on a significant body of newly available evidence, and drawing in particular on the memories of the men and women who played out that drama in the months leading up to January 2007.

Part 1 of this book contains edited transcripts of interviews with the president and twenty-seven top officials who participated in the complex and secretive series of reviews and meetings leading up to Bush's surge announcement. Aside from Bush, these officials include Vice President Dick Cheney as well as Secretary of State Condoleezza Rice, Secretary of Defense Robert Gates, Chairman of the Joint Chiefs of Staff Peter Pace, and National Security Advisor Stephen Hadley. Military commanders and diplomats who served in key positions in Washington and in Iraq described their views of, and role in, the president's decision-making process. Top aides from National Security Council staff, other officials from the Departments of State and Defense and the intelligence community, and key players outside the government similarly recounted how they worked toward a new strategy for Iraq. These are detailed oral history interviews, which address the nuances and complexities of the decision-making process and provide unprecedented historical insight on that process. The editors of this volume subsequently arranged this "evidence," as in all works of history, to tell what they consider an insider's history of the surge.

Collectively these interviews provide not merely a narrative of events, but also a broader resource for future students and scholars of how Bush came to make one of the weightiest decisions of his presidency. They have been edited in this volume only for length, not in any way for substance. Full transcripts (and in most cases video) of those interviews are being simultaneously published online with this book as part of the Center for Presidential History's "Collective Memory Project," a broad oral history of the life and times of the Bush years. Founded in 2012, this center provides nonpartisan historical assessments of American history and of its national leaders. Partners from the University of Texas–Austin, Duke University, Johns Hopkins University, and Harvard University, including veterans of the Bush administration, were consulted for their unique knowledge of the national security process within that administration. Our shared goal: to couple free and unhindered academic inquiry with the singular expertise that can come only from firsthand participants.

Interviewees were thus offered the opportunity to tell their tale, in their own words, to teams of interviewers. The interviewers included both participants in the surge process and historians unaffiliated in any way with the administration. Their questions were designed neither to praise or indict but to elicit full responses, and with an eye toward compiling a useful resource for future generations. The most critical stipulation guiding the process was that interviewees agreed to go "on the record," without opportunity to subsequently sanitize or alter their testimony. In all but one case (President Bush), the full interview is wholly available and accessible to the public. In all but two cases (President Bush and Vice President Cheney) these interviews were videotaped; in only a handful of cases were our requests for interviews declined.[5]

Part 2 of this volume complements the oral history narrative with analysis and interpretation of the interviews. It includes a firsthand account of the decision-making process in the White House as recalled by Stephen Hadley and two other key architects of the surge strategy: the deputy national security advisor for Iraq and Afghanistan, Meghan O'Sullivan, and the special advisor for strategic planning and institutional reform, Peter Feaver. Seven leading historians and political scientists, experts with long pedigrees in intelligence, security studies, foreign policy, and civil-military relations, then provide their respective assessments of what these oral histories reveal. These scholars, with full access to the interview transcripts, assess the decision-making process and place it in historical and strategic perspective. For most of the interviewees, the war in Iraq offered the critical moment of their careers; for these scholars it was but one, granted a contemporary one, of a long series of crises faced and decisions made by American presidents through time. To judge the surge, in other words, one must appreciate not only its peculiar and particular context, but consider comparable moments as well.

This book thus offers a new account of presidential and administration decision making in the run-up to a momentous change in America's war in Iraq. To be clear, this book is not a history of the subsequent implementation of the surge by US military forces and civilian personnel in Iraq. Neither is it designed to assess the outcome of the surge or adjudicate the wisdom and necessity of the Iraq War itself. Those questions will no doubt be exhaustively assessed by future historians. Moreover, given the complexity of the implementation of the surge and the debates surrounding it, the Obama administration's later decisions regarding troop deployments in Iraq, and the rise of the Islamic State, among other ongoing regional quandaries, including the ensuing Syrian civil war, any rigorous assessment of the surge's effects will require additional volumes. But we cannot begin to grapple with the history of the surge without understanding how it came to be in the first place. Telling that story is the purpose of this book, and this project.

The history of the surge must begin with another presidential address to the nation. A little after 10 p.m. Eastern time on March 19, 2003, George W. Bush announced that "American and coalition forces are in the early stages of military operations to disarm Iraq, to free its people and to defend the world from grave danger." The Iraq War had begun.

Although Bush warned the country that military operations in Iraq could "be longer and more difficult than some predict," it certainly did not appear that way in the spring of 2003. The American invasion of Iraq was a military marvel. Although planners had hoped for a two-front attack against Saddam's forces, Turkey's refusal to serve as a launching pad for the US assault caused a last-minute change of plans for Operation Iraqi Freedom (OIF). Nonetheless, the relatively small invasion force—fewer than 150,000 American troops supported by 20,000 British and coalition troops—a small fraction of the number of forces the US and its allies had used to evict the Iraqi military from Kuwait in Operation Desert Storm in 1991—raced toward Baghdad.[6] The invasion force, purposely limited in size to preserve agility and strategic surprise, routed or bypassed Iraqi forces and quickly shattered Saddam's regime. Early premonitions of severe fighting in Iraq's urban centers, and of thousands of Iraqi and coalition casualties, turned out to be overstated—for the time being.

On May 1, President Bush flew to the aircraft carrier USS *Abraham Lincoln* and declared an end to major combat operations. With this phase of OIF complete, American planners looked forward to a rapid drawdown that might see as few as twenty-five thousand US troops left in Iraq by the fall of 2003.[7] But preinvasion plans had overestimated the level of stability that would follow Saddam's defeat. As one history of OIF, drafted by the Center for Army Lessons Learned, put it, "the great challenge of OIF" would prove to be not the campaign to topple Saddam, but the "struggle to create a new Iraq in place of the Saddam regime."[8]

If the United States had been well prepared to topple Saddam's regime, it was not adequately prepared for the task of creating this "new Iraq" in its place. Prewar planning for the postwar phase of the conflict had focused largely on issues such as the treatment of large Iraqi military units that were expected to surrender en masse, as had happened during the Persian Gulf War, and with avoiding a humanitarian catastrophe. Those plans did not adequately deal with the scenario that ultimately emerged: the removal of

Saddam's regime effectively brought down the entire structure of Iraqi government beneath him and unleashed significant disorder and even chaos. Nor did the administration's plans fully grapple with the daunting complexity and difficulty of transforming Iraq—a country riven by sectarian and ethnic cleavages and traumatized by decades of tyranny, with little history of pluralistic governance—into the functioning democracy Bush and those around him envisioned. An alarming level of looting, violence, and general public disorder prevailed instead almost from the outset following the invasion, and American officials consistently found themselves behind the curve—and working with insufficient levels of troops and other critical resources—in grappling with this and other problems of occupation.

This situation created a serious challenge for the Coalition Provisional Authority (CPA)—a temporary government for occupied Iraq headed by Ambassador L. Paul Bremer III. Contrary to the expectation of US military planners, Bremer was convinced that the establishment of a new and effective system of governance in Iraq would take time and require the sustained presence of US troops. In mid-May, the CPA—after hasty and apparently somewhat ambiguous consultations with President Bush—issued its first two orders designed to root out the remnants of Saddam's Baathist dictatorship and create the political conditions for democratization. CPA Order 1 mandated the "de-Baathification" of Iraqi society—that is, the removal of thirty thousand members of Saddam's Baath party from positions of responsibility.[9] CPA Order 2 effectively disbanded the Iraqi military—or rather, made clear that the CPA had no intention of reconstituting an Iraqi military that had essentially dissolved in the course of the invasion and its aftermath.

Both orders had major consequences for the occupation, and particularly for Iraq's Sunni population. Saddam had used his party and the armed forces to elevate the minority Sunnis above both the more populous Shias and the Kurds of Iraq. By removing the Baath Party from power and dismantling the armed forces, the CPA achieved some success in convincing the Shia and the Kurds that the United States was not simply propping up Saddam's henchmen and planning to replace him with a new Sunni strongman. These previously disenfranchised groups were thus persuaded to play a role in the country's emerging political structure.[10] The CPA also planned a series of elections and a process for writing an Iraqi constitution, the goal of which was reestablishing Iraq as a self-governing state.

It would not prove that easy. Throughout the spring and summer, insurgent attacks against American troops and their coalition partners increased in number and scale. By July 2003, the commander of US Central Command, John Abizaid, declared that Iraqis were fighting a "classical guerrilla-type campaign" against the coalition, even as other officials, particularly Secretary of Defense Donald Rumsfeld, took pains to deny that the United States confronted anything other than embittered elements of the former regime.[11] Looking back in 2004, a US Army intelligence officer charged with leading a "red team" to study the deteriorating situation in Iraq noted a connection between the two CPA orders and the guerrilla campaign, now increasingly referred to as "the insurgency." According to the intelligence officer, CPA Orders 1 and 2 effectively stripped the Sunni minority of the power they once held in Iraq and "flipped the social, economic, and political order on its head."[12]

De-Baathifcation, it seemed to David Petraeus—the general who was charged with pacifying and administering the city of Mosul during the aftermath of the invasion, and who would later command US and coalition forces during the surge—caused the Sunnis of Iraq to lose hope, by demonstrating that "there was no place for them in the new Iraq." Such disaffection, he pointed out, "obviously made for fertile ground for AQI"—that is, al-Qaeda in Iraq, a new source of violence that would soon push Iraq to the brink of civil war.[13]

By the summer of 2003, coalition forces and other institutions associated with the occupation were under attack. In August, Baghdad was rocked by two spectacular and deadly attacks, one against the Jordanian Embassy and another against a United Nations compound. Seventeen perished in the first, with dozens wounded. The second cost twenty-two lives, including the UN's Special Representative in Iraq, with more than one hundred additionally wounded. Abu Musab al-Zarqawi, the Jordanian who led AQI—itself a mix of Iraqi and foreign fighters—claimed responsibility for the attack on the UN compound and was assumed to be responsible for the attack on the embassy.[14] But by the autumn of 2003, coalition troops saw evidence that foreigners were not the only targets of attacks. Growing evidence emerged of interethnic violence—Iraqis killing Iraqis. In isolation, these events suggested a continuing absence of security and an increasingly explosive situation.

Conditions, however, were not universally dire. There were also positive trends at work in the early days of the occupation. By the end of 2003 and into 2004, Iraqis seemed to be making political progress as the CPA's election and constitutional plans moved forward. Attacks declined in number, if not in lethality. When Saddam Hussein was captured near his hometown of Tikrit, after being found in a "spider hole"—a small concealed dugout—it seemed that the former regime had been fully put to rest, and that Iraq's fortunes could finally improve.[15]

The new year, however, began inauspiciously. In January 2004, US forces intercepted a letter from Abu Musab al-Zarqawi to the leadership of al-Qaeda. Zarqawi, a thug-turned-jihadist, planned to draw the Iraqi Shia population "into a sectarian war" by "striking religious, political and military symbols."[16] In early 2004, foreign fighters and al-Qaeda affiliates, like Zarqawi's AQI, were small in number, even if their attacks captured headlines.[17] Zarqawi would continue to plan assassinations and try to spark civil war in Iraq—something he would nearly achieve in 2006.

Through 2004, the basic paradox of US policy in Iraq persisted: the political situation seemed to improve, but security deteriorated. In March, Iraqi political developments took a step forward with the approval of the Transitional Administrative Law—a temporary constitution that would take effect when Iraq achieved sovereignty. Yet just a month later the situation took a step back, and parts of Iraq descended again into violence. In April, after Sunni insurgents killed and mutilated four American security contractors, US forces, supported by recently trained elements of a new Iraqi security force, responded with an attack on the city of Fallujah. The first battle of Fallujah (as it came to be called) revealed glaring flaws in the training and commitment of the new Iraqi forces and ended in a major embarrassment for both the Iraqi government and US forces when political pressures forced the assault to end with insurgents still in control of the city. Failure to dislodge them, and misleading media reports suggesting that US forces had shown a wanton disregard for civilian suffering, constituted a propaganda coup for anti-coalition forces and polarized opinion in Iraq. As one CPA advisor put it after the battle, "Two weeks ago Iraqis wanted to see us make promises and deliver on them—rebuild, improve—but then they saw pictures of US bombs falling on a mosque in Fallujah. Now they want us out."[18] The role AQI played in the fighting at Fallujah transformed it into the most dangerous element of the insurgency.[19]

Around the same time US and Iraqi forces were fighting the Sunnis in Fallujah, American forces came under attack by Shia forces elsewhere. Muqtada al-Sadr, a Shiite cleric, had gained a large political following and militia, the Jaysh al-Mahdi. In April 2004, the CPA, concerned by Sadr's strident anti-American rhetoric, moved to close his newspaper, while an Iraqi judge issued a warrant for the cleric's arrest. In response, Sadr directed his Shia forces to attack the coalition in and around Baghdad.[20]

In June 2004, and in accordance with the political timeline the CPA had been working toward, Ambassador Bremer formally handed sovereignty back to Iraq. The security situation was becoming so dire, however—with US and coalition forces facing attacks from elements of Iraq's Sunni and Shia population—that he pushed the ceremony ahead of schedule by two days to prevent any attacks from tarnishing the symbolic moment.

With Iraq officially sovereign and the occupation formally ended, the United States created new structures for its diplomatic, political, and military efforts. President Bush appointed an ambassador to Iraq, whose embassy was paired with a new military command structure. The first commander of this Multi-National Force–Iraq (MNF-I) was General George Casey. MNF-I's goal, according to the command's "initial campaign framework," was an Iraq "at peace with its neighbors and an ally in the War on Terror, with a representative government that respects the human rights of all Iraqis, and security forces sufficient to maintain domestic order and to deny Iraq as a safe haven for terrorists."[21]

Yet the change in command and political structures brought this goal no closer to realization. Violence continued to rise; the formal end to occupation provided no reprieve. August 2004 saw the most attacks against coalition forces in more than a year.[22] That summer, another "red team," this one studying the insurgency, reported to Casey that the source of the violence was "rejectionists"—Sunni Iraqis who had lost power in their own country.[23] Casey and his staff agreed, however, that the strategic "center of gravity" for the MNF-I's campaign was not in Iraq but in the United States. Presuming they would succeed in stabilizing the country if given sufficient time, they ranked American public support for continued operations in Iraq as the most important ingredient for success. Within Iraq, the command decided, the theater-level center of gravity was the interim Iraqi government. The coalition, Casey decided, would work to enhance the legitimacy of the Iraqi government so that it could take primary responsibility for protecting its own people.[24]

Casey's plan fit with the "antibody theory" developed by General John Abizaid, commander of United States Central Command: "Foreign forces are always rejected" in the Middle East, Abizaid argued. "They're like a disease that enters into the organism, and then all the antibodies form and try to reject it." Ultimately, Casey and Abizaid believed that "we had to really move [American and coalition forces] out as quickly as we could to make the transition to Iraqi security force capacity."[25]

By the end of 2004, the centers of gravity in both the United States and Iraq showed minor cracks, but ultimately held. In November, US Marines and Army forces, joined by some Iraqi units, attacked Fallujah for a second time. The Iraqi government and their American allies, with an eye on the upcoming January 2005 elections, believed it imperative to ensure no major Iraqi city was under insurgent control. The second battle of Fallujah was more successful than the first, breaking open the insurgent safe haven. The same month, President Bush won reelection, but the war in Iraq was a source of controversy throughout the campaign. In December 2004, as the US Embassy and the MNF-I prepared for the following month's Iraqi National Assembly election, there was hope but also worry that Shia success in the election might further embitter Sunnis.[26]

The January election proceeded as planned, with the selection of 275 parliamentarians responsible for drafting a permanent constitution. Drawing on recent political progress in Iraq, and stirrings of political liberalism elsewhere in the Middle East, Bush proclaimed in his second inaugural address a new "policy of the United States to seek and support the growth of democratic movements and institutions in every nation and culture, with the ultimate goal of ending tyranny in our world."[27] The speech thereafter became known for heralding his "freedom agenda."[28]

Security continued to lag behind political progress in Iraq, however. As early as January 2005, Casey argued that it would be longer than expected before Iraqi forces were ready to maintain security. The US ambassador in Baghdad, John Negroponte, agreed and suggested the mission might take another five years, at least.[29] In February, Philip Zelikow, the counselor of the Department of State, visited Iraq and wrote to Secretary Rice that "Iraq remains a failed state shadowed by constant violence."[30] By August 2005 an increasing overlap had emerged between the work of insurgent, organized criminal groups and AQI. The Center for Army Lessons Learned would later identify seven distinct "major insurgent groups" at work during this period, running the gamut from Sunni to Shia, religious to nonreligious, Iraqi to foreign.[31]

The signals from Iraq were confusing. Why was violence still on the rise? Zarqawi publicly declared war on "Shia infidels," and suicide attacks continued as he worked to ignite a sectarian civil war. Coalition forces found that the Shia-dominated Ministry of the Interior had been mistreating, even torturing Sunni detainees.[32] The violence, then, had multiple sources and consisted of a large number of disparate conflicts, even if the violence occurred in a relatively small fraction of the country's geography. The seemingly unending chain of violent events in Iraq led to growing political critique back in the United States. In November, Democratic congressman Jack Murtha's call for the withdrawal of troops from Iraq raised concerns within the Bush administration about continuing public support for the war, especially given Murtha's stature on defense policy. Still, the calendar of Iraq's political milestones was unfolding according to plan, with more elections scheduled for December 2005.

In late 2005, members of the Bush administration, and particularly within the National Security Council staff, were therefore faced with a puzzle: Was there actually a problem with the US strategy in Iraq? If so, what was it? Acting on the belief that American strategy was still viable—but was simply not being properly explained to the American people—they undertook a major public relations campaign, producing a public "National Strategy for Victory in Iraq" (NSVI), which recast the two intertwined strategies the US had been pursuing for years. The political strategy was premised on the idea that strengthening moderate groups and politicians would isolate extremists. The strategic plan for security was to continue training Iraqi troops for domestic security responsibilities, in order to allow the gradual withdrawal of American forces, while US troops targeted al-Qaeda members.[33] Together, these twin strategies—essentially those pursued since 2003—rested on the conviction that an improved political process and stable government would solve Iraq's security problems and bring American involvement in the conflict to an end.

In December 2005, Iraq held its first general election under its new constitution. There was limited violence during the election, and high total voter turnout—2005 even came to be called the "year of the purple fingers," for the dyed digits used to mark those Iraqis who cast votes. This apparent political success revived hopes that Iraq's liberation from Saddam's rule might yet spark a broader democratic transformation throughout the Middle East.

Still, despite the high overall turnout and relative peacefulness of the elections, large parts of the Sunni population boycotted the vote. The American ambassador, Zalmay Khalilzad, worried that the election had increased the sense of disenfranchisement among Sunnis and also revealed growing Iranian influence on Shia politicians.[34] The new parliament was deadlocked, too, meaning that Iraq would not have a prime minister for months after the election. While the political process stalled, ongoing security problems collectively tore the country apart.

In February 2006 an explosion demolished the al-Askari mosque in Samarra, one of the holiest sites for the Shia. Suspicion immediately fell on AQI.[35] Officials and analysts then, as now, debate whether the attack on the mosque was a cause or symptom of internecine killings. Either way, the bombing was a milestone for a new period of intensifying violence, one that would bring the US mission in that country to the brink of failure—and one that would, ultimately, catalyze multiple internal reviews leading to the surge.

The remainder of this book describes that process of review and decision—first through oral histories that have been condensed and edited to provide a narrative of that process (part 1), and then through analysis and debate regarding the decision-making process and its outcome (part 2). Chapter 1 of the oral history traces the emerging concerns and contradictory signals reaching the president up until the end of 2005. While the political process continued along schedule in Iraq, violence also increased; at home, public support for the war seemed to waver. As NSC official Peter Feaver put it, "At that time I thought we didn't have a strategy problem, we had a failure-to-explain-our-strategy problem."[36] The administration persisted in its basic strategy in Iraq, while attempting to explain it more effectively at home with publication of the NSVI.

Chapter 2 examines the Samarra bombing and the resulting debates over its significance. The winter and spring of 2006 was a time of conflicting signals and conflicting efforts in Washington. Some officials—particularly on the NSC staff—began to believe that the strategy in Iraq was not working. The predominant view in the intelligence community, according to David Gordon, vice chairman of the National Intelligence Council, was that "we were transitioning into something very different, that we were really transitioning from insurgency to a civil war."[37]

Around the same time, the failings of the US mission in Iraq led a number of retired generals to publicly call for the ouster of Secretary of Defense Donald Rumsfeld. Unknown to its advocates, the public "Revolt of the Generals" actually undermined ongoing, internal efforts to replace the secretary of defense—and thus, ironically, delayed rather than accelerated a review of strategy in Iraq. Meanwhile, efforts from within government to rethink US strategy remained nascent and largely disconnected. The successful seating of the Iraqi government and a new prime minister, Nouri al-Maliki, and the success of US forces in locating and killing Zarqawi, undercut arguments that the war was failing, and in particular derailed efforts to kick off a major strategy review beginning with a high-level meeting at Camp David in June 2006.

Chapter 3 examines debates over US policy in the summer of 2006, focusing particularly on the unhappy results of military efforts to tamp down violence in Baghdad. Two major military operations—Operations Together Forward I and II—were launched, intended, as the chairman of the Joint Chiefs of Staff, Peter Pace, recalled, to "begin the process of turning over the battlefield responsibilities to the Iraqi armed forces."[38] Both were clear disappointments, however, revealing how unprepared Iraqi forces were to assume responsibility for their country's security. Iraqi forces themselves were, in the words of the National Security Council's Meghan O'Sullivan, "perpetuating acts of sectarian violence" and were "as much part of the problem as they are a solution to the problem." Throughout the summer, NSC staff thus sought to press the Iraq country team for a review of Iraq strategy, and pushed the president to ask General Casey harder questions about where the current approach was leading. But MNF-I and the US Embassy in Iraq continued to champion existing plans, believing that the existing strategy merely required more time.

Despite this resistance from the Iraq country team to reconsidering fundamental strategy, by late August and into the early fall of 2006 the internal impetus for change was growing stronger across the government. The core premises of NSVI were no longer tenable, recalled Feaver. "None of us believed those assumptions anymore."[39] These officials also worried that Washington had only limited time to make a course correction before the violence in Iraq spiraled out of control. Chapter 4 details a low-profile but intensive effort by NSC staff to review US options. Some officials believed it was necessary to increase US forces in Iraq as part of an overall change in strategy. Whether or not any such forces were available was another question entirely, and so the NSC staff undertook a clandestine effort within the US bureaucracy to calculate just how many additional troops might be available.

Chapter 4 also examines concurrent reviews, including one launched by the chairman of the Joint Chiefs of Staff. The chairman's group, known as the Council of Colonels, was formed to discuss the broader war on terror. As one member recalled, however, the group "simply could not get over the argument about 'what do we do about Iraq?'"[40] It was a remarkable aspect of the Iraq strategy debate that so little of these policy discussions leaked to the public, or were even known to those involved in parallel strategy reviews. This chapter offers explanations as to why these various reviews operated independently and discretely.

Chapter 5 begins with two trips to Iraq, the first by Secretary of State Rice, and the second by National Security Advisor Hadley. Hadley's trip in November 2006 was particularly crucial—it was meant to gauge prospects for a change in course, and to determine whether Iraqi prime minister Nouri al-Maliki was a viable partner. Back in Washington, the Republican Party's loss of control of both houses of Congress in the midterm elections, along with Bush's eventual firing of Rumsfeld, interacted with the growing intellectual ferment inside government and led Bush to launch and publicly announce a formal review of strategy in Iraq. Rumsfeld's replacement, Robert Gates, while named to the post in early November, would not formally take charge for another month. Time was now of the essence for the president. He was losing the war in Iraq, and, as Stephen Cambone, the under secretary of defense for intelligence, put it, "he was losing the war here at home."[41]

Chapter 6 examines this review process, highlighting a series of high-level interagency meetings (along with intensive accompanying staff work and bureaucratic jockeying) as the members of the review group debated the status of US efforts in Iraq and began formally to consider alternatives. By Thanksgiving of 2006, the review group was wrapping up its work, albeit without a clear policy recommendation, and divergent reviews remained among Bush's advisors. In retrospect, some of the president's advisors now believe that Bush himself was already leaning toward increasing US forces in Iraq as part of a new strategy; at the time, however, many thought the president had not made up his mind and that the deliberative process had simply deadlocked. As Deputy National Security Advisor J. D. Crouch recalled, the "document that we generated . . . was called, 'Iraq the Emerging Consensus'—no greater oxymoron had ever been created in government than that document."[42]

Chapter 7 traces a series of climactic meetings of the National Security Council in December 2006. By December, Vice President Cheney thought it was "pretty clear that we've got to do something different than what we've been doing. December was then devoted to sort of nailing down what that was going to be." The president and his advisors discussed fundamental issues regarding American goals and responsibilities in Iraq and increasingly concluded that only a surge option, as part of a change in military strategy and an effort at bottom-up political reconciliation in Iraq, could salvage the American mission there. That same month, the president visited the Joint Chiefs of Staff in their meeting room—"the tank"—to hear and address their concerns about whether an intensified military effort in Iraq might overtax the US military and even "break the force." In December, too, public discussion about the American future in Iraq was fueled by reports from the congressionally mandated Iraq Study Group, which advocated for a regional diplomatic strategy to help quell violence in Iraq—but did also mention the possibility of a temporary increase in US troop levels—as well as from the American Enterprise Institute, which advocated increasing US forces in Iraq and pursuing a proper counterinsurgency strategy. The impact of these external reviews on the eventual surge decision remains hotly debated; this chapter helps place these efforts within the context of the internal administration policy process and Bush's decision making.

Even by late December, just what the surge would mean in terms of the number and timing of troop deployments remained uncertain. Chapter 8 describes the trip by the new secretary of defense, Robert Gates, to Iraq, his recommendations regarding the surge, and the deliberations by the president and his advisors as to just what means would be available for a new American strategy. By January, however, as Bush publicly announced the change of direction, he had made the crucial decisions to adopt a new counterinsurgency strategy, which included committing up to five brigades, enlarging the overall size of the Army and Marine Corps, and appointing a new country team for Iraq—David Petraeus as commander, MNF-I, and Ryan Crocker as ambassador. Moreover, the president had largely unified the executive branch—which had just recently been riven by disagreement on Iraq—in support of this new strategy. By January, recalls Hadley, the president had "brought his national security team on board; he's brought his military on board; and he's got a strategy. . . . The effect the president wanted to achieve has been achieved."[43] The surge had been ordered.

Part 2 of this volume offers overlapping and at times competing analyses of the story revealed through these oral histories. First, three former National Security Council officials and seven leading scholars put the surge decision in historical context, analyze its strategic implications, and assess the policy process and role of the president. Drawing from the same data, they offer diverse and often widely divergent appraisals, particularly regarding the quality of the administration's decision-making process and ultimate product. With this range of assessments, our contributors demonstrate the respectful debate and probing inquiry that are hallmarks of academic research.

President Bush's national security advisor, Stephen J. Hadley, and two NSC staff members, Meghan O'Sullivan and Peter Feaver, begin part 2 with a participants' account. They offer firsthand insights about the logic of the surge strategy and the process by which that strategy emerged, as seen by three of its principal architects.

Cambridge University's Andrew Preston then compares Bush's decision-making process with that of another president in an earlier war. While not setting out to equate the Vietnam War with the Iraq War, Preston contrasts and compares Bush's decision to surge troops in 2007 with decisions taken by Lyndon B. Johnson in both 1965 and 1968. Columbia University's Robert Jervis, too, sees connections to Vietnam, as well as things to praise in the administration's decision making. He notes that the perceived lessons of Vietnam were in the back of policy makers' minds as they considered the US predicament in Iraq, and additionally notes that this episode demonstrates the power of bureaucracies in shaping information flows and policy options, as well as—paradoxically—of presidents in using their power and persuasion to bring reluctant bureaucracies along.

Richard Betts, also from Columbia University, places the surge decision in the context of the broader history of the Iraq War and offers a modestly positive appraisal. He examines various dilemmas and challenges that the war occasioned—of relating strategy to both operations and politics, of promoting democratization in Iraq while also seeking some control over Iraqi decision making, and of seeking to exert presidential command over a complex decision-making process. He argues that the surge decision reflected a "delicate and skillful exercise in leadership" given civil-military tensions, but questions how well the surge answered the broader strategic questions surrounding American involvement.

American University's Joshua Rovner also considers the relationship between strategy and the surge, but disputes the idea that the surge constituted a new US strategy in Iraq. He considers it instead a "decision to put strategy on hold." The surge, he argues, encouraged a perverse strategic effect—by obscuring the political objectives of the war, it undercut efforts to forge competent and self-reliant governance in Iraq and contributed to the breakdown of the Iraqi state in the face of the subsequent rise of the Islamic State.

The International Institute for Strategic Studies' Kori Schake, herself a veteran of the Bush and Clinton administrations with tours at the Pentagon, the State Department, and the NSC, offers another—albeit different—revisionist take on the surge, using the new evidence to challenge the notion that the effort emerged from a process characterized by high degrees of internal dysfunction and civil-military discord. Instead, she points out that the challenges and frustrations in the Bush administration stemmed primarily from difficulties among the president's civilian advisors, not between civilians and the uniformed military. She thus perceives a healthier and more constructive process than is generally appreciated.

Temple University's Richard Immerman also examines the policy process but delivers a far more critical assessment. Taking issue with the fact that a number of key participants in surge decision making subsequently lauded that process on both procedural and substantive grounds, Immerman—using the Eisenhower administration as a model of peacetime national security decision making—argues that the process displayed by these oral histories was in fact idiosyncratic, excessively compartmentalized, and profoundly flawed. If the decision-making process was successful, he argues, success was due to individuals who adapted an ad hoc system when the regular policy process was too polluted to be effective. Immerman dedicates his chapter to the memory of Fred Greenstein, an exceptional scholar and mentor whose influence is evident throughout the chapter.

Finally, George Mason University's Colin Dueck focuses on the role of Bush himself, arguing that by 2006–2007, the president had become a more mature and assertive commander-in-chief who asked hard questions of his military commanders and pushed the policy process to deliver strategic alternatives. The president successfully related the policy advice he received to the political requirements and constraints he faced to fashion a new strategy for the Iraq War. His success in doing so, Dueck argues, might constitute the basis for a modest form of "Bush revisionism."

These perspectives are as rich as they are diverse, their authors finding common ground on some issues even as they disagree on many others. Readers can thus trace their themes and debates through the chapters that follow; nonetheless, five overarching issues might be flagged at the outset.

First, all the authors—as well as the editors, interviewers, and interviewees—are aware that oral history couples limitations with potential benefits. These words represent how the men and women involved remember those difficult months. These are their words, quite literally, and interviewers strove to encourage these participants to history to tell their story, in their own words. This is the tale of the surge as told by those who conceived of it, and most importantly, of those who influenced the man who ultimately ordered it. It is their story.

That unique perspective is the good part; now the bad. Memories can be hazy and, indeed, sometimes incorrect. Participants can be convinced that they were at the center of a policy process that had more moving parts than they realized. As part of his interview, James Jeffrey makes an important point: to the historian, the history of the surge decision may appear as "a discrete set of meetings, speeches, announcements, troop deployments, elections, and other things, and it looks like heartbeats, boom, ba-boom." But this is misleading; the process was not as clear as a cardiogram. "To somebody who's doing this every day, either in Washington or in Baghdad, it's all a blur, and for everything that I would be able to tell you in the two hours or in twenty hours, there were one hundred other things we were doing that seemed to be the most important thing in the world."[44]

The oral history process, at least, allows for participants to try to explain what the blur looked like or felt like; they can capture the mood and the energy that is sometimes absent from a purely documentary approach. They can agree and, as readers will see, frequently disagree over timelines, motivations, perspectives, and even the efficacy of the entire policy-making process. That is their right, and our goal was to record those thoughts for history. A thousand (if not more) dissertations lie within the stories told in these pages, and even more topics for study. That is why the full transcripts of these interviews and, crucially, video documentation of them, are available to all. There are undoubtedly more individuals who participated in the debates and planning leading up to the surge than could be interviewed for this project, and we encourage others to continue to add their voices to the record.

Just as crucial as the archival record will be for the study of this era broadly, the value of oral history is that it captures things left out of the paper and digital records. As David Satterfield mentions, "Papers and events are the product of near continuous verbal exchanges, e-mail exchanges, policy exchanges and discussions—some on paper, some not on paper—that proceed and that follow all of this."[45] Though they constitute only a part of the overall wealth of evidence historians will eventually employ to understand this critical period in American history, the oral histories below capture intimate impressions of these exchanges—this blur of activity—directly from those involved.

A word then about who is *not* heard within these pages. Several key participants—Donald Rumsfeld and George Casey in particular, secretary of defense and commanding general of the Multinational Force in Iraq respectively—declined multiple invitations to retell their story for this project. Their perspectives would undoubtedly have changed the ensuing narrative. Our invitations remain open should they or others engaged in this moment of history choose to add their perspectives.

Readers hoping to hear the words of key participants in the surge's implementation, General David Petraeus and Ambassador Ryan Crocker in particular, who oversaw operations in Iraq following Bush's January 2007 speech, will be disappointed. Theirs is largely a different story, one of development of counterinsurgency doctrine and its deployment. The question that animated this project, and this book, was subtly but critically different: how did a president come to change course in the midst of a war many of his closest advisors believed lost. It is a question of presidential decision making. Neither does this study seek to answer the question of the surge's ultimate utility, the efficacy of subsequent American policies in Iraq or toward the broader Middle East, or even Bush's critical decision to go to war in 2003 in the first place. Questions abound, but ours was one of presidential decision making, and the cast of characters interviewed reflects those who helped Bush decide.

Vietnam offers a second critical theme, its long shadow pervading many of these essays—just as it pervaded the debate over Iraq in the period leading up to the surge. Both the historians and political scientists writing in this volume see resonance and reminders of the Vietnam War, though the scholars use these comparisons to elucidate the dilemmas faced by Bush and his advisors rather than to argue that Iraq was simply a replay of Vietnam. During the Bush presidency, of course, there was much talk by pundits of an Iraq "quagmire" that paralleled Vietnam; to say such comparisons were unwelcome to the administration is an understatement. And yet, it is clear both from the interviews and the scholarly assessments that the legacy of defeat in Vietnam nonetheless loomed in the background of the surge decision-making process. The chairman of the Joint Chiefs, Peter Pace, and the former vice chief of staff of the Army, Jack Keane, both make reference to their tours in Vietnam to explain their thinking about Iraq. So does the senior State Department official and later ambassador to Iraq James Jeffrey, who served as an Army officer in Vietnam during the Nixon years. The president himself was conscious of comparisons with President Johnson's experience as a war president, and one of Bush's most decisive interventions in the surge debate—the idea that it was not a surge, but rather defeat, that would break the American military—drew directly on his understanding of Vietnam and its lessons.

The role of the president himself in the surge decision is a third theme at the heart of this volume. Overall, most of the interviewees—no matter their position on the surge at the time the decision was made—speak of the president's courage in making his decision, and the skill with which he managed a fractious national security team. Some of the interviewees identify a change in the president during the course of his administration; they perceived a second-term president with a different, less deferential approach to military advice. "George W. Bush," recalled Secretary Condoleezza Rice, "was a different president in 2006 than he was in 2003."[46] The scholars also grapple with the president's role, with most—but not all—commending his decision and particularly his ability to unify a divided bureaucracy behind a controversial change in policy. Perhaps, then, one can see the seeds of an emerging Bush revisionism in this episode.

Fourth, the scholars and interviewees offer sharply diverging assessments on one of the most contentious elements of the surge decision—the quality of the process that led to the increase in troops. Was this a "textbook" policy process, as described by Secretary Robert Gates? Or did it take too long to develop, and risk losing the war in the process? Does the near total absence of Donald Rumsfeld mean that the process itself was dysfunctional, or was the fact that it went on without him a tribute to adaptation and creativity? What was gained—and lost—by the compartmentalization and secrecy within the process? And who led the process? The president, or his national security advisor, Stephen Hadley? The president's interview helps resolve some of these questions, in revealing that he knew the power of a few well-placed questions to drive a major review of wartime strategy. But just as the surge itself was controversial when announced, the quality of the process leading to the surge remains a subject of enormous debate many years after the fact.

Finally, can the quality of the decision-making process be considered separately from the quality of the president's ultimate decision to surge troops to Iraq? Although the interviews and scholarly assessments presented here focus on the decision itself, interpretations of whether the surge ultimately succeeded unavoidably loom large in any retrospective assessment of the process leading to the surge. The scholars are, unsurprisingly, divided on this question; most of the interviewees view the surge positively, but not all. The issue was put most directly by Douglas Lute, who served as director of operations on the Joint Staff at the time of the surge decision. He would later go on to oversee implementation of the surge as deputy national security advisor for Iraq and Afghanistan—the "war czar." Lute turned the tables on his interviewers, asking, "Was it a stroke of strategic brilliance that reversed the course in a war that was failing, or did it, in a temporary way, sort of mask the fundamental flaws of the Iraqi government and the Iraqi security forces, . . . giving us an opportunity to exit with our heads up . . . ? And I think that's the debate, right, between those who say it was a success and those who say, you know, it wasn't, and we shouldn't have expected it to be."

We leave the answer to that question to future scholars, who will be better able to assess the effects of the surge on the basis of new sources and greater perspective. But we suspect that here, as in so many cases, the surge will remain as consequential and controversial in retrospect as it was when first announced by President Bush in January 2007.

PART 1

CHAPTER 1

America's War in Iraq

2003–2005

Two years after he stood before a banner that read "mission accomplished," George W. Bush's war in Iraq dragged on. Military officials and intelligence analysts warned of a growing insurgency as early as late 2003. Others hoped political developments would slowly, but surely, overtake opposition, bringing peace and stability to the country.

Mixed signals abounded for any who sought to predict Iraq's future. Sectarian violence spiked anew by the summer of 2005, especially in Baghdad, and with particular barbarity. Political milestones also dotted the landscape, including November's "National Strategy for Victory in Iraq," the White House's effort to shore up bipartisan support for the war through a clearer explanation of US policy in Iraq.[1] We plan to "clear, hold, and build," Secretary of State Condoleezza Rice told Congress.[2] Nationwide elections in December suggesting improved governance in Iraq might yet, she and other administration officials hoped, drain momentum from the current wave of violence.

American commanders in Iraq, and Defense Department officials in Washington, disagreed with Rice's optimistic characterization, revealing that American strategy was anything but agreed upon in Washington.

The Insurgency Emerges

LIEUTENANT GENERAL DOUGLAS LUTE, US Army, director of operations, Joint Staff: [The insurgency] was unanticipated. We didn't expect it. So from the summer of '03 to sort of the summer or fall of '05, the American forces, the multinational forces, were going through a major transition internally, from what we thought we were going to be doing in Iraq to what we were actually doing. This was not a counterinsurgency army; we didn't have a counterinsurgency army. We developed one on the fly, under fire, between the summer of '03 and the summer of '05, and that's not pretty, and there were a lot of mistakes made, and the transition was not smooth.

GENERAL JOHN ABIZAID, US Army, commander, US Central Command: I was a deputy commander during the invasion of Iraq, and after the invasion of Iraq I became the CENTCOM [United States Central Command] commander, and this was about three months afterward, and we were in the process of pulling forces out on the orders of the secretary of defense. We were going to leave a very small, residual force behind, and it was clear that that was not going to work, so we had to reorganize the force.

JOHN HANNAH, assistant to the vice president: In my own view, you know I distinctly recall in late 2003, certainly after the UN bombings in August of 2003, after the bombing of the head of the Supreme Council [for the Islamic Revolution in Iraq, Ayatollah Mohammed Baqir al-Hakim], his assassination by car-bombing in Najaf, around that same time in 2003. One has a sense that things are not going well, that something is emerging here in terms of the insurgency that looks like it could be a strategic threat to the American effort in Iraq, if and only if, because by that time already, it seemed to me at least, that you had a steady drip, drip, drip, of American casualties, virtually every single day or every other day; one, two, three Americans being killed, and that just seemed to be that over time, would be entirely corrosive of the effort. It wasn't what the American people had been prepared for, and I didn't think you would be able to sustain that over time in terms of achieving our objectives in Iraq. I think that only sort of escalates, and that feeling of unease continues throughout 2004, 2005. There's always a hope in that period, that the political progress that we are seeing being made, in terms of handing over sovereignty back to the Iraqis in 2004, in terms of the series of elections we held through the end of 2005, that that political process is going to be the thing that kind of stanches the insurgency and allows us to begin building that vision of a more representative, inclusive Iraq that is going to be an ally of the United States in the broader region and the broader war on terror. And yet, I think there's a lot of unease in the government, that as each of those milestones passes and the insurgency only appears to worsen, that that in fact is not the case, that there is a fundamental problem of first order, in getting on top of the security situation in Iraq and understanding what the insurgency is and how it might be defeated. And until you can provide Iraqis, at least the vast majority of the population, that fundamental sense of security, our ability to marginalize the insurgency and really proceed forward to develop that model of a representative Iraq is not going to get very far.

RICHARD CHENEY, vice president: [There were] arguments being made that . . . there was an inconsistency between what you needed to create a democracy and the role of the military, having a strong military. From the perspective of that view, that the [Iraqi] military was a negative, the military was a force not for good, but something you had to make certain didn't interfere with the political process domestically, inside Iraq. Some of the early debates, as we look back on them, began to take place around that subject. We ended up with the belief, for example, as I recall, in the interior ministry, and if we just go through and get rid of the bad guys at the top, the Baathists, the Saddam Hussein lovers, pull them aside, then you'd have a bureaucracy there and you could get good people in charge, and that unit would begin to function the way it should in the government. It turned out that wasn't valid. So there was an inherent conflict to some extent, and when we got into this debate of what comes first, the military or the civilian, and then if you go back to the original arguments, I think some of those occurred in that first year, and in the immediate aftermath of that, with this debate that wasn't really much of a debate, the [Iraqi] military ended up being basically disbanded and the troops went home. At the same time, we're trying to make progress on the political front, but they were viewed as inconsistent or incompatible somehow, and we had to get around that obviously, if we were going to before we could solve the problem.

PHILIP ZELIKOW, counselor of the Department of State: President Bush was passionately interested in what was going on in Iraq, cared deeply about it. He would chair NSC meetings on Iraq virtually every single week, without fail. He was asking Meghan [O'Sullivan, assistant to the president and deputy national security advisor for Iraq and Afghanistan] to write him, like, daily notes, like what happened in Iraq every day. He's intensely curious about what's going on. . . . But despite scores of presidential meetings on Iraq, these readings—these meetings, by '05, had acquired a stylized, routine quality. . . . How can you meet on Iraq forty or fifty times and not discuss these basic issues? And then you have to kind of understand the stylized and routinized way the process was working then, in which . . . you do the briefing on all the things we're doing, and all the little tactical things that go with that, which can easily burn up all your time. And the dog barks and the caravan moves on.

HANNAH: I guess the thing that perplexes me more than anything else is probably just how long it took, when there was obviously, again, this unspoken feeling amongst a lot of smart people inside of the US government, not to mention outside of the US government, who just knew in their bones that things were not going right in Iraq, in that 2004, 2005, early 2006 period, and yet it took, you know at least two years, if not longer, to begin righting that ship of state and begin taking the decisions that led to the surge and the necessary course correction. You know, figuring out why that took so long is, like I said, a bit of a mystery to me. . . . I'm speculating, but based on some knowledge, that there was, in the administration, and I think properly to some extent, a strong desire and urge to defer to our commanders in the field. In particular, somebody like General Abizaid was, I think, a really strongly respected figure who, if you asked any of those principals, John Abizaid understood the Middle East in general and probably understood Iraq specifically, far better than anybody else sitting in that Situation Room. He was the man who had the responsibility of trying to carry out the president's orders and achieve the president's mission in Iraq. These guys were the experts at the art of warfare, and therefore, I think there was, properly, a strong urge to give them a lot of authority and to stick with them and back them up.

My view is that that was the wrong strategy, and yet taking on the military commanders in that way, I think has got to be a difficult thing for a president to bring himself around to doing. Again, even as you have this track of the security situation deteriorating so steadily and dramatically over time, you did have milestones being achieved at some level, on the political front, and that allowed you to kind of attach yourself to those things and always believe that just the next milestone. Get us through this political transition to Iraq, to a permanently elected parliament and prime minister, and everything on the security situation will become much more manageable and we'll then begin to get on top of that because the politics will have moved to the place where it itself will begin to become a major factor undermining the insurgency and taking the energy out of the insurgency. And so it just took a matter of time. The US government is this huge bureaucracy, and fighting a war is no different, perhaps even more intense, than any other sort of normal events, and trying to turn that around when you have that much at stake and that many people involved in the process, I just think became a very difficult thing to do.

ABIZAID: I went to Secretary [of Defense Donald] Rumsfeld and the president, and I said . . . it was my opinion that we were in a long war situation and that there would be no early victory anytime soon, that it was going to be a long, hard military slog, but the real work that had to be done was political work. . . . There was a lot of consternation about whether we called it "insurgency," not on my part, but on the part of many of the political leaders. But I thought it was important to make sure the political leadership had an idea that was going on. . . . I don't think it was a surprise to them, they just didn't want to hear it. That's one of the great benefits of being a military commander; your job is to give military advice, and you have to tell them what you think. You try to do it privately, and Secretary Rumsfeld was very unhappy with me when at a press conference I used the term "insurgency." And then we went through a period of back-and-forth over whether it was an insurgency or not, and finally I said to him, "Look, Mr. Secretary, we're fighting an insurgency. A counterinsurgency. You can call it what you want to call it, but I have to fight it the way our troops know to fight it, and it's a counterinsurgency, and those are the tactics, techniques, and procedures we're using, and I'm not going to change how I talk about it." They were using terms like "dead-enders." . . . This was really not so much the president as it was Secretary Rumsfeld. . . . When I told the president I thought it was a long war, I laid out a briefing for why I thought that. I told them I thought there was a struggle here that just wasn't about Iraq; it was about the struggle against Islamic extremism. And he had me go to all of our allies and explain to them the long-war strategy. No one liked it. It's not that they disagreed with the premise, but they didn't like the idea of a long war.

Contradictory Signals

Though Iraqi politics frequently concerned the Bush administration, the president had politics of his own to worry about in the fall of 2004. Iraq played a central role in the close-fought election between Bush and Democratic challenger Senator John Kerry. Bush won, and as is commonly the case, key personnel retired or shifted responsibilities for the second term. Secretary of State Colin Powell retired. National Security Advisor Condoleezza Rice took his place. Her deputy, Stephen Hadley, replaced her at the White House, overseeing at once an optimistic yet trepidatious period in the president's international agenda. On the one hand, Iraq's future, and with it American blood, treasure, and prestige, remained in doubt. On the other, Bush proclaimed at his second inaugural a new "freedom agenda," promising the United States would strive to end tyranny around the world.

"We are led, by events and common sense," he proclaimed, "to one conclusion: the survival of liberty in our land increasingly depends on the success of liberty in other lands. The best hope for peace in our world is the expansion of freedom in all the world."

No president had ever promised something so ambitious. Even as the situation on the ground in Iraq, the signature foreign policy arena from his first term, continued to unravel, American strategists engaged in a critical if indecisive debate: whether security would flow from political stability in the occupied country, or whether political instability would lead to an increasing loss of security. More ominously, was Washington's strategy producing neither security *nor* stability? Bush was unsure which path to follow as his second term began, nor was he convinced he had yet assembled the right team for the job. Indeed, having changed leadership at the State Department and the NSC, his staff reached out to a potential new leader for the Pentagon.

> STEPHEN HADLEY, national security advisor: I remember a meeting with [Robert] Blackwill [deputy national security advisor for strategic planning until 2004] right after I became national security advisor, who said to me, "Your number one job is to get Iraq right. We owe it to the men and women in uniform. It is important to our country, and it's important to this president because this president's legacy is going to be about how he managed Iraq." So with that ringing in my ears for four years, whatever the other distractions, Iraq was always going to be at the top of my agenda.
>
> J. D. CROUCH, deputy national security advisor: I think about the period of '05 really, to some degree, as one of quite a bit of hope and optimism. . . . There was kind of a general sense, amidst problems as

well, that things were heading politically in a positive direction. There were also counter sides, and you know, one of the things that . . . is difficult [is] to sort of read the distinction between those two things. We're also getting, I think, fairly positive views from the leadership team that was forward deployed, Ambassador [Zalmay] Khalilzad and the commanding general . . . George Casey.[3]

DAVID GORDON, vice chair, National Intelligence Council: In late 2005, we saw some contradictory things happening, actually. Late 2005 was a time when the sectarian part of the conflict was really beginning to get a lot more intense. A lot more intense. But late 2005 was also a time when finally the efforts, particularly by the [Central Intelligence] Agency, in Anbar Province and western Iraq to mobilize forces against AQI [al-Qaeda in Iraq] were beginning to gain some traction. So late 2005 was a funny time, because there were some interesting positive things going on. They were basically not in the public domain, so the picture that most people were getting was one that was pretty negative. My view was that there were some very contradictory things going on. But . . . I think there was a lot of uncertainty about the military strategy in particular.

CHENEY: My recollection is that as we went through '05, a couple of things stand out. One were the elections, worked basically on the theory that if we could get elections, a democratically elected government, turn things over to the Iraqis as soon as they were able to put together a government, a functioning government.

Part of the difficulty was we were having to deal with the Iraq, Shia-Sunni conflict, and we were in a position where, because of the progress we were making politically, elections, you end up in a situation where you have the country . . . that had been governed by the Sunnis, power shifting to the Shia, there were more of them, they that won the elections, and that complicated the progress toward our objectives, and I don't think that we went into it with as comprehensive an understanding of the politics inside of Iraq. I think sometimes that was reflected in the military view, as our military view, that the State Department or the civilians in the business couldn't get it right and therefore they were having to deal with a very difficult situation. I think our military, based on tradition, based upon the way they're trained and what their focus is, they win wars. They don't have a heavy emphasis on setting up and running governments, and so I think that there was a natural built-in conflict there.

KARL ROVE, senior advisor to the president and deputy chief of staff:
And the question was—and I think this was weighing in the president's mind—will the success on the political side, the organization
of the government, the holding of the elections, which was a powerful moment, and the expression of the Iraqi people was just jaw-droppingly awesome. This was something they clearly wanted, the
right to participate in the formation of their own nation. But was
that political success, that political advance, I should say, or progress,
was that at risk because of some underlying problems with security?

So the question was, would the political success take care of the
security problem, or did we have to have security before we would
see permanence in that political process? And my sense was . . . —this
is episodic contact with the president in an informal way, either in the
Oval [Office] or when we're traveling—but my sense was that even
then there was something stirring in him that said I think we've got
something. Our strategy is not going to be sufficient. Great for political process, great for meeting these so-called metrics, but there was
something that was eating at him . . . something led to him in 2005
saying, OK, if I wanted to make a change at DoD [the Department of
Defense], do I even really have an option? And the option is [Robert]
Gates, so go find out if Gates is available.

The president was concerned about Rumsfeld, and asking a question of is it time for a change. And he had me reach out to Gates,
whom I had a relationship with . . . and Gates says no. I remember
this because I call Gates while I'm on my son's college tour . . . and
Gates returns my phone call and basically I say, "Would you be open
to this if the president were to explore this option? Is this really an
option?" And he said, basically: I'm in the middle of some things at
[Texas] A&M, and it's not possible for me to contemplate a quick
departure.

Explaining US Strategy

American public opinion faltered a year after Bush's inauguration, which
proved the high point of his second-term popularity. Policy makers in turn
feared they would lose political support at home before Iraq itself had time
to stabilize. "Those inside the administration felt pretty strongly that we did
in fact have a strategy," the NSC's Meghan O'Sullivan recalled, "and that
we were executing the strategy." Their problem in part appeared to be one
of communication, prompting administration officials to publicize their

National Strategy for Victory in Iraq (NSVI). The cacophony of concern grew as casualties continued to mount, with no clear sign of decline on the horizon. Echoes of Vietnam in particular surfaced by year's end, embodied by the stinging criticism of Pennsylvania representative John Murtha. A decorated Vietnam veteran, indeed the first veteran of that conflict elected to Congress, Murtha demanded a complete withdrawal of American troops. "The war in Iraq is not going as advertised," he railed, calling the entire campaign "a flawed policy wrapped in illusion."[4] By the beginning of 2006 Bush's advisors started to wonder whether their problem was not merely one of political communication, but if their strategy was flawed as well, something top leaders at the Pentagon were not keen to see discussed publicly, or at all.

PETER FEAVER, special advisor, National Security Council: Now, my surge story, I would begin it with the Aspen Strategy Group in August of 2005. I went representing the Strategy Office from the White House. The conference was four or five days of blistering critique of the administration, the failed Iraq policy, failed this, that, and the other. But then when they recommended . . . what we should do, what I kept hearing were the main elements of what I knew to be the strategy that the administration thought it was implementing. So, strong critique, but then when it came to recommending what to be done, it sounded very much like what we were trying to do.

It was a strategy that was premised on getting political momentum which would create a political home for the Sunnis who were the natural supporters of the insurgency. They would see that they had a future in the new Iraq. This would siphon off the support that they were otherwise giving to this insurgency. That over time this would lead to a decrease in the sectarian violence that was fueling the insurgency.

I return from [Aspen] and I talked to Meghan and Steve Hadley about it, and I said, there is a bipartisan consensus on what should be done in Iraq. That bipartisan consensus, at least at the kind of expert level, tracks pretty closely to what we're trying to do—what the formal papers describing our strategy are. I said I think we could capture that bipartisan consensus, maybe even relaunch a little bit of it, if we could better explain what our strategy was.

Now I knew there were other voices inside the government that thought we had a strategy problem, but at that time I thought we didn't have a strategy problem, we had a failure-to-explain-our-strategy problem. There was a coherent strategy we were trying to

follow. There might be resource issues, there certainly were implementation issues, but at the strategic level there was a logic to it,
and it resonated with what experts outside were asking us to do.
They just didn't know about it, or we weren't doing a good job of
explaining. I suggested that we release an unclassified version of
the underlying classified documents. That effort eventually became
NSVI, which was released in the end of November.

We thought that the strategy as outlined in NSVI was finally
beginning to show fruit with all of the political milestones that were
achieved in 2005.[5] We had a large public messaging push that came
out of it as part of the release of the white paper [NSVI], and the
president gave three, four big speeches. We had a follow-up series
of engagements planned, bringing together all of the former secretaries of state, secretaries of defense. A series of meetings with
members of the Hill, and outside experts, in a way of hearing their
critiques of the strategy, but also explaining to them what we were
trying to do.

HADLEY: [NSVI] was an effort both to improve our strategy, consolidate our strategy, explain our strategy, win support in the public and
Congress for the strategy. In this period of time, you know, it was
not clearly working the way we had hoped. . . . I carried around with
me all the time and updated each month the chart that showed the
incidents of violence in Iraq from 2003, when the initial invasion
occurred. And that line was steadily going up in this period. And I
remember saying to members of the staff, "I'll believe our strategy
is working when that line starts going down." And this period all the
way through the surge announcement in January in 2007, that line
continued to go up.

MEGHAN O'SULLIVAN, deputy national security advisor for Iraq and
Afghanistan: [NSVI] came about, as I remember it, primarily because
the administration was under constant criticism that it didn't have a
strategy. And those inside the administration felt pretty strongly that
we did in fact have a strategy, and that we were executing the strategy. And so there was a real need to communicate this to a broader
public. . . . So while I did see it as largely an effort to put together a
document which could explain to the public what we were doing, I
was hoping [it] would also catalyze some real hard thinking about
where our strategy was. . . . It was clear that there were some dis-
connects between what we were doing and what we were talking
about. And my hope was that the NSVI could expose those and lead

Average number of daily attacks per month

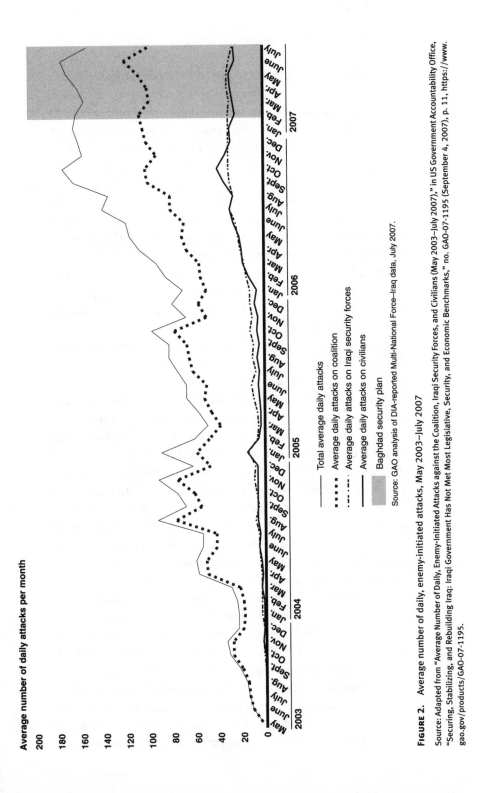

Figure 2. Average number of daily, enemy-initiated attacks, May 2003–July 2007

Source: Adapted from "Average Number of Daily, Enemy-Initiated Attacks against the Coalition, Iraqi Security Forces, and Civilians (May 2003–July 2007)," in US Government Accountability Office, "Securing, Stabilizing, and Rebuilding Iraq: Iraqi Government Has Not Met Most Legislative, Security, and Economic Benchmarks," no. GAO-07-1195 (September 4, 2007), p. 11, https://www. gao.gov/products/GAO-07-1195.

to something more strategic and concrete in nature than just a communications effort.

FEAVER: Right as we were finishing up [NSVI], Jack Murtha, a member of Congress from Pennsylvania, came out with a press conference where he basically called for the US to get out of Iraq within six months, or some very, very rapid timetable. He's no lefty. He's a Vietnam vet and was known sort of as a blue dog Democrat, hawkish on defense. Here he was calling for basically, I think his words even said, "The troops have done everything that could be asked of them. It's time to bring them home." Words to that effect. That dramatically moved the Iraq debate leftward, because it created safe political space for a "get out of Iraq now" wing which previously had been just the hard left, but now there's political cover.

Then, frankly, the situation in Iraq, it becomes clear as '06 goes on that we don't have a message problem, we have a policy problem. We don't have a failure-to-explain-our-strategy problem, we have the failure of strategy problem.

That was dramatized for me in the March, April, May time frame. The president does another series of big speeches on Iraq, but that gets almost no attention; no penetration, no movement in public attitudes, or public sentiment. It's as if the president is losing his ability to connect with the American people on this Iraq question.

ROVE: Look, I can't speak to Jack Murtha's intentions, but I look at Jack Murtha and see—he's got to, having seen Vietnam, he had to understand that a precipitous withdrawal would've plunged the country into chaos and given us a moral setback and a defeatist setback that would be as bad or worse than Vietnam. So I think this was politics, at the end of it. . . . I don't know why he ended up there, but he had to know the consequences of that, both for the region and the United States, would be disastrous. It took us twenty years to work our way out of the aftermath of Vietnam. It would've taken us longer to work out of the aftermath of a precipitous withdrawal.

CONDOLEEZZA RICE: secretary of state: By the time I got to the State Department in 2005, I thought we really had two problems. Not only was the strategy not working, but we couldn't explain to anybody what it was we were trying to do. In a now fairly infamous testimony before the Senate Foreign Relations, I tried to describe what it was we were doing. I had the advantage of having [then–Army lieutenant general] Ray Odierno as my liaison, from the Joint Chiefs of Staff. He had of course been in Iraq at the time of the invasion, and together with Phil Zelikow and some others, we came up with the idea of clear, hold, and build, which we thought described what we were doing. I think at that time, we were really trying to clarify precisely what we were trying to do. Were we trying to just get deaths down, from a point of view of American forces? The security situation wasn't improving, not just in terms of the population, but we couldn't get reconstruction projects going, because they were under constant fire from what was becoming a significant insurgency. So I would say that this was a rather gradual process, of beginning to reevaluate the strategy, and by 2005 the efforts had really started to accelerate to do so.

I think our problem was that we were sort of stuck in a situation in which there were those in the Pentagon, and particularly some of the younger officers in the Pentagon, who were recognizing that we had to move closer to a counterinsurgency strategy, which is how I could describe clear, hold, and build; it's really counterinsurgency strategy. But it was neither adequately resourced, nor, did it seem to me, particularly supported in some of the higher echelons of the Pentagon. I do think—I call them the counterinsurgency generals, but really, they were the ones who had gone, in effect failed, and had come back. Odierno, [then–lieutenant general David] Petraeus, [then–lieutenant general Peter] Chiarelli, all of whom had been associated with the heavier initial invasion footprint, you know the effort to pacify by out-and-out force, Fallujah and places like that. That strategy had clearly not worked, and there was a lot of churning in the Pentagon. We were more than aware of that churning at the State Department, because Ray was my liaison.

And so I would describe it as an effort to explain to the American people and to the Congress what it is we ought to be doing, some elements of which were in place and many of the elements were not really in place. We weren't trying to clear, hold, and build, although if you listened very carefully, to especially the generals who were trying to carry this out, that's what they thought they were trying to do. They were under-resourced to come even close. You know, holding means you have to leave people behind, and we would essentially clear, go home, and the next day we were clearing again because in the interval, when we went back to bases, the insurgents had gotten the upper hand overnight again.

I think it's fair to say that no one had been very satisfied with what was going on in Iraq for a very, very long time; probably dating all the

way back to 2004. . . . I think we'd all expected that once we transferred sovereignty and the political situation had begun to change,
we would be leading up to elections in 2005, and yet the security
situation really wasn't getting better.

ZELIKOW: So basically in '05, we come to the conclusion that the situation for the president is becoming desperate, the absence of a strategy. And the communications people are really intense about this,
because the president is just visibly just getting beaten up as '05 goes
on. The president keeps giving speeches essentially saying why Iraq
is important, but he's been giving those speeches for years, and he's
made those arguments, and actually, the American people are willing
to concede Iraq may be important; they just want to know what's
your story for where this is going. And we don't even have a story to
tell. The president can't describe the strategy.

Rice is very reluctant to step out to offer a strategy, not because
she's shy but because fundamentally ascribing a military strategy
for Iraq, or a political-military strategy, should principally be led by
the Defense Department, it has to come somewhere from the commanders. And she's reluctant, as a secretary of state, to basically step
in and say, "Well, since you can't do it, I'm going to do it." But we
decide that we actually do need to do that. Now, . . . this is preceded
by a fairly important trip that I made in September of '05, . . . after
which I write a fairly lengthy paper with a number of recommendations, including recommendations to begin confronting Iranians
directly and violently on the battlefield, as the Iranian problem is
becoming really quite dangerous by September of '05. . . . The paper
doesn't say we need more troops—it says, I think, that Casey doesn't
want more troops—but it's very hard to read through the recommendations and not think. . . . It clearly calls for a redoubled effort
without doing troop-to-task analysis, which I was reluctant to do. . . .
Condi asked me to brief that paper around town, and asked people
to see me. And so doors were opened for me, and I developed a set
of slides, which were more forthcoming than the paper, and which
were not given to Bob Woodward [associate editor at the *Washington
Post* and author of several books on the Bush administration], which
plainly called—we need to have a massively redoubled effort in Iraq,
we need to plan it now in the fall of '05 so that it is ready to go and
launches in March of '06, in conjunction with the election. The time
to make these decisions are now if you want something ready by
the spring. And that's briefed to Steve Hadley, to the Pentagon, to

[Deputy Secretary of Defense] Gordon England and [Chairman of the Joint Chiefs of Staff] Pete Pace, [the vice president's chief of staff] Scooter Libby, to the DNI [director of national intelligence], others.

Then, Condi decides that she's going to go ahead and make a statement about strategy in the testimony she's been invited to give in October of '05. I draft that testimony. That's the testimony that then has the "clear, hold, and build" phrase, which I drafted. Actually, I drafted initially "clear and hold," and when I was sending the draft around in the darkened airplane in which this was being done, Ray Odierno said, "No, you have to add 'build.'" So I put in "build," so it's "clear, hold, and build." And that was a deliberate effort to find some way of synthesizing an easy catchphrase to describe a positive, affirmative military strategy. It was not a deeply original and creative concept, to have a strategy for counterinsurgency of "clear, hold, and build." . . . There is this violent reaction from Secretary Rumsfeld, and from General Casey, more privately, to the State Department's articulation of the strategy. The White House backs—essentially, the White House backs Condi up and says, "Yep, 'clear, hold, and build,' and we're going to incorporate that now into the NSVI, the National Strategy Victory in Iraq, documents." And then Rumsfeld has this amazing press conference where he—you just really have to read to believe—in which he says—he denounces this, saying this is all Iraqi strategy. . . . We're two and a half years into the war, and he thinks the Iraqis are doing the military strategy in the field? That is so weird that we need different kinds of specialists to understand this.

But the consequences are significant. Because it means that rhetorically we've now moved to an affirmative statement of this strategy, with White House endorsement. It doesn't translate into action in the field. Rumsfeld and Casey basically, to a significant practice, ignore this and do nothing concrete about it. . . . This is really the first concerted effort to get a big, massive, redoubled effort going in Iraq, and it kind of fails.

JAMES JEFFREY, senior advisor to the secretary of state: I saw signs, as did others, that in particular in the military side, the security situation was not getting better, it was getting worse. And we culled this from the details of General Casey's reporting. While the above-the-line summaries were all positive, because that's how the US military's culture is, and that's also how the expectations were when you have 130,000 troops and many tens of billions of dollars invested in something, and you don't have total disaster staring you into the face, you tend to be optimistic. But in looking at the metrics and looking at the detailed analysis of what Casey was trying to accomplish, against the goals, it was clear in September of 2005 that he wasn't meeting the goals of his own military operation. My view, and I think Phil Zelikow shared it to a very large degree, was that this was because we were not pursuing an insurgency. I had a fair amount of experience in that in Vietnam. I thought we were still in the Westmoreland rather than the Abrams phase.[6] We were not protecting the population, we were going after the very elusive bad guys, and that was even more difficult in Iraq than it was in Vietnam. And as a result, the support for the government, its ability to deliver services to jump start any kind of civilian activities, was being eroded by the insurgents, who of course were targeting that with a vengeance, and we weren't doing enough to stop that.

I could see an erosion of our position slowly, and thus I, along with Zelikow, advocated very strongly with Secretary Rice to speak out. This was very difficult. . . . That led to her using the "clear, hold, build" term in congressional testimony, and then getting the president to use it in a speech. . . . General Casey was personally unhappy. He called her [Rice], because Casey is that kind of guy, and he felt that he was blindsided on—why is the secretary of state suggesting military strategy? Again, Casey knew, Casey was all about, to the extent he could, clear, hold, and build. What he didn't need was the secretary of state raising it. It put him in a very awkward position. I still justify her doing it, because there was no other way to get attention, and to get Bush. The problem is after he did that, there still wasn't the follow through, and I could give examples of this, that the bureaucracy was not able to overcome the resistance of DoD to actually do a true clear, hold, and build.

CROUCH: The politics inside the government of how ["clear, hold, and build"] kind of got spilled out onto public, into the public, made it challenging for it to get much traction. . . . My recollection of clear, hold, and build, though, however, is that it was certainly not a call for something like what was executed in early January of 2007. In other words, it was not the surge strategy ahead of time. But it was a recognition, I think, that there were deficiencies in the security environment in Iraq, and it was a recognition that the current strategy had weaknesses.

ABIZAID: The notion of "clear, hold, build" was a legitimate notion, but I
think it's important for you to understand . . . [the] secretary of defense
and the president and General Pace, and [former chairman of the Joint
Chiefs of Staff] General [Richard B.] Myers before him, all were very,
very concerned about casualties. And the instructions that they conveyed to me and General Casey were to do whatever we could to minimize our casualties, for obvious reasons. . . . I mean, both the president
and the secretary were both very, very engaged with the parents of the
fallen and the loved ones of the fallen. They visited troops that were
in the hospital. My own son-in-law was seriously wounded in Iraq; the
president invited him and his family over to the White House once he
had recovered enough. So they were very compassionate, they were
very concerned, and the president in particular kept on saying, "Why
aren't the Iraqis doing enough to defend their own country?" So this
notion that "clear, hold, build" would somehow or other minimize
casualties was a problem. "Clear, hold, build"—"build" was going to
cause casualties to increase, not decrease.

The Iraq Study Group

Perhaps fresh eyes would provide an answer. Congressman Frank Wolf proposed a bipartisan panel to assess the war in Iraq. Eager to find a new strategy,
and for it to garner broad bipartisan support, respected Washington insiders
from across the aisle, led by former secretary of state James Baker and former chair of the House of Representative's Foreign Affairs Committee Lee
Hamilton, convened a broad Iraq Study Group. Its charge: a top-to-bottom
assessment of American goals and policies for Iraq, developed by a roster
of experienced officials beyond reproach. One in particular would ultimately
have a larger hand in executing their recommendations than he originally
envisioned.

Not surprisingly, not everyone in the Pentagon, or the White House,
embraced the idea at the heart of the Iraq Study Group: that outsiders, or
Congress, or for that matter public opinion, might ultimately dictate American strategy overseas.

FRANK WOLF, member of the House of Representatives: I always go to a
hospital when I go to a place, and there are [Iraqi] guards running in
before we went into a room, they were . . . putting guns in the faces
of women and children, and I said, "This is crazy, let's go." . . . The
very fact that I had to go into a hospital in Tikrit, and I had armed

forces, private security people putting AK-47s in the women's faces, was not a positive. I knew this thing was unraveling.

I came back, and I said, "We need fresh eyes." . . . because many of the people who are making these decisions are not really there. We spent night after night with sheiks, and in people's homes, and we listened to them, and so I said, "Something's wrong." And I've always been supportive. I like President Bush, I've been a big fan of President Bush, and I really admired his dad. And, so I said, "We just gotta change this thing." . . . I don't know that I know the answer, but I think we need fresh eyes. There was really pushback from the administration. They didn't want to do it. There was not any particular great interest in the Congress, either, and then I put the bill in [to create the Iraq Study Group]. I was the chairman of the [House Appropriations] Subcommittee [on Commerce, Justice, Science, and Related Agencies], and I just didn't check with anyone, and we put it in. Steve Hadley, I think, was very good on helping the Bush administration to come around.

HADLEY: Baker-Hamilton's [Iraq Study Group]—the reason we got that was it was pretty clear when we set it up that we might need to have a new strategy, and that it would be controversial. And that it would be helpful if we could harness some, you know, respected national leaders and national security Republicans and Democrats to sort of construct a landing pad out there in the public debate that we could go to when and if we decided to change the strategy. So that was the purpose of it. It was in some sense to clear the way and to begin clearing the space for the strategy where we would end up.

RICE: Well, I had convinced the president—been one of the people to convince the president—to go along with supporting it, because he was immediately suspicious, not of Jim Baker, who he liked tremendously, not of Lee Hamilton, who he liked tremendously. But it was a sort of "Oh, right, so the Congress is going to appoint somebody to tell me how to do my job." Steve and I had both said to him, this is a real opportunity to kind of reset, these are wise heads, they're not going to come up with anything crazy. . . . It was a chance to reset, to give Iraq another look, to give fresh air, I guess.

Is There a Strategy?

ABIZAID: The strategy was: transition both militarily and politically over time; increase Iraqi security capacity over time; and as conditions warranted it, to move toward an opportunity for drawdown of American forces, handover to Iraqi forces, but really the most important thing was handover to Iraqi political authorities. . . . Look, the idea is in the Islamic Middle East, the Arab Middle East in particular—foreign forces are always rejected. They're like a disease that enters into the organism, and then all the antibodies form and try to reject it. And if you don't really have a very, very highly developed, well-coordinated, political, military, diplomatic, educational, informational intelligence program, and you just try to do it with military force alone, it's very unlikely to succeed. So it was my opinion, and George Casey agreed with me, and so did Secretary Rumsfeld—that we had to really move out as quickly as we could to make the transition to Iraqi security force capacity.

ZELIKOW: I came in assuming that we had some kind of strategy for Iraq, and I just needed to figure out what it was. And I would say probably not until the summer did I actually finally begin coming to the conclusion that there is no there there, that there really was no strategy.

Now, I can imagine people sitting in a chair talking to you who would violently object to that statement. "Well, of course we had a strategy." So let me just explain what the way I would think of a strategy is. The way it looked to me is we're training Iraqis and we're going to get out. And Iraqis are going to take over. We're building up the Iraqis so that we can get out; that's the strategy. To me, though, that's not a strategy for the war. In the war, what are your operational objectives for military operations, and then the political things that would go with that? I mean, what are you actually trying to do substantively in the war? You couldn't say, "Well, we don't have a strategy for the war; the Iraqis have a strategy for the war, because we're training the Iraqis to fight." OK, well, what's the Iraqi strategy for the war? But actually, that's a silly question to ask because the Iraqi army had no strategic capability. That is, we had amputated the higher-order functions of the Iraqi army. We were training field combat units, but all the higher-order functions of where to deploy units and what their goals would be and all of that were being performed in the coalition command at Camp Victory.

JEFFREY: Based upon our assumption that the military side of things wasn't doing well and that there was no way that either the Iraqi political system, economic and such, or our nonmilitary aid, assistance, development, and such, was going to compensate for that military lack of success, and in fact our own efforts and the efforts of the Iraqis were being undercut by the lack of security, because the military was not delivering security, we realized that we had a fundamental problem. But then bureaucratically, we in the State Department had a fundamental problem with our fundamental problem, because this was, from our point of view, primarily a military problem. Now the first difficulty is that's out of Condi's lane, and she heard this from several people, including military officers as well as Rumsfeld, in very direct and dramatic ways. Secondly, it was very easy, because there were lots of good examples, for the military, beginning with Rumsfeld, and he would do it all the time, to blame the State Department for everything. This is an insurgency, it is a social-political extraordinary thing that we were trying to do in Iraq, and at the end of the day most of it was nonmilitary.

There's a whole chicken-and-egg thing in the insurgency. If everybody loved each other and the government was not corrupt and inefficient and all of that, people probably wouldn't have been shooting at it. Actually, they would have, because they thought we were occupiers, so there was a whole different dynamic. But it was impossible for the Bush administration at the highest levels to understand that we were perceived as occupiers, they just couldn't do that. So therefore if there was underlying insurgency and violence and quasi civil war, as Zelikow would put it, it had to be because there were failures in the political-economic-social order. Well, who's in charge of that? Not Don Rumsfeld—Condoleezza Rice. So that was her first problem. Her second problem was who was she to tell the military how to do things. In "clear, hold, build," two-thirds of that, well, 60 percent, is military. Clear is essentially all military, hold is mainly military, and build is only slightly military.

DAVID SATTERFIELD, senior advisor to the secretary of state: Now, the US had been engaged for quite some time in a training effort to build up Iraqi armed forces, to build up Iraqi police forces, intelligence capabilities. This effort . . . had focused primarily on statistics. How many units had been trained to an ostensible, given level of proficiency, and then set out into the field? There was a high focus upon stoplight charts. X number of Iraqi were on red, yellow, or green in terms of their standing in the training process and their ability to deploy to the field capable of independent, quasi-independent, or not-independent action. In late 2005, almost by coincidence, a question was raised in interagency . . . as to, not how many units were being trained or how many units had graduated training and were now, ostensibly, in the field taking up their mission, but a different question. How many Iraqi forces could be accounted for in the field at a given moment? And the answer came back: only a relatively small percentage—somewhat higher than one-third—were actually accountable in the field.

This opened a quite profound debate in Washington and in the field. You mean, we have been training and reporting as green X—tens of thousands of Iraqi soldiers who cannot be accounted for? They don't exist in the field? Well, yes. And this was never an issue of feedback or report back. As I like to present it, you know the inputs, how many people have gone into training. You know the outputs, how many individuals, at what assessed level of proficiency, have emerged from training. But what about the outcome? How many units are actually in the field, effectively deployed? Great statistics on the first two. Very vague understanding or assessment of what really matters—the outcome of this whole costly, elaborate process. So, here you have in late '05, the beginning of significant questioning as to the entire process of training up Iraqi security forces to be able to take the fight vice [in place of] the US, which was planning, throughout '05, on a progressive drawdown of forces. Don Rumsfeld's intent was to pull out US forces at the fastest pace possible, consistent with the stand-up of Iraqis. As Iraqis stand up, we will stand back, and then we will stand down, was the rubric applied.

Beginning of '06, all of the trend lines that I've just described—emerging sectarian violence, serious questions about the Iraqi police and security to achieve effective actions on the ground to counter these trends—began to explode. February is the Golden, or Askari, Mosque explosion. Why? Why target that mosque? That explosion was the most dramatic demonstration of what intelligence had been suggesting for some time before, which was that the leader of AQIM [al-Qaeda in the Islamic Maghreb] was intent on provoking Sunni-Shia civil war in Iraq.

CHAPTER 2

This Strategy Is Not Working

January–June 2006

Tragically, even as American officials slowly realized their need for new strategies for Iraq, the country's religious and ethnic violence deepened still more. The insurgency—as most were now comfortable calling it—threatened to expand into a widespread civil war. Zealots on the ground welcomed the renewed bloodshed, eager for their own religious or ideological reasons to see the country further rent by war, and Americans further bloodied as well. Abu Musab al-Zarqawi, a key Sunni militant, orchestrated the destruction of Samarra's Golden Dome Mosque, a pilgrimage site of tremendous historic and religious significance for Shias Muslims. Violence surged in response, leading one American policy maker to the difficult conclusion that no matter what optimists might offer, "the current approach wasn't working, and we needed a fresh look."

From Insurgency to Sectarian Struggle

CHENEY: We had intercepted a letter, as I recall, that [Zarqawi] was sending back to the home office, where he talked about trying to foment civil strife between Shia and Sunni. His basic approach was to commit outrages on the Shia population, in the hopes that he could provoke a retaliation by the Shia, against the Sunni. That had been going on for a period of time, but we'd been generally successful at the Shia holding back and not taking the bait. Blowing up the Golden Dome and the mosque at Samarra sort of ended that. It seems to me that was the period, the trigger, if you will. After that, the Shia jumped in, in a big way, in terms of responding, retaliating, attacking the Sunnis. He had some success with that basic strategy, pitting Sunni against Shia, and that helped precipitate, if you will, the concerns then, as we got into later on in '06, when we were trying to deal with an increased level of violence: violence against our troops, violence against Shia and Sunni, and so forth.

GORDON: I was concerned that we were transitioning into something very different, that we were really transitioning from insurgency to a civil war, and that was definitely the predominant view in the intelligence community, that we were in that transition from insurgency to civil war.

ROVE: I mean, this is one of the most important symbols, one of the most important shrines in the entire Middle East, and the central government could not protect even this hallowed place. A lot of people paid attention to the Shia versus Sunni, but my suspicion is that as equally dangerous, or even more damaging, was the belief that our Iraqi government cannot protect us, the average Iraqi citizen.

O'SULLIVAN: I remember that morning quite well. I remember that was the first thing I heard when my alarm went off. And I knew that this was something that had the potential to really escalate what was already a declining trajectory. And I think we all had the sense that this was a potentially really calamitous moment, but feeling that the Iraqis actually recovered from it initially quite well.

RICE: We all held our breath, because it looked like for a short period of time, they had avoided the worst disaster. I remember when it happened, I was actually on an airplane, on my way back from the Middle East, and I got Zal [Khalilzad] on the phone, and he said, "Well, the good thing is, they've all decided to visit the mosque together, they want to show unity." Sunni, Shiite, Kurds, and all. And for a short period of time, it looked like it was going to hold together, but then after that . . .

ZELIKOW: I want to comment here that there is a widespread view in the literature that, Oh, Samarra, there's the . . . attack on the mosque in Samarra, and then, you know, the equilibrium we had in Iraq was shattered. I think this is significantly mistaken. The civil war had already begun by September of '05. I wrote in my report and

I briefed very candidly, and everyone in Baghdad knew, that there was already widespread interethnic killings going on in Baghdad in September of '05, that Interior Ministry death squads were picking up people in vans. We were discovering there's lots of pretty gruesome stuff. I was close to some of this, and really gruesome stuff was being done to people, torture, kind of laboratories and stuff in which we knew the Interior Ministry was deeply involved. And I used the term—"death squads" are, you know, going around killing people in Baghdad—with Steve Hadley in September of '05 when I briefed him on this, because I remember it because . . . I sensed that he had not heard that. But that's five months before Samarra.

SATTERFIELD: Now, civil war is a term that should be used advisedly, and not a casual reference. What Iraq was experiencing was an ever-higher level—particularly in Baghdad, but not exclusively in Baghdad—of overtly sectarian violence, killing, sectarian movements, and cleansing, as neighborhoods which were previously mixed in Baghdad became entirely Shia or entirely Sunni. The complex mix of Baghdad's intertwined communities was quickly dissolving, but dissolving at the point of a gun, at the blade of a knife. More and more of the counts we received each morning in Baghdad were of how many bodies had been found washed up in the water treatment center, dumped into canals—dumped into the river and caught as it entered the plant. This was extremely distressing, because if it continued, a true civil war was actually possible. That is, what Zarqawi, the leader of AQIM [al-Qaeda in the Islamic Maghreb], was seeking could well have been potentially achievable. Now, [Ayman al-]Zawahiri, the functional head of core al-Qaeda, was greatly concerned by all of this. He did not believe this was an appropriate tactic for al-Qaeda to be engaging in, and could ultimately revert back in a negative fashion on al-Qaeda. But Zarqawi broke away and would not follow the guidance from core al-Qaeda. . . . So, civil war is looming. The security forces are ineffective in confronting it, or are complicit to some extent, in the violence.

The hallmark here was a series of negative directions in term of the following: ability of the Iraqi security forces to assume real responsibility for maintaining security and stability in the country, particularly in Anbar-Nineveh Province and in Baghdad itself. Second principal problem, or negative trend line, the emergence of distinct sectarian markers to the violence—the beginnings of what, in 2006, emerged full bore as population cleansing or separation under force with considerable causalities. High lethality in Baghdad itself, but not only in Baghdad—that is, Shia-Sunni fighting with a distinct sectarian edge; the emergence of both indigenous and Iranian-backed and -directed Sharia militia—quite violent in their conduct—from the South, the Basra area, through to Baghdad and other regions where sectarian seam lines existed.

LUTE: I think maybe the genesis, the original genesis—that things were not going well, and maybe slipping out of our control came with the bombing of the Samarra mosque in what was early, early '06. I think by then it became increasingly clear that we weren't dealing only with the Sunni insurgency, but we are dealing with a combination of factors that were approaching the point of being overwhelming, OK. So we had the Sunni insurgency, we had al-Qaeda in Iraq, sort of the extreme of that insurgency. We had the rise of Shia militia, Jaysh al-Mahdi—or JAM, as we referred to it—led by Muqtada al-Sadr, which represented the most virulent part of the Iranian influence on Shia, on Shia militias. And then we had a very unhelpful neighborhood, with Syria being essentially the highway through which foreign fighters flowed to al-Qaeda in Iraq, unimpeded, and sometimes even, perhaps, assisted. And then, to the east—so that was Syria to the west—to the east, we had a very uncooperative, destabilizing Iran with the provision of support and training to the Shia militia, and very telling in the course of 2006 the rise of what we called explosively formed projectiles—EFPs, which were these shape-charged roadside bombs, which were especially lethal, even to our armored vehicles. So, by way of Iran's support to the Shia militia, but also by way of providing these very dangerous munitions, Iran was playing a very unhelpful role, as well.

On the Iraqi side you had an emerging Iraqi security force in the army and the police. I think it was, at this point, about three hundred thousand strong, but it was still being trained, leaders were being developed, and so forth. It was only just emerging. And you had a government under [Nouri al-]Maliki, which had—which showed promise, in terms of what it, what it was committed to doing, but really was not able to cross the sectarian divide, and take some very tough steps that would've maybe given the Sunnis hope that they were part of the future of Iraq. So a very emergent Iraqi security force, a very sort of promising-in-rhetoric-but-not-yet-delivering Iraqi government, confronting an overwhelming set of security challenges, and we probably at that time had maybe 150 or 160,000

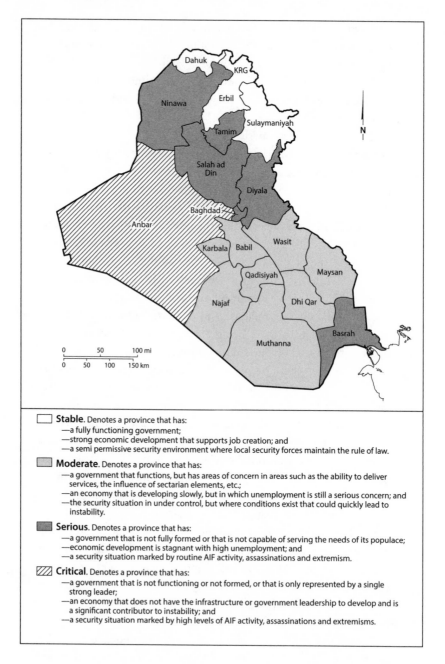

Stable. Denotes a province that has:
 —a fully functioning government;
 —strong economic development that supports job creation; and
 —a semi permissive security environment where local security forces maintain the rule of law.

Moderate. Denotes a province that has:
 —a government that functions, but has areas of concern in areas such as the ability to deliver services, the influence of sectarian elements, etc.;
 —an economy that is developing slowly, but in which unemployment is still a serious concern; and
 —the security situation in under control, but where conditions exist that could quickly lead to instability.

Serious. Denotes a province that has:
 —a government that is not fully formed or that is not capable of serving the needs of its populace;
 —economic development is stagnant with high unemployment; and
 —a security situation marked by routine AIF activity, assassinations and extremism.

Critical. Denotes a province that has:
 —a government that is not functioning or not formed, or that is only represented by a single strong leader;
 —an economy that does not have the infrastructure or government leadership to develop and is a significant contributor to instability; and
 —a security situation marked by high levels of AIF activity, assassinations and extremisms.

FIGURE 3. Iraqi provincial stability in March 2006, as assessed by a joint US Embassy–Multinational Force–Iraq team

Source: Adapted from "Iraq Provincial Stability Based on Governance, Security, and Economic Conditions, as of March 2006," in US Government Accountability Office, "Rebuilding Iraq: Governance, Security, Reconstruction, and Financing Challenges," no. GAO-06-697T (April 25, 2006), p. 11, https://www.gao.gov/products/GAO-06-697T.

Americans . . . on the battlefield. So that was what—that was the context such that when the Samarra mosque was bombed—and I believe the record shows that that was an al-Qaeda in Iraq attack, specifically against one of the holiest Shia sites in, in Iraq—that really set off and really sparked in a major way sectarian violence, which then raged throughout the rest of 2006 and led into the review process here in Washington that suggested that the current process wasn't working, the current approach wasn't working, and we needed a fresh look.

GORDON: I went to Iraq twice in the first half of 2006. . . . We were getting a lot of different views from the military on the ground on how things were going, what was going well, what was going less well. I think there was a broad view that the engagement with the Iraqi military was simply not robust enough to generate the kinds of advancements that people thought were going to be necessary if you were really going to sustain a momentum.

Revolt of the Generals

Frustration within the American military erupted in the spring of 2006, led by retired officers who felt emboldened to criticize the Pentagon's civilian command in ways their active-duty brethren could not. Rumsfeld was "incompetent strategically, operationally, and tactically," the retired major general in charge of training the Iraqi army charged. A former commander of US Central Command similarly condemned the "poor military judgment [that] has been used throughout this mission." Some even questioned publicly for the first time Bush's decision to invade Iraq in the first place. "I now regret that I did not more openly challenge those who were determined to invade a country whose actions were peripheral to the real threat—al-Qaida," retired Marine lieutenant general Gregory Newbold wrote.

Washington had not seen such tension in civil-military relations for more than fifty years. The last time military officers so publicly challenged their civilian masters was in 1949, when a "Revolt of the Admirals" pitted naval officials against a Truman administration keener to fund a larger air force than the new breed of large aircraft carriers sailors desired. "This, too, will pass," Rumsfeld told a national radio audience, dismissing their critique. The commander in chief similarly showed little interest in engaging the brewing "Revolt of the Generals" publicly. "I'm the decider," Bush said in response. "And I decide what's best. And what's best for Don Rumsfeld is to remain."[1]

In truth, albeit in private, Bush had begun to question Rumsfeld's interest in divining a new way forward in Iraq, but feared that saying so publicly might further undermine morale among American troops in harm's way. Ironically, then, the now infamous "Revolt of the Generals," orchestrated to encourage Rumsfeld's removal, instead ensured his survival for the time being. "There's no choice," the White House chief of staff, Josh Bolten, advised Bush in its aftermath. "What this means is that any consideration of replacing him at this point has to be put on hold, that you cannot be seen to allow the politics of the day . . . or people who were formerly in uniform to try to dictate what the president does in his civilian role as commander in chief."

Uninterested in further undermining Rumsfeld and others at the Pentagon by discussing the merits of their chosen strategies in public, Bush and those closest to him at the White House nonetheless pushed for just that sort of discussion behind closed doors. "Hadley," Bush conceded, "this strategy is not working."

> HADLEY: There was some discussion . . . whether Secretary Rumsfeld could remain in office and we could still have a real relook at our strategy in Iraq, because he was very committed to the existing strategy that we had. And I think that the "Revolt of the Generals" actually made it impossible for the president to think about getting rid of Secretary Rumsfeld, because the last thing he was going to do was establish the precedent that some retired military officers could go to the press and force out a secretary of defense. That was not the president's view as to how he would manage senior leadership. While the "Revolt of the Generals" was an effort to provoke a relook of the strategy, I think it actually had perversely the opposite effect and actually delayed the process.
>
> JOSHUA BOLTEN, White House chief of staff: So, yes, we did have conversations about replacing Secretary Rumsfeld. . . . I was among those who felt that both for political and substantive reasons, . . . it would be useful to make a change in the [secretary of defense] role, and so I did advocate for that with President Bush. He said that he had had that in mind, but that he had enormous respect for Secretary Rumsfeld, as I did, and that he was unwilling to make a change or even suggest that he was willing to make a change, until there was a more effective successor. . . . On my first day as chief of staff, the [retired] generals came out with a sharp critique of Secretary Rumsfeld, which didn't surprise me but did shock me. . . . I remember saying to him [the president], well, first of all there's no choice. You have to give Secretary Rumsfeld one hundred percent support, and number two, what this means is that any consideration of replacing him at

this point has to be put on hold. . . . The president was way ahead of me; he said, "Yeah, yeah, I got that." He said, "Go execute that," and we put out the word of full confidence, et cetera, et cetera. I called Rumsfeld to assure him and so on. That basically put into the, if not into the freezer, into the fridge, any serious consideration of replacing Secretary Rumsfeld at that point.

GENERAL PETER PACE, US Marine Corps, chairman of the Joint Chiefs of Staff: For retired general officers to think that they could somehow unseat a serving secretary of defense, in my mind is egregious. . . . So when I was asked my opinion from the White House, about what we should be doing about the retired generals' comments, my comment was, I do not know what the president intends or does not intend with this secretary of defense, but it's got to be at least six more months before, if he wants to replace him, that he replaces him. Otherwise, it will look to everybody like these generals somehow influenced who ought to be the secretary of defense.

GEORGE W. BUSH, president of the United States: I'm not going to have the generals force my hand. I thought it was a PR stunt, and it made me very sympathetic to Don Rumsfeld. It had no influence on me whatsoever.

But they didn't know that I was looking for a replacement.

Something New?

HADLEY: The question about a radical new look at the strategy I think does not really begin to emerge until early in 2006. You have in February of 2006, the bombing of the Golden Mosque in Samarra. And people think maybe this is the point where it's all going to start coming apart. And initially, it didn't. . . . And I was quoted on a Sunday talk show saying, "Iraq looked into the abyss, and it decided to step back." That judgment was premature. I think in April and May, finally the unity government is in place, but the violence continues to escalate in this period. And it's in that time frame, in spring of 2006, that really two things happen. One is that I remember the president in the morning, when he's looking through the blue sheets, which have the record of casualties and incidents in Iraq as well as other breaking news intelligence of the morning, there was again an uptick in violence and casualties. And the president looked up and he said, "Hadley, this strategy is not working." And I said, "You're right,

Mr. President, it is not." And he said, "Well, we need to find a new one." And that really, from my way of thinking, started the process.

BUSH: It was violence. The casualties, the violence, the stories of refugees—the papers were full of horror, you know. . . . Twenty people beheaded—there's a lot of brutal violence. Plus intelligence of Iranians moving in, creating instability; Sadr.

Now, when Hadley came to see me, as I recall, you know, I said, "What the hell are we going to do about it?" It wasn't like, "Oh, you know, damn, it's failing." It's, "Let's put a plan together and make sure we don't fail." And I think that was the beginning of the team he put together. Now you've got to keep in mind during this period, there was a lot going on in the presidency. . . . As president, you don't have a single focus. As a matter of fact, it's really important to rely upon others, and . . . I was a seasoned enough president that I had great trust in the people that were around me to the point where I was willing to delegate. Once the president says, "What are we going to do about it?"—in other words, the point is develop some alternatives. . . . I was dealing with a lot of other stuff and can't remember the timetable, but I do know that when Hadley, whose judgment I trust a lot, came in and said, "We're going to have to do something, it's falling apart," that was a seminal moment. In other words, up to that point in time, we were hoping things would get better, and they weren't.

HADLEY: We were in the Oval Office to prepare the president for a conversation with Prime Minister Maliki. And the president said in his sort of jocular way, "So, Meghan, how are your friends in Baghdad doing?" And Meghan says, "Mr. President, they've never been so frightened. I have never seen them or heard them this concerned about what's happening in Iraq." And that, I think, pushed the president even further down the road that we need a new strategy, because here's someone he knew was committed to the Iraq project and knew Iraqis, and she was saying to him, "Mr. President, it's deteriorating. It's not getting better." So I think it's in that spring time frame, April, May of 2006, when it becomes clear we need a new strategy. And that's what really begins the process, from my vantage point.

O'SULLIVAN: I think there was a group of people who felt like US actions did or could have positive ramifications on the situation in Iraq. And that group ended up being sort of the cornerstone of advocating the surge.

I think our State Department colleagues felt a little bit more strongly that we could throw a lot of resources at this problem, but it was so much bigger than us and that in fact it became a question about are Iraqis killing one another because this is a primordial hatred question? Is this something that's been going on a thousand years? We've all heard that. Sunni, Shia. Nothing we can do is going to influence the course of that conflict. Or is this a conflict that is fueled by extremist groups? And if you can inoculate the rest of the population from those extremist groups, you'll see a massive drop in violence. And so that was just two different diagnoses of the same situation, which had vastly different prescriptions follow from them.

FEAVER: What happens over the spring of 2006 is that, the two pistons that were firing our strategy freeze up. The first of the pistons was the belief that we could have political progress and that a steady drumbeat, really, a drumbeat of hitting political milestone after political milestone would propel Iraq forward and create the political momentum that would bring along the Sunnis, and that piston freezes. We have an election, but we can't seat the parliamentary leader because it's hung. That process goes on for months and months and months.

There had been an elaborate hundred-day plan that was going to be kicked in place as soon as the new Iraqi leader is in place. We'll implement this hundred-day plan, and it will allow us to get political momentum, security momentum, economic momentum, etc. We can't implement it, because we don't have a leader.

That's the one piston that's frozen. The other one is, the idea that we would be buying off Sunni anger; the opposite is happening because of the growing spiral of sectarian violence, and in particular the Golden Mosque. It's not just that. It's a steady drumbeat. As part of my job, I'm reading the nightly notes that Meghan O'Sullivan— we called them the POTUS note. It was a nightly summary of things going on in Iraq with graphs, and a review of all the lines of action: security, political, economic, and diplomatic, and so forth. It's a pretty dismal picture.

O'SULLIVAN: It was quite a frustrating period for me and for many people. From my perspective, I became increasingly convinced that our strategy was failing during that period of time. I became very convinced that our strategy was based on a set of assumptions that were no longer true. And the assumption that we had been building our strategy on really since 2004 was that the political process was going to be the driver of security gains, that this was a conflict about power and resources, so we needed to focus on politics. And if we got the politics right, the security would flow. We also assumed that the driver of the violence was primarily an objection to a foreign occupation. And finally, there was the assumption that whatever we could do, Iraqis could do it better.

All the effort was always to get Iraqis to do more and Americans to do less. And these assumptions had led to a strategy that fairly obviously was focused really heavily on the political process, was really focused on pulling back from cities and trying to distance the engagement between Americans and Iraqis. And it was focused on transferring responsibility to Iraqis really whether or not they were ready for it. My sense was . . . that the situation had changed pretty dramatically in Iraq, and we were still executing a strategy that might have been suited to some realities back in 2004—but in 2006, it was totally out of whack.

And a lot of this came from speaking with Iraqis that I had known over the course of my time in Iraq, and from a visit that I made in the spring. . . . I got . . . the sense that you couldn't expect politics to drive security gains, that almost every conversation we were having with Iraqis about politics was interrupted by a bombing, someone being assassinated, a raid, somebody rushing in with news. . . . In that environment, I could see people were drawn more and more into their sectarian identities and their sectarian affiliations. And the idea of political compromise was much, much harder and seemed so irrelevant. And so I returned thinking, if we don't have a floor, the security level isn't at a certain minimum level. We can't expect people to make really hard compromises in the realm of politics.

[The] nightly notes began because President Bush wanted to get a daily update. He used to read them first thing in the morning. . . . We tried to give the president and others who read the Iraq note a quick snapshot, a window into what was happening on the ground. . . . I think that when historians go back and read these hundreds and hundreds of notes, they'll really see that we tried very hard not to sugarcoat anything. . . . And I would say, with all due respect to everyone involved, I think there was a sense, particularly over this period of time, that the president wasn't getting unvarnished views of the situation on the ground in Iraq. . . . We were portraying a very deteriorating situation on the political, economic, and military front.

The president, and to some extent Steve [Hadley], increasingly would ask me for my views after NSC meetings or other meetings where there would be briefings from the field. So from MNF-I [Multi-National Force Iraq], from our ambassador, but particularly on the state of the security situation. . . . I was fielding an increasing number of questions [from the president] that tried to reconcile the quite dire picture that our note was painting with the assessments that came from the field.

BOLTEN: What I saw being briefed to him by the military commanders was what you always get from people who are in the field, which is an optimistic shade on what it is they are doing currently, on current trajectory, which is completely natural because you've got to believe in what you're doing, especially if you're putting people's lives at risk, in order to sustain doing it and doing it in the best possible way. So I did perceive early on, that that's what he was getting from the military commanders, was a realistic view, from their standpoint, but their standpoint is very much colored by the imperative to make the strategy that they were in succeed. The reaction I had to that was, he needs to have a broader aperture on the kind of information he's getting about how it's going, and it's hard to do.

I did notice something when I came in, and noticed it from, for the first time, being privy to all of the president's briefings: the security briefings in the morning, the meetings with the secretaries of state and defense, and the national security advisor, and in particular his usual videoconference meeting with the military, with the combatant commanders and things like that.

I remember in particular, very early in my tenure, a video conference. . . . I remember coming away from that a little bit startled that the president that I saw in every other context, that is to say non-Iraq issues, was a different person than the one that I saw in the Iraq meeting. . . . The president I saw at those war meetings was, to me, noticeably different from the one I saw in every other context, where he was in charge, he was challenging everything. He was keeping people on their toes, they had to satisfy him. In this meeting, I remember thinking he's in this meeting to encourage and satisfy them, that he's viewing his role as supporting the military, because they are the ones sacrificing, they're the ones with this very hard job. My thought at the time was that I should, in my role as chief of staff, in my role as the new set of eyes, that I should try to help bring the guy that I knew as president in all those other contexts, into this context as well. . . . I encouraged what Steve was already doing, which was trying to ventilate the process, trying to give the president more avenues of information, trying to make sure that he was hearing more directly, and with more force, the bad news, that everybody who was watching TV and reading the newspaper was seeing, rather than doing everything he could to support the commanders who were saying we're not doing great but we're just about to turn the corner, we think we've got the right strategy here, and exercise his own judgment, which I trusted enormously from all the other contexts I had seen, and I know Steve did too.

He took his role as commander in chief so seriously. He felt the pain of every family's loss, when he signed the letters or met with the families of the fallen, and he had such respect for the people who were in uniform and doing this incredibly hard job of trying to manage this unmanageable conflict, that I think he did not want to interpose his own judgment ahead of theirs nearly as aggressively as I saw him do in almost every other context.

ROVE: Yeah, at some point in 2006—2005, 2006; I think it's the early part of 2006—people began to just sort of shut down. . . . Ordinary people, American public. It was sort of like we've now completely soured. We were down on it, and now we've crossed over that invisible line, and don't talk to us anymore. . . . Only events, only events are going to influence them. Speeches had lost their ability. They no longer had any purchase. He would go out and say things, but it couldn't change opinion. Only events would.

O'SULLIVAN: I was thinking about the need for something much bigger than something I could do at my level in the steering group that I . . . chaired. But this type of review had to do with changing our overall mission in Iraq, and to a mission which is potentially a lot more resource-intensive. . . . And of course I'm not the only one who was thinking along these lines. But I thought maybe there are some other ways that we can get this review process going. So, . . . I wrote a memo just laying out my sense that our strategy is at fundamental odds with the realities on the ground. We are exacerbating a failing situation rather than contributing to its improvement.

I was hoping, along with others . . . , that we could use a Camp David meeting that had been set for June as an opportunity to try to get some new thinking into the system, and use that as a moment in which we could really force a strategy review, rather from the top down, the bottom up.

New Thinking at the State Department

The White House was not the only epicenter of concern that Iraq required a new strategy. Secretary Rice at the State Department longed for one as well, as 2006 began and the violence in Iraq surged. The current situation appeared intolerable, but also provided an opportunity to put to good use her experience during Bush's first term. "I have to admit," she said, looking back, "that maybe a little bit of it was as national security advisor, feeling that perhaps I've not really done the kind of red-teaming that we perhaps should have done, and this time I was determined, from a different perch, that we were going to be able to red-team. Red-teaming means that you think about everything that's possible."

Put everything on the table, she consequently told her advisors, though others in Washington desirous of a new strategy found one option wholly unpalatable. "What I did not want to see, from my experiences in Vietnam, was a defeated American military," James Jeffrey later recalled. "I did not want to see us withdraw defeated out of there." But "it's hard to justify keeping troops, perhaps more troops, which means more casualties."

RICE: I think everybody was distressed. The president was distressed. I know Steve was distressed. I had a conversation with Steve at one point, and I mentioned to him that every morning, when I was national security advisor, I'd go in to see the president, and he would say—you know, he looked very down and he would say, another hundred people, another fifteen soldiers, you know this is just going on and on and on. And I said, I dreaded walking into the Oval and seeing the blue sheet in front of him, because I knew that it was always bad news, and Steve said, "Well, you should be here now, it's that times ten." So I knew Steve was very worried. I knew that Pete Pace was very concerned, and the chiefs were very concerned by what they were seeing.

I couldn't read Don [Rumsfeld]. On the one hand, Don kept expressing confidence that what we were doing was working. George Casey seemed to be expressing confidence that what we were doing was working. I knew that Zal [Khalilzad] was not at all confident about what we were doing. So, I had a sense that nobody was really satisfied, but the Pentagon was hardest to read.

When I asked Philip [Zelikow] and others to take this on, I really just wanted as out-of-the-box, broad a look, at what was possible.

Philip had a conversation with Doug Lute, because I think, in my way of thinking about it, and I think I communicated this to those who were going to do the out-of-the-box look, we really had three options by this time. One was to just keep churning along and hoping for the best. The Pentagon kept saying, from 2004 onward, well, when the politics straighten out then the security will straighten out. The politics were getting somewhat better, but the security situation wasn't straightening out. But that was an option, just stay the course. The second option was if you could get more forces, then you could really institute clear, hold, and build. The third was, if you couldn't get more forces, it made no sense to keep going with what you were doing, and then you ought to think, perhaps, about other kinds of strategies, including other political strategies. I think that's sort of the guidance that I gave to the think-out-of-the-box people, but beyond that, they were free to think about anything from doubling down, tripling down, to complete and total pullout.

ZELIKOW: Also, at this time [in the spring of 2006], I was desperate enough about the need to articulate a strategy that I actually sat down and drafted a paper and then got Jim Jeffrey to look over it and join me in sending it to the secretary. That actually wrote out a strong military strategy. . . . [We] broke it out into here's an all-out counterinsurgency approach, an all-out clear, hold, and build; here is what we call the selective clear, hold, and build approach, and by selective—in this case, you only pick three to five major sectors in which you're going to make a ramped-up effort to really hold them. And then we identified what we thought if you did that, and here they are, and listed them, and kind of then listed the requisites that went with that. And then there would be a third approach as kind of a more minimalist approach. . . . We wrote in the paper, if you want to do either of the first two options you're going to need—and I don't remember the exact word, but you're going to need a significant increase in troops. . . . We gave it to Meghan and the NSC staff. No particular response to this.

JEFFREY: There were three centers of gravity in this thing . . . the military campaign, social-economic-political reconciliation effort among and by the Iraqis, and the American public. We had finally, after a long struggle, got a new government, Maliki. So we were hoping to have a new way forward, because you always get hopes when you get a new leader. . . . But also we were aware that things were—now we were in something approaching a civil war, or at least threatening a civil war, for the first time, in my mind. . . . By this point, I had become skeptical.

And the third center of gravity was the American people. On all three fronts, things were even gloomier in June of 2006 than they were in the fall, when we came up with clear, hold, and build. I felt that the chances of the Iraqis, who couldn't even see that they were descending into civil war, functioning and pulling themselves out, [were] less than before. The war was becoming ever less popular in the United States . . . so that center of gravity wasn't doing well. And then the first and most important of them, the security situation was deteriorating right in front of us.

My feeling was also—and here I was wrong, this is important— that to the extent we could get any success, Bush would swing back to his I've got to make this a Sweden, because that's what's going to solve the Middle East and make it the next great success story after Eastern Europe. And I was afraid that he still had this *idée fixe*. . . .I felt that this was totally unrealistic, and our efforts to try to do this would undercut a kind of sorry half-assed success, that was the best we could get, I was afraid that even if we could get ourselves back on the road to sorry half success, it would then simply encourage the president and some of the people around him to think that they really could turn this place into Sweden, and that would lead them to do things that would be counterproductive. So I was in a pretty grim mood at this point, and I think that's reflected in the memo.

I felt we needed more troops. . . . I knew this was never going to turn out to be Sweden, so I knew that the real geostrategic, the global goal, I won't even call it a strategic goal, the global goal that the president had for Iraq was never going to happen, and I think I'm right there. Secondly, even a strategic role of . . . a more or less stable Iraq that isn't being torn apart, that is sort of a friend of ours, I thought that that was extremely doubtful. But, what I did not want to see, from my experiences in Vietnam, was a defeated American military. I did not want to see us withdraw defeated out of there. I wanted to see, if possible, if there would be a way to at least beat these guys down enough so that we could withdraw with honor, at least. . . . Those people who were more invested in the surge than I was really did think that they were going to score a strategic victory, and that this would have been worthy of our troops. I cannot emphasize too much in the minds of the US military and people who felt beholden to the US military, which is much of the civilian Iraq-oriented population, the need to have a result that justifies and is worthy of the sacrifices of our troops. We told those young men and women that they were going in there to make democracy possible and to protect the Iraqis and to solve their problems and everything, and these people were out there risking their lives because they believed us. And therefore, to simply do an almost Nixonian thing of, well, we're going to have to stay on because . . . America isn't about losing wars, and we get too many enemies or potential enemies . . . out there, we can't afford to lose a war. That was my argument. But that's a realpolitik argument. I could get away with it because I had been one of the troops sent out there to actually risk my life in '72. I have a lot of respect for that argument, but I know it doesn't sell well in America, so I was kind of cautious on that one. That's why we kind of jumped around. We gave a series of options, none of which were particularly cheery to Condi.

Few commodities in Washington are scarcer than a president's time, and Iraq was not the only issue on Bush's agenda in 2006. Nonetheless it was critical enough for the White House to arrange an intensive strategy review in a venue designed to eliminate distractions. They chose Camp David, but soon found the process even of finding time for an open airing of ideas offered political minefields.

Lead-Up to Camp David

O'SULLIVAN: We realized that here's an opportunity. The president's going to sit down with his national security team for a day and a half and talk about Iraq, and do it away from Washington. . . . How can we inject a few new things into the conversation so it's not a briefing, an update, but it's actually a look at some of the things that have created an impasse here or an impasse there?

I had all these different groups in the Inter-Agency working on reviews of their particular sector, looking at the economic plan. What was working, what wasn't working, what could we propose, the political plan. We tried to do it on the security front as well. There was a huge effort on the part of dozens or hundreds of people to come up with briefs that were hoping to spur conversation . . . among the president and the principals. . . . If you're trying to instigate a conversation that goes beyond the, What happened today? What happened yesterday? What can we expect next week? . . . you need to present somebody with something else. And you also need to actually try to tee up the conversation with all the people who are going to be in the room, not just the president.

There was a lot of effort that went into that. Many, many papers written, briefings done, conversations had among my counterparts, among their principals. And the hope was that this would be a moment where we could really take stock.

FEAVER: As the spring is going on, it's becoming clearer and clearer to me that Iraq is not going well, but it's not clear to me what we should do about it. . . . I had a pretty free rein to speak to a wide range of people, and I'm hearing credible, persuasive critiques of our strategy.

I told Meghan, why don't we tee up a debate between Mike Vickers [then a senior vice president at the Center for Strategic and Budgetary Assessments], who's sort of the "we have too many troops," with someone who says we have too few troops. This would be a way of surfacing the issues that there's a growing . . . outside consensus . . . that our strategy is not working, although there's no consensus about what's the right way to do it.

Meghan liked that idea, and we pitched it to Steve Hadley and suggested this Camp David meeting. We had Mike Vickers already for the "go light." . . . His recommendation was that we had to move even more quickly to a light-footprint approach, one that would remove the occupational sting, the occupation narrative of large US forces. The large US forces had sort of created their own antibodies, so resistance to US. His argument was you've got to go to a light footprint, special forces training the Iraqis to do the counterinsurgency mission, etc. It was a strong critique of what we were currently doing, and an intriguing policy proposal.

The obvious person for the "go heavy" was Fred Kagan, who had been arguing this for quite some time. I was concerned that in that debate that Mike Vickers, who had already met the president and really connected with him well, might have an unfair advantage over Fred. . . . I suggested bringing in Eliot Cohen [Robert E. Osgood Professor of Strategic Studies at Johns Hopkins School of Advanced International Studies], who was Mike Vickers's dissertation advisor. I knew that he could keep Mike Vickers under control. I also knew that he tilted in the direction of pro-surge, so I thought that would even it up, and I felt we could get a vigorous debate between these two positions.

The hope was that this would persuade the president and the national security team that they needed to authorize a more thoroughgoing in-house review. We knew what was said by the outsiders and one single meeting wouldn't be adequate, but it could trigger . . . an internal review.

This was very sensitive . . . because it was a critique of our existing strategy. This is happening within six weeks or so of the famous "Revolt of the Generals," when you have retired generals calling for Rumsfeld to resign. There was some concern in the White House that if we do something like this, particularly in front of the national security cabinet, it will look like we're ambushing Secretary Rumsfeld. . . . What Vickers and Kagan and Cohen had in common is they had all strongly criticized Rumsfeld, and we didn't want it to look like an ambush of Rumsfeld, so we added [Robert] Kaplan [foreign affairs correspondent for the *Atlantic Monthly*]. That had the effect of diluting a little bit, perhaps, the sharpness of the analytical debate.

As part of this effort, Meghan and her team teed up a full terms of reference for a follow-on review. . . . Our expectation was the president would say, I'm not sure which of these guys is right, but we've got to do a thorough review. . . . Then, the paperwork for that review was already all planned, and Meghan had a pretty elaborate series of review efforts that we thought would be launched right on the cusp of, or on the heels, I should say, of the Camp David meeting.

BUSH: See, that's interesting. This is interesting to me because I wasn't a part of any of that stuff. I mean, it was very conniving of you two [Feaver and O'Sullivan]. [*Laughter.*] So that was foreign to me, I mean.

ERIC EDELMAN, under secretary of defense for policy: There was a lot of resistance to the idea of plussing up, increasing the US force at all. And the opposition came from General Casey and from Secretary Rumsfeld for a couple different reasons. One, General Casey used to say that if you bring an additional unit out here [to Iraq], it grows roots, and then it's very tough for me to get them out of here. Because he was very focused on getting down from fifteen brigade combat teams to closer to ten by the end of 2006. . . . He had reservations about bringing on additional forces except for very specific purposes like plussing up the security of the Iraqi election process in December 2005, which we did. We brought in an additional brigade, and we extended a couple brigades so there'd be more overlap, and we were able to plus up the numbers.

Second, he [Casey] and Rumsfeld were very concerned about plussing up the numbers of troops because of the impact it would have on the rotation base. . . . In the case of the Army they'd . . . have twelve months out, but then come back for reset and retraining and whatnot. For the Marines it was seven months out and then back. And then if you extended those tours from twelve months to fifteen months or seven months to nine months, as we ultimately had to do in part as a result of the surge, you put enormous stress on the force in terms of personnel, which was a legitimate concern obviously for the secretary and his commander to have.

HADLEY: I thought that the strategy review process had to be presidentially led. It had to be something that the president called for, that had his support. . . . Because my view was we only had one more bite at this apple, given how long the war had gone on, how attrited the public support was . . . we only got one more chance to get it right. It was about the president's legacy. It was also one of the most important decisions he was going to make in the second term. And again, the American people—the only person in this whole constellation that had been elected by the American people to make these decisions was the president. My view was it had to be a system—a process within the system, not outside the system and that was focused on the president and getting him the position where he could make the decision he needed to make.

It was going to be delicate. . . . We had earlier tried to make some suggestions to Secretary Rumsfeld about how to relook at some of strategy in Afghanistan. . . . And I thought on the theory that, you know, we're all one team—I asked the president of the United States if I had his permission to go to Secretary Rumsfeld and present these ideas. And we did, and I went into the SecDef's conference room, and it was the chilliest reception I've ever received in the SecDef conference room, and I've been there a lot my career. And we explained our ideas. And at the end, the secretary said, "If you and the president have lost confidence in the ability of this building to do military planning, then you should get yourself a new secretary."

O'SULLIVAN: It's impossible to group everyone at the Pentagon into the Pentagon. But if my memory serves me right, people were mostly frustrated with the lack of the political progress. And that was the real focus. The lens was on, Why can't you civilians get a government in place, and then we can have some political stability, and this will have positive reverberations for the security realm. And of course that's true, but it's also a lot more complicated than that.

CROUCH: I think Defense still at that point believed that there was a good chance that the current strategy was going to work. . . . One

argument you could make is that . . . the strategy that they were executing might have worked, but that the timeline on which it would
have taken to work was politically not viable.

ZELIKOW: We need to set up a meeting in which the strategy will be
pulled up by its roots, and we're really going to have the heart-to-
heart. The president and his advisors are going to get together for
days out in Camp David, and they are really going to have the blunt,
all-out conversation that they have long needed to have so this strategy can be pulled up and thoroughly reexamined. We believed that
the NSC staff was on board for this, and kind of gets this. During
this, I'm urging Condi to talk to the vice president. . . . And by spring
of '06, I'm actually lobbying to get the bureaucratic clout of the vice
president to help get a strategic review, because I figure remembering Dick Cheney from when he was secretary of defense, like, you
know, he gets what strategy is. It's like, how can he be content with
this? And we need his bureaucratic clout to help, because this is a
really hard problem now.

HANNAH: Certainly by that time, [the vice president] was completely
convinced that something had to change. Again, we were providing
him with an awful lot of information in 2005 and early 2006, that
things on the security front were going badly. . . . [The Office of
the Vice President] saw [the Camp David meeting] as a potentially
important event, perhaps even a key turning point in beginning to
do what we thought was necessary in terms of turning American
strategy in a more productive direction.

I know within our office, and I'm sure throughout the US government, we did a tremendous amount of preparation for the vice president, put together some very serious, at least I think, two very large
briefing books filled primarily with intelligence reports and assessments and analyses of just how bad things were going; the kinds of
levels of violence that we were seeing, the fact that the approach
being pursued by our forces in theater was not in fact working. We
were not getting a handle on the insurgency and reducing levels
of violence. On the contrary; levels of violence were increasing
quite dangerously and dramatically. We had had an ongoing conversation with a number of people who I think in some ways had
a better understanding of what was happening perhaps than some
of our commanders on the ground in Iraq. People like Colonel [H.
R.] McMaster, like the DIA intelligence official Derek Harvey, like
Colonel John Nagl.[2] These were a series of informal conversations

that we'd had, at least since 2004, with people who had experience on the ground and understood how dire the situation was and how negative the trends were on the security front, despite the achievements we had achieved in the political realm. So, we kind of tried to compile all of that together before that Camp David meeting in June of 2006.

CHENEY: We were trying to stand up the Iraqi government and Iraqi security forces, so that they could take over responsibility so we could leave. The normal way that would operate once the president signed off on a strategy, then everybody else better be out there pulling their fair share of the load, following the president's instructions and executing on his strategy. So, I didn't see it so much as resistance, but a lot of people trying to do their job, to do what they thought the boss wanted. Gradually, over a period of time, it became clear that that wasn't adequate to the task. We weren't winning.

There was a feeling on the part of the military that State wasn't doing enough. There was an argument that really went back to Afghanistan. And the view the Defense Department had was that they ended up having to do things that were more of a civilian nature, in terms of working with the locals; things that should have been done by AID or by the State Department, and so there was controversy there.

There was the view in the Defense Department that the key was to turn things over as quickly as possible and reduce the US presence. I think John Abizaid, I can recall him talking about that, or General Casey, George Casey, also held similar views, that the key was the transfer of power, the transfer of responsibility. And as we talked about that, it became increasingly clear that some of us believed that that wasn't the right objective; the right objective was to do that, but after the Iraqis were in position to carry forward on the mission, and to be able to secure their own territory, to be able to cope with al-Qaeda and so forth.

War Council

Outside experts—Vickers, Kagan, Cohen, and Kaplan—were called in to spark discussion, and specifically to present different points of view. Bush's advisors expected two days of frank discussion with their commander in chief, hoping to probe the very core of their strategy toward Iraq. They instead got one. Unknown to most of the discussion's participants, indeed in a development known beforehand to only a handful in Bush's inner circle, the president had other plans.

FRED KAGAN, resident scholar, American Enterprise Institute: We each had a certain period of time to make our pitch, and we did it, and it was, you know, as I recall it, it was very respectful and professional and oriented on the principals, because of course it wasn't just the president, as you know, I mean it was the whole war cabinet there.

The notion that you can get after even terrorist groups, let alone insurgencies, with special forces leading decapitation raids, has been about as thoroughly disproven as it's possible to disprove any theory, and I refer anyone who has questions about that to Stan McChrystal's memoir, in which he describes . . . the phenomenal damage that he and his team did to AQI senior leadership, and concludes that we were nevertheless losing at the end of all of that.[3] Mike [Vickers] was proposing something that was a lot less intense than what McChrystal actually did, and I didn't think what McChrystal was doing was going to work either.

The conclusion I came to was that it was two-thirds of a strategy, that, you know, General Abizaid, from the outset, was emphatic that if we put too many forces, we have too much of a presence, we're going to create antibodies, we're going to create hostility, which is true. That is a phenomenon observable throughout counterinsurgency; it's not arguable that that happens. And he was also concerned that if we did too much, we would create a perennial dependency on our forces and the Iraqis would be stunted in their development and they would never be able to take over, and that's also true and has been demonstrated repeatedly in the history of counterinsurgency. So, we started with two premises that I absolutely agreed with, but my study of counterinsurgencies told me that there was a missing third component, which is that if the counterinsurgent is not providing security, then the whole thing will go off the rails even if you avoid those other two traps, and that in fact the real art is in balancing these three mutually contradictory requirements of providing security, without having too heavy a footprint, that you create too many antibodies, without creating dependency, but without allowing stability and security to collapse. On the military side, I felt like there was a very sophisticated approach that was just missing a piece or overemphasizing two pieces.

You had Mike Vickers there recommending the exact opposite, and vociferously. I would say I was on one end. I think Eliot [Cohen] was generally pretty close to where I was at, I think. Mike was on the other end, and Kaplan was moderate, sort of. So I mean, it was very far, I think, from being a clarion call for a massive surge. I mean a number of different perspectives were offered, as would be appropriate in that environment. I certainly did not walk in there feeling that I had a phalanx at my back, to go make the case for the surge.

One of the things that really struck me was that after the meeting was over, the president came over and shook our hands. . . . I think Eliot was the one that he was most interested in talking to, and one of the questions that he asked really struck home, and it was, how do I know? How do I find out what's really going on? There was nothing disloyal in it, there was no indication that he was saying he didn't trust his subordinates or anything. It was just, how do I, as president of the United States and commander in chief, how can I really dig beyond what I'm getting? How can I really understand what's going on, on the ground?

HANNAH: It wasn't my impression there was any real theme that emerged from that [meeting with the experts], nothing that sort of hit the president or the other principals in the head and said, my God, we've got to do something, and this is the thing that we've got to do, a range of views and sort of confirmation that things were not going as well as they needed to go, that there needed to be some corrections. But no real sense of urgency coming out of there that this is what we're going to do, that we're going to review these policies from A to Z and figure out a new course ahead that would improve the situation on the ground in relatively short order. That did not emerge from that session at Camp David, in part, I think, because the president disappeared on the second day that was scheduled for that event and showed up in Baghdad and had what might have been an important PR event with the new Iraqi cabinet, the prime minister, that perhaps was important for the American people in trying to bolster support for the policy, but I felt that Camp David effort was—I was disappointed in what emerged out of it in terms of results and new thinking in the US government, and at least I considered it to have been a lost opportunity.

Missed Opportunity?

F. KAGAN: You know . . . if the situation were such that an hour and a half meeting with four outside experts could change the course of the strategy of the war, with nothing else going on, we would have been in a really weird world. I didn't have that expectation at the time, and I don't think that was a reasonable expectation. I think fate and a somewhat unfortunate decision by the president conspired to make that meeting pretty meaningless. The fate was that we killed Zarqawi a couple of days, at most, before the meeting. . . . I had the impression that the president felt that that was a very positive moment and a potential turning point, and so his openness to believing that things were really fundamentally off the rails was relatively lessened, because Zarqawi was in fact a real bogey, and certainly no one outside of maybe a handful of people in the intelligence community, if that, knew that, in fact, Abu Ayyub al-Masri would be a much more dangerous and effective foe. So that, I think, reduced the intellectual valence of [the Camp David meeting] a little bit for the president.

But then there was the fact that he had decided to pull a whizzer on everybody by, you know, leaving at the end of the first day and turning up in Baghdad. It was pretty apparent to me, after I saw that happen, that there was a certain giddiness in his demeanor that was driven by the fact that he was pulling a whizzer over on his team, and I think that was an unfortunate decision. As is so often the case with this president, there were very admirable attributes in that decision, but . . . if the president is going to decide to devote two full days to really sitting down and talking strategy, that was not a good use of that time.

CHENEY: The message might have been obscured in part because we just got Zarqawi . . . killed the leader of al-Qaeda in Iraq. That was a major success. It wasn't as though there was just an unending string of bad news coming in, for those who were worried about the strategy or trying to organize debate and discussion about the strategy, their efforts were, to some extent, pushed aside perhaps, because of the success that we were having in some of the areas. . . . I always thought of the victory over Zarqawi as a very significant event. We'd been trying to get that guy for a long time. I've still got a brick on my desk, in my office in Washington, my home, that's got MBZ 6-7-07, the date he was nailed by our special ops guys. It was an F-16 with a couple of five-hundred-pound bombs. That was a milestone event. Somebody presented me with that brick.

ABIZAID: Decapitation does not work. . . . It just doesn't work. You have to have a long-term strategy and a long-term presence that allows you to be able to drain the swamp of the ideological fervor that moves it forward.

BOLTEN: I see [the Camp David meeting] almost as a middle stage in the president's process. . . . I think the efforts that Hadley, supported by me, were making, was where the president was going anyway. . . . I saw a pretty clear continuum, where there would be moments of optimism, like the appointment of Maliki, with the selection of Maliki, like the appointment of his cabinet, where we thought, OK, finally, now this will be—he's promised and put together an inclusive cabinet. We made a trip over to visit with the cabinet, one of the great planning coups of all time.

I would have been much more concerned at that meeting, not listening, not so much about the conversation that was going on, which was an important conversation, a lot of which happened around the dinner table at Camp David, but I also would have been very concerned with the logistics of what I think was an extraordinarily clever plan, to get the president into Baghdad, meeting with the new Maliki cabinet, without blowing our cover and letting everybody know that the president of the United States was coming in there.

RICE: It's very easy, when you're doing this every day, to get stuck in a particular place, and you're just trying to grind through and make it work. I don't know how many times I've said plan B is to make plan A work. You get into kind of that mind-set, and so opening the aperture was really very important. I don't really remember if I thought going into Camp David, we might open a chance for red-teaming. I certainly didn't come out of Camp David thinking that we had, and it seemed to me, if anything, Camp David rather kind of affirmed that we were probably going to stay the course.

HADLEY: The problem was that that meeting at Camp David really got hijacked by another idea, which was to have the president of the United States convene his meeting for a strategy review on day one at Camp David and then fly overnight and to appear and join Prime Minister Maliki in his cabinet in Baghdad on the second day, and have the two cabinets then have a video link and begin to talk to one another. It was a way of showing support for Maliki, support for this new government. It probably was a higher priority, but it had the effect that the president in day one was not really focused on the kind of strategic thinking we wanted him to do, because he was kind of looking forward to his meeting in Baghdad. And of course, on day two it was completely hijacked by a very different agenda. So that was our effort to begin an interagency-wide discussion about a new strategy, and it really was stillborn because it was kind of overcome by the need to connect with the new Maliki cabinet.

JEFFREY: I hated the summit, and I hated the idiot trip to Baghdad thereafter, because it was all about, as far as I was—my take on this whole goddamn thing? It was sucking up to Don Rumsfeld, the civilians aren't doing enough. That's why we're not succeeding in Iraq. So we brought in all of these agencies who don't know shit from Shinola when it comes to Iraq, with some exceptions. . . . I saw no sign that that had anything to do with our military strategy. . . . And that's the thing that we needed, so therefore I just dismissed the whole thing as a waste of time, and I tried my very best to duck out of anything involving this thing, because they knew it was all going to come down.

CROUCH: I think that [Bush's Baghdad trip] was a judgment call. And I wouldn't second-guess it today, because I think it was really important. . . . To lay the foundation for what subsequently came was important to that relationship, again, on the first start.

CHENEY: I thought it was very important for him to go [to Baghdad]. He worked that account very hard. When I think of all the hours we spent on the SVTS [secure video teleconference system] with our people, especially later on as part of the surge, with Maliki and his folks, it was a sort of a hands-on way of doing business, and that's the way President Bush liked to operate. He enjoyed that kind of contact. He felt very strongly about Maliki, and that he could help shape the situation in Iraq by working with him, by having a personal relationship. . . . I would have said it was more important for him to be over there meeting with Maliki, while we do our thing here. He can meet with the cabinet any time, his National Security Council. It took some effort to put together a session with the leader of Iraq, and under the circumstances that, it made it possible for us to sort of encourage them down the road, and we wanted them to travel, and there was nobody better to do that than George Bush.

BUSH: In order to affect how another leader behaves, you have to court that person and you have to befriend that person, and you can't do it by hectoring or lecture. It's really like, "You're important, you're elected and you're important, and I'm curious to know about your decision making, and, you know, why are you making these kinds of decisions? Don't you think you ought to try this?" . . . Both [Maliki] and [the president of Afghanistan Hamid] Karzai were taking over a young democracy, and it was, a lot of it was foreign to them, and I fully understood that their governments weren't going to look like ours. On the other hand, decision making has got some commonalities to it, and that's what I tried to get Maliki to understand.

SATTERFIELD: I believe strongly that the drafting of the Iraqi constitution, the elections, indeed, Maliki's initial assumption of office were in fact positive developments. . . . They didn't confuse the security issue, though. Those successes stand on their own, but they were being countered and challenged by the fundamental deterioration of security and stability in Iraq. . . . Politics would not matter. Politics would be submerged in the flood of violence and division.

CHAPTER 3

Together Forward?

June–August 2006

Sectarian violence continued to worsen in Baghdad and elsewhere in Iraq as the summer of 2006 progressed. The situation continued to look bleak by other measures as well. Joint US-Iraqi military efforts (Operations Together Forward I and II) revealed Iraqi military deficiencies. In some cases, Iraqi security forces, acting in a sectarian manner, actively made matters worse.

Bureaucratic silos continued to hinder open consideration of new strategies. Elements of the National Security Council, for example, encouraged the "country team"—General George Casey, commander of Multi-National Force Iraq (MNF-I), and Ambassador Zalmay Khalilzad—to request a new strategic review, reasoning that such a plea, and perhaps only such a plea, from the people on the ground in Baghdad would catalyze action. The president, after all, had already made plain his unwillingness to do anything that might undermine military morale, or worse yet make it appear as though politicians back home were taking control of the war from the war fighters. This had been a central lesson of Vietnam for those of Bush's generation: that the cause was lost in large measure because of undue meddling from the home front. Right or wrong as a matter of history, it was a lesson from the past Bush was determined not to repeat. "Our commanders on the ground will determine the size of the troop levels," he had recently said.[1]

Efforts to encourage calls from Baghdad for a strategic review failed. Casey opposed any change in strategy that might undermine his troops or his command, though even this stalwart warned that scheduled troop withdrawals would have to be delayed, given the lack of progress on the ground. Rebuffed in Baghdad, those near Bush who sought a new strategy turned closer to home. The goal, as Chief of Staff Josh Bolten observed, was to produce "if not a consensus, at least some critical mass of support for a dramatic change in strategy." At least enough of a consensus to persuade his boss.

Dismal Start to Summer

GEN JACK KEANE, U.S. Army (Retired): What the Sunni insurgency and the Al-Qaeda are trying to do is undermine that government's effectiveness before it even gets connected to the people. They wanted the people to have no confidence in this new democratic government that they just elected. They wanted to sever that relationship before it actually got started, and that was a brilliant strategy in my judgment and a strategic one and one that they were able to achieve. The United States responded with Together Forward I, which failed, [. . .] and then they tried Together Forward II later in the year. I think it was in the late summer, fall of the year, and that failed as well.

F. KAGAN: We were observing at the time, from outside, this phenomenon, that we were having sectarian cleansing going on, that we had militias. [. . .] We were able to track pretty well, from open sources actually, where the fault lines, where the fighting was, where the sectarian fighting was, because there was—I mean, you know, if you read into the reporting, if you read into what the media narratives are, about what's going on, on the street, you can draw some conclusions that did not make sense in the context of the theory that was driving these operations.

SATTERFIELD: We had been so focused on getting out of Dodge, on producing the metrics—the endless metrics which would demonstrate X number of Iraqis trained to Y proficiency, thus allowing Z numbers of US forces to first pull back, and then depart—that we had not, as I noted as early as latter part of 2005, pulled our own lens back and taken a deep look at exactly what, in the real world of the Iraqi field, was going on. . . . I had reservations as to the ability of the military to get this right, or to self-assess.

O'SULLIVAN: The request or the intention of General Casey in June of 2006 to bring home two brigades . . . intensified this feeling of we've got very different views, there are very different views in the government about what's actually happening here and what's going to make sense.

ABIZAID: I got the impression that people in Washington had the impression that our troops were sitting around on their base camps, not moving around and fighting, and that was crazy. Our casualties were going up, they weren't going down, and troops were out there fighting. But there was a hesitation, until we heard it from the national command leaders, and we didn't really hear it until the president made the decision about the surge, that he would underwrite the additional casualties that would surely come from that.

Operation Together Forward I and II

Two joint operations in particular consumed military commanders on the ground in the summer of 2006, each symbolically named to highlight that neither Washington nor Baghdad could solve this problem on its own: Operation Together Forward (which commenced on June 9) and Operation Together Forward II (which began two months later). Unable to bring peace, they instead revealed deeper structural flaws within the Iraqi military, including the vacuum of experienced leadership that plagued the institution since its de-Baathification after 2003. The result was thus more violence, some perpetrated by the military itself, rather than the calm and security desired. "By August or September," Condoleezza Rice recalled, "I was pretty worried that we—well, I thought we were losing, flat out thought we were losing."

PACE: As best I recall, the purpose of [Operation Together Forward] was to begin the process of turning over the battlefield responsibilities to the Iraqi armed forces, and the way to do that, that I recall, was not going to be just one day we've got it and the next day you've got it, but to start working side by side, until we were able to feel the comfort level, both in Washington and in Baghdad, that the Iraqi forces were ready to take it on by themselves.

LUTE: Well, in a real strategic sense, that had to be our approach, because we weren't going to colonize Iraq. We weren't going to stay there forever. It had to be eventually a strategy of transition to Iraqi security forces. That was the only thing that was going to be authentic and durable. The challenge is that I think in '06 it became clear that they were not standing up fast enough to allow us to stand down fast enough, both for domestic political reasons, but also because over time the tolerance of the Iraqi people to our presence of 150,000 American troops was waning. Some described this as "the clock"; you know, the clock was running against our presence in Iraq. And I think that that's generally right. So the thing that's very hard to escape is this underlying appreciation that our time was limited. And when you describe that by way of a running clock, or a closing window of opportunity, there's this sense that at some point, certainly by '05 and '06, our presence was generating part of the problem, and was feeding the insurgency.

Sometimes the surge debate loses the point that in the long term of course we were going to transition. It was a question of how fast in the face—and what were the odds of successful transition given the challenges we faced.

Efforts to stabilize Baghdad [Operation Together Forward I and II] focused on increased Iraqi security force presence in Baghdad, and the problem was that it was, perhaps, too little too late, because the sectarian violence, the sectarian cleansing, if you will, of Baghdad neighborhoods, was so far advanced, and in some cases promoted by the Iraqi security forces—I mean, in particular the Iraqi police—that just adding more Iraqis to the mix I think just was insufficient. . . . In fact, there was even at one point a Baghdad Security Plan III—under consideration. Now, I also remember that we had a hard time— General Casey, I believe, had a hard time generating the Iraqi forces that were promised for these Baghdad security plans. So even if—my belief is that it was—this was—the problem was beyond the Iraqi capacity to deal with it, but even if they had a chance, under-resourcing the Iraqi forces committed to this very tough task just proved too little too late.

SATTERFIELD: The US begins a Baghdad focused series of operations. The latest of which were the Ma'an ila Al-Amam, the Together Forward Operations. The operations built by the US military—its command in Iraq as well as the Pentagon—as the necessary joint operations to both establish confidence and effectiveness in the form of Iraqi forces, and stabilize the situation in Baghdad, fail. And I use fail in the clearest possible term. They fail disastrously.

JEFFREY: Everybody was focused on this Together Forward thing. This was going to be the flagship of how we would do things, and it failed. Tens of thousands of US troops and tens of thousands of Iraqis, and we didn't accomplish anything.

KIMBERLY KAGAN, adjunct professor, Georgetown University: So the Iraqi security forces were in Operation Together Forward I and Together Forward II, going into some of the most dangerous neighborhoods, particularly in Baghdad. And what would happen in those neighborhoods was that the Iraqis would go in, and they would be indiscriminate in their fire. They would shoot a lot. They would not shoot only bad people, and they would, in some cases, actually facilitate the movement of some of the Shia militias, including the Iranian-backed Shia militias that were engaged in extrajudicial killings, executions, in some of the Sunni neighborhoods of Baghdad.

O'SULLIVAN: The Iraqi forces just did not appear to have the will or capability to do what they needed to do. General Casey had plans that were utilizing American forces but also relied heavily on Iraqi components to the plan.

. . . Those Iraqi forces were coming from parts of the country, other parts of the country. And they would leave, say, Basra, and never show up in Baghdad. . . . It was a pretty massive non-showing-up. It was pretty clear that the Iraqis were not there in the capacity that we needed them to, to do this joint operation. . . . This was another lesson, like how far are we from actually reaching the stated goal of our strategy, which is to transition security and other factors to Iraqi forces?

FEAVER: Together Forward I, the unit didn't show up. Together Forward II, it showed up but then operated in what was perceived to be a sectarian fashion. And so raising the idea that they're either not going to show up or they will show up and be unreliable for the plan.

O'SULLIVAN: At this point I think we're getting a much greater appreciation for the fact that actually, Iraqi forces are as much part of the problem as they are a solution to the problem as they're currently constituted. . . . There were significant parts of the Iraqi security establishment which were perpetuating acts of sectarian violence.

There was this . . . idea of like, well, let the Iraqis fail, and then they'll learn from the failure. And at some point I think some of us started to say, look, there are certain things that are too important for us to let the Iraqis fail right now. There was a feeling, at least on my part and people that I was working with in my office, that we had just taken this transferring things to Iraqis at all costs much too far much too fast, and that it risked even destabilizing the entire effort.

F. KAGAN: We were so fixated on the insurgency, and we were so fixated on al-Qaeda, al-Qaeda in Iraq, that we did not recognize the role that the Iranian-backed Shia sectarian militias, many of whom, in 2006, were actually in the security forces, were playing in driving the sectarian conflict. Now at the time, without the full context, I, like many others, largely thought that the sectarianism, the real bad sectarianism that we saw, was driven by the destruction of the al-Askari mosque in February of 2006, and so forth. I now understand that that's not the case, that we'd had really serious sectarian actors in the force from early on, avenging themselves, avenging the Shia on Sunni populations, which was driving the sectarian conflict, so that it was even deeper than I thought it was at the time.

The problem with Together Forward is that it didn't recognize that at all. The premise of that operation was that the Iraqis are blue, the Iraqi security forces are blue, and they're fighting al-Qaeda in Iraq, which is red, and we're backing blue against red, period, full stop. What we're actually doing was backing Iranian-backed-and-controlled sectarian Shia militias that were engaged in vicious sectarian cleansing of Sunni neighborhoods that looked like an existential threat to the inhabitants of those neighborhoods, who then allowed al-Qaeda in Iraq to come in to defend them, because it was the only force that could defend them, and in some cases replace them. One of the problems, of course, is that as we were not, as our troops were not living out with the population and were not engaging regularly enough with who was there, we didn't have a sense for who actually belonged in the neighborhood.

. . . You had neighborhoods that were fundamentally depopulated, and then they were repopulated by various extremists and so forth. You would go in and you'd think that you would be talking to the population, but you're actually talking to terrorist squatters. The Iraqi security forces were not helpful because they were ready to tell us, especially the sectarian elements among them, that any particular Sunni that they were looking at was an al-Qaeda terrorist and we needed to kill him. Together Forward just enabled this on a grand scale, and it basically drove off the military-age males in the Sunni communities, established Iraqi police units, including the Wolf Brigade basically, you know, the Badr core sectarian cleansing machine, in Sunni heartland areas, where they began to do unspeakable things, and drive things even worse. It was absolutely a counterproductive operation that was driven by a, at this point I've got to say, pretty blind acceptance of our own theories of what was going on, not enough in touch with what was actually going on.

LUTE: I think the other thing that began in '06, in my recollection, is that we began to appreciate just what we were up against in forming the Iraqi security forces. And so this process, in my view, got started late. It was underfunded. We provided insufficient resources to the advisory effort. . . . For years advisors were sort of ad hoc teams that came together in the States. They didn't know one another. They weren't trained to be advisors. They just kind of slapped together, assembled out, thrown into the mix with Iraqi battalions and brigades. In some cases they were advising the Iraqis on roles that they had never performed themselves. Many of these jobs went to the reserve component forces. Why? Because the active component forces were busy in the one-to-one rotation. . . . So the stress on the force began to play out, because we economized with the building of the Iraqi security forces. It was years after the invasion of Iraq that we actually got serious in terms of resources in the advisory effort. And I can remember throughout my time at CENTCOM one of the persistent demands on the system was for more capable, more coherent advisors, in teams that were serious. . . . But we economized for a couple years. By '06, '05 and '06, I think we were beginning to understand the price that we paid for taking that economy early on, because they were not developing at the pace that we imagine, they were not absorbing the training as well as they should have. . . . We began to appreciate just how hard the leader development part of force development was, and especially in the face of de-Baathification, where, you know, much of the military culture, the institutional knowledge of how to be an army, had been legislated away by way of de-Baathification. So this really became apparent when complete units of especially the police just loaded in and piled on the sectarian violence, and actually became, you know, in some ways, some of the worst perpetrators of sectarian violence. So there's this underlying appreciation, growing appreciation, that the vehicle, which was supposed to take us from stand up / stand down, was flawed at its core.

FEAVER: In the late July time frame . . . there was a military incident [at Gaziliyah] where they tried to move Iraqi units to come to the aid of a particular battle. The Iraqi units didn't show up, or didn't show up in force. It dramatized the idea that we don't have enough reliable Iraqi forces to provide adequate population security.

. . . That validated all of the arguments that I had been hearing Meghan and the other NSC directorate-level folks making for we don't have enough forces.

ABIZAID: I am not on the ground saying, Put these forces here, go to—
Guys on the NSC staff were doing that, and I wish they hadn't. . . .
In one of these big operations you have too many people who don't
know what they're doing with their fingers in the pie, and that was
certainly the case from the NSC, both under Condi Rice and under
Steve Hadley. When they did know what they were doing, dealing
with strategic political issues and diplomatic issues, they were excellent. But arguing with us over whether or not we had enough forces
allocated to Dora district of downtown Baghdad was—there was
nothing, no insight that they had was any better than any other person in downtown Washington, DC. And I trusted our commanders
on the spot to be able to know what was going on there. . . . George
[Casey] and I chafed at the meddling from Washington. There were
crazy things going on, where people from the NSC staff would call
down to subordinate commanders in the field and ask them how this
was going and that was going.

It was clear that we were entering into a period where we had to
reassess what we were doing and how we were doing it, and we were
not satisfied with the performance of the Iraqi defense forces—first
and foremost the police, secondly the army, although the army was
not nearly as bad as it subsequently turned out to be. . . . In the
2006 period, where the sectarian violence was really getting intense,
particularly in the Samarra/Baghdad, the Baghdad area—and really
I'd say what we were seeing was a Shia offensive to isolate Baghdad,
to ethnically cleanse Baghdad—the Kurds asked me to come up to
Sulaymaniyah and have a discussion about what they thought was
going on, and they were of the opinion at that time that the government had become so sectarian that something different had to be
done. . . . We had gone from what was, I would characterize in 2004
and 2005, primarily a Baathist-led Sunni insurgency to, by mid-2006,
it's a Islamic extremist al-Qaeda / al-Qaeda in Iraq insurgency with a
lot of Baathist participation.

HADLEY: I remember very clearly a conversation that I had with
Meghan, because we believed that in order to control the sectarian
violence, there needed to be a neutral law enforcer, a neutral provider of security. And my view was of course that's what we were
doing in training and equipping the Iraqi army; it was to be a nonsectarian army loyal to the national government, trusted by the people
in bringing order to the country with—regardless of the sectarian
identity of the population in which it was deployed. That was our

goal, and that's what I was focused on. And so when people talked about, you know, we need a neutral provider of security, my view was it actually wasn't going to be the US Army, it was going to be this Iraqi security force.

But Meghan convinced me in the summer—that while that was where we wanted to go, it was not where we were or could get in any short-term time frame. And in fact, the only force that was going to be accepted by the communities was actually an American force. And that's why the surge in the end of the day had such a strong American component. . . . I became convinced that actually to bring down the sectarian violence, the United States Army didn't need to get out of the way. In fact, the US military needed to inter-position itself and of course provide security to all three communities. And that of course was the essence of the change of strategy that was associated with the surge.

Fifty Questions

FEAVER: During this time, Meghan hasn't given up on the idea of a thoroughgoing review, but instead of launching it in a formal interagency way, she hits on the idea of teeing up the questions that had been the terms-of-reference questions for the review, giving those to the president for him to ask Casey directly in his weekly SVTS. And that, over the course of July, the questions get a little bit sharper, more pointed, probing Casey on getting to the logic of the existing strategy, and questions that invited Casey to think that the president's doubting whether this strategy is going to work.

O'SULLIVAN: I remember we put together these questions, which was quite a long list of questions. And the idea was to ask some sort of fundamental questions about our strategy, slightly different than the kinds of questions that generally were asked in the weekly meetings which . . . could feel routine because they happened every week.

This was an effort to really ask . . . more probing questions, and to do so in a much more private setting. This is really Steve asking these questions on behalf of the president. The hope and expectation was that this would trigger some thinking. At this point, I think Steve is feeling really uncomfortable with where things are going, and the president's feeling really uncomfortable. And we're looking to the field at this point. . . . We would have been thrilled to get an acknowledgment of a strategic impasse.

I really knew how hard it is when you're there day to day, how hard it is to note you're in a strategic impasse. Because every day is consumed by things that are totally unexpected, and it's very hard to anticipate everything that's happening. And you can have a very clear vision of how what you're trying to do might work out, it just might require twelve or thirteen things to happen. And it's harder, sometimes you need a little distance to say, OK, well, what are the chances of those twelve or thirteen things all happening to make it work out?

I think the questions were really an effort to get an acknowledgment of a strategic impasse and to create kind of a very nonhostile strategic review. And they didn't achieve that.

HANNAH: Everybody had sort of come to the realization that the dramatic deterioration in security in the Iraqi capital was going to be a make-or-break game for us, that we needed to get on top of that. We certainly saw that effort with General Casey, as kind of the next opportunity after that Camp David event, where we'd had enough of General Casey's new battle plan for Iraq, we'd had enough experience with it and the results were disappointing enough, that it was sort of the next big opportunity for the VP, from our point of view, and perhaps from other principals in the US government, to really begin to press and make clear to the command in Iraq that there was kind of a fundamental unease in Washington, with the current state of affairs, and that we really needed to begin thinking about new directions.

HADLEY: There were some briefings that were attempted to be provocative and to get General Casey and Ambassador Khalilzad to respond to questions that would have hopefully provoked them to take a strategic relook. Because it was my conviction that the best way to get this done would be for Casey and Khalilzad to decide we needed to relook the strategy. And for, of course, the senior leadership at the Pentagon to believe that they should initiate the process of doing a strategy review, so it would not have the "not invented here" reaction that Meghan and I got when we brought some constructive ideas over about Afghanistan. But that process was unfortunately not provoked by the Camp David meeting.

The second round was the so-called fifty questions exercise, where we took the kinds of questions that we had wanted to be discussed at Camp David and put them in terms of a list of questions that I was authorized by the president to put to Casey and Khalilzad in the presence of Secretary Rumsfeld. And I don't know whether Condi was on that call or not. I think not. That was an effort, again, through some fairly hard-hitting questions, to see if we could provoke Khalil-zad and Casey working with, of course, Secretary Rumsfeld, to initiate their own relook at the strategy. And it probably helped in that process, but it was really a kind of second-best alternative. We got some interesting answers; we wrote them up; we circulated them to the principals; we provided them to the president; and I think it provided some grist for those informal strategy reviews that were going on in the summer both at State, at the NSC, and at the Pentagon.

I think that they were surprised by [the fifty questions]. I think they were more pointed than they expected. I think they were surprised to hear them from me; I don't have, exactly, that kind of MO or manner. But I was pushing them, and they read it that way, and whatever they might have thought privately, they responded as the professionals they were and provided as good answers as they could. I think it was a very useful process. But it was unusual, and I think it was noticed. We were pushing them with the president's blessing. And they knew that. And I had informed them that this was something that had been blessed by the president, and indeed that we had given the questions that we were going to ask to the president. I'm not sure he read them, but he had them. Again, this was all part of, this needed to be the president's review. This needed to be something he was calling for if it was ultimately really going to be taken seriously by all the participants.

RICE: I think in part, people kept expecting that there would be some event that would trigger a better result. We had the elections in Jan-uary, then we had the formation of the government. Then we have a constitution. And so every time you had one of these events, because to a certain extent, I guess we all bought in a little bit, to the idea that the politics would improve the security situation. So with each one—oh, then we killed Zarqawi, all right, so we sort of thought that would have the effect. And so probably, because it's so hard to turn an aircraft carrier like this around, the tendency is to stay with a strategy and to expect the next event to improve the situation. I think I've been describing for you that underneath, people were starting to think about a different approach.

As national security advisor, you also have a very delicate situ-ation, because the Pentagon was supposed to be in charge of this operation. The president had been very clear that the secretary of defense was first on when it came to issues of reconstruction, issues of security, and so if the secretary of defense doesn't want to change strategy, it's going to take some work to change. And when Steve told me his little gambit, of I'm going to ask, whatever it was, fifty questions, I thought well that's kind of a clever way to get the Pentagon to rethink this.

SATTERFIELD: When I initially come back [to the United States from Iraq] in July, there is deep concern. Concern at State, in the person of the secretary herself; concern at the NSC; throughout the Iraq team and beyond, about where things are going. This does not look like it is leading to a success by any definition—much less the president's own declared definitions of success—and that leaving Iraq under these circumstances is really not something that can be contemplated. The issue is, what do we do? Now, there are not, initially, in July and August, clear lines of thinking as to, there are four options, three options, five options. But one begins to hear the emergence of broad trends in the interagency senior-level discussions.

The first big question is, is there anything at all that we can do, other than mitigate damage to broader issues in the Middle East? Try to mitigate damage within Iraq? Focus our efforts on the things that we might be able to do? Stop the worst potential disasters in Iraq? But not try to stage manage, intervene, or affect everything. Not because as a policy matter we should not, but because we may not have the capacity—despite the will—to effect that goal. Secretary Rice is deeply, personally concerned that, in fact, we are failing. We may not have the ability—literally, may not have the ability to affect events by the selective application, or the different application, of military force. She, at this point—which is now latter part of summer 2006, but not yet the fall—is deeply skeptical of the military's ability to actually address the emerging sectarian pre–civil war, proto–civil war situation in Iraq. And she is very keenly concerned with the impact of an exclusive focus on Iraq on other regional developments. Iraq is taking the air out of the room on every other policy issue the US has in southwest Asia and the Middle East. . . . There was very much a sense that we, as a nation, were being viewed exclusively through an Iraq success-or-failure prism. And we ourselves had cast that prism and were keeping it in prominent position. With every speech, with every iteration of maximal goals and achievements in Iraq as the measure of a success or failure, we were setting ourselves up for problems elsewhere in the Middle East.

And the Middle East had many problems. Not just the Lebanon development, but Iran-related issues. Other questions—both CT [counterterrorism] and non-CT—that Iraq was dominating. Not because Iraq itself was a factor in these other issues, but the ability, the bandwidth available to the US government to manage other issues—and the consumption of our key partners in the Middle East by our own focus on Iraq—made dealing with those other pressing and significant for US national security issues more and more difficult. We could not pull back the policy lens, because we kept it almost exclusively focused on Iraq.

BOLTEN: I think at that point it was really Steve, I think very expertly, managing the system, with a strong staff, to try to change, or at least to try to give the president the option to change course, when the people actually manning the tower on the ship were highly resistant to it. So it required some very skillful work within the system, by Steve and others, to try to start to build, if not a consensus, at least some critical mass of support for a dramatic change in strategy.

Anybody who says the president was distracted from Iraq by Cuba or stem cells has no idea what was going on inside the White House. . . . The president's focus throughout that period, beginning at six forty-five every morning, when he read the blue sheet, was making sure that he was doing his best for the troops in the field and making sure that the Iraq conflict came out right. If something was going to interfere with his ability to do that, it was only going to interfere momentarily, and neither the president nor I, as his chief of staff, would have allowed it to interfere comprehensively.

RICE: One thing that is relevant here is that I was really seized with this [Iraq] until, in July, Lebanon broke out, and for six or seven weeks it was all Lebanon all the time for me, because I was trying to negotiate an end to the conflict there. You know, it wasn't that I was not concerned about what was going on in Iraq, but I had one problem on my desk every morning. I was in the region twice, I was in Europe twice, to try to end the Lebanon war. So, I didn't check back into the issue until mid-August, when we achieved the cease-fire in Lebanon.

I remember following relatively closely, but Operation Together Forward II—as I said, I was consumed with what was going on in Lebanon, and I came out of that period and thought, my goodness, not only are things not—things hadn't changed, and in this circumstance, hadn't changed meant they were getting worse.

More Troops?

PACE: It was about August of that year when John Abizaid and George
Casey, together in Baghdad, called me on the phone and said, you
know, we think that this is not going the way it should be, obviously it's not going the way it should be. We are supposed to be
sending troops home this year, we don't think we'll be able to do
that, and we may have to come back to the president and ask for
more troops.

When they called me with that, sometime in . . . August, I told
them OK, when we get off this phone call, a couple things are
going to happen. One, I'm going to see the secretary of defense,
and tell him exactly what you just told me. There's no doubt in
my mind that the secretary is going to want to go to the president
and tell the president, and so that will get done sometime in the
next couple days, with the president. I said, I would ask you to do
this, George and John, if you would: General Casey in Baghdad,
start working on what you think the proper solution to the current problem is. General Abizaid, in Tampa, you please do the
same thing. I will do the same thing here, with the Joint Chiefs,
and what I'd ask is that for the first month or so on this, that we
keep our efforts totally separated, so we don't end up sharing ideas
too soon and perhaps preventing ourselves from having the best
solution.

Listen, we were all together every day, all day, and certainly inside
the building, the secretary of defense, the DepSec [deputy secretary
of defense], the chairman [of the Joint Chiefs of Staff], the vice chairman, and we were with the president many times a week, and we all
knew that this was not going well right now. So if anything, I think it
was probably a reaction, at least for the secretary of defense, of OK,
we now have a process ongoing now, we're going to give ourselves a
good scrub. To my recollection, there was no negative reaction to the
possibility of needing more troops. Nobody looked forward to that
opportunity, but it was not, Oh God, you can't be asking for more
troops.

I'm with [Rumsfeld] hours every day, but he also wasn't about
to go, you know, taking his checkbook out and writing a number
of troops on it, without knowing what the plan is. So, clearly, he
wanted, as did the president, to know, how is this going to work,
what's the plan? How many troops are you talking about, over what

timeline are we talking about it? But I didn't, I never felt that Secretary Rumsfeld was opposed to it.

When I went to the report that to the president, with the secretary, it did not surprise the president. . . . I think we all collectively knew, without having to say exactly, this isn't going well.

Chapter 4

Silos and Stovepipes

September–October 2006

It is no easy thing to change course in the midst of a war. The way ahead is uncertain, but so too is the path already taken stained with the blood and sacrifices of one's own troops. Too radical a correction, therefore, risks undermining their morale, and their confidence in the leadership they had thus far served—and died—under. "It sends the wrong signal to our troops," Bush explained, to radically change course midstream or even to engage the possibility of withdrawal, as critics increasingly suggested. "We've got young men and women over there sacrificing. And all of a sudden, because of politics or some focus group or some poll, they stand up and say, 'We're out of there.' I can't think of anything more dispiriting than—to a kid risking his or her life than to see decisions made based upon politics."[1]

Yet Bush and those around him suffered no illusions by the autumn of 2006 that their present course would lead to victory. Initial reviews of the failing Iraq strategy thus demanded secrecy, lest word of their very existence hinder the ongoing war effort. By late fall of 2006, the NSC had its own internal review under way. So too the State Department and, to a lesser extent, the Pentagon—which in fairness was constantly reassessing strategies and priorities. The chairman of the Joint Chiefs of Staff, for example, contemporaneously appointed a "strategic dialogue group," later known as the Council of Colonels, to examine United States strategy in the global war on terror, but this body came to focus exclusively on Iraq. The colonels famously described three strategic options: "go big" and significantly increase operations in Iraq; "go long" and plan for a lengthy commitment; or "go home" and exit Iraq. The colonels took their ideas directly to the Joint Chiefs. "Anyone could speak," Colonel Pete Mansoor subsequently recalled, and every proposition was open for debate. "You had colonels challenging the thinking of four-star generals and admirals."[2] This was not the way military discussions typically progressed, but these were not typical times.

Further scrutiny only caused opinions to diverge. The NSC largely grew convinced that only a new strategy with more troops could save Iraq from civil war, and the United States from its first real military defeat since Vietnam. Officials at State reached a starker conclusion. Once in favor of a more robust strategy, many in Secretary Rice's inner circle believed nothing could stave off defeat by this point. A rapid exodus might best preserve what remained of American credibility, and at the least save American lives and treasure. Though much ballyhooed, the Council of Colonels, some of whom advocated a position akin to that of the NSC, had little direct impact on the thinking of the Joint Chiefs of Staff.

Politics too played a role in keeping the majority of these reviews from public view. The midterm elections approached, and many troops and their families found themselves pushed past their breaking point by the stresses of repeated and extended deployments since 9/11. "We're out of Schlitz," a director from the Joint Staff lamented. The administration risked a backlash if it asked more from those who had already given so much.

At least, that was the conventional wisdom about the Army, although policy makers internally debated if those in uniform might be asked to do yet more. "This is about will," a former general countered. "This isn't about capacity. It's about will. So, we had the troops." One thing was certain: beyond Iraq, and the fate of the US military, Bush increasingly believed his presidency to be at stake as well.

NSC Efforts

O'SULLIVAN: Even the initiation of a soup-to-nuts strategy review suggests the strategy is failing. And so Steve's first impulse was, Can we get the field to bring this to us? So that was the first, and we actually went down that road in the summer [with the fifty questions].

You had the Baker-Hamilton report that was launched in the spring sometime. And so there was a sense, hey, there's already a strategy review under way. And there was a sense in the White House, and probably more generally in the government as well, [that] maybe we can make this into an opportunity. I don't think there was huge excitement about it when it was launched, but then these are very serious people, and maybe this can be an opportunity.

And then, lastly, this is the summer before the midterm elections. And I think that it would have been potentially awkward for there to be a strategic review of our Iraq strategy publicly out there in the run-up to the elections. I think people might have thought that. I think in retrospect it might have been helpful.

So I think those were three reasons why in the summer, especially in July when I was writing memos saying, "Here are the reasons why we really need to do a strategic review," that the response was "OK, let's try to elicit this through other means." And in the meantime, in my office, . . . was to show to Steve Hadley, "This is what a review might look like." . . . So we presented him—and he knew we were doing this—we presented him with the results of a review that was done largely just within my NSC office. And that was of course very private, and that preceded the more formal reviews.

FEAVER: JCS and DoD are strongly committed to the existing strategy. The State Department seems to be moving in a different direction. So the question in the August, September time frame is . . . how do we launch the review of our strategy that we tried to launch in May, June. How do we do it? Meghan and I make the decision that we're just going to start it under our own authority. We'll start building terms of reference, and start the analytics that we can do, and then seek top cover from, or authorization, from Steve Hadley to actually do something bigger.

One of the first things we do is take the National Security Strategy for Victory in Iraq, NSVI, take it and go through all of the assumptions. Part of the thing we had done in the NSVI is make explicit the assumptions of our strategy. . . . Do we still believe them? One by one it was clear that none of us in this little group—and this was Meghan, me, Kevin Bergner, and Brett McGurk—none of us believed those assumptions anymore. We couldn't credibly defend those assumptions. That suggested that, well then, on our own terms, we must not believe that the existing strategy is going to work, because they're the premises for the strategy. That was a very clarifying moment.

O'SULLIVAN: We put forward kind of four—I thought of them as stylized options. . . . One was accelerating the transition, which was essentially saying it's status quo, maybe with a little extra oomph behind it. And then . . . one that was called "A Step Back" or "Pull Back," which was basically saying let's minimize the risks at the time and minimize our commitment. And that again more with the idea that we can only make so much of an impact. And that's partially a reflection of David Satterfield being part of this review. Then there was the double-down strategy, which is what we were calling the surge before it became the bridge and then the surge, which was the idea of let's renew the commitment, and actually shift to a strategy where we're really focused first on providing the security and then hoping—not hoping, but with the emphasis that that security will help with the political realm.

And then there was one called "Bet on Maliki." And that was the idea of OK, let's relax this enormous effort that we've been making since 2003 to put an effort on a unity government, to really underscore the importance of a unity government and say instead, "OK, focusing on a unity government in divided society has created a situation in which you have inclusivity at the expense of any kind of efficacy." And so let's just say, "Maliki, you're our guy, and you know, how you want to govern, we're going to support you."

FEAVER: I think that Casey, who's reviewing the strategy on it on a daily basis, is seeing that Together Forward I doesn't work, so he changes it to try Together Forward II. I don't think that there's a fundamental difference in our assessment of the current situation. I think the difference is that Casey was arguing: Well, it's a long, hard slog. War is tough, and as long as we tough it out and stick with this, we can see this through. And the best way out is to stand up Iraqi forces so we can stand down, because the US forces are themselves producing resistance. They're reinforcing the occupation narrative, and they're reinforcing the Iraqi dependence. It's the hand-on-the-bicycle argument. They [MNF-I] are seeing those downsides, and I think we're seeing those downsides, too. That was a plausible argument. Indeed, it was the one that we had endorsed even a year before. I think that the difference is that we're coming to the conclusion that this is no longer a case of long, hard slog, just tough it out. That if we continue on this path we will have strategic defeat in Iraq. We have a closing window to change that narrative. There's basically one chance to do something big, and we need to seize that chance now.

What to do about it was another question. The Iraq office [of the National Security Council] had concluded that a surge was what was needed. Brett McGurk would talk about this battle, I think it was in

Gaziliyah, where repeatedly we would do clear, and then we couldn't hold. Then we would leave and the terrorists or insurgents would come back and kill off all the people who had helped us during the clearing process. Then we'd come back and clear, but of course there was less help for us the second time around. Repeatedly, we needed enough troops that we could hold. We needed more reliable troops, and as we learned from Together Forward I and II, we couldn't count on Iraqi troops being there. In the long run, yes, but in the near term we couldn't count on them. The question was, where can we get the troops? At this stage there's a sense, the sense we're getting from DoD is that there are no more troops.

Out of Schlitz?

ZELIKOW: In September or October 2006, I get clearance following some sort of Condi discussion with Pace to go directly and sit with the J3 [Lute] and the J5 [John Sattler]. . . . Just the three of us, OK, no staff, and—which I—kind of going through, you know, the arguments. . . . And this is actually the point at which for the first time they are really candid back with me, OK. . . . And this is when Lute—and Lute's role as the J3 is very important. You understand this, but more important to me than the J5 role, because he really understands what's available, and he says two key things to me, which is, one, to do Baghdad and control the violence in Baghdad will require—and I think the number he used, which I repeated later to Steve—was four to six brigades. Maybe it was three to five brigades, but I think he said we need an additional four to six brigades for Baghdad. And then he just said flatly to me, "Philip, we're out of Schlitz." I remember that phrase. It was a vivid phrase. Just, "We don't have troops."

RICE: I do remember Philip coming back and saying, you know, "I don't think the Pentagon will support more forces."

KEANE: Can you imagine President Roosevelt saying to George Marshall, "I think we're going to need some more troops," and George Marshall coming back and saying, "You know, Mr. President, there are no more troops"? I mean, what an absurdity that is. We've got the whole Army. It sits at five hundred thousand and something at this point, and we've got the entire National Guard and Reserves, and we've got the whole Marine Corps sitting at around two hundred thousand. Add all that up and we've got over a million people under arms who are a ground force alone, so we've got plenty of troops, plenty. The issue—this is about will. This isn't about capacity. It's about will.

JEFFREY: [In] 1968, Tet, we needed more troops. The Eighty-Second Airborne Division was the holding ground for troops that had just come back from Vietnam. We had no choice. A brigade of that division was tapped to deploy within days. Johnson flies down. He gives a rousing speech, as he should, to men who had just come back from Vietnam. Vietnam was a lot more dangerous then than Iraq was. We were now going to turn around and go back and fight again. And then they got in the planes, and Johnson went from plane to plane, holding the hands of these guys, praying with them, cheering them on. There's always more troops, OK. Take a look at how many brigades we had in the National Guard. People think, well, but they haven't gone through the training program. We stopped North Korean tanks in the Pusan perimeter where we almost lost four divisions. With training units out of Fort Knox, who were told that you've suddenly become a tank battalion, take your M-26 tanks and deploy right now. We had 1.3 million active duty and reserve Army and Marines. If the president wants to send them into combat, he sends them into combat. We had 130,000 troops in Iraq at that time, and maybe 30,000 or 40,000 in Afghanistan, and we had 28,000 in Korea. What the fuck were the rest of them doing? I'm sorry. There's a thousand bureaucratic reasons that everybody says no, you've got to have a fifteen-month thing, and then they haven't gone through the TA-23, you know, gas mask training, and a thousand other reasons. Those people had all had multiple tours in Iraq and Afghanistan. They would have gone out there, and they would have done well. We could have sent ten brigades. The only limitation was we didn't have brigades—then we could have formed them up. That never crossed my mind for a moment. I heard it all the time, but I immediately thought, I'm a student of military history. We formed security battalions in Vietnam in '72, when we woke up and realized we were faced with the North Vietnamese Army and the Viet Cong, and we had sent all the combat troops home. So what did we do? I was a lieutenant in one. I was a platoon leader captain in one of them. We just created them. This is what you do in an army, this is what you have armies for, that's what you have generals for. The president wants you to come up with five brigades, forty thousand troops, you come up with five brigades and forty thousand troops.

LUTE: Well, it's always a possibility, right? Because, I mean, on one extreme of the range of options is the World War II model where you go to combat and you don't come home until the war's over, OK, but that was not an all-volunteer force. And one of the things that loomed for the Joint Staff was, yes, the national importance, the national interest in succeeding in Iraq, but looming just behind that was the strategic interest in holding together the all-volunteer force. And at this point, the force had been into successive years of combat, and we were rotating divisions back for second and third combat tours in Iraq. So what that meant is to sustain the fifteen brigades in Iraq, and I think at that point we had two in Afghanistan, and to meet other global commitments, if you were in the US Army you were in combat for twelve months, you were home for twelve months, and then you were going back to combat. So we were in what we called a dwell ratio of one-to-one: months in combat, months out of combat. And it's revealing to remember that inside the twelve months of off time, or dwell time, at home, you didn't really have twelve months of dwell time. What you had was you came back, you reassociated with your families and so forth, but probably six months into that twelve-month break, if you will, you started gearing up for the next rotation, which, in many cases, took you away from your families for months at a time as you went to training centers and went through live-fire gunnery processes and so forth. So it's a little bit artificial, unless you were inside that actual rotation, it's a little bit artificial to say you had a year on and a year off. It was really more like a year and a half on and six months off, and this was beginning to show.

There were signs of stress beginning to show on the force, so family problems, substance abuse, and so forth. Frankly, what surprised me in the all-volunteer force is we never suffered a retention problem. I would've thought that at some point in this labor market of the all-volunteer force that you might see signs of soldiers voting with their feet, right, and just taking their lives in a different path. But frankly, the services, in particular the ground services, sustained their retention quite well. But I do think that there were health considerations, mental health considerations, and certainly family health considerations that suggested that this pattern of year on, year off was not indefinitely sustainable.

PACE: Well, there was more than that available. The president could have said everybody who's there stays, everybody who's not there, goes. We could have doubled the size of the force if the president wanted to, and then they would have all stayed until he decided they would all come home.

To take all the ground forces of the United States and put them in one place for X number of years, when they are an all-volunteer force, and we have other threats around the planet, would not have been prudent. You can certainly go for a period of time, but you also have real requirements globally, for places like Korea and elsewhere. If you got to a point where you believed that was necessary, and I would have certainly done what I was told, and the next request would have been for conscription—if the nation is in that place, where it needs to send all of its troops to one location on the planet, then the nation is in a place where it needs to do more than just take volunteers. It needs to do what nations do, which is grow their armies, grow their Marine Corps, grow their force. But just inside the constraints of what was physically available, the president certainly had the authority, if he had wanted to, to take that risk, take the global risk and reinforce.

CROUCH: The phrase we heard many times later on, is, you know, "We're out of Schlitz," that we're breaking the force, that this can't go on this way, there's no more capability that we can bring to bear here. . . . And you know, the mantra, the sort of the sub-theme of that, was you're never going to get rid of the violence until you have a political settlement, right? And so, of course, the flip side argument to that is, you're never going to have a political settlement until you bring the violence to a particular level, right? . . . I mean, it really came down to where did you put some weight in sequence? Nobody disagreed that you didn't have to have a political settlement, right? Nobody disagreed with that. Where we disagreed was what the sort of a sequencing of it [would be].

Checking the Math

FEAVER: In early September I went to my office mate, who was Lisa Disbrow, who was a detailee from the Joint Staff, and she was in charge of programs, implementation, and execution. . . . I asked Lisa how would we find out what is the true amount of available troops, because I'm hearing from Meghan and her office, we need more troops. We are hearing from DoD there are no more troops. . . . Do you know how to answer that question—find out if there are more? Lisa says, "Actually, yes." That was her job when she had been in Joint Staff. I said, . . . very, very quietly, can you figure out what is the number? If we were to send more troops, what's the maximum number we could even send?

She did . . . a force generation bit of analysis, and she was very quiet, because first of all, we had no authorization from the suite to do this study. Second of all, this was certainly not where Secretary Rumsfeld and the Joint Staff were. But we just wanted to get an independent assessment. What is that number, and what are the assumptions for generating that number.

She comes back to me with the number five. That we could, with great pain, mobilize five BCTs [brigade combat teams]. Now, shortly after this time, so in early October, Bill Luti gets the authorization to do this study. Bill Luti was the senior director for defense policy and arms control. He is tasked with doing the force generation study, but the person on his staff who can do this is a guy named Mark Gunzinger, Gonzo, and Gonzo knows that actually the person who knows how to do this at the White House is Lisa Disbrow. Gonzo comes to Lisa Disbrow and says, "Do you think you could help me figure out this question?" Lisa says, "Well, as a matter of fact, yes. Here's the answer." She had already done the analysis that said five.

That convinced me in September that if the president authorized a surge, that there were five combat brigade teams that we could do. The information was kept very, very compartmented, though, in part because it was very sensitive, and this kind of planning from the White House was probably leaning forward or maybe falling too far forward of our skis. Also, we hadn't been authorized yet to do a full-up review. We don't migrate that information into the rest of the strategy review process until we get the authorization that comes from Steve through Bill Luti to do that study. However, the result of Lisa's analysis is, yes, you can do this, but this is going to be very, very, very painful. Very painful to the ground forces, because of the stress on the PERSTEMPO. Lisa and I talk about what could we do, what can be done to alleviate that. She says, "There's only one way and that is to raise the top line of forces."

So this is when I went to Josh Bolten, who was the chief of staff, and I told him, this is the situation. There's belief that the Iraq strategy is not working, and we're going to have to do something. There's a belief that the best solution is the surge, but surge is going to be very, very painful. When the time comes, the president is probably going to want to have the ability to raise the top line, and thus alleviate some of the pressure. Otherwise, it's going to be a very hard sell with the military. I said, we have someone on the White House staff who can do the analysis, but that's traditionally done in DoD, and this would cause a lot of heartache if it was done at the White House. Do you want me to do this? And Bolten authorized it.

HADLEY: It was pretty clear that the NSC staff was moving toward a surge kind of option, which was fine. I didn't want to get captured by the staff in that option, which . . . Meghan and her team were getting a lot of conviction in. It wasn't that I thought it was wrong; I wanted confidence that it was right because I thought we would have only one shot at getting this right. Secondly, we weren't military planners.

I asked J. D. Crouch to ask Bill [Luti] to put on his force planner hat and use his informal contacts over at the Pentagon and design a surge. What would it look like? What would the—what forces would you need? How would you deploy the forces? And what would the surge look like? And could it succeed? . . . I didn't want to do it through Meghan's shop, and I didn't want Meghan actually to know about it, because it was really a check on the process. I wanted to be completely independent. And he came back with a piece of paper that he briefed J. D. and me on, which basically said, surge is a good option. Here's how you would do. You need five brigades to do it. It was focused on Baghdad. And it really validated where Meghan and her team were going. . . . I then shared it with Pete Pace, because I had been meeting privately with him about what options they were looking at. I wanted to make sure he had the benefit of the work Bill Luti had done. He'd already been informally seeing what Meghan was doing. So I gave . . . a copy of that to him and ultimately had Bill share it with Meghan and his team. . . . It validated the work and the conviction that Meghan and her team had developed in the notion of a surge. But I thought it was very important, that we needed to have a formal process where this would all be brought together, that it was not going to work if we were to end around the process and try to jam the surge down the throat of the military.

I said to the president that I thought, in order to make it salable to the military, he was going to have to couple it with an increase in end strengths of the force so that we could ease the pressure. . . . He needed to show the military that he was willing to give them some relief from a terribly—intensive rotation schedule. And so I said that to him at the time, and he said, "That's right. Good idea. We will keep that in our back pocket."

RICE: I was aware of it [the force generation studies], but I thought that Steve had to use that just to check his own thinking. That would have been death for a national security advisor, to say I've got an answer as to where our troops are coming from. . . . Would have crossed all kinds of lines . . . because the president has a secretary of defense, and he has a chairman of the Joint Chiefs of Staff, and in a properly functioning national security system, questions about why you go to war, where you go to war, against whom you go to war, are questions for the civilian leadership, led by the president. Questions about how you go to war are questions that you ask the military, and what the national security advisor can do is to push and prod. I mentioned the trouble we had before the invasion, getting them to really look at how they were going to backfill. So, in a properly functioning system, those answers really come from the Pentagon. The president can ask hard questions and check, but for the president to substitute, through his national security advisor, his judgment about issues like deployment schedules and where you would take troops from, it's not appropriate. President Bush, probably as much as any, didn't believe in doing that sort of thing. I remember when we were doing Afghanistan he said, "I'm not going to be Lyndon Johnson, choosing targets from the basement of the White House."

CROUCH: In any interagency context, you have different ways of getting the information that you need. And sometimes you do it through formal taskings, and you do it at DC meetings, or principals' meetings, or assistant secretary level meetings, or whatever. And it's done in a very formal way. And other times, you, you know, it's a judgment call—is that the best way to work? Is that the best way to get the answers that you're looking for? Because those can be much more public; they're much more likely to leak. . . . I think there was a sense that we would get a more cooperative response from the department by doing it that way; that it was a better way to sort of control the information, and it was also—it gave us the ability to decide how we wanted to use that information.

O'SULLIVAN: I didn't know about that effort [the Luti study] at the time. . . . We were putting forward these four options, and we were clearly saying, "Look, this double-down option is the option that's actually—these are the prescriptions that are consistent with our analysis of the problem." . . . So we're advocating this particular approach, the surge approach, the double-down approach. And my memory is that Steve was understandably very nervous about this. This was a big deal, asking the president to go against basically the entire public opinion to take what some would perceive as a big gamble.

Increasingly convinced the situation demanded a new strategy, yet fully aware of the potential pitfalls, White House staffers begin coordinating with colleagues in the State Department and the vice president's office, albeit quietly. As one of Donald Rumsfeld's chief aides would later explain, "I had a principal who did not find the subject or the process congenial, and was making it plain that he wasn't going to be an active participant in that undertaking." Rumsfeld had plans, and a review, of his own.

NSC Informal Review Grows

BUSH: It's very important to understand that the worst thing a president could do is butt into meetings where people are trying to come up with recommendations, because people tend to preen for the president. No matter how seasoned they were, there's kind of a blanket effect on the ability for people to put their opinions out there because they end up speaking not to the issue but to the president. It's just a natural phenomenon. . . . Why would you want homogenized opinion? I mean, you want these different national security heads to work the issues on their own terms, not trying to coordinate it and figure out, you know, what's he going to say, therefore let's say what he says or what she says. That doesn't bother me on the surface. . . . Sometimes decisions require kind of a homogenized approach, but this was so big a decision that you want distinct opinions that have been debated, and so in a sense they were compartmentalized that meant they were less homogenized, and that's fine with me.

FEAVER: Meghan and I, and Kevin Bergner, and Brett [McGurk] are still doing our own strategy review, and after about a week or two of that, we explain to Steve Hadley what we're doing, and don't you think this is a good idea? He says, "Yes, that's a good idea. I want you to do it, but I want you to bring in John Hannah." And he says, I want you to just have these people: I want you to have John Hannah, Bill Luti, Kevin Bergner, Meghan, and me. We say, well, OK. At least we've got top cover authorization. . . . We got permission to add Brett McGurk. Then a week later, or very shortly thereafter, he says, "I've talked to Condi about it. I want you to bring in Satterfield, who is Condi's Iraq coordinator."

HANNAH: I personally have a very strong—maybe it was just because the vice president did, that we would have to move to a surge type of option. I have a strong feeling that whether or not Steve said it, certainly the people around him in the NSC, I think [Peter Feaver], Meghan O'Sullivan, Brett McGurk, all knew that was the direction, if we were going to salvage this, that [we] needed to move in terms of providing security and protection to the Iraqi population. I certainly got a very strong vibe from Steve, that that was the president's strong inclination as well.

I can sort of speculate, sitting here now, that there was a general view that the leadership at DoD and certainly the leadership of our command inside of Iraq, there was a view probably that they were not enthusiastic about a fundamental change in strategy in Iraq, from one of kind of building up Iraqi forces and drawing down American forces, kind of handing over the security situation to Iraqis as quickly as we could. I think there was a sense that that's where the Pentagon was on this, as well as the command inside of Iraq, and that if we were going to convince them to change their views, there was a first-order need for other people in the US government, who weren't necessarily as wedded to their particular view that DoD had, to kind of get our act together and get our arguments together on why you really did need a quite dramatic change, shift in strategy, in Iraq.

STEPHEN CAMBONE, under secretary of defense for intelligence: We at Defense were not in that flow of conversation. This conversation about the surge was taking place between the State Department, the White House, and people on the outside. . . . That was perfectly understandable. I had a principal who did not find the subject or the process congenial, and was making it plain that he wasn't going to be an active participant in that undertaking because he . . . had a plan, and they were following it and doing what needed to be done.

ZELIKOW: We were out of the loop on so much of this, and therefore could not form a coalition to better help the president, because of the compartmented way—perhaps because of how eccentric and unusual this decision-making process was. It was handled in such an eccentric way that we actually—we were kind of in these interagency meetings working with people who, aside from the NSC staff with their own constraints, we couldn't work with, in making our ideas better. See, like, we write a paper—in an ideal world, we'd write a paper, and the military people would sit with us, and they'd help edit it, and they'd mark it up, and we'd tear it up, and it'd go through five drafts, and get a lot better. But see, that never—none of that ever happened, and that's what I missed.

Council of Colonels

KEANE: I took [Rumsfeld] through what was wrong, why it was wrong, and what we needed to do about it, and I told him that, from the— the thing that got his attention—I told him from the outset, "We have never had a strategy to defeat the insurgency." He said, "What do you mean by that?" I said, well, our strategy has two major pillars—you know, trying to simplify what it is. One is political, to stand up a democratic form of government that will represent all the people and connect the people to this government in a way that they've never been connected to their previous governments. . . . Number two, from a military perspective, our strategy is to train the Iraqi security forces as the priority military mission so that they can defeat the insurgency. I said that is our strategy. So, by definition, we do not have a strategy to defeat the insurgency. We have a strategy from a military perspective to train the Iraqis so they can defeat the insurgency. I said that's fundamentally flawed, and here's the reason. One, the Iraqis do not have the capability to protect the people, and we have chosen not to protect the people. He said, "What do you mean, 'protect the people?'" I said, . . . if you're going to defeat an urban insurgency, by definition you have to protect the people, and we have chosen not to do that. . . . I said, to be able to accomplish that kind of insurgency strategy requires more troops, and I think it's eight to ten brigades is about what we need. It's just back of the envelope. . . . His reaction to that—that whole thing—was nonverbal, because I know him pretty well. It was a general resignation. You know, I think he knew that things were obviously going bad. He had heard.

LUTE: We had this view from CENTCOM that our time was waning, and the clock was running, the window was closing, whichever metaphor you're attracted to, it seemed rather a stark recommendation to essentially reverse course, dramatically reverse course, and, rather than working with a fifteen-brigade start point, imagine how you would gradually decrease that US presence as you handed off responsibility to the Iraqis. But to go from that basic concept . . . to a sense of, "Well, no, let's reverse course 180 degrees, and let's add five brigades." So it was a pretty stark change. I think initially it served a very important purpose in the Washington discussion, and General Keane's very persuasive, makes a very persuasive presentation. But it served the purpose of shaking up the thinking, and presenting a very stark assessment that we're losing. And that in itself, I think, was very, very helpful.

RICE: [Pace] said, "I've deputized some colonels to take a look at it," and I said, "Funny, I've deputized some people to take a look at it, let's keep in touch." . . . I didn't think there was any harm in having everybody look at this separately for a little while. You didn't want to come to a too-soon conclusion about what was possible or what you ought to do. I had complete visibility in what the NSC was doing, because Steve Hadley was my closest colleague and one of my best friends.

PACE: We told them [the colonels] to go and just start with a complete blank slate. . . . I think the colonels, understandably, weren't quite sure how to be talking to six four-stars who were the Joint Chiefs. So I went down a couple times to where they were working and said, listen, when we ask you for your opinions, we mean your opinions. If we ask you to be critical, we want you to be critical. We need your unvarnished advice. Don't tell us what you think we want to hear; tell us what you know we need to hear. And it took a couple iterations like that for them to, I think get the comfort level, to really kind of take the gloves off and give us a really good product.

COLONEL PETER MANSOOR, US Army: I was watching a football game on Saturday night; I'm a big college football fan, and I get an e-mail from General Petraeus basically saying, "You need to be in DC on Monday, and I can't tell you anything about the group, but I've been told to nominate a couple of smart people to it." The other one he nominated was H. R. McMaster and said, "Pack your bags." When I got there and got together there were about fifteen of us, plus or minus. There was a group that the Joint Chiefs—the chairman—had formed, in order to help them reconceptualize the long war against Islamic extremism worldwide. . . . As I recall there were three Army colonels, there was an Army colonel from the Joint Staff who was considered a Joint guy, there were three Marine colonels, three Navy captains, and the Air Force being the Air Force sent five Air Force officers. Then there was a Navy captain, Mike Rogers, . . . who was the group's informal leader because he was the chairman's executive officer.

We were given a very broad mandate, to just relook the war against Islamic extremism around the world, and so we started on that. We brought in subject-matter experts from all over the place—historians, intel officers, politicians, experts in Islamic jurisprudence. . . . But as the weeks rolled by it became pretty clear to us that we just simply could not get over the argument about "What do we do about Iraq?" It's fine that we're talking about worldwide jihadism or we're talking about Afghanistan or whatnot. Remember Afghanistan in '06 didn't look as bad as it did three years later, but what do we do about Iraq? So at some point I think in mid-to-late October we went to the chairman and we said, "We'd like to focus just on Iraq because we can't get over that discussion," and he agreed.

We came to, I think, a consensus, which we shared with the chiefs—much to their consternation—that Iraq was in the midst of a civil war. I think this was the first time anyone had told them that. And they said, basically, "Are you sure?" And we were like, "Yeah, pretty much." And they said, "Is this the consensus of the group?" And we said, "Yes, pretty much." Then we told them we are not winning; therefore we are losing, and time is not on our side. So General Pace shared that with the president, and the president came out in a press conference and said, "I just talked to General Pace, and he put it this way, and I agree with him, 'We're not winning and we're not losing,'" and I was like, "How about the last part about time not being on our side?"

I do know that the country was just tired of Iraq at that point and wanted out. That was one of the three options that we actually teed up for the Joint Chiefs—go home. Get out; contain the conflict within the boundaries of Iraq. Keep US forces in the region in case we had to fight Iran and contain the mess. I didn't agree with it. I don't think the Joint Chiefs, in the end, would have agreed with it either. But that certainly was one of the options we gave them.

The nation we talked about the most was Iran. I think especially the Navy and the Air Force officers said, "We have to get ready to fight Iran if it comes to that, and we can't do that if we're embroiled in this messy war in Iraq." So I think there were more Navy and Air Force officers that skewed toward the "go home" vision of containing the mess in Iraq and getting ready to fight a more conventional conflict against Iran than the Army and Marine officers who said, "No, we need to fight the war we are waging right now and win it."

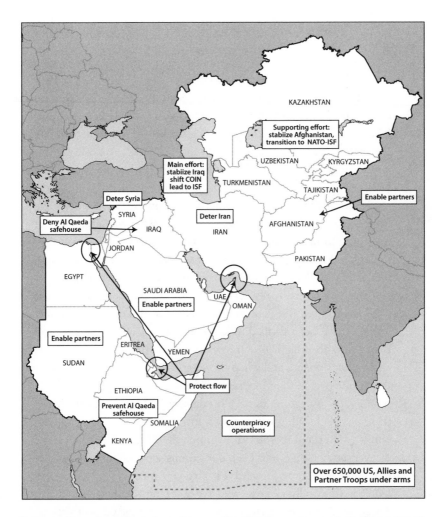

FIGURE 4 Lines of operation in Central Command's regional war on terror, adapted from a Council of Colonels briefing slide

Source: Adapted from "RWOT Lines of Operation," in "Strategy for the Long War, 2006–2016," presentation prepared by the chairman of the Joint Chiefs of Staff's Strategic Dialogue Group (the "Council of Colonels"), September 26, 2006, p. 11, released via FOIA as 09-F-0423 Strategy for the Long War 2006–2016 Joint Staff Briefing Slides, http://www.esd.whs.mil/FOIA/Reading-Room/Reading-Room-List/Joint_Staff/.

The Informal Process

Politics, both public and bureaucratic, kept Washington's various reviews of the situation in Iraq disjointed and separate. Critics might consider this inefficient, even dysfunctional. The administration's proponents might note the opportunity separate reviews offered for generating truly original ideas. No matter one's view, cooperation, collegiality, even friendship at the top helped bridge the divide.

HADLEY: The process got a big uptick when, to his credit, Pete Pace went to Secretary Rumsfeld and suggested that DoD needed to do an internal look at Iraq strategy. And to his credit, Secretary Rumsfeld agreed. So we got a process going within DoD, within the State Department, and of course, within the NSC staff. And during this period from the spring really until November, what we were doing was encouraging those reviews to go on independently and in sort of parallel action with a fair amount of communication among the leaders of each of those reviews so we knew what was going on. But it seemed to me, in order to get everyone to the point where they understood a change needed to be made, we needed to go through those individual, informal processes within the individual agencies.

O'SULLIVAN: There was really very little, I would say no visibility in the NSC about what the Pentagon was doing at the time. And in fact I would have been thrilled to know about that review. But, as you know, how the chain of command works is that things go up the chain of command, and when they come over to the White House, they come over at the more senior level.

PACE: [Hadley] was going to have his deputy, J. D. Crouch, run that [a review], and I said, great, if you want some military guys, I'll certainly assign them to you. All I would ask, Steve, is what I've asked of everybody else, is let's keep our groups separate initially, let's let different ideas come forward. I'll give you military guys, but they won't be the military guys who are working for the Joint Chiefs. These need to be military guys who are not tarnished, so to speak, by the thinking that's going on inside the Pentagon. So we did that, and for the first month or two, each of the groups stayed separate and did not, to my knowledge, share ideas. . . . It was not meant to keep anybody out. It was meant to not pollute the pool.

O'SULLIVAN: I think it [keeping reviews initially separate] allowed for a little bit more creativity to flower and a little bit more deep thinking to occur. That said, what's the counterfactual like? What if I'd known about the Council of Colonels' review and the options they put forward and the go-long strategy? . . . Maybe things might have happened more quickly. It's possible. Maybe it would have been squashed more quickly. . . . The downside of this approach was it was fairly slow. It's like you repeated the review three or four times.

So there's clearly a downside, but I'm not yet willing to argue that there was unquestionably a better structural approach.

SATTERFIELD: It was the need to organize at a political policy level as opposed to uniform service level—certain frames of reference, questions to ask. But it was also—and again, I can't avoid this—a clear perception that many of the critical interlocutors in DoD, from the chairman down, were constrained by Secretary Rumsfeld from expressing a position which contrasted or contradicted Rumsfeld's doctrine of standing down in Iraq as rapidly as possible—shedding missions, detainee, security, and others as quickly as possible. That was real. And it had been building since the latter part of 2005, that you could not get a frank appraisal—in a policy sense—from what ought to be the most responsible interlocutors, because of fear of contradiction of Secretary Rumsfeld.

HADLEY: Pete Pace was separately having his own conversation with Condi Rice. And he was separately having his own conversation with me. He would come over, and we would sit down and talk about the reviews. . . . Pete was the guy that was going to have to bring the Pentagon along in this effort. And he was my principal partner, and his view at that time was, "We're not done with our internal review. Let me keep going with what I'm doing. Don't force me too soon into an interagency process." And I took that advice.

The Emphasis on Secrecy

HANNAH: The explanation I heard was that the president, particularly with regard to the military, if he was going to make this kind of dramatic shift in strategy, at a time when it would be so incredibly controversial, when he and the administration had been so weakened, when public support for the effort in Iraq was draining day by day, and for the president to make such an announcement without as much solid support from the military and the Pentagon as he could muster, might itself almost be a step too far politically and might actually damage and undermine the effort. He already knew, I'm sure, that this was going to be incredibly difficult, incredibly controversial, and this decision to surge forces was going to generate a huge domestic backlash, and in order to face that, he was going to need, as much as he could get it, a unified government, particularly the people in uniform that were going to have to actually implement and carry out the strategy.

I think Steve Hadley [was] articulating . . . a concern about going to the Pentagon too quickly, going to the generals too quickly. You need to be able to bring them along. There was a choreography, bureaucratically, within the US government, as much as conversations that we were having in the Iraq Review Group were no doubt important. They were a good way to air out, to let people have their say, to put various options on the table. As much as that substance was important, there was an important bureaucratic and political choreography—the way you did this, the way you presented it.

FEAVER: I know that there was great reluctance to do anything formal, because it could leak. The concern was once you start second-guessing your strategy, you cannot go back to that strategy. This is one reason why it had to be kept so compartmented. You can't then turn around and tell the troops, "Oh, yeah. No, we still think—yes, last week we told you we're doing a zero-based review, because we have no confidence in the strategy, but guess what? We've decided this is the best one anyway, so go back and fight for this one." It was a point of no return.

BOLTEN: Had it been more widely known early on, the nature of the shift in strategy that Steve was beginning to build critical mass for, I think it would have been badly undermined and resisted, and I think would have caused a rift in the national security team and apparatus, in the midst of trying to fight a war, that the president would have found not just disappointing but dysfunctional to the continuing operation of the war. So I think the shift in strategy had to be done, because the war was ongoing, that it had to be done in a way, in a fairly contained fashion, and then when it was ready to go, build support among those who needed to support it.

The public angle would have been terrible as well. There was little enough support for what was going on in Iraq as it was. It was very important to us that we maintained at least a baseline minimum of support for prosecuting the war in Iraq, within the Congress, because we were always at risk of having the money just cut off and having the Congress step in and make it impossible for the president to actually execute in a way. This is the way in which politics was important. Politics was otherwise irrelevant to President Bush. He was oblivious to concerns about how he might be seen, how his party might be seen. He was aware of them, he knew how damaging what was going on was to both him and his party, but he was very consistent in not allowing those considerations to color his judgment about what was best for the prosecution of the war and the national security of the United States.

I think where the president would have been focusing, I think correctly, is that that same person in the field just lost a buddy, and to have the president of the United States say oops, you know, by the way keep doing what you're doing, but I'm thinking this is like totally messed up, having lost the buddy in the field and continuing to do what you're doing, without the new strategy in place, I think the commander in chief has got to recognize that that's potentially very demoralizing to the guy in the field. When you've got the new strategy and you've got agreement on the new strategy, all in.

HADLEY: It's a real dilemma for a president because we're in the middle of active hostilities, and if it comes out that you're rethinking the strategy, it's an incentive to your enemies—who think that they're winning—and if the issue is a review of strategy and one of the options was going to be withdrawal, and if you looked at American public options, it was clear that one of those options would be withdrawal, then you incentivize your enemy to start killing more and more of your men and women in uniform in order to strengthen the hands of those who say the war is lost, we ought to pull out. It also undermines the confidence of your friends and allies. It undermines the confidence of the wives and husbands and children of the men and women in uniform who serve. On the other hand, it requires you to continue to reflect publicly confidence in a strategy in which you have increasing discomfort and lack of confidence. And it is not a perfect solution. And so it leaves people to say, "Well, did the president mislead the American people by indicating he was committed to continuing the project in Iraq?" We talked about [how] he should talk about that, to not give a hint of the strategy review, but also to not say something that would raise credibility problems after the fact. It's one of the dilemmas you have in these situations. I think we did the right thing in terms of how we handled it, but we did want to keep it bottled up for those reasons and not have it become a public conversation.

Morale

Not everyone agreed with the argument that troop morale demanded a continuation of the present course, or that the existence of formal reviews needed to be kept secret.

ABIZAID: Oh what bullshit. The morale of the troops was just fine. The troops were fighting well, performing well. This whole notion of this legend that's developed around this is just kind of crazy to me. Where was there any example of American morale anywhere in the theater, over sixteen years, being at risk? . . . That's the great thing about a professional army. You fight as long as the president tells you to fight. This wasn't World War II. Look, by the way, so we all are clear here . . . I was very much against going into Iraq. And yet when it came time to go to Iraq, I threw my hand in the air and begged to go, because that's what soldiers do.

MANSOOR: I'm dumbfounded that we would even think that. The soldiers on the ground knew things weren't progressing very well in Iraq, and in fact when we got there with a new strategy and a new doctrine, there were a bunch of troops who said, "This is great, we finally know what to do now in order to win."

PACE: I mean the president's actions were always extremely supportive of the troops. . . . I actually appreciate the fact that some folks in the White House were feeling that perhaps there could be a morale problem, but from my perspective, the morale problem was, we're not doing well. The troops on the ground know when things are going well and when they're not going well, and it's obvious to them that the plan we're executing isn't working the way we thought it would. If anything, if somebody in the theater were to hear that the president was rethinking, if it happened to be a guy on the ground with a rifle, you're probably saying to yourself, thank God.

KEANE: If somebody unburdened the soldiers who were executing the flawed strategy—and believe me, having sat in many of those vehicle convoys with those guys going through those towns and going through those cities in that vehicle, that is a very intimidating experience because you feel so vulnerable. You know you only have passive protection with you—in other words, the protection the vehicle affords and whatever you can possibly see or detect, which isn't much from a Humvee, and you're doing that every single day. You don't think those soldiers say to themselves, "You know, there's something not right about this. Whose idea is this, anyway?" I mean, of course they do. . . . They'd say—I think they would—their reaction would be, finally, somebody understands this is all effed up, because that's what they're saying. This is all effed up, and somebody's actually thinking about maybe fixing this. Great!

MANSOOR: The Bush administration did not want to come out publicly in saying, "Yeah, we're rethinking the strategy for the Iraq war." They kept talking publicly about, "Well, we can readjust tactics, if necessary." Of course that means a whole different thing, and it wasn't until the elections were over until they said, "Yeah, we're looking at strategy." Had they done that before the midterms, they would have been open up to accusations that the war was lost and we should just get out. So I can see why they did that.

Looking Forward

ROVE: I'm not aware of any decision that said let's not discuss this because it has to do with politics. [The president] may have had that instinct, but I think it may have also more likely been, I want to have clarity in my own thinking, and I've got a sufficient range of people right now that we're discussing this change among without broadening it.

BOLTEN: I saw a president who was basically making up his mind over that period, in a way that in reality was probably ahead of the process. . . . Maybe even earlier than [September–October] he was coming around to the view that of the options, the only one that had a reasonable prospect of the kind of success that the US needed from this, in this situation, was something like the surge.

I saw a president who was coming around, by the process of elimination, to go big, and recognize that it was a big risk. But he also, I think, understood, again, in the way that people thirty years from now should understand about presidential decision making, that sometimes you have to take a big risk, because the even bigger risk is doing the less risky things, the things that seem at the moment to be less risky.

I mean, I knew there was consideration going on to well, if we go big, how big is needed to really make this effective, and do we have the manpower for it, and do we have the money for it. I always kind of had an instinct, from my days as budget director, that there's a lot more elasticity in the system than people think, if it's really a priority. I always felt like if you can get people bought in, or enough people bought in to the underlying strategy, there will be a way to find the sufficient manpower, there will be a way to stretch the force, and there will be a way to persuade the Congress to put the money in. You can't do that with many things, but if it's really the top issue, then you can succeed in doing that. And so, from the political side, I always tried to be supportive and optimistic of, you know, you guys decide what needs to happen and then leave the politics to the president and others, to make it happen. Do not censor yourself on the strategy based on what you think the rest of the political system will let you do.

FEAVER: This is the challenge, right? We're exploring options that are not being generated by the interagency. We're trying to create those options, we're trying to call forth those options from the interagency, but we're not succeeding in that. We're doing some of the analytic work, at least the preliminary analytic work, for those options. . . . The NSC role is starting to shift out of that honest broker mode, just a little bit.

HADLEY: The review within the State Department was going to come out with an option of pulling back, preserving major institutions, not getting in between what was a sectarian war, and let it "burn out." And that in the end of the day the Iraqis would have to solve this issue. And it was pretty clear to me that neither of those were going to work. . . . At that point, we needed a formal review because the informal reviews were not going to take us to where we needed to go. On the other hand, they had started the dialogue within their agencies, and it was accepted that we were going to have a new strategy. And, you know, that's of course the first step in getting a new strategy.

CHAPTER 5

Setting the Stage

Early November 2006

November brought dramatic upheaval, changing Bush's political and strategic calculations. Republicans took a "thumping" in the midterm election. Democrats picked up thirty seats in the House of Representatives and for the first time since 1994 controlled both houses of Congress. The election results were widely considered a referendum on the Iraq War, with exit polls showing a majority of voters dissatisfied with the conflict or hopeful of an immediate troop withdrawal. Six in ten polled believed, moreover, that the conflict in Iraq had diminished the nation's overall security.[1]

Secretary of Defense Donald Rumsfeld proved the election's most visible casualty, resigning days after the final votes were tallied. Before the election, Bush had met secretly with Robert Gates—then president of Texas A&M University and a former director of central intelligence—who had agreed to replace Rumsfeld. A few days after accepting Rumsfeld's resignation and announcing that Gates would take over as secretary in December, Bush publicly launched a new interagency review of strategy in Iraq. In the immediate aftermath of the election, with Rumsfeld remaining in charge at the Pentagon until his replacement could formally assume his responsibilities, Bush's top advisors met to discuss the terms of a review of US strategy in Iraq. Many traveled to Iraq as well, to hear from the troops in the field, but also to build consensus for new approaches to the war. Talks with Iraqi leaders did little to improve their optimism. "And as far as I can tell," Secretary Rice told her hosts, "you're all going to be swinging from lampposts the next time I come."

Rumsfeld too offered suggestions for a new way forward, albeit quietly, the news revealed only in December.[2] Still, despite the growing consensus within the government regarding the profound need for a new way forward, the direction remained unclear. Reviewing options, however much it seemed a bureaucratic victory to some, did not ensure they would settle upon a better one.

Trips to Iraq

RICE: It was the worst trip. . . . I went, and [Ambassador] Zal [Khalilzad] had had a group of Sunnis there first, and they all brought horrible pictures of severed heads of children, and this is what the Shiite are doing to us. And then the Shiite showed up, and they had severed heads of Shiite children, and this is what the Sunnis are doing to us. And I remember saying to Zal, "Are the Kurds next?" He said, "No, they're not coming." I was so furious at them, because they couldn't focus, and this is all of the leaders. . . . I finally said to each of them, and I said to Zal, "I hope I didn't embarrass you," because after they'd gone through these horrible soliloquies of what everybody was doing to them. I said, you know, we have a saying in the United States, "You can hang separately or you can hang together," I said, "And as far as I can tell, you're all going to be swinging from lampposts the next time I come." I was really unnerved by it, furious about it. I talked to Maliki, had a kind of similar conversation there about hanging separately and hanging together and swinging from lampposts, and I came back and I remember being very tired.

I'm pretty hardy, and I was never terribly exhausted when I came back from these trips, but I mean, I was really tired and I hadn't slept very well. I think I met with the president, I got home maybe nine or ten o'clock the night before, and I got into the Oval shortly after he got in, so probably seven o'clock in the morning, and I said to him, "It's coming apart, you know, it's not going to hold together." I felt bad, because I think it was the only time in our time together that I expressed that kind of dismay and distress, and didn't have an answer about what to do about it. I remember he said, "So what should we do?" And I said, "I've got to go away and think about that."

FEAVER: This is the phase of the project, September or probably October by this point, when we're taking the options that the Iraq group had developed. . . . It became clear that a critical piece of this was Maliki, and our uncertainty about Maliki. That if Maliki was one kind of leader, then some strategies had no hope of success. If he was another kind of leader, then other strategies had no hope of success, but we were unsure of Maliki. Out of that assessment came the idea of . . . taking Steve Hadley to Iraq, for him to take the assessment of Maliki on the president's behalf.

O'SULLIVAN: Out of all the meetings that we had [in Iraq] . . . the one that struck me as potentially a really big turning point was one that we had with commanders in Baghdad. And there was a certain point where I think that we asked people who I seem to remember were generals to step out and just have the brigade commanders talk to Steve. . . . At this point, I remember there was an active debate. We were hearing clearly and consistently from the leadership of MNF-I that the root of the violence was the American presence. . . . And so even in October, at the end of October, that was still the view that was coming to the White House most consistently, which was the only way you're going to bring down levels of violence is to bring down levels of US forces. And in that meeting . . . I think I asked them just to say, "Can you tell us how Iraqis react to you when you go into their neighborhoods or you leave them?" And to my memory, every single one of those commanders said that they were welcomed with open arms when they arrived and people begged them not to leave.

And this really ran in the face of the idea that we are the source of the violence. And what had happened over the period, the year or two, that we'd been implementing the strategy in that time was we had become the third force, the closest thing to a neutral force in these warring neighborhoods. Where you had Shia and Sunni extremists fighting and killing one another, it was the US presence which was the one that had the most calming effect.

And this was very important because another thing that we were hearing very clearly was that Maliki is a sectarian actor. And so if Maliki as prime minister is nothing more than an advocate for Shia interests and a suppressor of Sunnis, how are we going to throw more force and support behind this guy? . . . It was a very important thing to sort out before we started proposing solutions that would be empowering to Maliki. And so I think Steve felt that it was really important to get his own personal assessment of Maliki's character and his intentions and to bring it back to the president. And he came back saying, look, there are still real questions about whether there's a lack of will here or a lack of capacity. But I think the net assessment was this is actually someone who wants to improve the situation, is willing to work with us, and can be a partner. I think it helped open the door to Maliki as a potential partner, not unconditionally but not to dismiss him entirely.

FEAVER: I remember sitting in the Silver Bullet[3] on the way back, just wrestling with, discussing with Hadley and with Meghan O'Sullivan what were the different interpretations of who Maliki might be, and what the implications of that were.

The fruits of that are in a memo that he [Hadley] wrote to the president, went to the president I think within twenty-four hours or so of getting back. He then did a version of that for the interagency and sent it around to all the other principals. Someone who received that second version of it leaked it to Michael Gordon, and it shows up in the *New York Times*.

HADLEY: At one point in an interview with Bob Woodward, the president said, "Well, I delegated the strategy review to Hadley." And a lot of people said, "Well, he [Bush], you know, took himself out of it." . . . The president didn't delegate things, he tasked you to do something. And it was not fire and forget; he would want . . . ongoing reports. So in this period of time, I'm having an ongoing and healthy debate with the president, with . . . our staff, with Pete Pace, with Secretary Rice. So it's not a question of, did I decide? We came to a consensus that we needed to go to Baghdad, and the purpose was to try to get a sense of Maliki.

There was a lot of reports that sectarian activity has stepped up significantly. . . . Somebody had a sectarian agenda, and the question was, was it Maliki? And was this sectarianism that we were seeing a result of because he didn't know what was going on? . . . [Was he] a nonsectarian at heart, but didn't have the means to prevent the sectarianism that we were seeing? Or was it in fact this his sectarian agenda that he was in fact implementing? And the question that we were sent with was to try to answer that question, because it was critical for the president to know whether he was going to have a partner in Maliki for the surge that was beginning to take shape in his mind, or whether . . . Maliki was going to be a barrier.

I think the view was Maliki is not a sectarian. This is not being done with his active support, but . . . he does not have the wherewithal to stop it and is not stopping it. And therefore, the . . . Iraqis were not going to solve this problem themselves. And so it gave further grist, I think, for the kind of surge strategy and . . . in some sense [began] to lay the foundation for the argument for the surge.

I think I was quoted by somebody as saying, "I should have come [to Iraq] earlier." And I think that's right . . . but, you know the kind of job you're in, there are a lot of constraints on your ability to travel. But it was an eye-opener, and I think it helped, again, set up the process toward movement toward a new strategy.

CROUCH: And I remember the president turning to Steve [in the Oval Office] and saying, "We're going to do a review of this," and Steve looking at me and saying, "You're going to do this."

EDELMAN: J. D. [Crouch] . . . at one point had a conversation with Rumsfeld about that as well. I was there while he had it. . . . And Rumsfeld half listened but was not terribly interested in having another policy review, because I think he felt it would be a lot like the "National Strategy" [NSVI] again, that it was going to be a lot of other people trying to tell him how to run the war, which he didn't particularly want or felt that he needed.

The Upcoming Midterm Election

ROVE: It wasn't going to be a good election year. The second midterm election is almost inevitably bad. By then, already we were starting to see some sort of efforts inside the Republican caucus on Capitol Hill to sort of divorce themselves from the war, and to try and find some way out of association with it. And some of that was basically, Let me be critical of how the war's being conducted. Others were, Let's literally begin to bring people home. And the object was to keep them focused on victory, because if we allowed . . . that effort to divorce the Republican Party from the war, public support would've dropped even more. If they had cut and run on the president earlier than they ultimately did, then we would've had even bigger problems in sustaining public support. . . . If the narrative is, Republicans are breaking from the president on the war, and Republicans are running away from the Iraq War, that would bring back in the consciousness of Americans that we weren't committed to victory, and the American people, more than anything else, they're willing to sustain military action if the goal is victory. But if the goal is maintenance, and to get through the next election, and the president's own political supporters [are] saying this is a political loser, they [the American people] want to walk away from it. They don't want politics injected into war.

It's a weird thing. It's sort of like, OK, I'm for the war as long as it's not political, and as long as you're seemingly willing to fight it out. But if you appear to be weak on this, if you appear to be wavering, if your attitude seems to be we're trying to manage this, not get victory, then they'll say throw in the towel and get the hell out of there. It's not worth American lives and American treasure if the goal is something less than victory. The problem is in this kind of a situation it's hard to define what victory is.

CAMBONE: I think the big issue—look, the president had a strategic problem of the first order. He wasn't losing the war in Iraq, he was losing the war here at home, in the sense that the political support for what was being done was leaking out, and it was near to gone, all right? So he had to make a change. So, whether you thought what was being done at the time was adequate to the need was immaterial. I mean, this was a presidential-level strategic decision about changing the course of that war, and the secretary understood that, I understood that. So the notion of saying no, no, no, no, you can't make a change, I mean that was not only strategically a misapprehension. It was not helpful to the president, it wasn't helpful to the country, it wasn't helpful to the people on the ground in Iraq.

If we were going to have any chance of winning in Iraq, he had to address domestic issues here, he had to address the military situation on the ground. He had to deal with the issues having to do with the political situation inside Iraq and, oh, by the way, sometimes lost in all this, right, are coalition partners who are getting a little uneasy too, about whether this is turning into a morass that they're never going to get out of. Plus there's all the domestic politics in the region, where assurances have been given to the local governments, the regional governments. So when I say strategic, it's taking all of those things and pulling them together with an approach then that's going to be best suited to bring each of them to a successful—either a successful conclusion, or changing the nature of the debate.

The military was doing its job in terms of its combat operations, all those things, training the troops and doing all that. Where was the problem? . . . Time had run out on the current plan, I mean just time had run out, and if the situation was going to be reserved, conserved, then the president had to make a choice and a big one.

Replacing Rumsfeld

ROVE: My sense was Rumsfeld just—he was stuck. I don't know whether it was because he'd been there for six years and had sort of run out, or whether it was that he actually believed that merely keeping doing what we were doing would somehow or another at one point begin to click and work. . . . It's clear, Rumsfeld is going to be obstinate about a change, so these things would have to move together. So the president is thinking about a change in strategy, and thinking about a change in leadership, and then Hadley approaches Gates, Gates signals that it's possible.

BUSH: So I snuck him [Gates] over from College Station, where he was the [university] president. . . . I told him we needed, I thought we needed a change. First of all, he agreed to do it. I told him what I was thinking about, that the only way to win is more troops—I'm not sure how many yet, but there are options brewing. So I think at that point in time I had pretty much made up my mind, and therefore I wanted to make sure that the new secretary of defense wouldn't balk. One thing you don't want to do is change secretary of defense and say, we're surging, and the guy goes, "I'm not interested."

BOLTEN: I think the president, by that point, was pretty far down the track and on a new strategy. It actually coincided well with a change-over in secretary of defense, to implement a new strategy that was going to be easier on everybody—on the military, on the Pentagon, on the political system, to put a new face on a new strategy. So, I thought it all dovetailed pretty well. On the specific timing of Secretary Rumsfeld's departure, President Bush decided on that basically, really almost a month before the election, if I'm recalling right.

HADLEY: There are a lot of criticisms of the president, that he should have announced his intention to accept Rumsfeld's resignation before the election. I think the president rightly declined that counsel because he thought it would be viewed as playing politics with the Iraq War in order to enhance his prospects for reelection, because people would take that as a sign that maybe we were going to have a different policy in Iraq, and most people expected that that different policy would not be a surge, but would be a withdrawal. And the president didn't want to play politics with an important a decision as what our policy should be in Iraq, and I think he made the right judgment.

BOLTEN: We had in mind—and the president was very determined about this—we had in mind to make the announcement after the election. I remember [Counselor to the President] Dan Bartlett, the communications director, and I thought that this was very clever political strategy and so on, so that it would be clear, what the president intended, that he was not allowing politics to infect his decisions. It certainly would have been very popular with Republicans scrambling for reelection in 2006, and having enormous difficulty, many of them, because of the headwind of the unpopularity of the Iraq War. They surely thought it would have been very helpful to them, to dump Rumsfeld overboard in September or October.

We wanted to make a demonstration that the president wasn't going to let politics infect it, and the president was adamant about that. He said he didn't want anybody in the field to think that he was making his decisions about the command because of anything having to do with partisan politics. And so Dan Bartlett and I concocted the scheme where we would announce it literally the day after the election, so that it would be clear that the president didn't want that to infect the politics, but it would also be clear that we had made, the president had made the decision before the election, and wasn't blaming Rumsfeld for the defeat in the election, which we knew was coming.

It [the announcement] was a complete lead balloon, everybody was mad at us. In particular, the Republicans, who had suffered these big defeats, you know, the leadership in the House was just, they couldn't have been madder.

ROVE: I didn't want him to act until after the election because . . . politically it's damaging, because you have a major change that gives the other side the chance to be intensely critical of the policy. But he had a more important reason for not doing it, which was he didn't want the next secretary of defense to have to go through a confirmation hearing that would be colored by the politics of an election season. He wanted to make a change, but he didn't want Gates to come in having been tarnished and ripped up one side and torn down the other in the middle of an unnecessarily contentious hearing. His feeling was if it happened after the election . . . Gates would have a less difficult time in the confirmation hearing, and as a result be able to be a more successful secretary of defense, which was absolutely right. His instinct on this was absolutely right. You take a look at the hearing, and as tough as it was—there's that one moment where he is asked, "Is it working?"

and he says no it's not, which signaled to the country we're going to make a change. But that hearing was about as successful a hearing as it could possibly be, and the fact of the matter is that he then becomes the only secretary of defense in history, that I'm aware of, to have worked under a Republican president and been kept on by his Democrat successor. That says something about Bush's instinct, the president's instinct, about how to do this in a proper fashion.

ROBERT GATES, secretary of defense: I came to believe that the president had begun to have doubts about the strategy that we were then pursuing by late spring or early summer [of 2006]. . . . He said in our meeting, "Our strategy isn't working, and I think we're going to need to have a surge." He didn't elaborate on what the surge would be, how long it would be, how many troops were involved, just that we needed to change course, that what we were doing wasn't working.

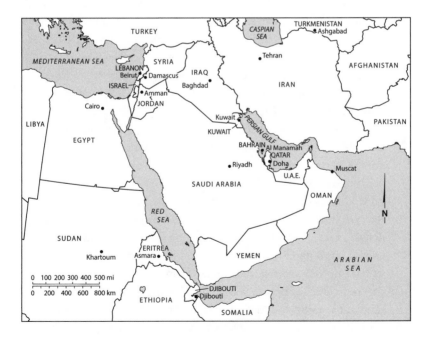

FIGURE 5. The Middle East
Source: Adapted from Cartographic Section Department of Field Support, Middle East—Map No. 4102 Rev. 5 (United Nations, November 2011), http://www.un.org/Depts/Cartographic/map/profile/mideastr.pdf.

Doubts at the State Department

RICE: I think some of the people who worked for me . . . had begun to think that we had to go to some other strategy. . . . The strategy wasn't just pull back. The strategy was pull back, say to the Kurds, the Sunni and the Shiite, You're going to have to take the head of this fight, and so organize yourselves to do this, and if the tribes want to take care of Sunni areas and the Shiite want to take care of Shiite areas. . . . I remember saying to the people who were talking about this, David [Satterfield] and others: this begins to sound like partition, because if you're effectively saying the national forces of Iraq can't do this anymore . . . you're going to tear apart the notion of a unified government, but beginning to think that maybe that was our only option, if the unified government and its security forces weren't going to perform. . . . The question was, if they were going to tear themselves apart as sectarians, could we do anything about it.

I remember saying, can't referee somebody else's civil war, because again, I'm a social scientist, I'm a political scientist, and there's a very important view that if you're going to be involved in a civil war, choose a side. It felt like we weren't choosing a side; we were trying to referee it, and we certainly weren't going to be able to referee it with the strategy that we had. And so my view, reflecting on what I think some of the State Department people were saying, really was about could you get the politics in place and was Maliki prepared to make the decisions he had to make, in order for us to actually be able to do something about the sectarian violence, or were they going to keep splitting apart, blaming each other, and you know, if they were going to be swinging from lampposts, I didn't see any point for us being there while they did it.

JEFFREY: I had been since the summer very discouraged, but I did feel that we should try some kind of limited surge to avoid a military defeat. I mean, I was basically channeling my whole Vietnam experience. . . . I thought that the American public had definitively turned its back on Iraq, so that that center of gravity was gone. I felt that the Iraqi center of gravity was going. I felt that a military surge could reverse the military situation sufficient to possibly buy us time for some kind of less-than-defeat exit, but that in the long run it wasn't just that George Bush's dream of an Iraq success was out the window. I had never thought that that was really possible. But that our hope, which we had all been involved in, that you would get the Iraq that . . . was kind of holding together in a constitutional, democratic fashion, with a low level of violence, that that was slipping away, too. . . . Satterfield and Phil [Zelikow] and the secretary were even more worried about Iraq and worried about the legacy and worried about this thing really pulling our whole global diplomatic and security system down with it, and therefore the secretary . . . was not enthusiastic about the surge. I, in the end, went along with Phil and Satterfield so that we'd have a unified agreement with her.

SATTERFIELD: Bottom lines up front, the US had helped Iraqis achieve significant political advances. Those advances were now being fundamentally threatened by sectarian violence; by the inciting and inflaming effect of AQIM [al-Qaeda in the Islamic Maghreb]; by the AQIM terrorist presence itself in Nineveh, Anbar; by the real possibility of dramatic and much increased sectarian cleansing, separation, in Baghdad itself. The possibility of a, quote, "Srebrenica-style" massacre in Baghdad. What could we do? [That was the] First bottom line.

Second bottom line: Could US forces in their current presence in Iraq—or augmented presence—achieve a different result than the results achieved previously? And now we come to what became the fundamental policy divide that moves into the fall—October and November—which really is, US forces have tried a variety of approaches, operationally, to dealing with sectarian violence now for over a year—because we're talking about the latter part of the fall of 2006. Is there a reason to believe that if one added to their strength or somehow redeployed them, they could be more effective or would be capable of even accurate assessment of degrees of success? In the end, our position was no. We could not have such confidence. That is a combination of pace of accelerating sectarian violence, pace of accelerating al-Qaeda incitement, presence of Iranian Shia accelerants of violence—but there's more to be talked about on that score in a moment—ineffectiveness of US military actions in the past, particularly the disastrous Baghdad campaigns—the Together Forward one, two, three—led us to believe we needed a different approach.

We are setting ourselves up for comprehensive defeat. And you are about to throw into that comprehensive defeat—the last US combat-ready ground forces in the world. Is this a wise action? Should hope triumph over experience? And I want to underscore here . . . we did not have confidence that by themselves, or by itself, a surge in US forces could have a decisive, determinative impact on the scope of sectarian violence, the scope of Nineveh-Anbar fighting, and al-Qaeda presence. That was it. That was the fundamental assumption State made. And I would say, today, looking back in retrospect—taken as just that isolated statement that by itself the introduction of an additional five BCTs [brigade combat teams], however managed, could achieve the effect we were seeking—I think that was an accurate judgment by itself.

ZALMAY KHALILZAD, US ambassador to Iraq: [The State Department's] idea [of a minimal or reduced footprint] could be relevant for consideration, in my judgment, if we saw the disintegration of the national security institutions. . . . But, the national institutions were holding. . . . I mean, because I was there, I had a much more fine-grained appreciation. [State's view] was kind of going with the media story, reacting to a media accounting of what was going on in Iraq. This was a [State Department] strategy appropriate to respond to the media articulation, or description of the problem, not to the real situation; it was bad, yes, but it wasn't what they had described the situation.

RICE: I said more troops—the one thing that I'd really become convinced of was more troops doing the same thing was just going to get more Americans killed, and that that was the one thing I couldn't support. This was a hard period for me, sort of September, October, November. The president and I had been together—as he said, he used to tell foreign leaders, "She's like my sister, we came into this together." I'd been with him since effectively, the end of '98, and we had rarely had differing views of anything. . . . Yet, I worried that in an effort to save this, he was going to throw, as I told him, his last card on the table, and if it was more forces to do the same thing, it wasn't going to work, and that would have been the greatest tragedy.

November 11 Meeting

The White House announced Secretary Rumsfeld's resignation on November 8, the day after the midterm elections. A new round of meetings designed to develop a new path forward began on November 11.

FEAVER: It's after the president has announced the review, but before the first day of the J. D. Crouch thing. So it's in that interval, between those two.

RICE: I really valued NSC and State having open communications on this, and being as close as we possibly could to understanding what everybody was doing, and so we agreed to meet that Saturday morning. We met for several hours. . . . And just reviewing everybody's concerns, reviewing what we thought [was] going on, kind of re-walk back through the history. We looked again, back at how to clear, hold, and build, and why the Operation Together had not worked, and then really just a mandate from Steven, from me, to really now go work. I remember saying nothing should be off the table; we should really make sure we've looked at every possible option for the president.

HADLEY: We had been looking at this issue separately, and I thought it would be useful for us to look at it together. . . . Also, you know, the president is very comfortable making decisions, but for the reasons we've already discussed, in this case, he wanted his decision to be something that all his cabinet secretaries would support. And it needed to be something that as much as possible all the military would support because it would not stick, it would not succeed if that were not the case for a whole series of reasons. So part of that reason was to figure out where Condi was and to start a process to try to bring her along.

And the results were not all that successful. They were wedded to this kind of stand back, don't get in the way of a sectarian battle, let it die out, preserve the democratic institutions, which I thought was not going to work. John Hannah—and I'm not sure John was speaking for the vice president, or whether he was speaking for himself—but his view was, you know, you got to go with the majority . . . we ought to be throwing in with the Shia. You can't ride all three horses. And I think my view was, the only way you're going to keep this country together and the only way you're going to get it stable is if you had an inclusive process in which all three constituencies were able to participate and had a common stake in a common future for Iraq.

So it did not provoke a consensus by any means. I think it helped, personally, me sharpen my own thinking. . . . And I think it was the start of a process of bringing Condi along to where it was pretty clear the president wanted to go.

FEAVER: Secretary Rice was arguing forcefully that the surge was not a viable strategy. It wasn't viable politically. The American people wouldn't put up with it, especially after the recent election, and it had these other problems with it. . . . I knew the way the political team would advise the president on this question. I remember, because I had heard this sort of argument from State before, so I remember going to Karl Rove and saying, if the president were asked this, what would be your political advice to him?

Karl's answer was the surge was the one that would be the easiest politically to sustain. It would be very, very hard to sustain, but the other ones would be even harder because you would lose Republicans who thought we had given up on Iraq. Once you've lost the Republicans, then you would have no governing coalition for support for the Iraq War.

RICE: I think my view was, you know, the polls be damned. I mean, just that this was not our writ, to worry about domestic politics. Now, I do remember thinking that the Congress might be a problem as a result. . . . I've always thought, even as a social scientist, that kind of polls about what the American people think about something as complicated as war and peace is not a very good bogie for what's really going on. But you did have a complete wipe of Republicans in 2006, a new Congress. Even Republicans were starting to look over their shoulder, because in testimony, in 2006, I just remember being confronted as much by Republicans as by Democrats, and having a sense now, that I do remember that the Congress, I thought might be a real constraint. . . . It wasn't so much just, in just a general sense the American people wouldn't support, but I do remember thinking [that] 2006 had made a sea change on the Hill.

ZELIKOW: On the substance of what to do in Iraq, it seemed . . . the White House now agrees we ought to have a new strategy, and is now ready to . . . sit down and talk about this, and talk about what, you know, what we could do. . . . This was the meeting where I actually went through these parameters. I don't think I outed Lute as the source, but I said, "We understand from the Pentagon that we require this many brigades to do Baghdad, to police Baghdad, and that they don't have the troops. And so . . . this is a problem." I do remember that at this meeting I think maybe McGurk spoke up, or someone, but somehow I associate in my mind with McGurk as speaking up in favor of a significant troop increase. And my immediate response to that was that they say they can't. Though intellectually, I really liked what McGurk was saying. We've been here for a long time, but kind of, "We're out of Schlitz."

O'SULLIVAN: I think it was a significant meeting. It was one of those meetings that tends to be unusual in government where you have not a lot, you have a small group of reasonably senior people. It was

Condi and Steve. So very senior people with [Peter Feaver], me, John Hannah, Phil Zelikow, Brett McGurk with enough time to really talk about what's happening, what's going on.

It was very interesting to get a window into what Secretary Rice was thinking at the time and assuming if she's thinking there are lots of senior people in our government who are still questioning the relationship between US forces and stability. . . . I remember reasonably clearly that she said, "We don't really see any correlation between US force presence and levels of violence." And this was running very counter to what we had been not only noticing anecdotally but then our office had started to try to map because we wanted to be able to actually counter that with facts and with diagrams. We'd been mapping a neighborhood called Gaziliyah. And Brett McGurk, he was like the Gaziliyah overwatch committee. And this was a neighborhood that had seen US troops come in and out and things transition to Iraqis.

And it was just dramatic how violence went down when the US force presence was there, and when it transferred over to Iraqis, violence spiked. This was very, very clear, this kind of correlation. . . . I said to Brett, "Could you share with Condi your study of this?" And so I think there was still a sense, which I guess makes sense because they've continued it in the State Department's position for a while, that what we did was sort of irrelevant, that our efforts weren't really fundamental to the trajectory in Iraq, whereas we're sitting on the other side of the table thinking, No, we actually know that it's possible to stabilize these areas, but we know it takes a different kind of commitment to do so, or at least we think.

RICE: The thing I remember most about just before that November 11 meeting, that we had a National Security Council meeting that week, just before it, and the metrics were surreal, I just remember that they were surreal. . . . Well, we had broken up this many caches, we'd killed that many terrorists, we've arrested this many people. The one that really always got me was we had all these Iraqi security forces, right? The numbers of Iraqi security forces just kept growing and growing and growing, but weirdly, they would never actually seem to be there, because they'd forget to come back after going home on leave or whatever. But the numbers were almost as if they were being created out of thin air. I remember going to Congress to testify, and it was a real turning point for me in 2006. . . . I remember being asked something about the numbers of security forces in Iraq and refusing to answer, dancing around it, because I no longer had any confidence in the numbers the Pentagon was putting out.

ABIZAID: I got a call from the chairman, General Pace, probably in October, November period. He says, "Hey, our casualties are way too high. Put more Iraqis out there." I said, "Well, where is this coming from?" He said, "It's coming from the president." I'd heard the president say that before. I had no reason to doubt that Pace wasn't relaying accurately what the president thought. And George [Casey] and I talked about it, and again, I went back to General Pace a day or so later and said, "Look, not going to work. We either have to get out there and in the middle of it and increase our casualties, because that's obviously what's going to happen, or we're going to have to just go ahead and withdraw to remote bases on the periphery of the fighting . . . and leave this to the Iraqi security forces to start getting under control."

Announcement of Formal Review

BOLTEN: I think politics may have played a role, and it's not very clear in my recollection, but it makes sense to me that the president was not saying "Snap" two days after the election, "here's where we're going." Again, not because he thought it would have been politically unpopular, which it certainly would have been and was, but because he thought that would then undermine political support for the effort, that he wanted to bring along as many people within the Pentagon, within the interagency process, so that there would be better support for the mission and so that there was a better chance of having the Congress give us the resources, and not block an effort that he knew would be deeply unpopular.

HADLEY: My view is there wasn't a delay. That we were moving forward in the way we needed to move forward if we were going to successfully change the strategy. Remember, it is not easy to change strategy in the middle of a war. And you think it would be easiest to change strategy in the middle of a war that you think you're losing. I think, in fact, it's in some sense the hardest to do that.

A case where the president and his military are at odds in the middle of a war is a constitutional crisis. And a situation where the military is split on the issue of conduct of a war is a kind of political crisis that will make it very difficult to move forward in any strategy. Because for something as controversial as Iraq, those divisions within the military would be used by critics of any engagement of Iraq to undermine the strategy and to force us out and to give up and basically come home.

So this was a very difficult process to manage, and I think the deliberate way we did it was not a question of delaying; it was exactly the process that needed to be gone through in order to bring us to a point where we could get a pretty good consensus behind a very difficult strategy and to be confident the strategy we came up with was actually going to succeed.

CHAPTER 6

A Sweeping Internal Review

Mid–Late November 2006

On November 10, just days after the election, President Bush officially launched a strategy review. It was to be led by Deputy National Security Advisor J. D. Crouch, engaging all relevant departments of the federal government. Participants differ when asked to recall and assess both its purpose and value, though all agree the review process was unlike any policy development process in their professional careers. For some the question was primarily about Iraq; others viewed that conflict as part of a broader series of regional problems. For some the question was how best to salvage the American effort begun in 2003; for others, how best to position the United States in a pivotal region going forward. This was grand strategy of the highest order.

The review culminated with a November 23 meeting in the White House solarium, the site of a famous foreign policy exercise held by President Dwight Eisenhower in 1953. The 2006 exercise left many participants wondering just what had been decided, and whether there was any consensus in government as to how to proceed in—or whether to exit—Iraq.

Mandate and Purpose

CROUCH: I had a very specific mission. I recall the president saying to me, "If we can win, I want to win. If we can't, we have to find a way to get out. And I don't want to spend any more blood and treasure on this." That was the strategic level guidance. And so I think what those [strategy review] meetings were trying to do was actually suss out that question. And was I looking for a consensus per se? No. . . . In the end, we didn't get a consensus.

HADLEY: It needed to be a fundamental look. We had to assess what [were] the assumptions we had with our current strategy, how events have changed since we started that strategy, given the new situation, what were the new assumptions we needed to premise our policy on. And then take those and say, so, in light of the assumptions we'd been working under, what is our operational concept? Now that the world has changed and that we have a different set of assumptions that are going to drive our policy, what are the new operational concepts that are going to work and be consistent with those assumptions? And then in light of that, what's a strategy that would sort of carry out and implement that. And that was the kind of process that we went through. And the briefings that were done and were prepared by J.D. and his team were used to drive and inform the conversations that the president was having with his National Security principals.

RICE: My understanding was that it was really almost as much as you can get to a zero-based review at this point; it was a zero-based review, and you know, you always have costs, you always have restrictions based on what you've already done. It's not really a clean sheet of paper, but this was supposed to be as close to a clean sheet of paper as possible, and that's what I told our guys they should do. This should be as close to a clean sheet of paper, and nothing should be off the table. We owed the president, to look at every possibility.

FEAVER: Our interagency group starts. That's basically all-day-long deputies committee meeting from that point on for the next month. Almost every day, morning session, afternoon session, just cycling through papers, and reports, and assessments.

CROUCH: I think there was a fundamental division in that room. . . . You can argue there was more than one. On the Defense Department side, there was the view that in this question . . . is it politics first? Or is it security first? . . . The State Department view that was articulated at the time was much more of, Things had descended so badly that we were now in a civil war. And so the debate was really over the question of is this a classic counterinsurgency problem, or is this civil war problem? Doctrine would tell you counterinsurgency;

you know, suppress the violence, control—secure the population. The internecine conflict will go down, confidence will be built in the local population, that you're here to help. They'll start helping you, blah blah blah blah blah—that's classic counterinsurgency doctrine. Civil war—that doesn't work. I mean, you can suppress and you can suppress and you can suppress, and I remember at least somebody articulating the idea that, you know, this had to burn itself out. And what we needed to do—we, America, needed to do—was step back, let it burn itself out, and only intervene to, you know, keep a really horrible thing from happening. . . . Focus on al-Qaida, but stay out of this internecine struggle. And you know, the truth of the matter is, nobody in that room really knew who was right, right?

If you talk about what actually happened in 206 [the meeting room number for the strategy review], there was not much talk about a surge strategy in that. There was more discussion about what are the fundamental problems, and what are the overarching strategies to deal with it? The surge is actually not about more force . . . the surge to me was about what were the objectives, political military objectives that you were trying to achieve, and then you looked at it and you said, I needed more force to do that, right?

If you could have achieved those political military objectives without more force, you would have done that. But nobody believed you could. In fact, we weren't even sure that we had enough force to do it, we thought it might even take more than the five and two thirds [brigades], or whatever it was, that ended up being deployed. So that was, to me, that I think the strategy review helped to suss out some of those questions about what were the things that were critical . . . on this question of counterinsurgency versus civil war.

GORDON: It was quite obvious to all of us involved that these weren't, by any stretch of the imagination, the only discussions going on, right? . . . I think what the president wanted to do was to sort of both set up this formal structure and process, but then also do a lot of other stuff himself, or with a more political audience. So I think there were a number of things going on here. I think that what we were told, I think accurately . . . your job here is to represent intelligence and to try to bring the best analytic view, and to give your judgments.

CROUCH: There were other lines of operation that were being discussed outside that room, and that would have been very difficult to discuss inside that room. And so I think—and there were discussions going back and forth—you recall the paper that came out of the Bill Luti brief was then handed by Steve to Pete Pace, I handed it to Doug Lute as well, in the same time frame, and said, "All right, you guys go back and take a look at this."

ROVE: I think it was genuinely open-ended, but I think there was a predilection for a preference for the surge. I think the president's mind, by the summer of '06, is already that the answer to this is that security must come first. That would require surging additional troops to reestablish security, that the security had to be in Sunni and Shia areas, and that all of the rest of this economic and political and cultural progress was at risk unless and until security was obtained, and that would only require putting Americans back into the fight, and with sufficient force.

BOLTEN: I saw a president who was basically making up his mind over that period, in a way that in reality was probably ahead of the process. The review was extremely important, but I think a fair reading of the review, if anything, was Steve Hadley, other folks, helping to lead the rest of the government, which is an important element, toward a conclusion that the president had already reached on his own.

Departmental Positions

O'SULLIVAN: There is a tendency in government and bureaucracies to try to move everything to the middle and find the compromise, and . . . here the differences were very stark.

The State Department position which was briefed by David Satterfield and Phil Zelikow was based, I think, on the idea that our capabilities to effect change were quite limited and that we should really be focused on minimizing our exposure and maintaining our ability to tackle other problems in the world.

We had the OSD [Office of the Secretary of Defense] and then the JCS proposal. I remember them as being essentially the status quo, with more acceleration of transfer of responsibility to the Iraqis.

There was a view from the vice president's office, which was a little bit more like the "Bet on Maliki," like "This is democracy. These people won the election. Let's support them."

SATTERFIELD: I think it's fair to say key points of policy difference emerged in the following way. First, the basic question. Was there more US forces could do? Not in a different role—that is, in a stand-back role, limited goals, limited triggers for intervention—but could the US actually affect, with . . . a steady state or with an increased . . . presence of forces, could it achieve the absolute goals? Stop this violence? Stabilize, in an enduring fashion, the situation in Baghdad? Address the shift, the violence, in Anbar and Nineveh directed against the Iraqi government and coalition? That is, basically, could we succeed on a big level—the president's big level—by adding more military forces? Shifting the way those additional military forces acted, but not diminishing the goals? That was one key division.

Second division, Baghdad. Could you ignore Baghdad? Could you, in fact, have a coherent, politically stable—marginally stable—Iraq if Baghdad wasn't stable? And what did it take to stabilize Baghdad? Which fed us back into the issue of US forces. So there was a challenge there to whether decentralization was even possible without fragmentation and further violence emerging. It was a fundamental challenge to the premise itself. So I think those, fairly said, were the key divisions here.

Defense

FEAVER: We had been avidly waiting for the JCS report, which we thought was going to be the Council of Colonels' report. We had seen a version of that. Pete Pace had briefed it to me and Meghan and Steve Hadley, so we knew what it was and we knew that it had these different options, including a surge option. That would be finally a paper that had a surge option that we could then—it wouldn't be an NSC option, it would be a JCS option that we could explore.

General Pace gave us a version of that. He said, "I haven't taken this into the tank yet,[1] but this is what the Council of Colonels have put forward." The day of the actual, JCS was scheduled to present their paper, it leaks, and I think Tom Ricks had the version of the study, the early draft of the Council of Colonels. It's in the *Washington Post*, and there it is: Go big, Go long, Go home. Those were several of the options.

MANSOOR: Basically in the end we said, "Here's three distinct options that we can present to the Joint Chiefs"—and remember that we were not a decision group. We weren't saying, "And this is our preferred option," we were just allowing them different options so they could discuss among themselves what was possible or desirable to do in Iraq.

As we were sort of putting the strategy in some sort of final form they said, "Well, how do we explain this?" and I got up to the whiteboard with a marker and I said, "H.R. [McMaster] wants to mobilize the American people, mobilize the reserves, put another 250,000 troops in Iraq—or put enough troops to raise it up to 250,000—we'll call that 'Go big.'" That would've required mobilization of reserves. We had discussions about should we have a draft. In the end I don't think we thought we needed to, but that was on the table. H.R., I think, was the proponent of We're in a war, we need to fight to win it, and we need to mobilize the American people behind it, and we need to mobilize our full capability. I think a quarter million or more was what he had in mind.

There were those of us—and I was sort of the leader of the middle group—that said, "Well, that's probably not in the offing. I just don't think the administration is going to do it, nor are the American people going to do it." Counterinsurgency wars are usually fought and won over the long term, and so what we need to do is . . . get the situation under control, but then configure our involvement in Iraq for the long haul, and I was thinking decades, not years—or at least a decade. So I said, "We'll call that one 'Go long,'" so it didn't rule out a surge to get things under control, but the long haul would've been staying in Iraq with tens of thousands of US forces or at least more than ten thousand. The sort of interim structure was ten brigades and a huge advisory group until the counterinsurgency war had been won and then drawing down to a sustainable presence but staying there, not leaving at the end of 2011 like we did. So that was sort of "Go long," and we've discussed "Go home," which was let Iraq go where it will and contain . . . it, contain the mess, and hold our fire for wars to come.

No one said, "Well, you know the American people aren't going to put up with a multigenerational presence or multiyear presence in Iraq." We thought the American people would, given what we had done in South Korea—we are still in South Korea today. We thought that actually if we could generate a bipartisan consensus in Washington, that the American people would eventually see the need to sustain our efforts there. No one really had an insight into what the Iraqis were going to think about that.

FEAVER: When Doug Lute presented the actual JCS paper, it was the existing strategy. It was Casey's next phase of his existing strategy. In other words, the Council of Colonels' study had gone through the tank, been washed out, and came out from MNF-I as "keep doing what we've been doing, only do it faster." I remember Meghan and

I were looking at each other saying, we just lost our surge option, because the JCS was no longer even entertaining that as an option.

LUTE: The Joint Staff just—simply represented Casey's position, and the theater commander, General Abizaid's position, and that was essentially holding to the current concept, which was stand up / stand down, holding to the provincial Iraqi control transition process, right? And supporting General Casey's position they didn't need more troops, and, in fact, Maliki might not accept more troops.

I would have considered an add-five-brigades option as an accelerant to the clock, that it would speed the clock up, that greater US presence would result in greater Iraqi intolerance, and eventually speed the whole thing up. . . . I knew that the force was stressed, I knew that we were actually encroaching on one-to-one, because the dwell one year was not really a year off. . . . The service chiefs were telling us that was really a stress, and we didn't want to break the all-volunteer force.

I believed that—and I still believe—that the burden here ultimately had to fall on the Iraqis, and if the Iraqis weren't going to do this, then that's a pretty fundamental strategic assessment, and adding five more brigades—arguably, from the outset we knew that wasn't going to be a long-term proposition. It was going to be hard to do once. It was going to be very hard to do if we were to sustain twenty brigades over, say, a couple years, right? It turns out we didn't do that, but that was going to be almost mission impossible. And so the notion of adding five very much, I think, came across as a kind of a quick fix, a temporary fix, a Band-Aid, if you will, and it wasn't clear to me that a temporary US surge—which even the term implies in and out, right?—would help things, as opposed to having a neutral effect or having even a negative effect. . . . I didn't think it was going to be successful, and I was not an advocate, and it was basically because of my belief that it would at most have a temporary, localized, even maybe tactical impact.

LIEUTENANT GENERAL JOHN SATTLER, US Marine Corps, director of strategy and policy, Joint Staff: I recollect both General Lute and I going in, talking with General Pace when he told us [about the review]. . . . I walked out of that meeting thinking that our position was, hey, the surge is a great idea, comma, but we just don't have the forces to do it. We're going to break the force, break the families, and we're going to break, you know, break the tone that we told the young men and women coming in. . . . I actually saw it in their eyes and how absolutely tired they were by the end of—when it was time to come home, it was like a pitcher going twelve innings. . . . No whining, no moaning. I don't want to paint that picture, but you could feel the fact that wow, we are stressing the force. . . . We're going to crush them.

For all intents and purposes we surged for the battle of Fallujah, it was just internal with General Casey. . . . We surged the Marines into Fallujah, we tightened our belt out toward the Syrian border. So that experience told me that—I am a believer that, if we have the resources, I believed it was a good idea, but I was convinced it would break the force going into the first meeting. . . . So I went in thinking surge, bad idea.

We never collaborated with Dr. Cambone and the OSD team. . . . General Pace wanted all chips on the table and candid discussions, so Doug and I were not influenced by anything that OSD was coming in. I truly . . . did not know OSD's position when we got in the room, and we were not handcuffed by having to tuck under it.

ZELIKOW: The Pentagon did not play in this review, in effect, which is in itself an astonishing statement. The command did not play. . . . And Lute—basically . . . stuck to the position of we don't have any troops available, or it would be very difficult to make more troops available. . . . They didn't really come in with a strong, affirmative strategy view of their own that would've come out of this colonels' review or something, and that just—that was deflating.

CAMBONE: The secretary [of defense] had a paper. It was called the plan, and it was being done, and that's what it was. So this was a question about what did other people have to say and what it is that they thought they wanted to do, and more to digest that and bring it home and allow him to do what he needed to do relative to both State and the White House.

From the point of view of General Casey, he was not of the view that it was time to change course in a substantial way. A little left, a little right, a little faster, a little slower, sure, but I don't think he was of the view that this needed to be scrubbed, top to bottom, with a wholesale change. And moreover, as I recall, I think from his point of view it was also a distraction. I mean, he's got a war on his hands, and now he's sitting in meetings going over people, you know, grading his homework.

HANNAH: With DoD . . . there was clearly concern about, and I think legitimate concern, about the health of the force. I mean, people call it big Army kinds of concerns, and no doubt the Marine Corps had it as well, that the stresses on the force by that time in Iraq were enormous. Adding new additional burdens to this would really endanger the force and endanger perhaps our ability to conduct operations in crises elsewhere in the world. So that was part of it.

But I think it also was in part a holdover that they just had a different view of the role of American forces in Iraq. . . . That in fact the presence of American forces that had been labeled as occupiers had fired up all kinds of antibodies in the Iraqi body politic writ large, that were reacting against us, resisting us, fighting us, and that in fact the way to get control of that was to actually do as much as you could as quickly as you could, to hand over to Iraqis, even if they weren't going to do it as well as we could. The political benefits in terms of potential reconciliation would be much greater in terms of getting the Iraqis to actually take responsibility for their own affairs and to do what was necessary to stabilize their own country, that the benefits would far outweigh the cost of drawing down our forces on a much more quicker time frame. . . . DoD and the Pentagon and the military in general were not particularly enthusiastic about the course that we appeared headed toward.

EDELMAN: Well, it was a bit of an awkward period in the sense that Secretary Rumsfeld had resigned, Secretary Gates had been nominated, and initially had not been confirmed, and then later was confirmed but didn't take office until mid-December, because he wanted to preside over the winter graduation at Texas A&M. And so that made it a bit of an awkward period for me, because you only work for one secretary of defense at a time. And Secretary Rumsfeld, as I've indicated, had some very strong views about not increasing the troops, about continuing to train and transfer and make sure the Iraqis took the responsibility for this fight themselves, not just push it back on the US.

In that period, somewhere in there in November, Ray Odierno, who was then down at III Corps as commander, but who was headed back out to Iraq to become the corps commander under General Casey, replacing Pete Chiarelli, paid an office call on me while this review was going on. And he said, "I've been doing a study of this, and I think I need more troops." . . . And I said, "Ray, I'm very sympathetic. Very sympathetic." I said, "But I've got a secretary of defense who doesn't want to have more troops out there. I got a new secretary of defense who's getting briefed up. I don't know what he thinks. I'm going to have to navigate my way through this."

This is one of those periods when civil-military relations and the lines become really blurry. What's policy advice? What's military advice in this context? I think General Pace, to his enormous credit, was trying to play it very straight and not prejudice people one way or another. . . . But basically, when asked, he would just be straightforward about OK, what do we have in the kit bag, what could we provide in terms of additional forces. He would play it very straight. As did General Lute whenever asked directly. But General Lute was, I think—made it very clear he had minimal enthusiasm for increasing the number of troops. I think very much in the Rumsfeld camp in terms of making the Iraqis step up and do their part.

CROUCH: The general view that I think I got from the Department [of Defense] in those meetings, in the trans-secretary changeover, was . . . still a belief and confidence that over time, the strategy would work, respectful of the fact that the president needed to have options and needed to get options in front of him, but at the same time wanted to make sure that there wasn't just a single-point solution that was being developed by the NSC, or somebody else, and that's very consistent, I think, with the way Secretary Rumsfeld always looked at issues. He wanted to make sure that all the assumptions got surfaced up. And there was still a very strong feeling, and this was not just on the political side, but on the uniform side as well, that the rest of the government had not shown up to this fight, yet. Rightly or wrongly, that was the view.

HANNAH: Once Secretary Rumsfeld went, I'm trying to think what kind of impact it had. I'm not sure because institutionally, I think at the Pentagon, I think there continued to be, throughout that period in November and December, and certainly amongst our commanders in Iraq, a great deal of reticence to look at any kind of dramatic changes in policy and strategy in Iraq, particularly ones that required a significant addition of US forces. Exactly where Secretary Gates stood at that point in time was unclear.

Intelligence and Regional Politics

GORDON: The intelligence community . . . paper that had been requested really look[ed] at what might the options be moving ahead, and the consequences of those actions. . . . We were actually quite negative in what we thought the implication of a troop withdrawal was. . . . A lot of people, particularly people who didn't know very much about Iraq, frankly, were of the view that things aren't going great, therefore the source of things not going great must be the [US] presence. We really didn't think that was the case. Earlier on, that was definitely part of why things went downhill in Iraq. We had not prepared adequately . . . for insurgency, and we hadn't really thought out the parallel processes of creating effective administration and building up Iraqi political institutions—there had been very little thinking done, this was done on the fly, basically. We were of the view, at the time, that if you actually took the US military presence out, that the civil war element would become more unbridled. I think in retrospect that was right. . . . And that in the absence of a US presence, sectarianism was likely to get worse, not better.

We considered regional politics, I think probably not as much as we might have. . . . I mean, our main concern here was . . . that the civil war continuing and rising was going to drive the Iraqis toward the Iranians, and that basically a context of rising sectarian conflict there was ironically something that was in the strategic interest of both AQI and Iran. . . . I mean, we had been burned in intel earlier on in Iraq by underestimating the degree to which Iran was going to be willing to confront the United States in Iraq. . . . But we were very, very, very worried that as the Shia got more and more fearful about their future, that it was absolutely inevitable that they would turn to Iran. And there was a lot of intelligence that I can't talk about the specifics of, of individual events and situations that showed that was happening. . . . And I think . . . that became a critical point in leading this group toward the surge concept, because . . . if it's the case, as you say, that a rapid withdrawal would have these very, very negative options, would a substantial increase have the obverse? Earlier on in the discussion, I don't think I was prepared to be so positive about this, but as the discussion went on, and as the situation deteriorated, I think it was this notion that the Iranians are really making headway here, and that the only chance of basically holding on to a policy that could offer a pathway forwards for both Sunni and Shia involved more, not less, resources.

CAMBONE: There was concern about the Iranians, and what they were up to, and how this would affect them one way or the other. Lost in a lot of things that are written about the time is the active role that the Iranians were playing inside of Iraq, and the danger that that portended. And the longer the unsettled state of affairs continued, the more likely it would be that the Iranians would have an advantage, more advantage than they already did. Meanwhile, we were losing people in what appeared to be circumstances that somehow or another, if you kept pulling the string, you'd find yourself back, worrying about whether the Iranians had been involved.

ABIZAID: In this period you have the Iranians actually killing American soldiers by proxy. This was new in 2006 and 2007. And so there was obvious need to prepare for the potential of conflict with Iran. We always were preparing for the conflict against the Iranians. And so I had my commanders prepare for contingency operations against Iran, ranging from kind of what I would call raids to send them the signal, to having to destroy their air and naval operations along the Persian Gulf. And it was a very, very major effort. And again, when I looked at what would be needed, should it come to that, that it would really have strained the armed forces without a mobilization. Nobody was going to mobilize. Not in the sense of World War II or Korea. . . . But the prospect that you could either miscalculate and go to war with the Iranians, or have to then have a campaign against the Iranians, was very real to me, and I had some very difficult discussions with people in the administration about the wisdom of provoking the Iranians.

LUTE: We persistently . . . through the surge decision process, and to a fault, considered Iraq in isolation of much of the regional context. So I don't remember the regional context playing a big role. As I look back on the surge, you know, I ask, OK, so let's get this straight: Iraq's not an island in the Pacific somewhere; it actually has neighbors, and the neighbors it has are all being unhelpful. And again, I've talked about Syria and the foreign fighters; I've talked about Iran, and the Shia militia, and the EFPs [explosively formed penetrators], and so forth. The surge wasn't going to do much of anything against that strategic set. I mean, those regional challenges were not going to be impacted at all. And so one of the concerns was that if we take this US step to send in five more brigades, how does it change the regional dynamics in a way that suggests that maybe this big effort—I mean, you know, this doubling down by the US—is going to have a durable impact. And to this day I can't cite much promise that adding five brigades would have any impact at all on this very detrimental regional set.

ABIZAID: You're looking through the soda straw at Iraq, right? And everything is "look in there," and all the people in Washington are

concerned about it, and all this other stuff is going on, but, we're trying to get ourselves unencumbered in Afghanistan as well. . . . And
what I was seeing, because I looked at the whole theater, I was seeing a clear movement of fighters that were no longer able to operate
the way they wanted to in Iraq to other places. In particular, they'd
come on down into Somalia. And so we were opening up a new front
in Somalia. We were seeing this from our outpost in Djibouti. We'd
see it in northern Kenya. We'd also see it in the Sinai in Egypt. And I
went to all these places to try to get some kind of judge on what was
going on. So while General Casey's worried about the deteriorating situation, which was true in Iraq, between Sunnis and Shias, I'm
worried about the deteriorating situation in the broader Middle East
about Islamic extremism in particular.

I had a very difficult time [trying to] convince people that there
was a broader Sunni Islamic extremist movement in the region
that required urgent attention. And so many of our resources were
focused on Iraq, it was very, very difficult to get at it the way that we
needed to. And I was constantly saying that to the secretary of state,
secretary of defense, and the president.

State Department

ZELIKOW: I began crafting a paper that is kind of starting from where
we had been in May, but now beginning to scale back what was possible. And Satterfield is wary, and I'm actually a little disillusioned by
this point, too. I've now taken a run at this three times. . . . To some
degree, I have failed three times. And now I've been told flatly by the
J3 that we have no troops.

So here's my point: I've got to write a strategy, and if I write a
strategy that the Pentagon says they cannot do—and by the way,
which I know they will not do—I'm not being very helpful to the
president in basically writing yet another quixotic strategy paper
that I know is unimplementable. So then I feel like my job is to be
practical and write a strategy paper that this government, as constituted, is able to implement and will implement. Again—later
I would discover that there was another guerrilla warfare operation on strategy that was going on, that was actually developing
out-of-the-box approaches to use more troops, but I wasn't clued
into that at the time, and thus could not ally myself with that and
run with that.

So I'm trying to write a paper inside the parameters I think I now have after these efforts, and so then that paper essentially said we do not have the troops . . . we can add to police Baghdad internally, and control the violence inside the city. What I did not want to do is destroy what we were accomplishing elsewhere in the country . . . in order to police Baghdad. So then the only alternative I could come up with is we've got to basically cordon the violence in Baghdad, which is just going to burn itself out, and our goal is to try to keep a lid on it and keep it from spilling over.

There was going to be an amount of ethnic cleansing we could not stop. It was already well under way, and had been under way, for a year. . . . People were dying at the rate of hundreds per week, and had been dying at the rate of hundreds per week for a year. So we needed to close off the violence inside Baghdad, hold all of our troop strength in, you know, Tikrit, Kirkuk, Mosul, Anbar, bolster the British as well as we could in Basra, and then the key also was hold the Baghdad belts, because the Baghdad belts were the big conduits to escalate, to stoke the fires in Baghdad, for infiltration, and so hold the Baghdad belts is also the key to holding Baghdad, while you basically try to let this burn out, because we don't have the four to six brigades that would be needed to go in and police Baghdad, and if you tried to do that by stripping the country you'll just make other things worse again.

So that's kind of the tenor of the paper that I'm drafting, and I don't remember the time frame, but it would've been around this period of late October, early November. . . . I'm drafting it, Satterfield is editing it, it's being discussed with Condi, among different approaches. . . . Condi was becoming—was also somewhat skeptical and disillusioned about what was possible.

SATTERFIELD: The State Department position, the secretary's ultimate position on that, was we could not be held responsible for the phenomenon of sectarian violence. It was the product of historical processes unleashed by the ouster of Saddam Hussein in 2003. The US, at best, could attempt to mitigate or to try to prevent the worst. And Srebrenica was always used as the trigger rubric here.[2] If we saw a Srebrenica-style massacre emergent, then we would have to intervene. US forces had a responsibility not to stand by across the river from Warsaw and watch the ghetto being destroyed—that they would have to intervene under such circumstances—but that the bar should be a very high one.[3] Not because it was not right to stop sectarian violence, but that the generators of sectarian violence were so profound, so intrinsic to Iraq and its fabric, and then inflamed from outside—Shia militias, Iran, al-Qaeda—that we simply didn't have the ability to do what otherwise we might, as an objective principle, want to do.

SATTLER: State Department had everything on the table, everything from status quo to precipitous withdrawal—I remember that with Philip and I going nose to nose on a—you know, "We'll order them out!" and I remember screaming, "That's an unlawful order. No Marine or soldier is going to— We put our arms around these people. We told them we'd be there. We cannot withdraw next week. That is an unlawful order." We got really into it, which you should in a meeting like that. . . . I just think it was healthy debate. . . . But that got real hot and heavy at the beginning, and then that kind of— precipitous withdrawal, just pull out, you know, head to Kuwait, load up the trucks, go to the airfield, it's all yours—discussed in detail, but I think we moved away from that as not being what we stood for as a country when we put our arm around somebody.

HANNAH: From early on, my impression of State, from the secretary on down, that they had sort of begun to arrive at a conclusion that— probably unfair to say that the situation in Iraq was lost, but the situation was pretty much lost as far as what the US could do at the margins to actually turn it around, that this was something that Iraqis were going to have to do, that they were right now engaged in something that was pretty damn close to a civil war. It was certainly a sectarian bloodletting. . . . So it was a pessimistic overall kind of view about what could be accomplished, and whether or not it was outright against a surge in forces and a shift in strategy toward true protection of the population primarily by—or with a major role by—American forces. It may not have been outright opposition, but it was deep, profound skepticism was my impression, where they were coming from.

KHALILZAD: My judgment is that it [the State Department position] had to do with two things. One . . . the institution of the State Department never bought into the Iraq project. They thought this was wrongheaded to begin with, we . . . shouldn't have gone in; and the building of democracy in the Middle East was a kind of oxymoron. . . . People never gave up completely on what the original position was, though that position did not prevail at that time, it's kind of a permanent struggle, policy making, where people who lost at one time see the circumstances change, and strike again, so to speak, because they lost in the last round, and I believe that they saw the increased violence [with] a bit of triumphalism that they had said from the beginning that we shouldn't do that.

SATTERFIELD: The presentation from the embassy in all of its dimensions—which included the military—was indeed, we thought, far rosier. To the point that, speaking from my agency, the secretary began simply to discount and dismiss what she was hearing. . . . We didn't see connectivity between these rosy projections of "we can make it work." Some of which were substantive, but most of which were personality-driven, I can make this work. They were no longer relevant. And this became much more of a Washington process than it was driven by the field.

National Security Council

ZELIKOW: And then the NSC staff was taking this interesting view of, here, aside from being the umpire of this process, is we want to be sure the idea of a significant troop increase is on the table. But I don't remember that Meghan or Brett would really do . . . a full-throated advocacy of how that option would work. . . . I think Condi's reaction, even more than mine, was we can't put the president in the position of basically doing, you know, this incredible high-stakes play unless we know where it's going to go. And see, at that point we weren't sure . . . that anybody was . . . willing to do what needed to be done to make something like that work. We now knew Gates [would be secretary of defense], but everybody else in the chain of command is opposed to this, and the Iraqi prime minister is opposed to it, too. These are fairly significant obstacles!

CROUCH: The notion of pulling back, however, I think—and I articulated this, I know, at the table . . . would have been a disaster, because Americans—America at home, and the Americans particularly on the ground who were executing that strategy, could not have sustained that. It would have morally undercut the purpose for which they believed that they were there.

O'SULLIVAN: The NSC staff doesn't have a position paper. . . . This is one of the very interesting things about this whole review, which . . . is the NSC and people working in the NSC are supposed to play multiple roles. And the very important role is to make sure that the system works and make sure everybody's at the table and everybody has an opportunity to put forward their views. . . . Our job is not to put forward a particular view or viewpoint; it's to manage the process.

On the other hand, the most senior people are direct hires of the president and that the president looks to us for his advice to him. And certainly this was a case where he wanted to know what people who work on these issues thought. And so he wanted to know, What would you do? What do you think is the best strategy? What are you advocating? And so there was this tension between those roles.

Steve Hadley let it be known to this group of deputies, OK, we can formulate these options, but if we're presenting options, we're going to have a double-down option in there just because we want all the options to be in there. . . . That's different than saying it was a decision and so it was just injected in there. . . . There wasn't anyone else who was advocating for it.

HADLEY: I do remember at one point meeting with J.D. and the team, the deputies-level team that was doing that important analytical work, and saying that you come up with a set of options for the president. It needs to reflect the full range of views, but it will contain a surge option. Because if it doesn't contain a surge option, we are not presenting the president all of the options, and that's what we owe him. That was really the only pressure I put in terms of an outcome.

I was wanting to make sure we had the kind of process that would be inclusive, that would be focused on the president, that would give him the right set of options and would put him in the position to make the right decision. I think he and I were both moving toward the surge as the way to go, but wanting to reach that decision through this process that we had described.

At one point in this process, when the formal strategy review is launched, it goes forward on two levels. It is focused on the president; it is going to have an important component of the president talking to his national security principals. And then it's going to be supported by the deputies' process that J. D. Crouch is running, which is going to run the numbers, do the analysis, and respond to the questions and insights of the principals and inform the principals.

So that's really how we ran that process. It was kind of a three-tier process.

BOLTEN: That speaks to the adroitness of Steve Hadley, in being perceived as honest broker while pushing the most radical option that nobody else supported—but he knew he was doing that on behalf of the president.

BUSH: If Hadley had his mind made up, how can he be an honest broker? And you know, he probably wasn't. On the other hand, Hadley's . . . very fair, and he wanted to make sure everybody—and that's what made him a really good national security advisor—wanted to make sure everybody's opinion was known. In other words, he didn't come in and say, "Dismiss Condi's opinion."

I was advocating. It's the victory option. What does it take? That's really the only, not to be a blowhard, but that's the only one that really matters. Therefore it made it difficult at the national security meetings to be an honest broker, but I wasn't at those meetings. I was at the meetings when I asked them questions. I'm a questioner. "Where are we? What are we doing? What's the process?" And Steve or Meghan or somebody else would say let's just slow down, President, we're making progress. I'm chomping at the bit, and they're saying ease back, we're not quite ready.

RICE: I thought Steve wanted to surge forces. I know him well enough. I think he was—the idea of changing strategy and properly resourcing it appealed to him. Now, I think the problem was, he wasn't quite sure whether he could get it properly resourced, and I wasn't sure he could get it properly resourced either, because I remember the initial Pentagon discussions where they made it sound as if we wouldn't be able to confront North Korea if we surged forces in Iraq. There was a lot of politics going on around this.

Was the Review Precooked?

SATTERFIELD: There has been speculation, which others in government at the time have raised, that the results of this process were cooked from the very beginning, or almost the very beginning. That Steve Hadley had decided that there was going to be a surge, the president had decided there was going to be a surge. And all of this was, essentially, window dressing, or trimming, to provide a plausible corroboration for a decision already taken.

I can't speak to the president's own thoughts during this time or to Steve's, but nothing in the conduct of the process would bear out that assumption. Whether it is right or not, I simply can't say. But I certainly cannot make that judgment based on any of the conversations.

CAMBONE: It's getting more intense in Iraq, business with Maliki isn't going very well. The [US] election was brutal, in terms of the criticisms of the president and the way things were going, and so forth.

So clearly, it was about making a change, and so the question was what kind of change was it going to be.

O'SULLIVAN: My view at the time was that if there was any sort of inevitability to the surge, I was completely unaware of it. In fact, I thought that the cards were dramatically stacked against that outcome for all the obvious reasons. . . . But a few things stand out in my mind. . . . First it's just my own interaction with President Bush. And he said something to me that I believe he also said to J.D. and maybe others. He said, "You know, I'm looking to you to tell me how we can fix the situation in Iraq, but I'm also looking to you to tell me if we can't." I remember him saying that because I remember it weighed on me really heavily, because we were all very emotionally invested in this. I asked myself, Am I capable of coming to that conclusion?

LUTE: It didn't seem precooked to me. I give J. D. Crouch credit for asking the hard questions, taking a very comprehensive view, taking a deliberate, time-consuming approach to hearing from the different perspectives around the table, asking for options, and giving the departments and agencies time to come back, and so forth. So, no, it didn't seem predestined in any particular way. I think there was a common view around the table that it was time for a fresh look, and that we were certainly not winning, and we may have been losing, and time was running out.

SATTLER: I think we had to get in there and bare knuckle it for a while. And I think Dr. Crouch teed it up very, very well, to kind of get, OK, we're getting a little donnybrook on the front side, then after we all know each other and we're a little worn down, tired of going at each other, then we're going to go at the problem. . . . I was influenced by that discussion over the course of the many meetings. I did listen to the facts—very persuasive men and women, the articulation brought me off of the position I went in with. I slowly morphed along the way to a more central position. . . . We started talking about really how many brigades were really available. . . . I believe, if I remember correctly, it might have been Meghan O'Sullivan or Peter Feaver that actually brought forth . . . an outside assessment as to where some of the brigades were. . . . I think Doug [Lute] went back and took a hard look at it with his team, and came out and said, "You know, this period of time, we can have five brigades who will have dwell [time at home], who won't break dwell if we go in and surge and we accomplish the mission in accordance with this timeline." . . . And I think at that point in time, the not breaking the back of the force and doing the surge became a viable option to me personally.

SATTERFIELD: I saw the NSC playing a role that was directly shaped by the concern that a fundamental US policy pillar which the president was personally involved in was being threatened. And the NSC, quite appropriately, took a significant lead in trying to provide a recommendation that would ideally be able to result in a strategy that would produce the effect, the outcomes which the president threw out all this time, would not waver from. And this is an important point. The president's language didn't alter in terms of victory, success. Whatever our concerns may be that a toned-down rhetoric was really more appropriate, he didn't. And of course, that is his prerogative. He's the president. And the policy process, I think, quite effectively presented to him different recommendations on where to go.

But I would say this. No one should ever underestimate the power of the president's own views to trump even the most senior level and profound interagency, principal level, debate or discussion. . . . President Bush believed to his core that success was possible. He also believed to his core that it would be inexcusable and irresponsible, in a historical context, for him having invested this amount of treasure, this amount of American, Iraqi lives since 2003—to hold back one final push to see if success could be achieved. Or put differently, even if you are recommending against doing this, if there is any possibility that these additional force elements can produce success, I have an obligation to what has gone before—and to history—to try it. And I think that's a pretty fair assessment of what he thought. And in the end, he got a fair presentation of his view and of differing views. He made his choice.

CAMBONE: What it boiled down to in the end was a position offered by State, which would have had essentially a withdrawal from the active combat operations and a pullback into the urban centers, and wait out, sort of, the outcome. . . . It was argued forcibly, but it always struck me more as a contingent kind of argument than as a preferred outcome. . . . But it wasn't long before it was clear it was either more or you're going to end up doing this contraction, and the contraction was not attractive. It wasn't in keeping with what was thought to be the whole purpose of the war in the first place. So it was nearly a default on a surge of some kind, and so then the question was how big, how long, to what end, and those kinds of things.

I don't mean to gainsay the process, but it was clear that it was going to be one or the other, that is to say the retrenchment or the surge, and there really wasn't much enthusiasm around the table to include inside the Department of Defense, either on the civilian or uniform side, for retrenchment. So then the question is OK, so how do you manage this surge business.

Solarium Meeting, November 26

EDELMAN: It was never very clear when the end point was going to be and when we were going to actually deliver ourselves a kind of product. And in a way we never really did. I mean it just evolved into a discussion of what are the options. What it really boiled down to in the end was should we move away from "train and transfer" and try and put some emphasis on population security until we can stabilize the situation.

O'SULLIVAN: I think we had done the deputies meeting for maybe ten days. And then this was the solarium meeting. And I remember Steve called me into his office and he said, "Could you draft a paper for the discussion in this meeting that we're going to have in the solarium? Call it something like 'The Emerging Consensus' and just put forward what the view is that's emerging out of this deputies meeting."

I kind of grumbled a little. I went back, and I started to write it. And I went back to Steve and I said, "Look, there is no emerging consensus. This is an impossible paper to write because the interesting thing is that actually nobody agrees with anybody about even foundational issues." That said, Steve wanted something that would be the basis for a discussion. So I remember writing this paper which J.D. briefed to the group, and I remember thinking it was absolutely the worst memo I've ever written in my life because to me it was not internally consistent.

CROUCH: The document that we generated for the solarium meeting was called, "Iraq: The Emerging Consensus"—no greater oxymoron had ever been created in government than that document.

O'SULLIVAN: It was a small meeting of basically the cabinet, the National Security Council, without their deputies or plus-ones, with the exception of J. D. Crouch and me, and I think that's it. Dan Bartlett, I think, was there as well. It was a small group of people. It wasn't the normal kind of NSC process.

I felt completely dejected after that meeting because I felt that I saw happening what I felt had happened on many occasions before, which is that everybody's differences had been obscured, all the sharpness of the debates had been papered over, and the net effect was an approach that was just an incremental change from what we'd already been doing.

There's no decision made. And to be fair, in retrospect, when I look at the meeting, I have no idea what was in the president's head at the time. The people I remember being most vocal and having the floor the most were Secretary Rumsfeld and Secretary Rice. . . . He was still involved. And I remember that there were a lot of the familiar arguments made, and Secretary Rice expressed her deep skepticism of our ability to do anything meaningful. And I remember feeling like a lot of the momentum that I thought had been building at least for a crisp, decisive conversation was really dissipated after that.

RICE: I knew we were in the midst of really trying to figure out how to change course. . . . It was a very good meeting in the solarium. It was a good presentation about kind of where we were and what the options were, and I just considered it yet another opportunity for the president to hear from people, but to start to really get to some answers about where he wanted to go. . . . I didn't feel that we came to a conclusion, except that we had to do something different, and maybe that was a conclusion in and of itself, that we were no longer in the "well, this might work one day" mode. Now that I think about it, I think maybe that was everybody in the room, for the first time, sort of saying that to each other.

CHENEY: By the time we get through the election and we have that meeting in the solarium, it's pretty clear that we've got to do something different than what we've been doing. December was then devoted to sort of nailing down what that was going to be, but that there weren't a lot of people in the room arguing that we shouldn't do anything. Casey may still be on the old track out in country. Rumsfeld wasn't much of a factor by then, he's gone.

RICE: Well, I don't think the president ever was—he wanted something different, he wanted to do something different. Quite unlike his reputation, he really isn't someone who's given to snap judgments, and I think he was rolling it over in his head, he was thinking. . . . I think he felt his greatest obligation was not to create Vietnam, not to lose. But I think he was trying very hard to find out what the best possible answer was, and one of the reasons that I wanted to push so hard was that I wanted to make sure that he was prepared to deal with the possibility that a more dramatic move would not work.

The worst thing—and I'd watched the Pentagon, in 2003, inadequately resource the invasion. Now, part of that was not their fault, because the Fourth ID [Infantry Division] got stuck, couldn't get through Turkey. I remember, I'd gone through this horrible fight about what we called rear action, rear area support. So, once our forces pushed through, who was going to stay back to maintain order. Steve and I had essentially lost that fight, it was always a different answer: Oh, the Iraqis will, or the British will, or somebody else will. I'd seen this movie before, and a surge with too few forces was going to get a bunch of Americans killed, particularly if it was at a time when the Iraqis were stupidly still fighting among themselves. And so absolutely, I was a skeptic of whether we could pull this off, and I told the president as much, but I told him privately.

Yeah, you won't see that in the State Department papers, and you won't see that in the NSC notes.

BOLTEN: [The solarium meeting's] significance probably would be exaggerated by historians. I think at that point, the president had basically made up his mind that he was fine-tuning and that part of the purpose of the meeting was to try to help build a consensus for where he was headed at that point, because that meeting was pretty late in the year. . . . I don't think the president wanted to communicate at that point that he had decided, but in my recollection and in my view, he basically had decided.

Chapter 7

Choosing to Surge

December 2006

The American people having vented their frustration at the polls in November, by the following month pressure grew in Washington for a change of course in Iraq. It was public pressure indeed. In early December, the Iraq Study Group (ISG), composed of seasoned policy makers, released its own report, bluntly describing the situation in Iraq as "grave and deteriorating." The ISG report focused heavily on a regional diplomatic offensive to help give breathing space to national reconciliation in Iraq. It made a minor mention of increasing US forces in Iraq in the short term. But the ISG's primary purpose was to provide a political off-ramp for Bush should he decide that withdrawal was his best strategic option.

Bush was not interested in finding an off-ramp, admitting defeat and leaving Iraq in tatters after three years of American occupation. Instead, in the first two weeks of December, the president and his NSC debated anew the very fundamentals of American strategy in Iraq, with a specific focus on the viability of adding more troops. Rather than folding, in poker terms, they debated pushing all their chips forward, even as respected voices inside and outside the Pentagon decried the military's exhaustion. In their view, Bush couldn't bet chips he did not have.

New players entered the debate. Jack Keane and Fred Kagan of the American Enterprise Institute (AEI) offered an opposing view to the Pentagon's conventional wisdom—for example, briefing senior officials in December on their work suggesting the feasibility of a troop increase in Iraq. They were publicly arguing what some in government already knew: a surge was possible, if deemed desirable. This has been seen in the existing literature as a crucial external intervention, a pivotal moment in the surge when outsiders changed the course of the war. Our oral histories suggest a different tale, however, arguing instead that the AEI's efforts dovetailed with and supported existing NSC proposals.

Bush's innermost advisors—Bolten and Rice especially—realized he preferred a surge strategy, but even they could not be sure it would ultimately prove his final choice. With Pentagon opposition to a surge still strong, Bush visited the Joint Chiefs on their turf on December 13. Flanked by Vice President Dick Cheney and both the outgoing and incoming secretaries of defense, Bush made plain to his top military advisors that he would not tolerate defeat or withdrawal. Going forward, despite the hardships, would be his option.

But he did not come to the tank—the meeting room of the Chiefs of Staff—empty-handed. He instead offered to endorse the Joint Chiefs' demand for increases in the overall size of the Army and Marine Corps in order to help compensate for the deployment of more troops to Iraq. It is an illuminating moment in civil-military relations. The president can order, but he must also convince. For a man who had repeatedly invoked one "lesson of Vietnam" as being a president's need to follow his military commanders' advice, it was a dramatic session in the extreme, repeatedly described by those present as "seminal" to the birth of the surge.

Of course, Washington was not the only political realm that mattered. The surge in US forces would do little good, even the plan's advocates worried, if it failed to coincide with new efforts on the Iraqi side. While bureaucrats within the beltway thus debated the size and scope of a surge, and its price, their counterparts overseas turned to ensuring support in Baghdad.

December NSC Meetings

BUSH: I remembered Lyndon Johnson picking out bombing targets in Vietnam. The way a commander in chief ought to be is, here's the objective, now show me the options to achieve the objective, and if it's military involved, the military's got to develop the plans. . . . What Vietnam influenced me on is the relationship between the president and the military. [You can't be] picking targets, micromanaging, letting politics decide. I remember the F-105 pilots, my instructor at Moody Air Force Base saying, you're not going to believe this, that, you know, that politicians decided that we could only fly certain routes and the SAMs [surface-to-air missiles] were all lined up for us, they knew we were coming. You know, the military's job is to figure out how to win. The president's job is to decide if we want to win or not, and if the strategy is not winning, then the president's job is to demand another strategy.

I never bought that we were contributing to violence. It's like saying that we created al-Qaeda by removing Saddam Hussein. Please. I don't buy that. Look, I believed and I still believe it today that most Iraqis want to live in peace. And the way I would put it is, mothers want to raise their child in a peaceful world, no matter who you are. . . . On the other hand, I always felt like if people want peace and the local authorities can't give peace, we could until the local authorities can, and that I didn't feel like our troops were creating problems. The critics would say that. I felt from anecdotal evidence that, and just a belief system that—you know, obviously some of the early disgraces like Abu Ghraib—but that our troops were basically a positive influence.

Well, the other thing is that we were also getting intelligence that there were foreign influences, al-Qaeda, that had nothing to do with our troop presence, or Iran. It had everything to do with our troop presence but for a different reason. They wanted influence, and we were influential, and so therefore they were stirring up problems to make life complicated for us.

O'SULLIVAN: We had some principals' meetings, and then we had the NSC meetings with the president [in the first weeks of December]. And one thing that I walked away from the solarium thinking very strongly was, OK, we can't just go to prescriptions. We can't just talk about what we're going to do. We still need the president to clarify for people how he sees the situation and what he sees US responsibilities as being.

There were dozens of papers that were written for those, I don't know, ten days or two weeks of NSCs, whatever they were. And those papers, to my memory, were all written on my computer, and I was not allowed to e-mail them to anyone. When they were circulated in the room, they all had numbers on the paper, and it was my job to collect them from everyone after the meeting was over. There was a real effort to make sure that nothing leaked and to have a conversation that was completely frank and valid and allowed for unfettered discussion.

A lot of what we discussed in that room wasn't just about the surge and the troop numbers. It was a lot about diagnosing the situation, considering other options, considering what the mission of our forces had to be, and then talking about what other components of the strategy had to be there to make that military mission ultimately be successful.

And in fact this wasn't about presenting options to the president. We started with a series of papers that basically, in my mind, we were going to try to move the conversation incrementally. And so the president would have a chance to hear people's views on various things, and then he would have a chance to say, "This is my decision" or "This is my assessment." And then we would go from there.

LUTE: And it was only in the course of these decision-making sessions—so by the time you get to the principals, and in particular the sessions with the president—we began to sense that he's not going to stick with the status quo, that it just wasn't satisfactory. I don't remember accelerating [the troop reductions], the accelerating option as getting serious mention, and so by process of elimination it became pretty clear. It was quite clear early on that the status quo option, in some sort of elaboration or augmentation of the status quo, wasn't going to be sufficient.

O'SULLIVAN: A conversation between Secretary Rice and Pete Pace in one of the NSC meetings . . . had to do with is it feasible for our troops not to be engaged in sectarian violence? The effort to kind of tamp down sectarian violence. That was part of the State Department proposal, which is this sectarian violence is not something that we can affect. We should therefore not try. . . . The reaction of General Pace and others was this is totally intolerable from a US military perspective, because US forces are not going to sit by and watch hundreds of thousands of people being killed and just say that's not our mission. That this was going to be incredibly demoralizing for our forces, and it was not a position that he or any other military person would put our forces in. And when that debate got to President Bush, he immediately understood that. And this was, I think, one of several knocks against that proposal. . . . Can the Iraqis, do they have the capability to actually quell sectarian violence on their own? And everybody said absolutely not.

So then the president was like, "Well, OK, so what does this look like? If we decide that's not our responsibility, they don't have the ability to do it, where does that leave us?" And then subsequently he made a very clear decision, in my mind it was a decision, saying we're going to take responsibility for this.

Once he said that, that shifted the conversation. If you decide that we're actually going to take on the mission of quelling sectarian violence because we see it as being fundamental to the larger mission of stabilizing Iraq, then you get into this category, OK, how can you achieve that? What kind of mission should our forces have? And that's how we got into the counterinsurgency option.

But even then in the counterinsurgency piece, we didn't talk that much in the formal process about troop numbers. There were a lot of conversations about troop numbers happening outside of that room, but it was more about what is the mission, how are they going to achieve it? And if that is our military mission, what other components are required to make it successful? Because no one was talking about that the end goal is just to bring down violence in Baghdad. The whole idea was this is connected to a political reconciliation of some kind.

FEAVER: Throughout this period, the papers that Brett McGurk had written, and all the things that Meghan O'Sullivan had developed in her office, were all about putting population security first and, with the associated changes in our approach, heavily influenced by Dave Petraeus's COIN manual.[1] Our view was that it wasn't just surging more resources, but it was changing fundamentally. In fact, this was a crucial part of the thing—changing fundamentally what was priority one.

This turned out to be the first and most consequential decision of the surge review, although at the time we didn't realize just how consequential it was. . . . NSC staff wanted population security to be the mission, but the MNF-I was saying, understandably, that the train-and-transition was the first-priority mission.

We teed that up as a separate decision, and finally President Bush—and this would have been in either late November or early December—decided it's going to be population security, but no decision on the surge.

We were afraid . . . that we had just gotten a decision to increase the mission without increasing the resources. In other words, exacerbate this ends-means gap that we were already struggling with.

O'SULLIVAN: It was simply flipping our old strategy on its head, saying we're going to focus on security with the expectation that this will be the foundation for political progress. So kind of a flip of where we had been for the previous two years. But then, of course, in this review and in this conversation with the president and his closest advisors, there were many, many different briefs that we put forward about, Well, what's the economic component of the strategy? What's the political component of the strategy? Is there a regional component to this? And we actually tackled a lot of issues that had been lingering out there but had just not been resolved. And one of them, maybe the best example, was that for more than a year we had had an issue with State Department people and military people having different . . . security requirements. They couldn't travel together and that the military could move more easily. The diplomats couldn't. There wasn't a lot of synergy between our civilian and military people in the field. And we tackled that in that setting and made a decision that on a military base, our civilian people were going to be subordinate to the authority of the commander. . . . And they were going to move as military people moved.

ZELIKOW: Another little decision is at some point during this process we made the decision to stand up to the Iranians . . . and that was essential that we do that . . . because remember all the doubts in the papers about were Iranians really responsible for all those killings of our soldiers. And I had seen this evidence close up—including the vehicles soaked in blood, and people going through the forensics of these munitions with me right out there in Baghdad. And this was a very constructive move, too, that turned out to be salutary.

RICE: I could sense that the president wanted to surge. I could sense it. He didn't say it, but I think he was becoming attracted to the idea that he was going to make one last play, and he was not going to lose this war, and this was his best option. Before he did that, I wanted to really be sure that he understood that that could fail.

Bob [Gates] had hinted as to what he thought he might do. He wasn't confirmed yet, so he had to be careful, but he had hinted at what he was going to do, and I had a pretty good sense of what he was going to do. It was going to be a new team, not just in Washington but in Baghdad, and so I was feeling more comfortable about that piece of it.

I had, by that time, very little faith in the Iraqis, and could they carry out their part of the bargain. So my concerns had shifted really, from the Pentagon and the military side, which I actually really thought they would get it right now, to could the Iraqis play their role.

I remember, in one particularly tense meeting, saying to the president, "You know it may just well be if they're determined to kill each other, we just have to let them do it." And really, he was really furious. I think it was the only time he was really angry at me, and he said, "So your view is you're just going to let them go at each other and they're just going to kill each other and we're just going to stand by and watch?" I sort backed off, but I followed him into the Oval Office afterward, and I said, in a voice that was almost kind of how dare you say that to me but not quite, because he was the president, I sort of said, "You know, nobody's had more involvement and more emotional involvement in this war than I, except maybe you, and how could you think that's what I'm saying?" He said, "Yeah, I know, I know." And I thought at that moment, he's just—this is just horrible, this is just horrible.

HADLEY: What's going on is the president is asking questions to get views and information to inform his decision. He's already pretty clearly leaning toward the surge, but he has not decided on the surge. But what's really going on underneath that is he is asking a series of questions that are going to put facts on the table, because he's also trying to bring his other national security principals to where he thinks he's going to come out.

It's been building over the two-month period. . . . He is pushing back and beginning to try to shape the views of his principals. Don Rumsfeld for a long time has been saying, "You know, we're teaching the Iraqis to ride a bicycle, and at some point you have to take your hand off the bicycle seat." And he's been saying that for months. And finally in this time frame, he says it again, and the president says, "Yeah, but Don, we can't afford to have the bicycle turn over. We can't start again. So if the bicycle starts to tip, we've got to be able to grab it." That's a very big break with this notion of handover.

Another thing the president's talking about, something he and I talked about, Don—and he said this—Don is basically right. Casey's basically right. Ultimately, Iraq is for the Iraqis, and we are going to have to hand it over. But we couldn't get there from where we were. There had been another assumption that there has to be a political solution, and once there is a political solution and a real unity government in which all three communities participate, then the sectarian violence will die out. But of course, the problem was that the violence was so great that you weren't going to get that kind of political solution because the sectarian groups were pulling back in their holes, waiting for all-out warfare. It became clear that you had to improve the security situation before you could get the kind of political dialogue that ultimately would lead to a stable situation. It's not that Don and George were wrong, it was just that we could not get there from where we were. And the president started talking about the surge as a bridge between where we are and where we wanted to be.

So that was the kind of the pushing back he's doing on terms of the military. The pushing back on Condi is very much [that] you can't simply let Baghdad melt down. One, it's not our tradition to stand back while people are slaughtering one another. We're either going to go in, or we're going to come home. That was not going to work. And second . . . what the president understood, and what I—can't differentiate what the president said or what I said because we're in a dynamic conversation of all of this—but I can remember saying, "You know, the whole country is watching their capital melt down in sectarian violence. And if Baghdad goes, the game is lost. So you can't just step out on the perimeter and let it burn out, because it's not going to burn out; it's just going to consume the whole country." And at one point, Condi says to the president, "Well, I'm willing to increase the forces, but they can't just do what they're already doing." And the president comes back rightly and says, "They're not going to just do what they're already doing. They're going to have to be doing something else."

In those meetings, he's bringing people along so that in the end of the day, when he makes the decision, I think he's increasingly confident. He doesn't have a split within his cabinet, and he's got cabinet officers who are going to be committed to implementing it. He's also—or we are also bringing in this strategy review process, we're bringing the Pentagon along. Because in my conversation with Pete Pace, he's coming in and I'm saying to him, "You know, if the president is going to order a surge, you know, what's the reaction going to be? What do we need?" And there are a couple things that Pete in this run-up, in this sort of November, December time frame—October, November, December. He says, "Well first of all, it can't just be a surge in the military. Where is—the civilians?"

And that of course gets into the work that J.D. is doing and percolates up to the principals that there needs to be a civilian surge. There needs to be a whole of government effort to bring civilian expertise to contribute to the post-conflict stabilization reconstruction. So we structure and Condi and her team put together a civilian surge. Box checked for Pace.

Another piece, Pace says, "It can't be just American forces. The Iraqis have to do it, and the Iraqis have to be willing to cooperate with the surge if it's going to succeed." So as you well know, the next box is we've got to get Maliki and Iraqis on board. And that process starts in . . . the Amman meeting, where the president talks to Maliki. . . . Maliki says, "I have a strategy and I want to brief it." And it's a surge strategy of sorts, not perfect, and Maliki says, This is the strategy and I'm going to do it. We're going to bring down the violence. And at one point, the president turns to Casey and says, "George, will this work?" And George says—publicly—he says, "Well, we've had a hand, and we've advised." And privately the president says, "Do the Iraqis have the juice to carry this off?" And Pace—and George Casey says no. So basically what the president says to Maliki is, "I agree with your strategy. Let us work with you on the fine points. But you don't have the troops to do it. Let me lend you my troops."

And he is in a process then of doing two things with Maliki from that meeting going forward: getting Maliki comfortable that there will be more troops moving into the country, that our end strength, in-country, is actually going to go up. And secondly, getting Maliki to agree to contribute troops, and I think they did five brigades and we did five brigades, something like that—in terms of the core force.

And then, three, get Maliki to agree that it would be done in a nonsectarian way. That it'll be a nonsectarian commander; that there will be no no-go areas like Sadr City; that this notion, if we pick up a Shia terrorist, we won't get a phone call from the prime minister's office to let him go; and that once we start, we're going to go to the end.

Maliki agrees to those things, and to lock him in, the president convinces him to give a speech publicly, articulating those conditions for Iraqi participation in the surge. He gives two speeches. The first one he doesn't give quite right; we have to send him back to give a second speech. The second speech he gets right.

All of that is presidential business in terms of bringing those final actors around. It's presidential business, but it also brings the president to the point where he's comfortable making the decision he's making. . . . Keeping the president at the center of an issue of this import is the only way it's going to get done. . . . It is a non-delegable responsibility by the president.

SATTERFIELD: The president was himself very skeptical about the ability of those forces to be efficacious in their mission minus an absolute and demonstrated commitment by Nouri al-Maliki that . . . the forces would be deployed against any element generating violence in Iraq—including Shia leaders. That was one explicit point. Secondly, the US would have command over how those units were deployed and acted, and how the Iraqi units working with them would flow. No more Iraqi units being pulled out of the fight when the targets were Shia figures that couldn't be touched. The president didn't just want this as an assurance from Maliki. He wanted to see a demonstration before those new US elements arrived, which couldn't be until the beginning of 2007. That there had been a shift in the way US forces and associated Iraqi forces were conducted themselves. Now, in this, we no longer have policy divides. This is a uniform, absolutely, need-to-do.

This gets us into the question of the president's famous trip to Sharm, to Aqaba, and then to Amman for the discussion with Maliki. Those were not easy discussions. Here you have the president now coming in . . . as a direct interlocutor and policy advocate. This is not being done through intermediaries, this is the president of the United States telling Nouri al-Maliki, I am willing to commit the last US combat-ready ground forces we have in the world, but only if I see you demonstrate the following.

Now, Maliki pulled back. He didn't say, "Well, sure Mr. President. Of course. We accept that." Maliki came forward with his own initiative. The famous bi-plan for Iraq, which would have US forces essentially screen the Sunnis out of Iraq, out of Baghdad, while Iraqi Shia forces fixed Baghdad. We all could predict where that would go, and we rejected it out of hand. And it was that act of No, you're not going to get any forces. You're going to lose Baghdad and your country if we don't come in, but we won't come in unless we see a shift.

Maliki finally came to a yes. Now, the yes infuriated Muqtada [al-Sadr], really, and the Iranians. And they brought everything they could bear to bring Maliki to a no, to reject this. Everything they could bear. It's to Maliki's credit—often forgotten in the later Nouri al-Maliki and his behavior. Maliki, at this time, was an Iraqi patriot. He stood up to the Iranians. He despised the Iranians, and he feared them. He had had a very bad personal historical experience with Iran and its clerical leaders. Very different from ISCI [Islamic Supreme

Council of Iraq] and their experience. It's why he broke. It's why he went to Damascus for the life—the miserable life—that he lived there, in Dawa. He did what he needed to do. And we watched carefully through those weeks that followed Amman, Iraqi forces, US forces able to conduct operations against previously off-limits Shia targets. And it was that that met conditionality to actually implement the surge. And I'm afraid in the historical record there has been a confusion that the decision to make the surge meant, now US forces are being sent willy-nilly. No. The president had absolute conditions which he personally advocated with Maliki—against pushback—and got. And that is what made those deployments—actually in the new year—possible to achieve.

RICE: [The president] had become pretty convinced that Maliki might be OK in being a partner in this, because at one point in that meeting [in Amman], what had impressed him—it's a funny thing, what impresses you. Maliki actually brought his own plan, and he put it on the table and he said, "Here's my surge plan." Because they knew this conversation was going on, you know they'd read it in the papers. He said, "Here's my surge plan." The president said, "Oh, that's interesting," and Maliki said, "Well, the only problem is it won't work without you, but I've got a plan at least." I think the president found that Maliki was more committed. He'd given him a list of things that had to be done, and I think he got the sense he [Maliki] was maybe more committed than he had been six weeks before or two months before. So the pieces were falling into place, but I think he wasn't just quite ready to pull the trigger.

GORDON: We [the intelligence community] were definitely skeptical on Maliki, although we agreed that probably the only strategy for handling Maliki was to approach him as a partner. We were asked: How do you think I should deal with Maliki? And I think the answer was that gaining his confidence in you as a partner and sharing your concerns and your desires, while at the same time trying to shape those concerns and desires, was the only way to go. But we were skeptical. I believe the president asked very directly, Will this shift the balance in Maliki's mind away from the Iranians and to the United States? And our answer was it would shift it, but would it shift it fundamentally to being more oriented to the US? And we went no. We definitely answered no to that. We did not think that was going to happen, and of course it did not happen.

Report of the Iraq Study Group

The Iraq Study Group finally released its report in December, painting a dire picture. It was also a picture, we now know, that both fed enthusiasm for a final last-ditch surge of troops in Iraq, and which in part was shaped by policy makers who longed for that outcome. As one noted, "Nobody at the end of that year, with the publication of that report, could pretend that the war was going well for the United States."

> RICE: When it was about to come out and they came to brief us about it, the president was put off by some of the elements of it, but actually, it sort of supported the surge in a kind of roundabout way, and so it helped a little bit, I think, with the surge. It helped to be able to say, it's part of a broader strategy, we're actually doing all these things that are in the Baker-Hamilton report, except we're not going to go talk to the Iranians, but other than that, we're pretty much doing everything that's here. And so I found it mildly helpful, I think the president found it mildly annoying, and everybody went on.

> HADLEY: Overwhelmingly, what the Baker-Hamilton committee recommended was things that we did. . . . In some delicate conversations I had with Secretary Baker, we actually crafted language in there—in the report—that supported the surge. He basically would run some things by me to make sure that they were supported by analysis within the government, which was a wholly appropriate thing for him to do. And he said, "We're going to have a paragraph on the surge." As which, you'll remember is a temporary increase in troops in order to calm the sectarian violence if requested by the commanders. I was feeling pretty good that, in fact, the Baker-Hamilton committee had gone and set a document out there, which would provide a support when we announced the surge, and therefore argued that we should embrace it.

> The problem was twofold. One, it became characterized by both countries in the region and by conservatives in the United States as a cover for withdrawal. All they focused on really was a timetable and a firm date for withdrawing forces. And so it became not a safe harbor for an alternative strategy; it became the poster child for cut-and-run and give up. And that's how it was viewed by the *Wall Street Journal* and conservatives in the United States. And that unfortunately was how it was viewed in the region. Well, with that characterization, we could not embrace. And therefore we had to distance ourselves from it.

HANNAH: Alas, when the report came out, I think, fairly or unfairly, it was thought of as kind of more or less reinforcing the approach that was already under way, that was oriented, as much as anything, to figuring out a way to get us out of Iraq, while doing the least amount of damage, rather than figuring out a way to truly achieve the president's objectives in Iraq. . . . Some of their other recommendations on the Palestinian peace process, that that somehow could affect the insurgency or affect the Arab world's attitude to actually assisting a Shiite-dominated government of Iraq, or somehow bringing Iranians and Syrians that for several years by that point in time . . . clearly had been dedicated to a strategy to destroy the American project in Iraq—that somehow bringing them into the process and empowering them to become shapers of Iraq's future at that point in time, when it looked like America was on the run, that those were actually probably not particularly helpful. Those were not the ways we were actually going to achieve success in Iraq, and yet once the report came out of course, you had something of a political issue, of how do you deal with it in a country and in a Congress that is already predisposed to, let's figure out a way to get out of this place, because we sure as hell can't win in this place.

DANIEL SERWER, executive director of the Iraq Study Group: The policy recommendations, frankly, are uneven. They were partly—I won't say dictated, but encouraged by the White House, especially the whole thing about reconciliation, and, you know, it was very much on General Casey's mind and the White House's mind. So I had the sense that a number of recommendations really came from the White House. But the first part of the report was, from the first sentences onward, was shocking. Because it said the truth, which was that things were going really badly. Remember, up until that year, Rumsfeld was still saying, "What insurgency?" . . . Nobody at the end of that year, with the publication of that report, could pretend that the war was going well for the United States. And that, to me, is vital.

CROUCH: I felt that you weren't going to have an effective diplomatic offensive with Iran and Syria unless you had reset the military political calculation in the region. . . . I remember the Syrians had been the major pipeline of foreign fighters going into Iraq, suicide bombers, and all that sort of thing. The Iranians certainly, in my view, didn't take a position that an unstable Iraq was not in their interest, let's put it that way. You know? I remember arguing at the time that they sort of viewed Iraq the way the French viewed Germany for about four hundred years, which was, you know, the more Germanys the better. And so the more Iraq that'd be kind of carved up—they didn't want it to be out of control, but they also felt that their interests were served by having a weakened Iraq. So that doesn't mean you can't have a diplomatic offensive. But you've got to set the conditions for a successful diplomatic offensive. And that was demonstrating to the region inside Iraq, to them, that you were here to stay.

AEI Report

Much like the Iraq Study Group report, discussions of the failing American mission in the country, and of potential solutions, themselves surged in the popular press and throughout Washington think tanks as 2006 came to a close. A well-known case in point is offered by the American Enterprise Institute (AEI), where Fred Kagan and other military analysts openly debated not only the necessity of a surge but its potential parameters. These debates had less influence on the Bush administration's thinking than previously reported, though they were remarkably detailed, given their reliance on publicly available information. "Really?" one former general involved remarked. "In my day, most of that [information] was classified, but now it's on the Internet." Being so public, these discussions went far toward educating the public and thus laying the broad political groundwork for Bush's ensuing decision.

Unknown to nearly all who participated in these public discussions, indeed unknown even to White House and Pentagon policy makers, Bush had already made up his mind. "We have a speech—a draft of the speech," Hadley recalled, designed to announce the new way forward in Iraq. "The president would have given it on the tenth or the eleventh [of December] . . . except he wanted to hold off until January so that Gates can have an opportunity to see things on the ground."

> F. KAGAN: At some point in the fall, my boss at AEI, Danielle Pletka, who's the vice president for foreign and defense policy, came to me with an idea and said, "Hey, Fred, why don't we run a war game on Iraq?" . . . A big part of the motivation for that . . . was simply incredible frustration at the level of discourse in Washington about the war. . . . What we really wanted to do was put out a serious report that would force other people to raise the level of their discourse.
>
> The weekend was the culmination of a lot of effort, a lot of intelligence-gathering effort, and there were a couple of different

kinds of intelligence that we needed to gather. One was, what's the situation in Baghdad, what's the situation in Iraq. . . . It was a very granular look at the violence from open sources, identifying where we could, street by street, or at least *mahallah* by *mahallah*, where this violence was going down, which gave us a pretty good view of where the sectarian fault lines were, because that's mostly where it was happening. . . . We were looking at Google Earth maps of neighborhoods and [saying], This is where the violence is. OK, well, what would it take to clear this neighborhood, based on your Tal Afar experience, based on your experience in Baghdad? How many Bubbas [soldiers], where do they need to go, how long? This kind of stuff. We went, neighborhood by neighborhood, and laid out, We're going to have to control these road junctions, we're going to have to—I mean, it was a very serious undertaking by people who did this professionally.

K. KAGAN: One of the chief problems was the question of should there be more troops, and if so, what would they do, and how would you use them? But I think the real blinder was, there was an assumption in Washington that there weren't any more troops to be had, that the forces could not be generated for a surge; therefore the option was not viable, therefore it was not worth considering. And so one of the things that the small group started to think about was, first, what forces are there available? What capabilities do they have? What is the actual problem that is transpiring in Iraq? Have we misdefined the problem in Iraq? Are we saying that the problem is that the Iraqis lack the will to fight, or that we haven't handed enough over to the Iraqis, when, in fact, the problem is one of having our own strategic approach.

KEANE: I received a call from Chris DeMuth, [president] over at AEI. I think it was November. He said, "You know, I've got some guys looking at the war in Iraq, and I was wondering if you'd come over and take a look." . . . I was very impressed, because their grasp on the enemy situation using open sources was nothing short of staggering. I mean, I was dealing with top-secret information, and they didn't have that but they had a very detailed resolution, which was surprising. Then, they had better resolution on US force availability than I had, you know, because I told Rumsfeld we needed eight to ten brigades. I reasoned that was about right. I think what took place—actually, I think I was pretty close. They said there were only five brigades available, and they told me what brigades they were and where they were. I said, "Where the hell do you get all that information?" They said, "Well, you get it off the Internet." I said, "What do you mean, on the Internet?" He said, "Yeah, the Army's whole, what do they call it, 'Force Generation Model' or something." He said, "It's on the Internet." He said, "So, we know what units are coming home, how long they rest, recuperate, when they start to get back, they start to get equipment again, when they start to build the organization, all the different phases that they go through leading up to deployment. Which ones are going to be deployed are all earmarked on the Internet." I said, "Really? In my day, most of that was classified, but now it's on the Internet."

But mainly what resonated between the Kagan team and myself was understanding how serious the problem was, the nature of the enemy, that this was very formidable, what we were truly up against. Our strategy was failing, and it was doomed to fail. There was no way they could succeed and that we had to put in play a counter-insurgency strategy for the first time to protect the people. So, we both independently came to that same conclusion with each other. I wanted the eight to ten brigades, and they said, "Well, they're not available. There are only five."

K. KAGAN: The workshop that we did at AEI focused on brigades rather than boots on the ground. . . . Discussion circled in on five brigades, five brigades as what was needed to handle the degree of violence that we saw in Baghdad itself, as well as perhaps . . . some of the changes or some of the touch-point areas outside of Baghdad, in Eastern Anbar or in Diyala. But the issue is Baghdad itself. Go back to the fact that Baghdad is a circle divided into quadrants. . . . What became clear was that in order to have the forward operating bases that were properly situated, and then all of these combat outposts, these hubs and spokes whereby forces could disperse from their headquarters, we actually needed to be in about four places in Baghdad, and we needed to have headquarters in about four places in Baghdad.

If you could put a brigade on one of those spots and kind of squish it down, you would actually take the pressure off of Baghdad itself. So we came up with five brigades, and it turned out that they were available. We knew this because there is a model of force generation that the Army has. It has the wonderful Army acronym of R4GEN. And as we were trying to figure out what units would be available, we went ahead and did research and found, on Wikipedia, the R4GEN model with the units available that were in rotation, those that were being rebuilt.

O'SULLIVAN: [Keane and AEI] played a very important and interesting role that I think underscores the value of outsiders to a formalized process. I guess the first thing to say that my sense is again, looking back with having more information than I did at the time, they were coming up with proposals that were very similar to the surge, to the application of more force, to embracing a counterinsurgency strategy. So I think certainly I would never say that we at the NSC were the only ones who had that idea. There's not a lot novel about that idea, right? The challenge is can the boat of government be turned in such a way that in the middle of a war the strategy can be changed and resourced. And that really required a decision by the president.

HADLEY: For me, when I finally meet with Jack Keane, the decision has largely been made. We have a speech—a draft of the speech; the president would have given it on the tenth or the eleventh [of December] . . . except he wanted to hold off until January so that Gates can have an opportunity to see things on the ground. And Keane comes in and gives us his briefing, and . . . it validates what we have come up with. It's not that it's the author of the surge; we've already developed the surge option at that point. But it's very much along the same line. So that's good. It's a validator. And we don't have a lot of people who were going to be external validators, and he's going to be one.

But there's a problem. His is a seven- or an eight-brigade surge; ours is a five-brigade surge. . . . And we sit down with Keane and Keane says, "No, you need seven or eight brigades." We don't have seven or eight brigades. So my problem is, if I'm going to make Keane a validator, I've got to walk him back down to the surge option that we know the president is going to pick. . . . It's not that he's telling me about this great option that becomes the surge; we've done all that. I'm trying to get him to the point where he will be a validator of what we're doing rather than coming out and saying, when everybody says this is too much, Keane comes out there and says it's not enough and we have no supporters. . . . He basically in the end says, "Well, you could do it with five brigades. There's more risk, but, yeah, this would work with five brigades." . . . So we've got our validator.

HANNAH: So that meeting in December with Keane and [Fred] Kagan was really an opportunity to go into detail about the strategy, to talk about the forces that it would require, that forces that were available, why those forces were sufficient for us to be able to make a real dent in the insurgency. I remember it being quite a detailed meeting, with a full-blown PowerPoint before us, in which both Keane and Kagan were very, you know, competent and aggressive advocates for the surge, which of course we had been pursuing, through the Iraq strategy review and elsewhere, in sort of parallel tracks; but having someone particularly of Keane's stature and what he represented, come in and validate all of the things that bureaucrats and staffers in the US government were working on, I think was a tremendous help.

ROVE: I have a minor role in that the president has arrived at this surge before the surge is formally declared, but there are people out there who are talking about doing exactly what Bush wants to do, and one of them was Jack Keane. But the president and I met with him, so I said, "Mr. President, we need to bring people like that in here so that if your idea is similar to their idea, you need to bring them in here so that they can tell you about their idea, so that when you do your idea, it's their idea and they defend it." . . . I know we brought Jack Keane in, and others. And it was helpful, because it helped refine the president's thinking, helped give him a greater sense of the strengths and weaknesses of this approach, the challenges and the opportunities, but it also helped create a corps of people who felt sort of in essence we've got to go defend this. . . . We had implicitly credentialed and deputized a series of explainers, like Keane and others, who made their way around Capitol Hill and were constantly reinforcing us.

CROUCH: You had people like Senator [John] McCain and others who were standing up and saying, well, somebody ought to look at this. Somebody ought to consider this. You had advocates and detractors and all those sorts of things, but at least it surfaced the argument so that it wasn't maybe quite as much of a shock when it came forward.

And it also gave people on the outside, particularly in the military, an opportunity to sort of, in a sense, vote on it, if you will. There was an opportunity there. As I said, there was dissension within our own military on did we need to do it? Should we do it? Would it work?

The Tank

Bush having decided meant he needed not only public support, but his own Pentagon's. Thus he scheduled a meeting with the Joint Chiefs. "He wants to send a message that he's hearing directly from the chiefs," Bolten recalled, "that he's going to their turf to hear from them," and Rumsfeld said, "I got it, it will be in the tank," the Joint Chiefs' meeting room.

He came with gifts, in the form of troop-level enhancements the Army and Marine Corps desperately wanted as compensation for the difficulty of immediate deployments to Iraq. He could have ordered their compliance, of course, but civil-military relations are never as simple as that. As Pete Mansoor explained, "The president can make a decision on strategy, and there's still people who disagree with it and will try to undermine it. And I just found that astonishing, but I guess that's life."

FEAVER: From the NSC staff point of view, the [AEI] proposal allowed us to go to the Joint Staff and say, "Hey, we've just seen this briefing. This was just in over here in the West Wing. What do you guys think about this? Give us your feedback." It was a stalking horse that allowed, rather than forcing the JCS to come up with a surge option, it was asking the JCS to comment on a surge option that had already been briefed at high levels and was getting some attention around town. That, I think, was an important catalyst for getting through the civil-military challenge of overruling generals on a strategic issue—overruling the ground force commanding generals.

HADLEY: We're actually ready to go with a decision at the end of that first week in December and . . . there's a draft of the speech. And on the weekend before—I think it was the Saturday or the Sunday—the president calls me. He says, "Hadley, I've decided I'm not going to give this speech." I said, "Oh, Mr. President, why not?" And he said, "I'm comfortable where we are. I'm comfortable where we are, but I want to give Bob Gates an opportunity, since he's new secretary of defense, and I want him to get an opportunity to assess the situation on the ground, come back, and give me a recommendation. It's such an important decision; he's going to have such a big role implementing it. I think I owe him that." So it's deferred. It also affords us to do the last piece we needed to do in terms of the process, which is the president's meeting with the chiefs.

GATES: He knew he was going to surge, but he didn't have any idea how much, how long. I don't think any of those details were clear in his mind at that point. He just knew that this was the only way forward. . . . If, to get the ducks in a row, including Maliki, required taking a little more time, that that was better than rushing it before the cake was fully baked, if you will. . . . He was talking about kind of how do we do it, politically how do we handle it, how do I get the chiefs on board? It was more, how do I bring this government together to move in this direction at this point? This was one of the things that I admired about the guy. It was clear that his decision to go for the surge was contrary to the recommendations of every one of the Joint Chiefs of Staff, to his Central Command commander and the field commander. His secretary of defense had only recently come around to the notion that maybe it was necessary. His secretary of state didn't think it was a very good idea. This is a period during which—and I think this is important from your standpoint, or from a historian's standpoint. This is a point at which the president of the United States is basically taking this whole thing onto his shoulders. Doing something that a couple of military people he respects think he should do, but his own instincts.

RICE: If Gates had shared with me that he was going to change the leadership in Baghdad, he'd undoubtedly told the president he was going to change the leadership in Baghdad, and I think the president was ready to see that. He had enormous respect, by the way, for George Casey, we all did, but Casey was operating with a pretty limited strategy, and if you were going to go to a broader strategy, you were going to have to change personnel. And so, I think he was feeling better about that. That probably gave him some confidence that he could surge forces, but I don't think he made a final decision, no.

The Pentagon had to tell him he could do it, first of all; I mean they were still sending over numbers that didn't make sense, right? . . . And still dealing with the fact that if he surged in Iraq, he might have to allow South Korea to be overrun by the North Koreans. There was a lot going on there, but I think he maybe understood that he would get there eventually, and this is where Pace just did magnificent work in sort of smoothing the ground to get realistic resourcing before the president, rather than what I think the system would have produced.

But I think he also owed it to Gates, to get the secretary of defense off to the right footing. If he, Gates, goes in, and his first job is to shove down the throats of the professional military something the president has told him to do, that's not a great way to start as secretary of defense. Bob is a strong-willed person, and Bob wanted to have a chance to really know that he was giving the president the best advice. So I had no problem with the delay.

BOLTEN: I called [Rumsfeld] to say that the president wanted to meet with the chiefs, to talk about a new way forward on Iraq, and he wanted to hear from them directly, and Rumsfeld said, "OK, I'll set it up in my office." I said, "No. The president wants to go to the tank," and I think Rumsfeld said, "But the protocol is that the secretary of defense sits between the president and the chiefs, and those meetings are held in the secretary's office," and I said, "He wants to send a message that he's hearing directly from the chiefs, that he's going to their turf to hear from them," and Rumsfeld said, "I got it, it will be in the tank."

PACE: About two days before we were going to brief the president at the Pentagon, and oh by the way, the president was very gracious to go to the Pentagon. We rightfully so should have been going to him, but he was making a statement, in my mind, of support for the troops, and showing them that he was willing to do this. I went in and briefed the president, and I said, "This is what you're going to hear from General Casey, this is what you're going to hear from General Abizaid," because they were going to do a VTC [video tele-conference] with him the day before.

ABIZAID: I think somewhere around November George [Casey] comes to me and he says, "I think I'm going to need three more brigades." . . . The guys in Washington, I understand, have the opinion that it was all their idea and that they fixed it. But I think it was a mutual sort of understanding of a deteriorating situation that had to be fixed, and that George Casey was coming up with many of the same ideas that were coming up in Washington.

PACE: General Casey and General Abizaid wanted two brigades, and by then, we had gotten to the point where we thought maybe five brigades [were] going to be needed. . . . Their response, General Casey and General Abizaid, being right there with the Iraqi government, they believed that asking for that many troops would be telling Iraqis that we didn't believe that they could do it themselves, that going forward together just wasn't going to work and that we did not trust that they could get the jobs off. So from their standpoint, with their needs to be able to be talking to the Iraqi counterparts day to day, they wanted to only ask for two brigades, because they thought that's all they needed.

I also told the president that when you come over to the Pentagon—and I had the slides that I had already shown Steve Hadley, and I showed the president—this is a recommendation slide: up to five brigades, and please, get Maliki on board, get our government on board, get us more soldiers and Marines. So the president knew, before he had any of these discussions, exactly what was going to be recommended to him. I felt that was important for me to do for him, so that (a) he wasn't surprised, (b) he didn't think about it, and know what kind of questions or directions he wanted to give.

The Joint Chiefs, with the help of the Council of Colonels, had gotten to the point where we believed—some chiefs believed and others believed otherwise—that five was right. Some believed up to five, et cetera. Part of my responsibility was to give the president options to choose from, but also to give him consensus, if I could get there, from his military guys. So, we weren't saying pick two, pick three, pick five. It took a long time. It sounds simple now, but it took a long time to get everybody comfortable with the phrase "up to five brigades." What that allowed the guys in Baghdad to say was, to their counterparts, we think we're only going to need two, but they're giving us this extra cushion.

There's guys like me, who believed that among very important things was my remembrance of Vietnam, which was just ten thousand more guys, just ten thousand more guys. We did ten thousand at a time until we got to half a million troops. I wanted to make sure we were not going to get on that kind of a thing either, so my recommendation was, I wanted to say we're going to have five brigades available, but it made great sense to say up to five. That way, if you needed three, four, and five, it was part of the plan, but if you said only two brigades and then you needed three and then you needed four and then you needed five—now this new plan isn't working at all. So eventually, we got the guys in Baghdad, the guys in Tampa, the guys in DC, the military folks, to agree with the phrase "up to five." Admittedly, and I told the president this, this phrase means something different whether you're in Baghdad or you're in Tampa or you're in Washington, DC, but this phrase is a phrase that I recommend we use, because it gives us off-ramps if we are really being successful, but it allows us to stay on course if not.

MANSOOR: I don't think the Council of Colonels had anything to do with the decision other than I think maybe perhaps we intellectually prepared the Joint Chiefs to accept it. Had they just been presented with a decision as a fait accompli without the background that we had given them, there might have been more resistance than there actually was to the decision to surge. Of course you don't want that kind of resistance inside the military and inside the government working against a decision the president has made. That's actually something

I learned during my fifteen months with General Petraeus in Iraq. The president can make a decision on strategy, and there's still people who disagree with it and will try to undermine it. And I just found that astonishing, but I guess that's life.

BUSH: First of all, it was very dramatic for the president to go to the Pentagon—you know, everybody snapping to, and there are lines of people, and you're shaking hands.

HADLEY: December thirteenth. And that of course is a very important meeting, because it is the one where the president finally brings to closure the process that Pete Pace has been running. So the chiefs are against the surge. President's leaning clearly toward the surge. The surge is now an option that has been fixed in the sense that it addresses all the concerns that we have heard from Pete Pace except, "You're going to break the force, Mr. President," which is the perspective of the chiefs, not because they are the war fighters—because they're not—but they're the ones who raise and man and train the troops. And it's the right perspective, and it needed to be addressed. It's the last piece. So the president goes in; he has his conversation; he and the vice president choreograph it in the car. The vice president is going to be kind of the bad cop pushing the chiefs initially; president engages in the conversation; we have this seminal moment where they say, "Mr. President, you're going to break the force." He says, "If we lose the war, that's what breaks the force. What do you need?" And they say, "We need, roughly, an increased end strength to give people hope that they're not going to be doing these kinds of long-service, short-rest deployment cycles forever."

At the end of that meeting, they know that he's going to pick the surge. He knows he's going to pick the surge. And he's really addressed through the conversation I'm running with Pete Pace and then finally face to face with the chiefs, he's addressed all their objectives, and he's brought them on.

SATTLER: We were trying to source both Afghanistan and Iraq, and we were short a training brigade inside of Afghanistan. . . . I went and saw Chairman Pace—General Pace—and I said, "Boss, the president needs to understand that there are consequences based on his decision. I'm not telling you which way it ought to go, but if we surge four brigades, we will have a brigade to go into Afghanistan to do the training piece. . . . I just think you need to ask the president to make sure it's clear to him, that that fifth brigade—that's a big one." . . . I remember I was up in the peanut gallery [in the tank], all the service chiefs were at the table, and General Pace said, "Mr. President, I want to make one point clear here. We're still under-resourced one training brigade—which we can hold. They weren't going to combat, they were just going to go in and work the Afghan forces. . . . You just need to know, if we send four we have one left to go to Afghanistan, but to support where you're leaning right now, all five will go into Iraq." And the president was pretty decisive when he said, "No, I don't want to leave any doubt that we under-resourced Iraq. We're going to win this one first, and then we'll move on over to the other side."

GATES: The chiefs basically were all aligned in opposition to the surge, and basically arguing that the force was exhausted. By that time, they had been at war in Afghanistan six years, three years in Iraq. And they were worried, as they would repeat over and over again, that he was going to break the force.

Or, Pentagon strategists worried, they'd invite aggression elsewhere in the world.

RICE: I remember the initial Pentagon discussions where they made it sound as if we wouldn't be able to confront North Korea if we surged forces in Iraq.

BUSH: Look, you know, the truth of the matter is if we were to be disgraced in Iraq, it may create the necessity for another theater. If we succeed in Iraq, it is less likely there would be another theater.

GATES: It was not a confrontational meeting. The president was there to try and bring these guys on board, not to confront them or to sort of challenge them. He was there to explain his thinking about why this was necessary and why they had to find the resources to be able to do it.

Officially, it's still an open question. . . . First of all, because of his concern about leaks, the president had been very careful about with whom he discussed his feelings and his sense of what had to be done. So at this point, for people outside of his inner circle, he is still debating this. This debate is still going on, and it's still an open question whether to do this, and not so much how. I think that was the atmosphere of the meeting in the tank, and it was also him trying to explain why he was leaning in the direction of a surge, and why he thought that the American military could do it, rather than sort of facing off with these guys. That was not his purpose in the meeting. And he did, I would say, on the civilian side, even though Rumsfeld and Cheney and Hadley and I were all there, I would say that the president did ninety-five percent of the talking.

EDELMAN: Well, my recollection is that there were two members of the chiefs who were most vocal about this. General Pete Schoomaker, the chief of staff of the Army, and General Jim Conway, who had just become commandant of the Marine Corps maybe a month earlier. . . . General Schoomaker was very concerned about public support and whether if we increased the size of the force in Iraq the American public and the Congress would support it. I think a lot of members of the military have this concern because of Vietnam and it's very deeply ingrained. I mean as I sat and listened to this I thought the president both very politely and very deftly handled this by basically saying, "Thank you very much for your political advice, General Schoomaker. That's my job. I'll handle that. I'll make the presentation to the public. I'll manage the Congress. And you'll have all the support you need."

General Conway made a slightly different argument . . . which is the rotation base and the stress on the force, and talked about how long we could go extending these deployments by three-month or two-month increments for the Army and Marine Corps respectively without some change in either the end strength or without breaking the rotation base.

But the president said, "Look, I get the stress on the force." He said, "I'm the one who goes out and talks to Gold Star families and has to comfort people who've lost loved ones. I recognize that this is very stressful on the force. But if you're talking about breaking the force, in my view, nothing would break the force like us walking out of Iraq with our tail between our legs. We don't get into wars to lose them in this country." And basically the chiefs all said, "Yes, sir, we agree with that. We can't lose." And that was pretty much the end of the discussion.

PACE: It was very respectful, it was very calm, it was very comfortable, but it was also very direct, as you would expect the service chiefs to be with their commander in chief. It was not all contentious at all, for sure. It was, for example—the chief of staff of the Army was Pete Schoomaker—General Schoomaker was very forthcoming about his concern about breaking the force. His guys had been on two, three, four deployments already, and their families—and we're talking about an all-volunteer force, that's now going to go back and go back and go back. So he was making sure the president knew that from an Army standpoint, if we did this, he really needed to have, if the president would give it to him, more soldiers. Same thing from the commandant of the Marine Corps.

But remember, they already voted, and I had already presented, the chief's position to the president, and we already put it on a slide-show two days before and had given it to Steve Hadley and given it to the president. This is what you're going to hear from your chiefs, we recommend we go do this. But in the process of telling the president what we recommended he do, the service chiefs, rightfully so, were also telling the president the impact that was going to have.

FEAVER: It was clear that the president went into the tank leaning toward the surge, and came out of the tank believing that he could do the surge without provoking a revolt of the generals.

PACE: When I briefed the president, pre-briefed him, when he went to the Pentagon, he knew that he was going to hear, we're going to need more troops, we're going to need, we're going to need that. But he also knew, at the end of the day, we were going to recommend to him this "up to five brigades." Whereas the vice president was not in that [pre-briefing] meeting, to my recollection, and therefore, when he [the president] went in and started listening to the chiefs [in the tank], when the president said—went around the table, "talk to me," when the Army chiefs started saying, I'm going to need more troops, we've got to be careful of morale, et cetera, the vice president was hearing it without—in my recollection—the certain knowledge of what the recommendation is going to be.

So if you don't know that we're going to be recommending let's do this, let's go up to five brigades, as you start hearing the concerns that the service chiefs—remember, the chief of staff of the Army is wearing two hats. As service chief, he owes the president what this is going to do to his troops, and his recommendation to what it's going to do to his troops. So the president heard from his Army chief, his Navy chief of naval operations, his Air Force chief of staff, and his Marine Corps commandant, as service chiefs, and then he heard from me as Joint Chiefs and as the representative of the Joint Chiefs, what our collective recommendation was. That to me is the best way I can come up with why it was the vice president came out of that meeting [in the tank] thinking that the chiefs had said they'd rather not, and why the president's book says he understood that we were going to make this recommendation, but what we needed, if we could get them, these special things.

GATES: And the truth is, that's what led to the decision to extend the tours to fifteen months, because we really were out of Schlitz. The reality of expanding the end strength in the near term was all about morale. That the cavalry was coming. But the reality was, the cavalry wasn't going to be there for a year or two. So the reality was, we were out of Schlitz with the surge, and the only way to make it work was either to cut the amount of time at home or extend the deployment. The Army's recommendation, which I agreed with, was it was better to extend the tours than to cut short the time at home. We either went to fifteen-month deployments or nine months at home. There was just no alternative. That's what we had to do, because as the chiefs were saying, we were out of Schlitz, particularly in terms of the Army and the Marine Corps.

PACE: It was going to take two more years, but the message wasn't so much [that] we're going to have these troops available. The message was really to the families and to the troops themselves that no kidding, your commander in chief understands that this is an extra rock in your pack, and he's going to do what he can to alleviate that strain long-term, but we need you to do this now, this very important part.

LUTE: Well, [the increase in end strength] didn't have any immediate impact. I mean—perhaps—maybe it's well described as a sweetener, because, look, we can't just turn the faucet on and increase the size of these ground forces. I mean, people have to be recruited. They then have to be trained through just the basic training, right? Then they have to be formed into units. So this was going to have a downstream impact, but it was going to have no impact on the surge itself.

RICE: The president can always just order, but it's not always the prudent thing to do or the right thing to do. You want your military really onboard with something. You want them to really give you their best professional judgment. You don't want to have them kind of half in, half out. You don't want any passive-aggressive behavior by some who might feel defeated. . . . And when you have professionals in the Pentagon who are taking the brunt of what's going on, you want to make sure that you're really on the same page and that they've really come to the right conclusion, and you want to give that time.

HADLEY: Yeah, it'd have been a faster process to get a decision, but it would have been a decision that did not have the full support of the agencies who were having to implement it and carry it out, and for which they did not have conviction. And remember, conviction is an important thing here. One of the things about putting the president at the center of this process is, when you're doing something very hard and trying to turn a war around, a war that you're losing, everybody is watching you to see whether you really have conviction, Mr. President or Madame President, in the decision you have made. And if you show any absence of commitment, everybody's going to start hedging.

One of the reasons the president has to be in the center of this process is he's got to be so committed to it and so visibly committed to it—and I have seen with my own eyes, in situations where, you know, it's very rough going—the president basically by his conviction and confidence holds the whole team together. So that process has to be one that produces in the president a real conviction. But also, this president in particular, he wants the whole team to be with him. He understands that he gets to decide because he's president, but this is going to have to be implemented both politically—sold to the American people, sold to the Congress—and then implemented effectively on the ground, otherwise it's not going to work. And there's no point having a good option where you check the right box, but because it isn't implemented it doesn't produce the effects you need on the ground and it does not work. That's the problem.

I think the best process is to take these cabinet secretaries who the president has proposed and who the Senate has confirmed and who the Congress has appropriated the money and the funds and allow them to speak directly to the president to make their views known. And the president then to interact with them and bring them along to the decision that works for the country. And that's the process we pursued. Takes a little time, but the goal of course is not to get a decision, the goal is to get success. And we got success out of this process in terms of the decision we reached and what happened on the ground in the implementation of that decision.

BUSH: I'm not sure how wise I was as opposed to practical, but yeah, cramming down an idea as big as this one down the throats of reluctant people is not good for team morale. And the other thing is that I knew this needed to marinate because otherwise there would be a lot of leaks in the press that would then undermine the capacity to fund. So if the administration were united into the funding battle . . . it would make it easier to get the Republicans on board to begin with. If we were divided going in, it would provide elected officials who would be reluctant, I knew, . . . an excuse not to go. In other words, you're trying to work with [the Senate minority leader] Mitch McConnell or somebody and you're saying let's go, we're going to go for a funding battle, and he says, well, I happen to agree with your vice chairman of the Joint Chiefs who was in the press, and so it's a pretty practical consideration.

CHAPTER 8

What Kind of Surge?

Late December 2006–January 2007

Having decided to surge, and having brought
the military on board, Bush still needed a clearer sense of what those new
troops would do in Iraq. How many troops would he ultimately send, and
what would their strategy be?

Many of those questions would ultimately land on Bob Gates's desk.
Newly sworn in as Rumsfeld's replacement, he flew to Iraq soon after assuming office, to see matters firsthand. It was his second trip that year, having
already visited Baghdad with the Iraq Study Group. Returning from his trip
as secretary in December, he recommended a modest troop increase, though
his own staff soon realized this was no time for modest measures.

The president needed to make a decision as well. Bush thus convened a
National Security Council meeting at his Texas ranch on December 28, 2006.
When presented with a range of options, "Absolutely not. No way," Bush
said when told of plans to send a couple of brigades, and to take decisions
on more later. "I'm not going to make this decision every month. Let's give
them everything we've got and take it from there." He insisted any surge
employ "decisive force" capable of changing the strategic equation in Iraq,
and ordered five brigade combat teams to Iraq, a move history has come to
know as the surge.

The formal announcement took place during a prime-time television
address on January 10, 2007. "The new strategy I outline tonight will change

America's course in Iraq and help us succeed in the fight against terror," he said. "Times of testing reveal the character of a nation."

Secretary Gates

GATES: I think that I was greatly advantaged when I was asked to become secretary by having served on the Iraq Study Group. . . . My belief, by the time we ended our session in September in Baghdad, I believed that there was the opportunity to stabilize Iraq and to bring it to a place where the United States' eventual departure would not be seen as a strategic defeat with either regional or global consequences.

About literally a week before National Security Advisor Steve Hadley called me and the president asked me to become secretary, would I do it, about a week before that call, I had sent an e-mail to both [James] Baker and [Lee] Hamilton, recommending a surge. I had been persuaded by our visits to Baghdad, by the conversations we'd had with everybody, that we had to improve the security situation, particularly in Baghdad, before we could begin to think about transition to Iraqi security responsibility and making any kind of political progress. I had recommended a surge in this e-mail in mid-October. Interestingly enough, so had two other members of the Iraq Study Group, just in our internal communications, Chuck Robb and Bill Perry. We each had a little different approach to it. . . . I just said I thought we would need twenty-five thousand to forty thousand troops. I had a pretty good feeling that the only way we could improve the security situation was through an increase in US troops.

Now, in my recommendations in the Iraq Study Group, I said the duration of the surge should also be directly connected to certain benchmarks for the Iraqi government in terms of things they had to do, like not interfering in the arrests of Shia who might be prominent politicians, were involved in the militias and worsening the security situation. By the very nature of the term "surge," I saw it as a temporary thing that would be required. This was really the advice and what we were hearing from most of the experts. You really just need to stabilize the security situation, because you can't make progress on anything else, including transfer of security responsibilities, until the downward spiral that began with the bombing of the mosque had been reversed.

O'SULLIVAN: I did not feel confident that it [the surge] was going to happen until, I would say, the second part of December. I think . . . when I really felt like this was going to happen was when the conversation shifted to talking about resources, to talking about when, how we were going to resource this. . . . I mean primarily forces. And so that happened, those conversations happened, in roughly the fifteenth through the twenty-second of December, or the second half of December is when we're having those discussions.

The proposal that came back initially from MNF-I was we can do this. I think it was first said we can do this with two brigades. We don't actually need the full contingent, all five that we understood could be made available. This can be done with less.

And at this point, General Petraeus was . . . the likely commander [to replace Casey at MNF-I]. And I did call him up, and I said, "If you were to be executing this strategy, how much force would you need?" And he said to me, "Everything you could give me." And so there were quite a few of us who had very strong reactions to the idea that somehow you could resource this in an incremental kind of way.

I remember having a pretty frank exchange with Steve [Hadley] about this in his office. And my feeling very strongly at the time was we have come this far to where the president is going to make a very bold, risky, and courageous decision to dramatically shift strategy, and then we're going to kill it by not resourcing it.

HANNAH: Again, my instinct, again, this entire period of several months, that at some level this was baked. The president could figure out a way to get from his desire for more troops and for getting on top of the situation, to bringing everybody else along, that he was going to do that. I think that only became more true as the process evolved and he spoke to more people, his advisors came up with concrete options, as that was validated by people, serious people on the outside, that the president was headed there, and . . . it was a question of how many and whether you could both get the new secretary of defense, but particularly the commanders that were still on the ground in Iraq, Generals Casey and Abizaid, to also come along with that recommendation. That's kind of the way I saw the mission. Exactly how many you were going to surge and exactly how they would be used, for what functions and what purposes, I think that, not in the president's mind, but in the commanders' mind and in perhaps Secretary Gates's mind, that was by no means assured.

EDELMAN: So when we were on the flight to Baghdad, I had gotten a set of the briefing slides that Fred Kagan had prepared for Jack Keane, that Jack Keane had basically drawn from when he briefed the president maybe a week or so earlier before we'd gone out, basically calling for an increase in the force and a change in mission. And I gave those to Secretary Gates and said, "I think you ought to take a look at these, because the president is getting this from other sources, and you ought to be knowledgeable and aware of it." Gates took a look at it while we were coming off the plane.

When we got off the plane and got to Baghdad, we were met by Generals Abizaid and Casey and Odierno, and we went off to Camp Victory and sat down with them and got briefed by Casey and Odierno. Casey at that point was saying, "I need another brigade." He'd actually come around to needing some additional forces.

General Odierno, interestingly, said, "I'd actually like to have two brigade equivalents. I'd like to have that additional brigade in Baghdad. And I'd also like to have two regimental combat teams of Marines, essentially Army brigade equivalent, in Anbar Province to support General Zilmer," who was the commander out there, "and help him reassure the Sunni sheikhs," who were part of the Sahwa, the so-called Sunni Awakening, "that we're going to be there to support them as they fight al-Qaeda in Iraq." This goes back to the Anbar-is-lost discussion from a couple months earlier, Colonel Devlin's famous intel analysis for the Marines out in Anbar Province.[1]

Interestingly, General Casey pulled John Hannah and me aside before we had dinner that night at his residence and said, "I want you guys to go down and sit with Odierno and Zilmer and run them through their paces." He said, "They want another. They're pushing for these two regimental combat teams. I'm not sure we need them." And so Hannah and I actually spent much of that evening at dinner talking to Zilmer and Odierno. And actually . . . I found that they made a very persuasive case for the two regimental combat teams. And I told Secretary Gates that.

Secretary Gates then launched into a series of meetings with Maliki, most of which ended up being one on one, where he pitched the notion of two additional brigades to Maliki, who was somewhat resistant. Not somewhat. He was very resistant. It took several hours for Gates to finish this discussion with Maliki. And in the end of the day he came out and said, "I think I've persuaded Maliki to accept these two increased brigades for a limited time span."

And so we got on the plane and we flew home and I drafted the trip report for Secretary Gates and reported in this conversation to the president with Maliki. And then he circulated, as was his wont, he wanted to make sure he had interagency comity as it were, on the plane. We were in a C-17, we were in the Airstream trailer, because you can't hear yourself think in a C-17, to have this discussion. So we went into—which is the bedroom and office for Pace and for Gates. And we went off to have a meeting with Kevin Bergner and Dave Satterfield. And he had circulated the trip report and asked for people's comments. And then I took all the comments and cleaned it up and gave him a final version of the trip report. And he discussed it with all the members of staff.

And I wish I could say I did it, but the one person who raised a concern was John Hannah, who said, "Mr. Secretary, this is great, two brigades. But I'm worried." And this was pursuant to a conversation that Satterfield, Bergner, Hannah, and I had while we were going over the draft and looking at the edits. And Hannah said to the secretary, "We've been failing here for some time to stem the sectarian violence. Is two brigades just enough to fail?" And Secretary Gates thought about it. He said, "John, that's a great question. I don't know the answer to the question. But I don't think I can persuade Maliki to take more than two brigades, even if we had more than two brigades to throw at this."

GATES: I had been secretary for, I think, thirty-six hours when I went to Baghdad. First of all, Casey and Abizaid made the pitch to me about maybe two brigade combat teams. But the thing that troubled me the most was Maliki's resistance to the idea of a surge. This was something that I wasn't sure the president had figured on. Maliki really didn't want anybody. He felt the Iraqi people were assuming America's troop presence was going to diminish, rather steadily. He thought that the American troops were a target, and created more violence because they were a target. He felt this was contrary to the trends that Iraqis were expecting. He was very resistant to the idea of any surge at all, anybody. Abizaid and Casey told me they thought they could work him around to maybe accepting one BCT, one brigade combat team, early on, and then maybe a second later. And I don't know the extent to which their thinking was influenced by Maliki's resistance. Never had that discussion. But that was the biggest takeaway for me, was the position of Maliki. . . . I reported to [the president] what I had heard from Maliki, and he acknowledged that that was going to be a challenge. And I told him what Casey's and Abizaid's recommendation was, and that I agreed with it. . . . I think he probably was very disappointed.

HANNAH: I remember having Secretary Gates previewing that for a group of us on the plane on the way home. I can remember, you know being a very lonely voice in saying that I was afraid this was not going to work, it was too little too late, it was incrementalism, that we weren't going to get another bite of the apple. I remember getting back to Andrews, going directly to the White House, close to midnight, going to my office, getting on the phone with Jack Keane. Jack Keane had already heard, I can't remember from whom, whether it was from Ray Odierno or General Petraeus, but from his sources in the military and perhaps some in Baghdad, that this was the direction, this was what Gates was coming home with. Keane confirmed all my suspicions, that this was not going to get the job done, or at least at too high a risk of failing.

I immediately, that night, wrote a trip report to the vice president, telling him that this was what was coming, and expressing all my concerns about it. I think we had a phone conversation the next day. He entirely agreed.

GATES: In the ensuing few days, as I talked to people like General Petraeus, and others, I very quickly tipped to the argument, if you start with two and then have to ask for the other three, it will send the signal we're failing. . . . If you start with five, you may not need all five. You don't necessarily have to deploy all five. But if you start with five, then you don't have that problem. And that just seemed eminently logical to me. So I quickly embraced that.

There's nothing deep about it. I was brand-new to the job. I'd been secretary of defense, like I said, for thirty-six hours. And here I've got two four-stars, one of them who's longtime expert in the Middle East, out there in Baghdad. I've also got Maliki saying he doesn't want anybody. So I accepted what they told me. I came back. Pace and I probably talked all the way back. And within a few days, I realized that the argument that I had just talked about was quite persuasive.

O'SULLIVAN: General Petraeus was someone who was very important to me in the process because he was someone that I had known since 2003, someone whose military advice I really valued, and someone who I had a good relationship with and so I could call him and ask him questions without feeling that I was going to upset anyone over at the Pentagon. . . . So he was someone who I would say repeatedly, throughout this process that we've discussed, who I would call and talk to him about things that were happening.

It was a very delicate situation because he had no formal role in the process, and he was not in the chain of command that was giving us the official military assessment. In some ways, he shouldn't have been giving input to the White House. I was reaching out to him and asking for it. Steve and President Bush knew that I was doing that but couldn't acknowledge it. And so there was this strange kabuki game where I would somehow communicate to them that I was getting this from credible military sources and they would know it was Petraeus, but there was never anything explicit.

ABIZAID: What was a surprise to me was the extent that Jack Keane and Dave Petraeus and others who were in the middle of all this apparently have an entrée, somehow or other. . . . And I thought that the fact that they didn't call and tell me about that, or they didn't indicate it, Petraeus in particular, I still take great umbrage at that to this day. I thought it was very unprofessional. . . . I recommended to the president that . . . General Petraeus go in to replace General Casey. Had I known what was going on, I would not have made that recommendation. . . . I'm shocked that he didn't call me, Keane didn't call me, or George [Casey], or somebody and let us know what they were working on and why they were working on it. It was rational, and we were coming to that direction. And then in the subsequent selling of the story, to claim that somehow or other we avoided defeat—we were never on the road to defeat.

Crawford

SATTERFIELD: I can recall [Secretary Rice] telling the president, "I know you don't like me saying this," or, "I know you are tired of me repeating this view. But I have to express my profound concern that . . . introduction of additional forces into this fight cannot predictably achieve the success we are seeking. But in the process of committing them, you will have made a final roll of the dice. There's no way back from this. And the magnitude, or character, of failure and the implications for broader global issues and confrontations will be profound." Those were her views until the moment of the president's decision.

Once the president made the decision, then a very different policy process, which we were all on board with, flowed. But no, there was no change in her views up until the actual decision was taken by the president. And I can recall very shortly before that decision, some very direct conversations between the two.

RICE: When Bob Gates got there, it became much less of a problem, because Gates was—in our first conversation, you know he was looking for another way to do it too, but he wasn't sure he could adequately resource it, because he was getting really strange readings from the service chiefs and others, about—and we were also, by this time we were starting to face the multiple deployments, which was starting to have an effect on the population. There were stories every other day, in the *Times* or the *Post*, about this soldier was on his fourth deployment to Iraq. There were questions that people had about whether we could adequately resource Afghanistan and do a surge in Iraq. American soldiers were dying in huge numbers, because the Iranians had really stepped up the improvised . . . explosive device.

So it was a real constraint, this question of the resourcing, but fortunately, Bob Gates was prepared to kind of push and prod as to how to get that done. Pete Pace did a great job too, of kind of smoothing the waters with the service chiefs, who really are the ones who have to answer those questions about resources, and with the combatant commanders, who were—the combatant commander was in favor, particularly once Petraeus got there, but the service chiefs were very reticent to start kind of altering deployment patterns and the like.

It was a breach of my own sense of civil-military decorum, to call Ray [Odierno] in the field and say to him, "I'm trying to get my head around this idea of surging forces, will it matter?" And when he said, "Yes, it would matter, particularly in Anbar." That was a big piece of the puzzle for me.

[The president] knew that I had concerns about deploying more forces. He knew that those concerns were largely abated by the appointment of Gates, and then Petraeus. He knew that I didn't really trust the Iraqis, and that once—I was in that meeting with Maliki—he felt that he'd gotten good answers from the Iraqis. And by the time that I talked to him in Crawford, I'd decided OK, this is the right thing to do, and he knew that. It's not as if the president has to say, Well, until the secretary of state is there, you know, I'm going to feel a problem. But we've been very close, and I think he recognized that my concerns were not knee-jerk, that my concerns were not gee, I think Iraq is falling apart, we just ought to get out of here, but I think he respected that I didn't want to jump to an early conclusion about the surge.

I always stayed at the governor's house [in Crawford], which is the ranch house at the end of the property. I drove up early that morning, and the president was out, walking around, and we walked down to one of his lakes, and I said, "I know you want to do this, don't you, you want to surge forces." He started saying something like, "Well, you know, I'm not," and I said, "No, you want to do this, don't you?" He said, "Are you OK with it?" And I said it was always about whether or not you were just going to do the same thing with more troops, and if you're not going to do the same thing with more troops, if you're going to do something different with more troops, maybe this will work, I said, "But it's your last card, it's your last card."

HADLEY: Gates now is fully on board with the surge; and the effect the president wanted to achieve has been achieved. He knows what he wants to do, and he's got confidence in it. He's brought his national security team on board; he's brought his military on board; and he's got a strategy. And he's already thinking about and starting to staff out the people he's going to need to make that strategy succeed, which starts with Bob Gates and then goes to Petraeus and then goes to Crocker. And off we go.

BUSH: Remember, we're trying to win—and the definition of win, by the way, we said this all along, is [for Iraq to be] an ally in the war on terror and a functioning democracy. It's not going to be perfect, but that was victory. And I also, by the way, was deeply influenced by my readings about Harry Truman and the presence of Korean troops [US troops in Korea] for years after a very unpopular war—and you know, my relationship with the Koreans was very strong. I was struck by the fact that during my presidency, I never had to worry about war in the Far East, and I ascribe that in part to the fact that they were functioning democracies. But those democracies would not have existed without a long-term US presence, and my view, we can talk about this, was that we needed to be there for a long period of time. . . . I mean, we've got a big presence in Korea and a big presence in Japan. It's just, I find it very ironic that my dad fights the Japanese, they're now our allies, matter of fact, not only our allies, that [Prime Minister Junichiro] Koizumi was forward leaning right after 9/11 to help us, and so you've got to ask why. And the answer is that free societies are peaceful. They end up being a part of

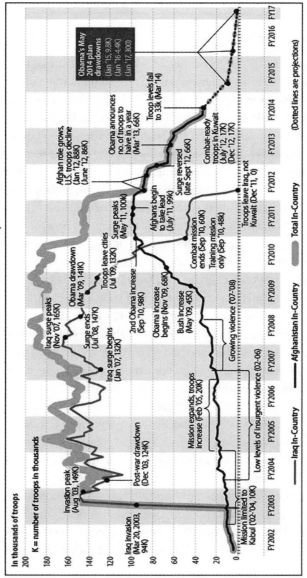

FIGURE 6. US "boots on the ground" in Iraq and Afghanistan, 2003–2008

Source: Adapted from "Boots on the Ground In-Country, FY2001–FY2017," in Amy Belasco, *The Cost of Iraq, Afghanistan, and Other Global War on Terror Operations since 9/11*, Congressional Research Service Report, December 8, 2014, p. 9, https://fas.org/sgp/crs/natsec/RL33110.pdf.

a foundation of peace. But it turns out if you look at history, there's only one force that can enable these recovering societies, and that's us. And so long-term I felt the Iraqis could deal with it. Short term I didn't, because the facts were so obvious."

The Announcement

HADLEY: The last issue in connection with the speech is, is it five brigades—two brigades now and three more if the commander needs it, or do we commit up front to five brigades and the commander can send them home if he doesn't need them? That's the difference. It is an issue in terms of the EXORD [executive order]—and I'm talking to Pete Pace over the phone about the EXORD that the secretary of defense is going to sign, committing the troops. And it's an issue of what we say about it in the speech. And Pentagon preference is five brigades available, only two committed, three more on call. Something like that. Or do you commit the five brigades now?

I have a recollection of talking to Meghan, who I knew was having discreet conversations with General Petraeus and others, and that I was delighted that she was, but for a lot of reasons I didn't want to know anything about them. And I said to Meghan, "How do you think General Petraeus—what would be his druthers?" And she said, "I think he'd like all five brigades." Which was what I thought. I went to see the president and said, "This is the issue." And I told him what I thought the incoming commanders wanted, which is what any incoming commander would want getting into a new situation where they hadn't been on the ground. Give me everything and I'll tell you if I need it all. But also the other argument I made to him was, you want to send a firm message that something is new, that it is different, and that we are committed to win. That's the question people are going to have. And the strongest statement you can make of your intention is to say, five brigades committed from the start. And of course, given the president we served, he said, "That's exactly right. That's what we'll do. Tell Pace we want EXORD to commit all five brigades." And that's what I conveyed back to him over the phone.

CROUCH: I think there was also an argument . . . that making the full commitment actually had more of a shock value in the region, remember? We were trying to get our Sunni allies outside Iraq to sort of say they're serious. We were trying to leave the impression with the Iranians we were serious. We were trying to make sure the Sunni allies inside Iraq thought, OK, they really are going to do something here. We were trying to convince the Shia, who were influencing Maliki, you know, that this was a big commitment.

HADLEY: Because one of the last issues in the surge discussion is, do you do Baghdad now and Anbar later? Do you do Anbar now and Baghdad later? Or do you do both together, which requires more troops—five brigades for Baghdad and some battalions of Marines for Anbar. And the president wisely decides, again very strategic, he's going to address his biggest problem, which is Baghdad and the sectarian violence there, and take advantage of his biggest opportunity, which is the Sunni uprising in Anbar. And he's going to do them both at the same time. That's the right decision.

FEAVER: I was able to talk to the political side of the house and say, "Do you think you could manage that strategy, or would you prefer to have to swallow the whole pill all at once?" For them it was a no-brainer. They want to swallow the whole pill all at once, so [I was] able to then inject that back into the discussion, saying, "This would be a disaster politically."

ABIZAID: At various times, various people would call me and George [Casey] from Washington—these are the guys that are dealing with all these policy reviews—saying, Do we support it or not support it? like we're congressional delegates or something like that. And I said, "Look, you guys—if you haven't figured this out by now, you're never going to figure out. Whatever decision the president makes, we're going to support it. We're going to support it one hundred percent." But I said, "There's a lot of different ways to look at this." It was clear to me that they had come to the conclusion that they were going to discount the view from the field. Because they thought that we were not moving the mission toward an outcome that they considered to be politically successful.

I said, "Look, if this is an effort to get us to leave, then I don't really think it's an effort that we should make. If this is an effort to achieve some sort of a long-standing strategic victory, then it's going to take more time, more effort, more energy, and a lot more political action."

And interestingly enough, the guys in Washington were fixated on military forces being able to achieve some sort of an outcome that I said to the president, "Look, military forces will only buy you time. So we'll buy you time. A five-brigade additional force that stays there for a year and a half or two years will buy you time. But it will not allow you to have strategic success unless all the other things we've been talking about for four or five years are put into the equation."

ROVE: There was difficulty in getting a commitment from DoD that there were five brigades available. I had two views. One is if there was difficulty in getting five brigades; they may pull them back. Better to commit to the five brigades at the beginning. And the second thing was, if you're going to say to the American people we're going to surge, then surge. And maybe it's easier to explain, Well, you know what, we decided that we were succeeding so well we didn't need the fifth brigade, than it was to say, Ladies and gentlemen, we need another brigade.

I was in favor of, if we have gone through all the effort to get the commitment to the five brigades, then say five brigades, and if you wanted to say "up to," fine, but say five brigades. I thought it would show determination. The enemy would hear it, and that's important. Will matters. If we had been wishy-washy about it, I think it would've had an effect on their mind-set, and if we showed we're coming strong, that would similarly have an effect on them.

And on the Iraqis. Are we in for a penny or are we in for a pound? And I think one of the things that the Iraqis were wondering at that point was, can the president of the United States sustain his support here, given the political pressures at home? Now they had political pressures of their own. They had the Shiite militias, they had Shiite paramilitary/political organizations growing. They had a keen awareness of political pressures, and it colored their view. Are these guys going to be able to stay with us, and how does that affect our internal politics as well?

Look, you don't advise [the president] on the political consequences of something. He may have an idea about what it is, but he didn't really care about the political consequences of this, if you mean Republican/Democrat partisanship. He did know that by saying that we need a change, that that would cause some pause on the part of the American people, but he felt confident that explaining what it is that he wanted to do—in essence, surge troops in in order to achieve a military victory, to stabilize the security of the country, and defeat and kill bad guys—that the American people, he felt confident the American people would say: You know what? If you're serious about it, then I'll support you, but if you're not serious about it I'm not going to support you.

ABIZAID: I said, "When we surge in Iraq, I'm going to have to divert special operating forces from Afghanistan, and I don't want to do that." I said, "We're finally starting to have an impact on al-Qaeda cells on both sides of the border, between Afghanistan and Pakistan, and I'm going to have to divert resources that are having very good effect out there, that are helping with the transition of NATO forces, and I think it would be a big mistake. And I don't want to sacrifice progress in Iraq or sacrifice progress in Afghanistan for what I don't think is a sustainable effort in Iraq."

I thought that the national command authority very much undervalued the threat of Islamic extremism. And I was very concerned about that. And I tried to convey that constantly. So I'm not sure that that ever quite got through. The amount of time that we'd spent talking about tactical problems in Baghdad was incredible. Not the president, but more junior people.

PACE: So, the recommendation was up to five. Oh, by the way, reality was, we could only get manned and equipped and send one per month. So, whether you said two, four, five, was going to be one, two, three, four, five. The president understood that. By saying up to five, which is what he said and what his guidance to us was, we got those mechanisms going. We then got all five brigades alerted, we had them all on a timeline, they all knew they were going, but we also had the opportunity to go back to the president and say, Mr. President, there are three brigades there now, the job is going fine, thank you, we won't need four and five.

BUSH: I remember somebody said, "Let's go ten thousand." I asked you [O'Sullivan] and Hadley, and you both said that we need thirty thousand, and I said if you're in, you're in. You don't tiptoe. . . . At this point, I'm not interested in tiptoeing. I've got a new secretary of defense, got a new commander on the ground, got a strategy I'm comfortable with, and yes, let's go.

BOLTEN: When he went to give that speech in early January, announcing the surge, [the president] was well aware of how very unpopular this was going to be, even within his own party, which was still smarting and blaming him for a very bad defeat in the midterms, which, by the way, could have been—it was dramatically contributed to by the party's own problems, not just Iraq, but the members and the leadership were focused on what a big drag the Iraq War had been on their political prospects.

GATES: I think we all knew instinctively that this would not be popular. I think we all underestimated the magnitude of the backlash.

BUSH: I wasn't nearly as emotional as I was when I announced we were first going in. I knew it was the best shot we had. I don't remember being very emotional about it. I think pretty matter-of-factly, and I also knew that people would not believe me until the results changed on the ground—that you can try to be persuasive all you want, but at this point in time, they had to see concrete results. And thankfully September of '07 there were concrete results. The biggest angst for a president, at least for me, about a decision was prior to making it. Once you make the decision you're relieved. There's a relief, particularly if you're confident that you've looked at all the options and you're making the best call you can make. If it's a haphazard decision, there's got to be a lot of angst. But I didn't know what the outcome would be, of course, but I knew that this was our best shot, only shot.

Excerpts from the President's July 10, 2006, Speech

Good evening. Tonight in Iraq, the armed forces of the United States are engaged in a struggle that will determine the direction of the global war on terror and our safety here at home. The new strategy I outline tonight will change America's course in Iraq and help us succeed in the fight against terror.

When I addressed you just over a year ago, nearly twelve million Iraqis had cast their ballots for a unified and democratic nation. The elections of 2005 were a stunning achievement. We thought that these elections would bring the Iraqis together and that as we trained Iraqi security forces, we could accomplish our mission with fewer American troops. But in 2006, the opposite happened. The violence in Iraq, particularly in Baghdad, overwhelmed the political gains the Iraqis had made.

The consequences of failure are clear. Radical Islamic extremists would grow in strength and gain new recruits. They would be in a better position to topple moderate governments, create chaos in the region, and use oil revenues to fund their ambitions. Iran would be emboldened in its pursuit of nuclear weapons. Our enemies would have a safe haven from which to plan and launch attacks on the American people. On September the eleventh, 2001, we saw what a refuge for extremists on the other side of the world could bring to the streets of our own cities. For the safety of our people, America must succeed in Iraq.

The most urgent priority for success in Iraq is security, especially in Baghdad. . . . Our past efforts to secure Baghdad failed for two principal reasons: there were not enough Iraqi and American troops to secure neighborhoods that had been cleared of terrorists and insurgents, and there were too many restrictions on the troops we did have. Our military commanders reviewed the new Iraqi plan to ensure that it addressed these mistakes. They report that it does. They also report that this plan can work.

This will require increasing American force levels. So I've committed more than twenty thousand additional American troops to Iraq. The vast majority of them, five brigades, will be deployed to Baghdad. These troops will work alongside Iraqi units and be embedded in their formations. Our troops will have a well-defined mission: to help Iraqis clear and secure neighborhoods, to help them protect the local population, and to help ensure that the Iraqi forces left behind are capable of providing the security that Baghdad needs.

This new strategy will not yield an immediate end to suicide bombings, assassinations, or IED attacks. Our enemies in Iraq will make every effort to ensure that our television screens are filled with images of death and suffering. Yet over time, we can expect to see Iraqi troops chasing down murderers, fewer brazen acts of terror, and growing trust and cooperation from Baghdad's residents. When this happens, daily life will improve, Iraqis will gain confidence in their leaders, and the government will have the breathing space it needs to make progress in other critical areas. Most of Iraq's Sunni and Shia want to live together in peace, and reducing the violence in Baghdad will help make reconciliation possible.

The changes I have outlined tonight are aimed at ensuring the survival of a young democracy that is fighting for its life in a part of the world of enormous importance to American security. Let me be clear: The terrorists and insurgents in Iraq are without conscience, and they will make the year ahead bloody and violent. Even if our new strategy works exactly as planned, deadly acts of violence will continue, and we must expect more Iraqi and American casualties. The question is whether our new strategy will bring us closer to success. I believe that it will.

Victory will not look like the ones our fathers and grandfathers achieved. There will be no surrender ceremony on the deck of a battleship. But victory in Iraq will bring something new in the Arab world: a functioning democracy that polices its territory, upholds the rule of law, respects fundamental human liberties, and answers to its people. A democratic Iraq will not be perfect, but it will be a country that fights terrorists instead of harboring them, and it will help bring a future of peace and security for our children and our grandchildren.

We go forward with trust that the Author of Liberty will guide us through these trying hours. Thank you and good night.

Conclusion

GATES: First of all, I think the process was, in some ways, nearly textbook. There were senior people studying this at the State Department, at the NSC, at the Defense Department. You had a lot of smart people working this issue for weeks and weeks before any—before it began to crystallize as a decision. You had a lot of interagency discussion. You had a lot of presidential interaction with the chiefs and with military leaders. And then you had the president making a tough decision. And, frankly, everybody pulling together to implement it. So I think in terms of process that it worked pretty well. The one piece that we probably didn't focus on enough at the time was how difficult it was going to be with the Congress.

HADLEY: I think this was more a function of how we were operating in the second term and the kind of process [the president] asked me to run. . . . After I was nominated as a national security advisor, I had my first meeting with the national security press, and . . . somebody basically said, Well, you know, the problem with the first term is that Rice wasn't able to knock heads with Don Rumsfeld and the vice president. And she's very close to the president. If she wasn't able to do it, how are you going to do it? And I said, "I'm not going to try. Those are six-hundred-pound gorillas, and you're suggesting I'm not one, but, you know, I may not be a six-hundred-pound gorilla, but I've got a twelve-hundred-pound gorilla down the hall who loves to make decisions. And if we have a disagreement among the six-hundred-pound gorillas, we're all going to go down the hall; we're going to have a conversation with the president of the United States; everyone's going to explain their views; he's going to make a decision; and all of them, because they're professionals and because they respect the president, they're going to salute, and we're going to move out. That's how we're going to do business. That's what it means to be an honest broker." And if you think about it, that's the outline of the process that we ran.

But the subtext I'm trying to describe it is, it's also a process of the president and me working together gradually to bring people to where the president thought we needed to be and to bring the military, both our outgoing commanders and the incoming commanders, where they needed to be so that we did not have in the middle of the war a split between the president and his military, or a split within his military, which is what we needed in order to succeed with the kind of bold strategy change he was going to make. And that's really what's going on.

So at the end of the day, when the president announces his decision, the country is shocked, speechless. It's not what they expected was coming, but I think we can say all of his cabinet secretaries supported; Condi and Bob Gates went together to try to sell it to the Hill, very uphill battle; and the military leaders, you know, were all more or less in the same boat, thanks largely to Pete Pace. Some leaned left; some leaned right. Casey thought we could do it with two brigades, maybe a third on call. The president at the end of the day thought we were going to commit the full five brigades; that's what Petraeus clearly wanted. So there were some disagreements, but everybody was largely in the same boat, and that protected the surge from being submerged or basically torpedoed by public disagreements among the military.

RICE: I'm very proud of the way that the surge decision unfolded. I know there will be those historically who will say it should have happened earlier, but it almost never does happen earlier than it has to, because there are so many costs to changing course, and the president owed it to his secretary of defense, to give him a chance to deliver on what he was doing. When the president decided he could no longer tolerate what was happening, I think a process unfolded that gave him every possible option. As I've said, I'm very glad that I withheld judgment on this until I could honestly say I was foursquare behind it. I'm glad the president waited until the military could be foursquare behind it, and I think because a process is not always as expeditious as people might like it to be, it sometimes is more effective, and I think this was a process that was immensely effective.

BOLTEN: If this was a question thirty years from now, I think thirty years from now, folks should look back and see an important example of true presidential leadership in an extraordinarily difficult situation, that put the interests of the country and the fighting men and women, and the national security of the United States, well above considerations of personal or partisan politics.

RICE: In 2006, he [Bush] had a lot more experience dealing with the military. He'd sat through those meetings. There's a joke that when the State Department gives an option, it says option A is bomb them into the ice age, option C is capitulate, option B is do what the State Department wants to do. The Pentagon is that way too, and you have to learn how to read the "Oh my goodness we're not going to be able to defend against North Korea," and I think in 2003, he was less willing to really push and press and prod on questions like how were they going to backfill when our forces went through. That's experience.

Sometimes wartime presidents have to go through difficult experiences. We know how many generals Lincoln went through before he finally got it right. In this case, it wasn't going through generals as much as it was, I think, going through a lot of very bad outcomes, a lot of false starts that those outcomes were about to turn around, and then eventually deciding that he had to make what I consider to be one of the bravest decisions that an American president has ever taken, which was to double down on a war that a lot of people thought was lost. So, we can talk about civil-military relations, we can talk about the role of the NSC, we can talk about the secretary of state or whatever, but it ultimately comes down to the president, and whether the president is willing to take tough choices.

ZELIKOW: I do recall believing that what the president was doing was an extraordinary act, unlike any I had ever seen in government. I had never seen a president defy so much of the institutional establishment in his own government to promulgate what I thought was courageous and instinctually correct strategy. As an episode in civil/military relations, it was remarkable. . . . And it was such a contrast with what had gone before. . . . I still to this day have the sense that this—at the time he made the decision at the beginning of January, it was a Hail Mary pass.

HADLEY: There's one thing that needs to be recorded for history, and that is right about the time he's clearly going to head and make the surge decision . . . he looks up and he says, "Hadley, is this going to work?"

In my recollections, I said, "Mr. President, I think it will work, but it's the last chance we have to get this right." And he says, "Well that's good." And he said, "But if you ever change your mind and think this can't work, you need to come tell me because I can't keep sending young men and women into harm's way if we don't have a strategy we think is going to give us victory." And I said, "Yes, sir." . . . You know, when [McNamara] was alive, they said, "Well, why didn't you go to Johnson with your views?" And he said, "Well, you know,

President Johnson was a difficult man to bring bad news to." And here was the president of the United States soliciting from me what would have been, if I'd ever had to bring it, the worst news that he could have heard, which was, "Mr. President, we've failed in Iraq, and there's nothing we can do about it." And basically, he was soliciting that bad news because of his commitment to the young men and women in uniform.

ABIZAID: Look, the process was not healthy, because the process did not use the whole of government approach to include the chain of command in a way that could have resulted in a different outcome. . . . I don't think I would have kept the commanders in the field so much in the dark as we were. It's not our job to read the minds of what's going on in Washington. . . . If you could think of the US military being defeated anywhere, please let me know where it is. It's not Iraq, it's not Afghanistan, it's not anywhere. It's all a matter of pain— how much pain can you assume? And once we set the pain levels, I think probably with the surge, we didn't set the pain levels high enough. Because the pain level, to maintain a bigger force over time, with more involvement with the Iraqis, and then more involvement with the political end of the spectrum, was what had to happen, and that did not happen. It really was a tactical solution to a strategic problem, and today, as we look back on it, it did not achieve strategic results. . . . I told the president back in November/December. . . , "I don't think that this is going to work strategically. I think it is chasing down the path that will allow us to withdraw a number of our forces, but I think ultimately it won't fix the basic problem, which is a political problem between Sunni, Shia, and Kurds."

CAMBONE: It was undoubtedly a success, and the president deserves a great deal of credit for having done what he did. . . . I think it is one of the model instances of presidential leadership in wartime. He, the president, knew that he had to make this decision, and he took it and put in place a process to bring him what he needed to make that decision, and then he made it. That's pretty good stuff and the sort of thing that those of us who have served or will serve in government need to appreciate about the responsibility of a president.

PACE: By the time we all got done with the surge briefings, it had been a very collaborative workup to this thing. Everybody knows the president can decide anytime he wants, but the way he did it had everybody together, everybody understanding where we were going, how we were going to get there, and doing the same planning, and everybody saying this is the right thing. Even guys who, understandably and knowingly, defined "up to five brigades" differently.

His result of how he did it was that he then had his entire military team recommending to him, and having planned through it, a course of action with which he was comfortable obviously, because he said go do it, and now we're all pulling on the oars together.

GATES: But the key is, how do you bring them along? How do you try and persuade them? At a minimum, it's how do you get them to a point where they at least acquiesce and don't actively resist? And I think he did that. The chiefs will—if they're consulted and brought in and have a chance to make their case, secretary and the president give them all kinds of time to make that case, access to make that case, they will almost always fall into line and be disciplined. But when a secretary, for example, overrides them, pays no attention to them, you have the same kind of relationship that existed between McNamara and the chiefs, where the chiefs went to the hill and McNamara was stymied, time and time again. Because the chiefs would galvanize support on the Hill. . . . So it's how you deal with these people and the respect you give them, treating them with respect and dignity, listening to them, that you bring them on board. Which doesn't mean that they agree with your decisions, but it means that they're willing to go along. And that's where I think the chiefs got to.

HANNAH: Whatever you think about the mistakes we made conducting this war, that—the decision that George Bush made in the fall and winter of 2006—is a genuine testament to presidential leadership and courage that had big, important, positive consequences for the country and our national security. He made it against the inclinations of a lot of his top advisors, indeed some of his closest advisors, you could argue. Had to make it against the inclinations of a lot of the US military, certainly against public opinion in the United States, certainly against the majority of people in the Congress, against the feelings of the international community. It was genuinely, in many ways, one of those singular, kind of lonely decisions that presidents are sometimes called on to make, and a lonely decision when, at least in terms of his political future and something genuinely important to the national security of the country, really seemed to hang in the balance. He seemed to really reach down and do what he thought was necessary and he thought was right, and I think, at least to some degree, history will prove that the correct thing to do. . . . I think people will have to look back at that, again, regardless of what else they think about everything that came before the war and everything that came after, when George W. Bush made that decision about the surge, he was genuinely a great president.

SATTERFIELD: The addition of US forces—or indeed, the efficacy of US force structure that existed on the ground, in our assessment—could not in itself fundamentally affect the direction of violence in Iraq.

The surge succeeded because of a reset taking place to the west of Baghdad in Anbar; by the tribes themselves, ever more decisively moving against al-Qaeda—not because of the surge decision, but outrage by al-Qaeda progressively shutting down, destroying, their structures of life, ways of living, cultural traditions, decapitations, fingers cut off, blocking the smuggling trade upon which they had relied. And a second development, which was the Jaysh al-Mahdi pulling itself out of the fight. Not because of the surge, but because of already progressively more effective US security actions and an increasing sense of insecurity on the part of Muqtada personally as to what his fate might be if he stayed in this fight. You had a perfect positive storm—not negative—building that came together post–surge decision, which made the surge a critical—but not the essential—element of success. I wish it had been the other way around, that, yes, we had seen all of these developments and figured, "Well, these five BCTs made a success."

Would we have had success without those five BCTs and a reset of what US force did? No. I don't think so. I think the ability to sustain, to project across the country these positive trend lines, could not have been done without the additional US force elements. But had it not been for the happy accident of two Sunni-Shia critical developments—which we did not know of—occurring, the surge would not have succeeded. So we were wrong in the recommendation against the surge, but for the right analytic reasons. The president, I would say, was right in his decision to go with the surge, but for the wrong analytic reasons. And you all can sort out—historians that you are—which of the two it's better to be. I would say it's better to be right for the wrong reasons than wrong for the right reasons.

Part 2

Chapter 9

How the "Surge" Came to Be

Stephen Hadley, Meghan O'Sullivan,
and Peter Feaver

The new strategy for Iraq that President George
W. Bush announced on January 10, 2007, shocked the country. The Iraq Study
Group chaired by former secretary of state James Baker and former congressman Lee Hamilton had just released its report a few weeks earlier. Many people had read that report as a call to scale back US objectives in Iraq and to
accelerate the withdrawal of American forces there. Instead, President Bush
doubled down. He announced a "surge" of almost thirty thousand additional
troops and, more importantly, a change in strategy. US troops would have
population security as their number one mission. This would require that
they be embedded with Iraqi security forces and deployed out among the
Iraqi people to protect them from terrorists, insurgents, and sectarian violence. This new security strategy would underpin a renewed effort to achieve
Iraqi political accommodation and ultimately a more sustainable relationship
between the United States and Iraq.

Despite congressional efforts to derail the surge, as the additional troops
were deployed and the new strategy was implemented, violence declined
dramatically. Soon it was at a level that could be managed by the Iraqi security forces largely on their own. The political process resumed. And a war
that most people thought lost was turned around.

In this chapter, we lay out the steps President Bush and his national
security team (on which we all served) took to assess the situation in Iraq,

determine a new course of action, and then persuade the rest of the government and the country to give this new course of action a chance to succeed. We cannot answer every important question about the Iraq War, but we do hope to answer the question that confronted President Bush in 2006: how can the United States shift the trajectory of a failing and unpopular war and find a path to success—all while avoiding a constitutional crisis? Against all odds, President Bush found a satisfactory answer to that question, but it was a long and tortuous process.

Why Was the "Surge" Needed?

The United States and its coalition of over thirty-five countries invaded Iraq because of serious concerns that Iraq's president, Saddam Hussein, was actively pursuing weapons of mass destruction (WMD), including nuclear weapons. As is now well known, the intelligence underpinning these concerns was wrong. Once coalition forces captured Saddam Hussein and the regime's archives, it became evident that the Iraqi WMD program was far less advanced than had been feared. Indeed, Saddam had apparently destroyed the stocks of chemical weapons, weaponizable chemical and biological agents, and delivery vehicles that he was known to have at the end of the Gulf War. Saddam was interested in and planning to reconstitute his WMD program when conditions allowed. But he was frustrating the demands of the international community to come clean about the WMD capability he was supposed to have destroyed under United Nations supervision out of fear that Iran would read Iraq's disarmament as weakness.

It is wholly legitimate to debate what the right course of action would have been had accurate information been available to policy makers. But the invasion of Iraq was a reasonable course of action, given what leaders and policy makers believed to be true at the time. Saddam's record of using WMD against his neighbors (Iran) and his own people (the Kurds), his invasion of Iran and then Kuwait, and his repeated threats against the United States and his neighbors (including Saudi Arabia and Israel) made his regime a serious source of instability in the region. Particularly in the wake of 9/11, American policy makers were reluctant to rely on deterrence if and when Saddam did acquire nuclear weapons and resumed his production of other WMD. They were concerned that Saddam not only might use weapons of mass destruction against his neighbors (again) but also might pass them to terrorist groups. Given the damage done by nineteen terrorists armed only with box cutters on 9/11—killing over three thousand people from over eighty countries—this was a risk that US officials were not willing to take.

Moreover, the international sanctions that had limited the resources at Saddam's disposal for such endeavors were fraying. Countries imposing the sanctions—even several on the UN Security Council—were dismayed by the humanitarian toll created by the sanctions and Saddam's manipulation of them. Many were also eager to resume normal business relations with Iraq.

Although WMD was central to the argument to go into Saddam Hussein's Iraq, it was not the only reason why many American and foreign policy makers supported military action against Iraq. Saddam had supported and financed terrorism. He had invaded his neighbors (Iran and Kuwait). He had brutally oppressed his own people, murdering tens of thousands—and by some counts even more. Iraq was in violation of sixteen UN Security Council Resolutions, despite a dozen years in which the United Nations, the United States, and other like-minded states had sought to obtain Saddam's compliance. They had deployed an extensive sanctions regime, three separate inspections regimes, no-fly zones over the northern and southern parts of Iraq, selective use of military power (under President Clinton in 1998), and various ultimatums. Nothing worked.

With the removal of Saddam Hussein in 2003 and the return of sovereignty to the Iraqis under the Iraqi Interim Government on June 28, 2004, it could be argued that the United States had achieved its national security objectives. Iraq would no longer be a threat to international peace and security: it would no longer pursue weapons of mass destruction, support terrorism, invade its neighbors, or brutalize its people as Saddam Hussein had done.

The aftermath of the invasion, however, had not worked out as the Bush administration had planned. Iraq proved much more difficult to stabilize than policy makers had anticipated. Thirty years of war, economic mismanagement, and repression—coupled with Saddam's plans to wreak havoc after his removal—made the challenges in Iraq particularly acute. But they were also exacerbated by some early miscalculations made by the Bush administration both about policy and resources. The United States learned a hard lesson in Iraq, which, regrettably, has been repeated elsewhere since: any vacuum created by the removal of a Middle Eastern regime will be exploited by extremists and outside powers, creating new security and other challenges.

For this reason, the removal of Saddam proved insufficient to meet the security objectives of the United States and its allies and partners in the region. Iraq also needed to be stabilized. The region needed an Iraq that could "govern itself, sustain itself, and defend itself," as President Bush put it in numerous speeches. Helping Iraqis build a representative government was a critical element in this vision for Iraq.

The United States did not, contrary to the beliefs of many, seek to impose democracy on Iraq or hope to create a Jeffersonian democracy on the shores of the Tigris and Euphrates Rivers. Rather, the impetus to help Iraqis create a representative government stemmed from two considerations. First, after decades of dictatorship, Iraqis made clear that they wanted a political system that would hold their rulers accountable. Second, in a country as fractious and divided as Iraq, with so many disparate groups (Sunni, Shia, Kurds, Turkomans, and various other minorities), the question was how to ensure stability. The only system that could ensure both accountability and stability was one that was inclusive of all groups, had checks and balances embedded in multiple institutions, and offered protection for minorities—key elements of a democratic state.

If there was to be a democracy in Iraq, the Iraqi people would have to build it. It would reflect the unique history, culture, and experience of the country. The United States could not impose a democracy upon them, build it for them, or guarantee that it would succeed. If it succeeded, however, it would prove that Iraq's various groups could work together in a democratic framework to build a common future. This would be a powerful example for the region.

The goal of an Iraq that could "govern itself, defend itself, and sustain itself" remained out of reach in 2004, 2005, and 2006. Despite elections, a peaceful transition of power, and the creation and approval of a constitution in 2005, Iraqi progress began to falter. Violence began to overwhelm even the best Iraqi efforts to construct a different and better future for their country. Al-Qaeda in Iraq (AQI), under the leadership of Abu Musab al-Zarqawi, began pursuing a diabolical strategy. It brutally attacked Shia in order to provoke retaliation against Sunnis. By this tactic, it hoped to touch off a civil war that would defeat the coalition-backed government in Baghdad, drive out American forces, and open the door to creation of the long-cherished dream of an Islamic caliphate—which AQI would control.

The Iraqi population was not predisposed to sectarian violence. Indeed, for almost two years the Shia population showed considerable restraint under the courageous leadership of Ayatollah Sistani. But that restraint was increasingly giving way as Iraqi leaders and the US-led coalition proved unable to provide security to Iraqi neighborhoods. After the bombing of a Shia shrine in Samarra on February 22, 2006, whatever restraint remained collapsed. Shia militia (especially those led by Muqtada al-Sadr) escalated their activities, responded in kind, and sectarian violence took off. By the end of that year, the country watched as Baghdad descended into chaos. The unity government that had emerged five months after the successful national election in December 2005 was unable to calm the situation. The political process of national reconciliation stalled. Sectarian groups began to look to their own survival as they prepared for sectarian war. The Iraq project was foundering.

What Was the "Surge"?

The "surge" is generally understood as the deployment to Iraq of 20,000 to 30,000 US troops in 2007 to supplement the roughly 160,000 already there. More importantly, however, it reflected a change in strategy in how US forces would be used. They would deploy with Iraqi military and police units and live out among the Iraqi people rather than on US military bases. Their priority would be to help Iraqi forces provide security for the Iraqi people. The "surge" in US troops would be accompanied by a "surge" in US civilian presence to help build Iraqi governmental institutions not only top-down from the national level but also and especially bottom-up from the provincial and local level. The anticipated improved security environment would be the foundation for more lasting and fundamental political compromises aimed at resolving the roots of violence in Iraqi society. These compromises had proven too difficult to achieve in the midst of escalating violence, which reinforced a zero-sum political mentality. What was needed was a "bridge" from the Hobbesian state of nature in which Iraq found itself to a more secure environment that would permit and encourage reconciliation and institution building.

The surge would also create more time and a better environment in which to build Iraqi security forces. Earlier efforts—in which Iraqi forces did not show up or fight, or were sectarian actors themselves—demonstrated the need for closer partnering with US soldiers in the field. Over time, Iraqi forces would gain experience and capability while helping to bring the fighting down to a residual level of violence that the thus improved Iraqi security forces could handle. That would allow them eventually to assume full responsibility for the security of their country.

President Bush's decision to launch the surge ended a major strategic debate within his administration. In particular, the surge decision resolved an internal debate about six crucial assumptions undergirding the pre-surge Iraq strategy:

- US strategy to this point had assumed that political progress would help isolate extremists and strengthen moderates—thereby driving security gains. It had become clear, however, that while this could be true over the long term, in the short run the lack of security prevented such political progress. ("Sometimes a security problem is a security problem.")

- There had been a largely unresolved internal debate as to the underlying causes of the conflict. The prior strategy had been developed when the main driver of violence in Iraq was a Sunni-led insurgency. Later, this insurgency attracted al-Qaeda, which took over the movement. The insurgency and AQI were undoubtedly the driving forces of violence in 2003, 2004, and 2005. But this reality began to change in 2005 and had certainly been altered by 2006, when the main source of violence had become sectarian fighting. The challenge for policy makers was to come up with a strategy that was effective against the insurgency, AQI, and sectarian fighting—all three elements fueling the violence. ("We needed a strategy that would work effectively against all causes of the violence.")

- The prior strategy had assumed that, because the insurgency was the dominant source of violence, US forces in Iraq were the main provocation for extremists. So the solution to the violence was to transfer security responsibility to the Iraqi security forces as soon as possible and draw down US forces. It became clear, however, that as sectarian violence became the more dominant element of the conflict, Iraqis increasingly viewed US forces more positively, largely because they were "neutral" in the sectarian struggle. US forces ultimately became essential to providing security reassurance to the various sectarian communities and avoiding an outright civil war. ("US forces aren't the security problem, they are the solution to the security problem.")

- Relatedly, the prior strategy had assumed that Iraqi forces would be useful in tamping down violence from any source—including sectarian violence. The Iraqi army proved on the whole to be helpful; its units had been painstakingly formed and trained to be national in nature. They were largely integrated, with Sunni, Shia, and Kurds throughout their ranks. Other components of the Iraqi forces—particularly the police, which had not been reconstituted after Saddam's removal—were instead viewed as highly sectarian and untrustworthy. ("The Iraqi forces were part of the sectarian problem.")

- The prior strategy had assumed that even at the risk of failure, the United States had to turn over full security responsibility to the Iraqi security forces. It was better to err on the side of transferring responsibility too quickly, rather than doing so too slowly. Otherwise Iraqi forces would become too dependent on US support and would never learn to stand on their own. It became clear, however, that the president was unwilling to take that risk and "gamble" with failure. ("You can take your hand off the bicycle seat and see if Iraq can ride on its own—but you can't let the bicycle fall over.")

- The prior strategy had assumed a limited and ever-waning tolerance of the American people for involvement in Iraq. It turned out, however, that the public would support deploying additional troops if the deployment was part of a new strategy that could produce success. As the strategy showed progress, the American people would give it more time. ("We had to buy back American confidence and support drink by drink, one success at a time.")

How Was the Surge Developed?

The essential feature of the decision-making process that produced the surge was that from the beginning President Bush was at the center of the process. It was designed to provide the president with facts, analysis, and opinions from a wide variety of sources that would allow him to be comfortable and confident making one of the most important decisions of his presidency.

But the surge also required the personal effort of President Bush. He had to lay the bureaucratic, diplomatic, and political groundwork for the surge and put in place the key elements that allowed the surge to succeed. We assess thirteen factors to be central to the success of the process:

1. *The president decided that the United States needed fundamentally to rethink its strategy in Iraq.* The administration evaluated the progress of the effort in Iraq on almost a daily basis and made incremental changes as needed. But by early in 2006, President Bush had become extremely uncomfortable with the trajectory of events in Iraq and had begun questioning the soundness of US strategy. In the following months, he came to believe that a fundamental reassessment of that strategy was needed—albeit done in a way that would not undermine the war effort in the interim. Each morning, President Bush would read two important documents before the start of his day. The first was the overnight casualty report. The second was a daily note written by the NSC staff Iraq team on the political, diplomatic, economic, and military events occurring in Iraq that day. At one point in May 2006, while reading these reports, President Bush looked up and said, "Hadley, this strategy isn't working." When National Security Advisor Stephen Hadley agreed, the president said, "We need to develop a new one." That started the process that resulted in the surge decision announced by the president in January 2007.

The urgency of the effort was underscored when the president asked Meghan O'Sullivan, the deputy national security advisor for Iraq and Afghanistan, how her friends in Baghdad were feeling. She replied that they have "never been so scared" or so pessimistic about their future. This moved the president. O'Sullivan had good contacts in Iraq from her prior service there and was a strong supporter of the US and coalition efforts. If she was worried, the president was worried.

2. *The president personally authorized the strategy review.* President Bush and his national security team met at Camp David in June 2006 to assess progress in Iraq. While there was widespread unease with the situation, the recent death of AQI leader Zarqawi and the formation of the new Iraqi government after months of stalemate gave some reason to hope that things could be turned around. General George Casey and the US ambassador in Baghdad, Zalmay Khalilzad, made the case for a renewed effort under the old strategy. Throughout the summer of 2006, the coalition executed Operation Together Forward I and Together Forward II to try to change the dynamics on the ground.

But the situation was so dire that, while the operations were unfolding in Baghdad, the NSC staff—with the president's knowledge—began a quiet effort to envision and develop the content of a possible broader strategic review. Soon after, Secretary of Defense Donald Rumsfeld authorized the Joint Staff to conduct its own review of Iraq strategy. Secretary of State Condoleezza Rice gave the same direction to her staff.

These reviews were conducted in parallel throughout the summer of 2006, but each was cognizant of the others at the principal level. The initial internal review by the NSC staff was held very closely. It was led by O'Sullivan and included John Hannah (national security advisor to the vice president), Peter Feaver (special advisor for strategic planning and institutional reform), Brigadier General Kevin Bergner (senior director for Iraq), and Brett McGurk (director for Iraq). Their mandate was to make a comprehensive and fresh evaluation of the existing strategy, examining the assumptions that had underpinned that strategy since 2004 and considering alternatives that had hitherto been deemed out of bounds for one reason or another. In addition, they were to develop alternative courses of action, identifying the strengths and weaknesses of each. While they sought to make the best case for each option, they concluded that the "surge" option—which they dubbed "double down"—had the best chance of success. Their assessment was based on the changed realities in Iraq—principally, that sectarianism had become the main driver of violence. As noted earlier, this effectively repositioned coalition forces from being almost parties to the conflict to more of a neutral third force.

In September 2006 the NSC and State review teams, along with a representative of Vice President Cheney's office, began to meet together to consider and refine the options developed by the NSC staff study. In October, Hadley asked deputy national security advisor J. D. Crouch separately to task NSC senior director Bill Luti (a former Pentagon planner) to analyze what a surge option would look like and how many US forces it would require. The purpose of this exercise was to make a judgment about whether adequate US forces were available to mount an effective surge option and complement the work of O'Sullivan's team. Luti came back with a concept requiring five additional brigade combat teams, which he believed were available from existing forces (but not without considerable strain). Hadley shared this analysis with the vice chairman of the Joint Chiefs of Staff, Peter Pace.

Hadley had been sharing with the president the results of these informal reviews. On November 10, 2006, President Bush directed a formal interagency review of Iraq strategy to be conducted by the deputies committee, chaired by J. D. Crouch. The deputies committee brought together the deputy secretaries and deputy heads of the relevant national security departments and agencies. The president announced the review during a meeting with the vice president, the secretaries of state and defense, the White House chief of staff, the chairman of the Joint Chiefs of Staff (JCS), the director of national intelligence, and Hadley and Crouch. President Bush thus put his personal imprimatur on the review. He would be its principal customer. This fact gave the review priority and importance within the interagency and with the NSC principals.

3. *The initial individual strategy reviews were kept separate and conducted in secret.* There were upsides and downsides to this approach. On the upside, early public acknowledgment that some form of review was under way would have undermined and discredited the existing strategy. It would have risked collapsing or at least damaging the ongoing effort in Iraq before the new strategy could be developed and put in place. It would have risked demoralizing our coalition allies, especially the Iraqis. It would have raised questions about America's staying power, given domestic pressures to withdraw US troops. It would have emboldened the enemy. Al-Qaeda in particular would have sought to increase American combat deaths and casualties in order to influence US public opinion to favor withdrawal. And early public disclosure would have created uncertainty in the minds of US troops deployed in Iraq and in the minds of their families back home.

Because the initial strategy reviews were so closely held, they never leaked. The president retained the maximum range of choice, including sticking with the existing strategy, had he chosen to do so. By mid-November, however, the secret reviews had yielded enough sound ideas that the president was confident that he would have good options to consider. Accordingly, the administration acknowledged the existence of the formal interagency review but gave the team strict instructions not to leak ongoing deliberations.

Keeping the early strategy reviews separate allowed each of the teams to conduct its own assessments. This gave each NSC principal an independent basis from which to participate in the formal interagency review. As the separate strategy reviews matured, gradually there was more informal cross-pollination, until they were pulled together and different courses of action debated in the formal interagency review led by the deputy national security advisor, Crouch.

The downsides of the early compartmentalization were that it slowed the process and denied each review the benefits of what was being learned in the others. The State Department, for instance, developed its recommendations without being aware at the staff level that there might be a way to generate additional US forces to resource a surge option. The NSC team was not privy to the details of the work of the JCS team until late in the autumn of 2006. Even then, there was important work being done in the Pentagon (like the work of the so-called Council of Colonels) that never reached the interagency, as it might have in a more regular process. The Office of the Secretary of Defense played only a marginal role until much later in the process.

The launch of the formal interagency review solved some of these problems but not all. At levels below the president, particularly at the sub-cabinet level, where much of the analytic work was being done, there were serious doubts even as late as mid-December as to whether the president would embrace a surge option. That was not altogether a bad thing, however. It kept the process honest—and it protected the president's options.

4. *Information came to the president from a wide variety of sources.* There were of course the "official" channels: intelligence briefings, military assessments, diplomatic reports, meetings with members of Congress, conversations with Iraqis and other foreign leaders, and memos from the president's NSC staff. But the president's chief of staff and national security advisor did not seek to be "information gatekeepers" and did not feel threatened by information flows from less official sources. Rather, they encouraged and facilitated "unfiltered" information from "outside the system" getting to the president. This could include advice and counsel from outside experts, columnists

and opinion writers, and members of the general public—including people standing in rope lines.

Vice President Cheney, Hadley, and the NSC staff in particular reached out widely to solicit the views of regional and military experts, and Republican and Democrats alike. Many outside voices offered insightful critiques, but the work of the team at the American Enterprise Institute (AEI) under the leadership of General (retired) Jack Keane and Fred Kagan was especially helpful as an external validation of ideas, concepts, and conclusions reached independently by the internal reviews.

5. *The deputies-level strategy review produced a full range of options that were debated at the highest levels.* J. D. Crouch and the NSC deputies conducted a comprehensive review of the then-current strategy. The deputies review included a hard-eyed look at the present situation in Iraq, identified what had changed and what had not, reexamined key assumptions, and developed options. The results of their work were fed directly to the president and the NSC principals, who in turn gave guidance for further work.

The Defense Department, including the Joint Chiefs of Staff, basically favored continuing if not accelerating the handover of security responsibility to Iraqi forces, with US forces in "overwatch" mode and gradually drawing down. The State Department felt the United States needed to step back from the conflict, avoid direct involvement in Iraq's sectarian "civil war," focus on protecting Iraq's key democratic institutions, and let the violence in Baghdad burn itself out—stepping in only if necessary to prevent sectarian genocide. While this reflected the positions of the principal NSC departments and agencies, it did not represent the full range of realistic options. Hadley met with the deputies on November 17, 2006, and told them, "You have got to give the president the option of a surge in forces." That option was then added, drawing on the work of the original NSC staff review.

This step was consistent with Hadley's view of the national security advisor as "honest broker" of the interagency process. He was not putting his "finger on the scales" and prejudging the outcome of the review process; but his responsibility as national security advisor was to ensure that the president would be presented with a full range of reasonable options. Without a surge option, what would ultimately have been presented to the president would have been incomplete. At the same time, Hadley's intervention also obviously reflected the fact that he knew the president was especially interested in how this option stacked up against the new assumptions about Iraq and other alternative courses of action.

6. *The president had intense conversations with his NSC principals.* The NSC principals are the senior-level officials who are confirmed by the Senate,

testify before Congress, and administer the funds and personnel that are the instruments by which American national security and foreign policy are carried out. The NSC principals include officials such as the secretaries of state, defense, treasury, and homeland security, the attorney general, the director of national intelligence and the director of the Central Intelligence Agency, and the chairman of the Joint Chiefs of Staff. These officials needed to be involved from the outset in any major change in strategy. They not only had a wealth of experience and judgment to offer the president, but were also the ones who would be charged with carrying out the new strategy. Their buy-in was essential to ensure any new strategy would be implemented effectively and with enthusiasm.

While President Bush's instincts led him to lean toward the surge option, he wanted a rigorous process that would provide the analytical basis for any decision and would allow him to weigh all options. This process would also be an important vehicle for ensuring that his NSC principals were on board with any decision he made.

President Bush held a series of meetings with his NSC principals beginning at the very outset of the formal interagency strategy review. Some were formal NSC meetings in the Situation Room, others less formal conversations in the Oval Office in the West Wing of the White House, and some in informal settings in the family quarters of the White House residence. This approach allowed the president to get information from various configurations of officials in a variety of settings.

President Bush held a particularly intensive set of meetings with the NSC principals during the first week of December 2006. Sometimes holding two meetings on Iraq in one day, President Bush and his NSC principals considered a wide variety of proposals and assessments, gradually concluding which options could be expected to produce the desired results. For example, in one early meeting the president and the NSC principals considered a paper posing the question of whether the United States should take on responsibility for helping Iraqis quell sectarian violence. Debate was vigorous over whether American forces could achieve this goal, and over various assessments about the ability of Iraqi forces to handle the challenges in the absence of coalition help. After much deliberation and discussion, President Bush decided that the United States would undertake a mission aimed at least in part at helping bring down sectarian violence. This was but one of the many issues debated and discussed, and it moved the conversation closer to a surge-like approach.

In these meetings, President Bush actively gathered information and opinions that would inform his decisions. But he could also be seen as bringing individual NSC principals along in the direction he was moving, as incremental decisions gradually narrowed the options in favor of the surge. Vice President Cheney, Chief of Staff Josh Bolten, and National Security Advisor Hadley were already favorably inclined toward the surge. Secretary of State Rice had to be convinced that the surge troops would be doing something different from what the troops already in Iraq had been doing—and that this new approach had a good chance of changing the situation on the ground. The military was probably the most reluctant, favoring the continued transfer of security responsibility to Iraqi forces. They were concerned that the Iraqi government of Prime Minister Nouri al-Maliki was not a reliable partner, but would instead seek to leverage increased US support to pursue narrow sectarian aims. And they feared that an increase in US troop levels would lead to a spike in casualties and strain US military forces to the breaking point. President Bush sought to address these concerns during the review process.

7. *The president brought Prime Minister Maliki along.* The US military was concerned that Maliki and his government were not interested in advancing the interests of Iraq as a whole but were more narrowly focused on promoting a Shia agenda. After the Samarra mosque bombing, the escalating sectarian violence had led to extensive de facto ethnic cleansing in Baghdad. The population had separated along sectarian lines, producing neighborhoods that were increasingly either Sunni or Shia. And predominantly Sunni areas were being denied government services. The question was whether this was the result of a conscious policy on the part of the Iraqi national government. In addition, US forces reported that the targeting information provided by the Iraqi government was all on Sunni perpetuators of violence—at a time when both Sunni and Shia actors were engaged in sectarian killings. Was Maliki a sectarian leader pursuing a Shia agenda? Or was he a leader who wanted to be cross-sectarian but simply lacked the institutional capability to carry out a more inclusive strategy? Or was he a leader who was simply out of touch and did not know what was going on in his own country?

At the end of October 2006, President Bush sent Hadley, O'Sullivan, and Feaver to Baghdad to try to answer these questions. They met with Prime Minister Maliki, other Iraqi officials, American diplomats, and military personnel from four-star generals to battalion commanders. Their conclusions were summarized in a memorandum to the president later leaked to the *New York Times* on November 30, 2006, the day before President Bush and Prime Minister Maliki were to meet in Amman, Jordan. They recommended that President Bush test the hypothesis that Maliki was more a leader who lacked institutional capability than a Shia-favoring sectarian. The memo outlined a series of steps that the United States and its coalition partners could take in exchange for appropriate cross-sectarian steps by Maliki. If he was willing to take these steps, President Bush could be more confident that Maliki—at least at that time—was willing to be a national leader, not just a Shia sectarian.

President Bush made his own assessment in his meeting with Maliki in Amman on November 30. He concluded that he could work with Maliki and could persuade him to move forward with a nonsectarian surge. In that meeting, Maliki presented his plan for quelling the violence. But when asked privately by President Bush, General Casey confided that the Iraqis did not have the military capability to execute the plan. President Bush then used the opportunity to urge Maliki to accept additional US forces, while contributing more Iraqi forces to the fight.

Maliki reluctantly agreed. On December 21, in a meeting with Secretary of Defense Robert Gates in Baghdad, Maliki formally agreed to accept two additional US brigade combat teams. By the time the surge got under way, and despite Maliki's reluctance, that number had been increased to five. And Maliki agreed to commit additional Iraqi brigades to match the additional brigade combat teams being committed by the United States.

Up to this point, coalition military operations had been hampered by restrictions imposed by the Iraqi central government (which, for example, barred operations in Shia areas of Baghdad like Sadr City) and political interventions seeking release of Shia suspects detained by US forces. This had to stop. If the surge was to succeed, it would have to be carried out on a strictly nonsectarian basis.

President Bush believed that a public commitment from Maliki to this effect was in many ways a prerequisite for his own decision to authorize the surge. He made this point to Maliki during secure video teleconferences between the two leaders on December 9 and 15, 2006, and again on January 4, 2007. Such a commitment would mean much more than simply putting Maliki on the record; it would require him to do something courageous and irreversible: take on the political party of Muqtada al-Sadr that had been critical in making him prime minister. Given that Sadr's militia were the main source of perpetuated Shia violence, there was no half way. If Maliki made the commitments that President Bush requested of him, he would be forced to turn to a different kind of politics—one aligned against sectarianism and committed to the defeat of one of the largest purveyors of it.

After an earlier first attempt at the end of December, on January 6, 2007, Prime Minister Maliki made a strong, nonsectarian speech to the Iraq people. Maliki had committed that any future military operation would be carried out on a nonsectarian basis. There would be no safe havens; Sadr City would no longer be off limits; Shia militia would be dealt with on the same basis as

Sunni militants; and Maliki and his staff would not intervene politically as military operations progressed. Four days later, on January 10, 2007, President Bush announced the surge in a televised speech to the American people.

The US administration was now clearly committed to Maliki. The process of coming up with a prime minister in the spring of 2006 had been painful and protracted. No one wanted to go through that process again. And President Bush was confident that he could bring Maliki along as a national Iraqi leader. He scheduled a secure video teleconference with the prime minister about every other week. They would discuss the problems each faced, and President Bush would offer counsel and encouragement. Bush was now "all in" with the surge, but so was Maliki—and the success of the surge depended heavily on the United States. Bush's approach to Maliki was that the two leaders were "in this together"—they would either succeed or fail together. Maliki seemed to respond positively, and the conversations seemed to suppress any sectarian impulses he may have had during this period.

8. *The president brought his military commanders along.* President Bush understood that a split in wartime on military strategy between the president as commander in chief and the military leadership was a serious constitutional crisis. The nation's experiences with such crises under President Lincoln during the Civil War and under President Truman during the Korean War were not happy ones. President Bush wanted the senior military leadership, including the Joint Chiefs of Staff and Generals John Abizaid and George Casey (the Middle East regional commander and in-theater commander in Iraq, respectively), to be on board with any decision he made. The president understood that he could simply order the change in strategy and expect his commanders to "salute" and obey. But he also understood that doing so would impose a great strain on his relations with the military. In addition, a surge decision would not be popular. Congress would use any split with the military—or split within the military—as ammunition in an effort to try to prevent a surge from being carried out.

Bringing the senior military leadership along depended critically on the ability of President Bush and his national security advisor Hadley to work with the chairman of the Joint Chiefs of Staff Peter Pace—and on Pace's ability to work with the rest of the Joint Chiefs to make sure their concerns were adequately addressed. This is why President Bush and Vice President Cheney (accompanied by Hadley and White House chief of staff Bolten) met with Secretary of Defense Donald Rumsfeld, Secretary of Defense–designate Robert Gates, and the Joint Chiefs of Staff on December 13, 2006, in the chiefs' conference room—"the tank"—at the Pentagon.

Two of the three concerns that the military had with a surge option were already being addressed. First, President Bush had already secured commitments from Prime Minister Maliki that any surge would go forward on a nonsectarian basis. Second, the chiefs had been pressing for any military surge to be accompanied by a "civilian surge" of personnel drawn from the State Department and other US government departments and agencies. This issue had been addressed in J. D. Crouch's deputies review. A civilian surge had been incorporated into the surge option they were developing, just as the military had requested.

The discussion in the tank therefore centered heavily on the third concern: the impact of the surge on the morale and readiness of the US armed forces themselves, particularly the Army and the Marine Corps. The leaders of these two services argued that a surge would "break the force" and demoralize the troops and their families. They would face the prospect of seemingly endless combat rotations, with too little time at home. President Bush responded that while he understood the problem, what really broke a military force was losing a war—implying that without a surge, that is what would happen in Iraq. The chiefs suggested that the American people and the Congress would not support a surge. President Bush replied that managing the politics was his job, not theirs.

But the concerns about the health and welfare of the armed forces were clearly valid. It was wholly appropriate for the Joint Chiefs to raise them. Indeed, to do otherwise would have been a breach of the duty they owed both the president and the American men and women in uniform. President Bush understood this and had already identified a way to mitigate the strain. Peter Feaver and Lisa Disbrow, the NSC staff's special advisor for implementation and execution, had already conducted the necessary analysis months earlier. So the president already knew a realistic increase in end strength was possible that would help alleviate in later years the strain a surge would cause on the force in the short run. He therefore offered to accompany any surge with a request to the Congress for a temporary increase in the end strengths of the Army and the Marine Corps. That helped reassure the chiefs.

Once President Bush announced the surge, the military leadership was on board. Their concerns had largely been addressed. The Joint Chiefs of Staff and the incoming and outgoing regional and in-theater commanders were all in the surge boat. Some leaned right, some leaned left, and not everyone was happy. But President Bush had skillfully avoided a split within the military and a constitutional crisis between the military heads and their commander in chief.

9. *The president required a military and political strategy to be devised in tandem.* The president and his national security team understood that the ultimate goal behind a strategy change was not simply to bring down the violence, but to do so in order to create the circumstance for significant and sustainable political compromises about how to share power and resources among Iraqis. Although the surge relied on the idea that greater security would be required before such compromises could be made, the new strategy carefully considered how the various components of the strategy could lay the groundwork for and encourage political compromise. In particular, the strategy considered how the surge could help strengthen the moderate political forces in Iraq at the expense of the extremist ones; how it could create incentives or imperatives for Iraqi leaders to identify themselves as nationalist rather than sectarian politicians; and how to marginalize the meddling of external actors in Iraqi politics. The new strategy also realigned US assets so that coalition military and civil personnel could work more seamlessly together to ensure that the political and military components of the strategy complemented one another.

10. *The president seized opportunity in Anbar Province.* The surge of five US brigade combat teams and change in strategy were designed first and foremost to deal with the greatest challenge facing Iraq—the tsunami of sectarian violence engulfing its capital. General Casey used to say that almost 80 percent of Iraq's sectarian violence occurred within one hundred kilometers of Baghdad. The people of Iraq were watching their capital descend into chaos.

President Bush could have left the surge right there, focused on saving Baghdad. Instead he decided to take advantage at the same time of the greatest opportunity in Iraq. This was in Anbar Province, located in the Sunni heartland of western Iraq. A senior US Marine intelligence officer had declared Anbar lost to AQI some months before. But the local Sunni tribes there, suffering under al-Qaeda occupation and brutality, had begun to organize against the terrorist group.

In September 2006, Anbari tribes launched a movement they called Sahwa. It came to be known in the coalition as the "Sunni Awakening." The Anbari tribes began to push back against al-Qaeda and enlisted some support from local US forces. It was still the early days, but those involved or closely watching Iraq saw the potential of a major strategic shift.

J. D. Crouch had traveled to Anbar Province, Mosul, and Basra in the fall of 2006 as part of the internal NSC review process. He was heartened by what he saw. But the Anbari tribes needed more US military support if they were to succeed. This support would not just enhance their military capability but would give tangible evidence of American political support.

President Bush wanted to reassure the tribes that they could count on the backing of the United States. With this American reassurance, they would have the confidence to continue their revolt against AQI. The president ordered several US Marine battalions into Anbar Province. These forces were in addition to the five brigade combat teams designated largely for Baghdad. The Marine battalions were to link up with the Sunni tribes in Anbar and provide them with training, equipment, operational planning, intelligence, and close air support. The Marines also offered assurances, backed by commitments from the Iraqi government, that when the fight was over, the Sunni tribes would not be abandoned by Baghdad. They would be given the opportunity to integrate into the Iraqi army, the Iraqi police, and otherwise have jobs in a unified Iraq in which Sunni, Kurds, and Shia would be full participants.

The effort paid off. The "Sunni Awakening" defeated AQI and restored Iraqi government control in Anbar Province. This success also aided the effort to reduce the violence in Baghdad, since much of the illicit weaponry flooding into Baghdad was coming from Anbar. Regrettably, the Iraqi government gradually backed away from the commitments of jobs and inclusion that had been made to the Sunni tribes. This in part explains why ISIS was able to take over the province in late 2013 and 2014 with so little local resistance.

11. *The president was the chief communicator and took responsibility for past failures and for his new strategy.* In his speech announcing the surge, President Bush took personal responsibility for the failures of strategy and policy in Iraq. He explained why the effort in Iraq was critical to the security of the United States. He described his new strategy in some detail. He called on Congress to authorize the temporary increase in the size of the Army and Marine Corps. And he asked the American people to stay with the Iraq project and support the surge.

This speech, and the presidential commitment it represented, were crucial to the success of the surge. As President Bush often told his staff, in time of war a president needs to be explaining constantly why the nation is engaged in the fight, what is the government's strategy, and why the American people can be confident that it will succeed. The enemy, America's friends and allies, and the American men and women serving in harm's way and their families all need to hear this message over and over again. And all need to know that the president is determined to press on to victory.

This was also important for a bureaucratic reason. With a war going poorly and a major bet being made on a new strategy, all eyes around the NSC table in the Situation Room were on the president. If he had shown indecision or hesitation—or lack of confidence in the effort or the strategy—it would have undermined the confidence of everyone around the table. His NSC principals, returning to their respective departments and agencies, could not have helped but reflect that lack of confidence within their organizations. Subordinates would have been asked to develop "fallback plans." Morale would have fallen. Eventually this lack of confidence would have crept out to the men and women in the field. That would have put the entire Iraq mission at risk.

When the nation is being asked to do hard things, often it is the sheer force of will of the president and the president's intrinsic power to persuade the American people that hold the effort together.

At the same time, there must be a realistic basis for the president's confidence. At one point, as he was going over the draft of the surge speech, President Bush looked up and said: "Hadley, do you think this surge strategy is going to work?" Hadley responded: "Mr. President, I think it will, but I do think it's our last chance to get this right." President Bush replied: "Good. If you ever decide that you think the strategy cannot work, you need to come and tell me, because I can't keep putting young men and women in harm's way if we don't have a strategy that we think is going to succeed." President Bush was soliciting the kind of bad news that a president, as invested as he was in Iraq, would never want to hear and that most people would be reluctant to bring to the president. But President Bush was saying: "That's the news I need to hear." It spoke well for his abiding concern for the country and particularly his overriding concern for those of its sons and daughters that his decisions had put in harm's way.

12. *The president announced new leadership.* To execute the new strategy, the president changed his team at home, with a new secretary of defense, Robert Gates, as well as in the field. The regional commander, CENTCOM commander General John Abizaid, and the in-theater Iraq commander, General George Casey, had agreed to President Bush's earlier requests to extend past their normal rotation dates. President Bush used the occasion of the surge decision to rotate in their successors. Admiral William Fallon took over CENTCOM, and General David Petraeus took over command in Iraq. As the same time, the president sent a new US ambassador to Baghdad, Ryan Crocker.

General Petraeus was in many ways a natural choice. Both the outgoing secretary of defense, Donald Rumsfeld, and incoming secretary, Robert

Gates, recommended him for the job. Petraeus had been in Iraq both as a commander in Mosul and as head of the effort to train the Iraqi army. He had then returned to the United States to head the US Army Training and Doctrine Command, where he helped write the manual for counterinsurgency operations. This was in many ways the doctrinal basis for the surge. He had literally "written the book" for the operation.

Ambassador Crocker was one of America's most seasoned and respected diplomats. He had always undertaken the toughest and most hazardous assignments: in Pakistan, Syria, Kuwait, Lebanon, and now Iraq. He and Petraeus formed an unusual partnership. They were "joined at the hip." This was essential, for the surge required an integrated and closely coordinated political and military effort. The two performed superbly.

They were aided by the fact that even before they had arrived, General Ray Odierno and other senior commanders in Iraq had been developing the operational concepts at the tactical level for implementing a surge of forces and a change in mission to population protection. The surge represented the happy convergence of both top-down strategy and policy change and bottom-up operational and tactical innovation.

13. *The president defended his strategy against Congress.* When he announced the new strategy in January 2007, President Bush knew that it was going to take time for it to unfold and to show results. It would be over five months before all the surge forces would arrive in Iraq, be fully in position, and be actively engaged in operations. The president also knew that because of the new force deployments and strategy, American casualties and deaths in Iraq would probably go up before they would go down. And the president knew that he would have to prevent skeptical elements in the Congress from strangling the surge baby in its crib.

Democrats in the House of Representatives in particular made a number of such efforts. They sought to defund the surge, requiring that no monies be spent to implement it. They sought to impose new operational constraints on the deployment and use of American forces in Iraq, which, if implemented, would have caused the surge to fail. And they sought early public hearings to draw public attention to the ongoing challenges in Iraq and to try to demonstrate that the surge was not working—even before the forces had been fully deployed.

Thankfully, most of the Republicans in the House and particularly in the Senate were willing to oppose these efforts—and the efforts failed. As the battlefield toll in Iraq mounted over the summer of 2007, political support for the surge became harder to mobilize. But the support held up just long enough. By the time General Petraeus and Ambassador Crocker returned to Washington to testify before Congress on September 10–11, 2007, the surge was beginning to show results. Violence levels were coming down. In a speech to the nation on September 13, 2007, President Bush was able to announce that some of the surge forces would not be replaced and that others would rotate back home before Christmas. US troop levels in Iraq were projected to return to pre-surge levels by July 2008.

In hindsight, it is evident that domestic politics factored in to the development of the surge, but in an unusual way. The president might have considered a change in personnel earlier in 2006. But that spring the so-called Revolt of the Generals occurred. A series of recently retired military generals came out with synchronized attacks in the media calling for Secretary of Defense Rumsfeld's removal. The president highly valued Rumsfeld's counsel and service to the administration. He also was not going to set the precedent of a wartime secretary of defense being pushed out by attacks from retired generals.

It is uncertain whether the president would have replaced Rumsfeld in the spring of 2006 but for the "Revolt of the Generals," yet their politically charged intervention hardly helped. Indeed, it may have unwittingly delayed the change until after the midterm elections that November. It is also worth noting that these critics were not recommending anything like the surge strategy. On the contrary, to the extent that they went beyond historical critique of decisions taken in 2002 and 2003, they were recommending precisely the strategy General Casey and Ambassador Khalilzad were seeking to implement.

Perhaps surprisingly, the "thumping" that his party received in the midterm elections did not cause President Bush or his senior White House staff to conclude that there was too little public support to undertake the surge. But it did convince them that the window for a surge was rapidly closing. The administration could not afford to wait and see if the existing strategy turned things around in 2007. If the president did not order the surge soon, there would be none. With the prospect of an upcoming presidential election in 2008, the political conditions would be prohibitive.

The White House staff concluded that the surge would be a heavy lift politically, but that the alternatives—particularly the strategy of hunkering down and letting the sectarian violence burn itself out—would be an even heavier and nearly impossible lift. Hunkering down would not win over any critics and would cause the remaining core base of support to collapse. While most Democrats would openly oppose the surge, they might temper their opposition, figuring that by taking the bitter medicine of the surge now, it would give them more options should they retake the White House in 2009—as they expected to do.

It is worth mentioning that these kind of political discussions almost never took place during NSC meetings in the Situation Room. President Bush was adamant that national security decisions would be made on their merits, not on domestic political considerations. But public support for the effort in Iraq was critical. The task for coordinating interagency efforts to explain Iraq policy to the public was undertaken largely by the White House chief of staff, first Andrew Card and then Josh Bolten, often at meetings held in their offices. The NSC staff members working on Iraq were told to focus strictly on proposals that would positively shift the momentum there. Indeed, once when Meghan O'Sullivan commented to President Bush about the political viability of an idea, he told her "not to worry about the politics—just help craft a strategy that can work, and I will handle the politics."

What Were the Results of the Surge?

The surge worked. It was an essential factor in changing the trajectory in Iraq for the better. Once the surge forces were fully deployed in the summer of 2007, violence in Iraq started to come down—and then came down dramatically. Sectarian violence all but ended. The results were evident as early as September. Whereas there were 3,700 civilian Iraqi deaths in December 2006, there were only 400 in October 2008. Similarly, there were 110 US military deaths in May 2007 and just 10 in October 2008.

It is often noted, correctly, that the drop in violence was the result not only of the surge and the shift in strategy that came with it, but Iraqi developments as well. This is undoubtedly the case. At least four factors also played very significant roles in dramatically bringing down the violence: (1) the so-called Sunni Awakening, which spurred similar anti-al-Qaeda movements in mixed and Shia areas as well; (2) Prime Minister Maliki's decision to go after Shia violators of the law as well as Sunni ones; (3) the decision of Muqtada al-Sadr to call for a cease-fire by his Jaysh al-Mahdi forces; and (4) the decision to confront directly malign Iranian activity in Iraq.

The intra-Shia dynamic reflected in several of these points—and the way Iran was manipulating it to undermine the US strategy—was crucially important and a major focus of analytic attention during the Iraq strategy review. Most of the outside commentary focused only on the Sunni dynamic, which was indeed important and recognized as such at the time. Yet to proponents of the surge, Sadr and the Iranians were at least as critical as potential spoilers.

What is often overlooked is the synergy between the surge and these four Iraqi developments. A strong case can be made that none of these developments would have occurred on a large scale, or even at all, in the absence of the surge.

First, as discussed above, the support given by the US forces to the Sunni Awakenings—initially in Anbar, but later elsewhere in the country—helped ensure, particularly in the early phases, that they were not extinguished by AQI as similar uprisings had been in the past. The enhanced US military presence of the surge gave these forces the confidence that they could defeat AQI. Later, constant US diplomatic engagement—from Baghdad and Washington—helped persuade a reluctant Iraqi government to accept and support the Awakenings, even though many Iraqis were reluctant to do so.

Second, as also discussed above, US engagement—by President Bush personally in particular—was absolutely essential to persuading Prime Minister Maliki to take on the Shia militia, and Muqtada al-Sadr's Jaysh al-Mahdi in particular, which had become a major source of sectarian violence in Baghdad. Maliki had become prime minister in May 2006 and owed his rise in part to the political support of Sadr. Maliki would simply not have been in a position to take on Sadr without the backing of the United States—militarily and politically—both during the surge and after. The significance of Maliki's move went beyond the security realm. Up until this time, the Shia had always competed in politics as one unified political bloc. The rupture between the prime minister and Sadr opened the door for Shia parties to run against one another for the first time—requiring them to appeal to potential voters as something more than simply being Shia.

Third, and relatedly, the cease-fire declared by Sadr in the summer of 2007 was hardly independent of the surge. From the arrival of the full contingent of surge forces until the declaration of the cease-fire, Sadr's Jaysh al-Mahdi took a persistent hammering from Iraqi and American forces working together. The cease-fire was a necessity for the survival of Sadr and his forces.

And fourth, the decrease in Iranian meddling was a direct result of the surge. The Iranians over time had increased their training and material support to various Iraqi Shia militias that were increasingly targeting and killing Americans. The Iranian Revolutionary Guard Corps (IRGC) had also increased its presence in the country. The pushback against these forces began shortly before the announcement of the surge. The change in strategy offered additional support—and the addition of the surge forces further enabled US commanders to target these militias and their IRGC patrons. Some IRGC agents were actually captured and taken into custody. Iran was told privately that continued targeting of Americans would have conse-quences for the Iranian IRGC presence in Iraq and potentially in Iran as well.

The success of the surge and related Iraqi developments cannot only be measured by the dramatic decline in violence. Part of the rationale for the surge, after all, was to reduce violence to the point where Iraqi politics could begin again to address the more systemic questions of power and resource sharing that were at the root of the violence. The Iraqis had made remark-able progress along the political front from 2003 to 2006—voting to approve a constitution and then conducting reasonably free and fair nationwide elec-tions under it. But the momentum had stalled in the face of the self-sustaining spiral of sectarian violence.

As it turned out, it took longer than hoped to revive the political momen-tum. Moreover, when political progress did come, it was not in the exact form that the Bush administration and Congress had been expecting. The long-sought-after metrics—such as an oil law or the full repealing of de-Baathification—remained elusive. But in other ways, political progress during the years immediately following the surge was equally significant.

After a lag, the much-improved security situation did provide greater space for Iraqi politics to grow out of the narrow, vicious, sectarian circles within which it had become trapped. The improvement in the political cli-mate was clearly evident in the results of the 2009 provincial council elec-tions and the conduct of the 2010 parliamentary elections. Iraqi politicians and political parties no longer organized themselves simply along sectarian or ethnic lines. Parties and coalitions emerged that touted nationalist—rather than sectarian—sentiments, and did extremely well with the Iraqi electorate. After years of devastating sectarian conflict, in a more peaceful environment, Iraqis seemed poised to build a new political future fashioned on more than the lowest common denominator.

The improved political and security situation also allowed the United States and Iraq to take important steps toward normalizing their bilateral relationship. From the legal transfer of sovereignty from the United States to Iraq in June 2004 until 2008, the legal basis for the presence of American and other coalition forces in Iraq came from the United Nations. Each year the Iraqi government sent a letter to the UN requesting the continued presence of these forces. This arrangement—which afforded all coalition forces and all contractors extensive privileges and immunities—increasingly became an irritant to the Iraqis.

During the summer of 2007, while the surge was getting under way, Presi-dent Bush sent Meghan O'Sullivan to Baghdad at the request of both Ambas-sador Crocker and General Petraeus. In addition to helping the US effort to work with the Iraqis, O'Sullivan was given a specific task by the president: to consult quietly with Iraqi leaders about the possibility of replacing the UN arrangement with a status of forces agreement (SOFA) as the legal basis for a continued US force presence. The SOFA would be supplemented by a strategic framework agreement (SFA), which would provide the basis for US-Iraqi political, economic, and security cooperation to help stabilize Iraq over the long term. The idea of the SOFA between Iraq and the United States was not new. It had been a key component of an agreement struck between the Coalition Provisional Authority and the Iraqi Governing Council on November 15, 2003. Yet, the worsening security environment had put this mutual ambition on hold until the surge.

A broad swath of Iraqi leaders—many of whom were understandably irked that the UN arrangement required the continued classification of Iraq as a "threat to international peace and security"—were very receptive to reviving the idea of the SOFA. So in September 2007, after much behind-the-scenes consultation, the Iraqi leaders came together and publicly announced their intention to seek a SOFA with the United States in the coming year.

President Bush believed that the situation in Iraq was still fragile and required a continued US military presence to make sustainable the progress that had been achieved by the surge. Yet the more secure environment put additional political pressure on Prime Minister Maliki, with many Iraqi political actors arguing that the dramatic improvement in the security situation meant that foreign troops were no longer needed.

The SOFA allowed Maliki to argue that he was normalizing Iraq's relationship with the United States, signing an agreement much like the one the United States had with more than one hundred other countries around the world. To those who were nervous that a "normal" relationship with America was not enough to ensure continued political or security progress, the SFA offered reassurance that the United States would continue to provide Iraq with extraordinary forms of diplomatic and economic—as well as security—support. The SOFA/SFA negotiations were particularly challenging, given that both the Iraqi government and Ayatollah Sistani wanted Iraq's fractious parliament to approve the agreements by a two-thirds vote.

There were extensive negotiations, not only between the Iraqi and US governments, but also among the Iraqi political parties. In order to reach the two-thirds threshold, Maliki felt that he needed the SOFA to include a specific deadline by which all US troops would be out of Iraq. The two governments explicitly discussed whether the inclusion of such a provision created an irreversible dynamic toward complete withdrawal—or whether a follow-on or replacement SOFA could be negotiated before the withdrawal deadline if all parties agreed. American lawyers advised that the deadline did not preclude such a negotiation.

President Bush was willing to draw down US troop levels based on the security situation—"conditions on the ground"—but strongly believed that Iraq needed a long-term US military presence, on the order of perhaps ten thousand to twenty thousand US troops. He was initially reluctant to set a firm date for withdrawal of US forces, but in the end he decided he needed to respect Prime Minister Maliki's political requirements. He accepted the end of 2011 as the purported deadline for the US troop withdrawal. The SOFA and the SFA were approved by the Iraqi parliament in November 2008, and both agreements were signed in December 2008.

President Bush's understanding was that Maliki was committed to negotiating a follow-on SOFA agreement before the 2011 withdrawal deadline. Indeed, at one point Maliki indicated that he could not negotiate the extension before the upcoming parliamentary election, but had every intention of doing so afterward. President Bush's NSC staff and others believed that Maliki was sincere in this regard. Under this view, the "out in 2011" provision of the SOFA agreement was more like a placeholder, pending the launch at an appropriate time of a new negotiation to extend the US troop presence—particularly if things were not going well as the 2011 withdrawal deadline approached.

There was now a clear way forward for US policy in Iraq. The surge resulted in the defeat of al-Qaeda in Iraq, brought an end to the extreme sectarian violence, and put the Iraq security forces in a position to provide for the security of their country. It also gave a boost to the political process seeking to build a more inclusive, secure, and prosperous Iraq for all its citizens. President Bush ended the war in Iraq pursuant to a surge strategy that his successor opposed and a withdrawal schedule that his successor did not negotiate but decided to accept. And President Bush left his successor with a clear way forward—at an appropriate point, negotiate an extension of the SOFA agreement to allow for a significant US military presence past 2011, continue the civilian surge working with the Iraqi government at all levels, and bolster Iraq as an ally in the broader war on terror. This was now a politically viable approach because the US effort in Iraq was no longer headed toward failure.

Could the Surge Have Come Sooner?

We have asked ourselves and one another many times whether the surge could have come sooner. Others have posed the same question. Some have suggested that the surge could and should have occurred as early as 2005. Others suggest it could have come at least by mid-2006. We think that both these suggestions are incorrect. While the surge might have been moved forward a few months, there were at least three critical prerequisites that had to be in place before any surge was likely to succeed. And they were not in place much before the announcement of the surge in January 2007.

First, a key element of the success of the surge was development of the resources and capabilities that were required for its successful execution. These resources and capabilities go well beyond the twenty to thirty thousand additional US troops sent into Iraq in 2007. Generals Abizaid and Casey, the men and women under their command, US intelligence officers, and coalition partners had skillfully developed these resources and capabilities, thus laying the foundations for the surge.

For example, by fusing intelligence with an extraordinary tempo of military operations, US special forces had decimated the leadership and key operatives of AQI. In addition, an Iraqi military force of over 350,000 had been trained in close partnership with US forces. And finally, the US Army as a whole had had to relearn the art of counterinsurgency, drawing on the lessons of Vietnam. All of this took years to accomplish, and the work was not completed much before the end of 2006.

Second, in addition to a military partner in the Iraqi security forces, the United States and the coalition needed a solid political partner in Baghdad for the surge to work. Prime Minister Maliki proved to be that partner, at least during the period of the surge. But he did not assume office until May 2006, after nearly half a year of political stalemate following the December 2005 parliamentary elections. In 2005, the Iraqi government was led by Prime Minister Ibrahim al-Jaafari, a Shia leader who did not have the confidence of the other Iraqi communities. He also had a mandate narrowly focused on the drafting and approval of a permanent Iraqi constitution. As the first Iraqi unity government taking power under that constitution, the Maliki government finally provided the United States a partner strong enough to make the tough decisions required by the surge.

Finally, the surge worked because it was based on a clear understanding of the new dynamics at play in Iraq and was designed with those in mind. Two were most important. The first new dynamic was that the main source of violence in the country was no longer an insurgency led by Sunnis bristling at the presence of foreign forces. The main source of violence was now sectarian violence. The second new dynamic was that US forces were no longer a key impetus for violence (as they might have been when the Sunni insurgency was the dominant driver of violence). As the violence became more sectarian, US forces became in fact an antidote to that violence—the only impartial "third force" able to dampen it. But these new dynamics only really came into play in 2006 and accelerated after the seating of the Maliki government in mid-2006.

In addition to these three prerequisites to the success of the surge, the enemy helped as well. Iraqis had recoiled at the brutal tactics particularly of AQI in killing innocents in order to provoke a sectarian war. AQI rule in Anbar Province had alienated the local population and set the stage for the Sunni Awakening. Iran and the Shia militia it supported had also overplayed their hands by that point. As a result, Maliki was willing to crack down on the Shia militia during the surge. Later, in March 2008, Maliki would personally lead Iraqi forces south into Basra to defeat and assert control over Iranian-backed Shia militia.

These essential elements were in place by the time the surge was announced in January 2007 but not much before then. Moreover, as described throughout this chapter, the new strategy was the result of careful deliberation, consultation, and consideration of options. Even more importantly, a successful surge required the careful and painstaking alignment of many elements in both the Iraqi and US governments. Even had Prime Minister Maliki been willing and able to agree to the surge immediately after taking office in May 2006 (a highly unlikely proposition), President Bush was not in a position to order the surge at that point. Had he done so without taking the time required to coordinate his own government and address the concerns of various US bureaucratic actors, the surge would almost certainly have failed. That process took until January of 2007.

What Happened to the Gains of the Surge?

The surge worked better than most advocates expected, and dramatically better than any of the numerous critics and opponents argued at the time. President Bush handed over to his successor an Iraq that was on a demonstrably better trajectory than it had been barely two years earlier. That new trajectory changed the US domestic politics of the Iraq War, enabling President Obama to abandon his campaign promise of a rapid withdrawal from Iraq and to shift to the slower timetable envisioned by the SOFA without paying any political price. In short, events in Iraq were headed in a generally positive direction between the end of 2008 and 2011. Not perfect by any means, with many political gains from the surge still waiting to be realized. But the United States had largely achieved its objective of an Iraq that could "govern itself, defend itself, sustain itself, and was an ally in the war on terror."

This positive trend was not irreversible, however, and in the end was disrupted by a variety of factors. The most significant was the descent of neighboring Syria into violence and an increasingly brutal and sectarian civil war. This opened the door for the resurgence of al-Qaeda affiliates in Syria in the form of ISIS. In 2014, ISIS swept across the border into Iraq. The Iraqi security forces largely fled, allowing ISIS to occupy about 40 percent of Iraq. Iraqi security forces, with the support of a renewed US military presence in Iraq, are now making considerable progress taking back their country from ISIS. But the ISIS invasion and occupation destroyed much of the progress achieved by the surge.

The second major development disrupting progress was the increasing sectarianism of Prime Minister Maliki—particularly after the withdrawal of all US military forces from Iraq at the end of 2011. By the summer of 2008, the political effort that had been revived by the surge began to show progress. However, in the years that followed, through a series of actions, Maliki alienated both the Kurds and especially the Sunnis. In addition, by politicizing the security forces, Maliki set up their collapse in Anbar Province in the face of the ISIS invasion.

Whether any of this could have been prevented if the United States had maintained a significant force presence in Iraq after the end of 2011 cannot be known. But there are good reasons to believe that a continued force presence would have seriously mitigated some of the factors that paved the way for ISIS and would have placed Iraq and the international community in a better position to respond to ISIS earlier.

First, a continued US force presence—even a small one—would have provided the United States some continued influence over Maliki. These US forces would have provided some additional military capability. In doing so, they would have given the United States grounds to maintain pressure on Maliki—as it had been doing for years—to refrain from politicizing Iraqi military appointments and intervening in its operational decisions. Even assuming that the United States would not have continued to be as successful as it had been in the past in curbing such behavior, some blunting of it would have helped.

Second, in withdrawing all US forces from Iraq at the end of 2011, the United States lost capabilities and relationships that had taken years to build. As a result, when the situation worsened to the point that President Obama decided that the United States needed to reengage in Iraq militarily, the

United States was required to rebuild these capabilities and relationships. This was a time-consuming and resource-consuming effort—and one that considerably slowed the US ability effectively to assist the Iraqis at a time when ISIS was overrunning large swaths of their country.

Finally, the full departure of US troops had a profound and negative effect on the political situation in Iraq. Since Saddam's removal in 2003, Iraqis had witnessed a contest between Iraq's old political culture—one of centralized power and authoritarian rule—and those Iraqis wanting to build a more accountable and inclusive Iraq. The United States clearly stood with the latter, and the US military presence was the clearest sign of that American commitment. The withdrawal of American forces in 2011 sent an unspoken but powerful message to Iraqis: the United States was no longer fully committed to their cause. This was a major psychological blow to those seeking to build a new Iraq, a boost to those who were happy to see Iraq return to its old political ways, and left the country open to Iran's influence without any credible and forceful counterbalance.

Some critics have tried to argue that elements of the surge strategy itself—for instance, arming the Sunni tribes and empowering Maliki—were poison pills that undermined the Iraqi government, contributing to the fragility that was vividly on display in 2014. This argument collapses under close inspection. The Sunni Awakening did not hollow out the Iraqi government; it brought a large part of the Sunni people on board the Iraqi project. It was Maliki's later decision to renege on commitments made during the surge period that produced the problems seen in 2014.

Of course, the surge did indeed empower Maliki. But while Maliki never performed exactly as American officials hoped, he was undeniably more effective and working in ways more consonant with American interests during the surge period than afterward. The combination of the surge, the high-level commitment of support and interaction from President Bush, and the effectiveness of the Petraeus-Crocker country team helped make Maliki on balance part of the solution rather than part of the problem. When US forces left and Maliki began to doubt the US commitment, he started underperforming. The surge made success possible. Later decisions, by leaders in Iraq and in the United States, made such success much less likely.

Conclusion: The Surge Decision in Context

The oral histories developed for this project have highlighted something that was obvious to participants at the time but seems less obvious to outsiders:

the surge strategy was very difficult to develop, and President Bush's decision was very difficult to make.

The new surge strategy required the president and his team to reach a series of conclusions, each one logically necessary before the next could be made. They included the following:

- That the existing strategy was not working and that a full-up review was needed going well beyond the normal policy or strategy reassessment. While some outside voices called for such a review, many were critics of the Iraq effort from the beginning. Their calls were seen as simply cover for forcing the withdrawal of US forces and abandonment of an effort in which they did not believe in the first place.
- That the existing strategy could not be rescued by trying harder or muddling through. This was not obvious. The US political and military leaders on the ground in Iraq were convinced that the existing strategy could work.
- That there was an alternate strategy that had a good chance of success. The president had to conclude that the seeming failure of the existing strategy did not mean that success was impossible. As put so well by Richard Betts: "Just because failure is unthinkable does not make success possible."
- That the additional US resources needed to implement the new strategy could be assembled. And that these resources could be obtained without doing irreparable harm to the force and without compromising other important national security interests and objectives.
- That our Iraqi partners could fulfill the higher demands that the surge strategy would place upon them. This included that the surge would proceed on a nonsectarian basis.
- That the rest of the US government could be brought to align behind the new strategy. And that it would do so despite the obvious weariness among Americans generally with the effort in Iraq.

Each of these conclusions rested on a set of analytical and political judgments that are more obvious in hindsight than they were under the conditions of uncertainty at the time of the actual review.

Moreover, reaching these judgments required most of the president's team to reverse their own strong convictions about the war. At the start of the informal review process, the president's top battlefield commander, the president's top military adviser, the president's top defense official, and the president's top diplomatic representative in Baghdad all believed that the existing strategy was working and that making a dramatic changes would be precisely the wrong step to take. Moreover, while the president's top foreign policy official came quickly to the conclusion that the existing strategy was not working, she initially believed that the surge was the wrong way forward and, if it failed, could jeopardize other key foreign policy priorities.

And reaching these judgments required the entire team to do all of this in defiance of the nearly unanimous (and loudly expressed) opinion of outside political leaders and experts. From mid-2006 on, the loudest voices outside the administration were calling for an accelerated withdrawal from Iraq. Defying that course of action required the president to have much greater confidence in the analytical foundations of the new strategy than other, less controversial strategy changes might entail.

The president presided over a decision-making process for the Iraq strategy review that did not match what is taught in academic textbooks. Yet it achieved the deeper goals that the more simplistic cookbook strategy reviews are intended to achieve. It surfaced a range of options, including options that key figures in the administration initially opposed. It subjected those options to rigorous scrutiny and cross-examination. It forged a consensus that allowed for unity of effort going forward and maximized the limited political space available for the new strategy. And it developed the new strategy without undermining the morale of the men and women risking their lives while still executing the prior strategy. One is hard pressed to think of times when the US government rose to a comparable challenge against comparable odds with comparably favorable results. And yet, in the end, it was President Bush's call. Under the circumstances, opting for the surge was an act of remarkable political courage and strategic foresight.

In hindsight, his decision has been largely vindicated. To have rejected the surge option in favor of the advice of his critics would have effectively abandoned Iraq to an even bloodier fate than what transpired in 2014. In choosing the surge, President Bush changed the trajectory of the Iraq War and created a real possibility for enduring success.

CHAPTER 10

Iraq, Vietnam, and the Meaning of Victory

ANDREW PRESTON

Beset by the problems of a failing war in a strange and distant country, the president faced a strategic dilemma. Three years into the conflict, American prospects for victory were diminishing with each passing month. It was clear to the president and virtually all his advisors that they needed to change course. But in which direction? Should he deploy more US troops to provide security and stability to a faltering ally, or should he cut his losses and find a way out of what was now essentially a civil war?

Neither solution appeared ideal. Surging troops carried significant risks, not least the prospect of seeing the United States lose a foreign war against unconventional, insurgent forces who were, by almost any statistical measurement, weaker than their American opponents. But withdrawal posed problems of its own, not least the projection of American weakness in a divided and hostile world. Surging troops offered the chance of saving an ally, albeit a frustrating and often unreliable one, while withdrawal almost certainly spelled defeat. And yet, perhaps accepting defeat now was the wisest course, for if surging didn't work America would become more deeply enmeshed in somebody else's civil war, perhaps beyond extrication. Even by the standards of the complicated global conflict the United States was in the midst of waging, it was a difficult decision.

This was the situation that faced George W. Bush in the fall of 2006. But without changing a word, it also describes the situation that faced Lyndon B.

Johnson during the Vietnam War—twice. The first time came in the spring of 1965, when South Vietnam was on the brink of collapse; the second came in the winter of 1968, the bleakest season of Johnson's political career, following the launch of the Tet Offensive in January. In both Vietnam and Iraq, the United States had to fight an insurgent campaign that was supported by powerful regional adversaries (China in the case of Vietnam, Iran and Syria in Iraq) determined to bring down a US-backed government. In both Vietnam and Iraq, America's superior military technology had limited effectiveness against an enemy who relied on simple but lethal weapons and could blend into the general population. In both Vietnam and Iraq, gaining the trust of that population was vital to the success of the overall mission yet proved frustratingly elusive. And in deciding what to do in response, the national security decision-making apparatus in both the Johnson and Bush administrations ultimately produced a consensus behind the president's decision, either to surge US troops to restore deteriorating security and political stability (in 1965 and 2007) or to begin the process of de-escalation and eventually withdrawal (1968). There were key differences, too, and they are explored below as well, but the similarities are uncanny.

The analogies between America's wars in Vietnam and Iraq have of course been examined thoroughly,[1] but the comparative dimension still retains its usefulness, not least because policy makers themselves often reason by historical analogy and precedent.[2] Bush's critics invoked the specter of Vietnam, yet so did Bush himself.[3] For him, Vietnam represented what the United States should not do when going to war. "See, I remembered Lyndon Johnson picking out bombing targets in Vietnam," he tells his interviewers. "What Vietnam influenced me on is the relationship between the president and the military. Picking targets, micromanaging, letting politics decide."[4] Bush's reasoning by historical analogy should come as no surprise—as two of his former staffers have noted, Bush thought in historical terms perhaps more than any other president since Harry Truman.[5] Yet the specter of Vietnam cast a shadow over his entire administration, particularly the uniformed military. For retired general Jack Keane, the references are intensely personal. General Peter Pace, who served in Vietnam during the war's bloodiest year, 1968, agrees: "There's guys like me, who believed that among very important things was my remembrance of Vietnam."[6] Perhaps nobody applied the lessons of Vietnam more than General David Petraeus, who wrote his doctoral dissertation on the strategic mistakes of the Vietnam War and later oversaw the surge in Iraq.[7]

Thinking about Indochina is almost impossible to avoid when thinking about Iraq, yet much of this comparative analysis focuses on Bush's original decision to go to war in 2003, and the difficult occupation that followed, rather than the surge in 2007. The process leading to the original decision to go to war in Iraq retains the lion's share of public and scholarly attention. It is not difficult to understand why: few wars have had such a controversial lead-up as the Iraq War did in 2002–2003. But even more, comprehending the outbreak of a war, any war, promises to reveal much about its internal dynamics; we can't grasp why wars unfold or end the way they do without first grasping their origins. For most wars, then, historians focus much more on the start rather than the middle or the end. Yet an interpretive understanding of a war's course and conduct is also essential—sometimes, it can even shed light on the original dynamics that led to war in the first place. The decision-making process on the surge has exactly this potential. In contrast to a narrow focus on 2003–2004, an investigation of the similarities and differences between 1964–1965 and 1967–1968 on one hand, and 2006–2007 on the other, can help us understand America's war in Iraq in its entirety.

Vietnam I, 1964–1965: Escalation and Americanization

In the winter of 1965, toward the end of January, Secretary of Defense Robert S. McNamara and National Security Advisor McGeorge Bundy backed President Johnson into a corner. In a memo that has justly come to be known as the "fork-in-the-road," Bundy wrote on behalf of himself and McNamara that the current policy was unsustainable. The prevailing approach, gradual escalation, had allowed US policy on Indochina to drift. Bundy and McNamara were now telling Johnson he had to take charge and decide on a clearer direction with greater US involvement.[8]

Since 1954, the United States had committed itself to the protection of an independent, noncommunist state of South Vietnam under the leadership of Ngo Dinh Diem. Initially that commitment meant political, economic, and diplomatic support. But in 1960, Hanoi oversaw the founding of the National Liberation Front (NLF), a leftist-nationalist movement that launched an insurgency against the Diem regime. The Vietcong, as the NLF was nicknamed, made immediate gains, so in November 1961 President John F. Kennedy authorized a significant escalation of US support for Saigon that was implemented early the following year, including a larger deployment of military advisors, much more economic aid, support for the Diem regime's counterinsurgency and land-reform programs, and the introduction of attack helicopters.

If we were to pick a year for the outbreak of the Second Indochina War, then, it would probably be 1962. The assistance Kennedy authorized proved to be of only limited effectiveness, however, and the insurgency grew in strength. Diem was overthrown in November 1963, which led to a power vacuum in Saigon and a revolving series of governments. Meanwhile, the insurgency continued to grow. Perceiving an advantage from the political instability in South Vietnam, and emboldened by Vietcong successes against South Vietnamese forces, in 1964 officials in Hanoi made the fateful decision to start moving regular Democratic Republic of Vietnam (DRV) troops down the Ho Chi Minh Trail. In the meantime, Lyndon Johnson gradually escalated US involvement, mostly by increasing the number of military advisors sent to South Vietnam, without making a dramatic gesture one way or another.

Thus by the time Bundy penned the "fork-in-the-road" memo in January 1965, the war in Vietnam had been going on for approximately three years. American prospects for victory had never been all that good, but by the winter of 1965 they had receded sharply. Whether Bundy and McNamara's hawkish advice was sound is highly doubtful, but they were right about one thing: Johnson's policy of giving marginally increased aid to Saigon, deploying small increments of additional advisors, and only responding to Vietcong/DRV attacks rather than taking the fight to the enemy had to change. It simply wasn't working. The president, Bundy warned, had to change policy, either by preparing the way for a US withdrawal or by making a bold military intervention.

If Bundy's memo was intended to shock the president into action, it worked. Johnson launched an immediate review of Vietnam policy, and over the next five months his administration underwent intensive deliberations. Once policy makers agreed that the status quo couldn't continue, the options before them were in essence very simple: should the United States commit its military power to preserve the government in Saigon, or should it find a face-saving way to withdraw and leave South Vietnam to its fate?

Between February and July 1965, several different policy reviews unfolded simultaneously, in Washington and Saigon, often in tandem but just as often in competition. In the first week of February, Johnson dispatched Bundy and a team to South Vietnam for a closer inspection of the war effort. Partly in response to their recommendations, and in the face of fierce internal opposition, Johnson authorized the Rolling Thunder bombing campaign and the deployment of the first regular ground forces, two battalions of Marines to Danang. In April, he paused Rolling Thunder and offered North Vietnam a grand bargain—economic development for peace—that Hanoi swiftly rejected. The US military presence grew in direct relation to the worsening situation in South Vietnam, yet LBJ still resisted the kind of massive commitment Bundy, McNamara, and some of his other top advisors felt was necessary to stave off total defeat. By June, it was clear that Johnson confronted precisely the same situation he had faced in January: escalate massively or withdraw. Key officials, including McNamara, were sent to South Vietnam for further consultations and inspections, and for much of July the Johnson administration was locked in debate. The entire process culminated with Johnson's announcement, on July 28, that he was raising US force levels in Vietnam to 125,000, an immediate increase of more than 50,000 soldiers and the largest such escalation to date. This marked the moment when LBJ Americanized the Vietnam War.

More than anyone, Bundy managed the process that led to this pivotal moment. He had basically invented the position of national security advisor in 1961: with Kennedy's encouragement, he transformed what had once been a clerical, purely administrative role into a substantive, policy-making one. Just as important, Bundy reconstituted the National Security Council (NSC) staff into a policy-making unit of its own that reported to the advisor and ultimately to the president.[9] From 1961 onward, the national security advisor had two roles that were sometimes in tension. First, the advisor was to act as a gatekeeper for the president by managing the policy-making process and controlling the flow of information to and from the White House. In serving this function, the advisor was to be an "honest broker" and ensure that the president had access to different, often contradictory sources of information from the various departments and agencies. Second, the advisor was to act as a policy maker in his or her own right and offer ideas on foreign-policy formulation and implementation. Obviously there is an inherent tension between those two roles. What should the advisor do when called on to monitor access to the president of views he or she disagrees with? Despite his disastrous counsel on Vietnam, by all accounts Bundy struck that balance extremely well. While many of his colleagues disagreed with Bundy's policy prescriptions, only Chester Bowles, who served a brief and unhappy tenure as undersecretary of state in 1961, felt that he abused his power.

Those who followed Bundy had a difficult time emulating his fairness. Walt Rostow, his immediate successor, was a policy maker without necessarily exceeding his authority. By contrast, Henry Kissinger and Zbigniew Brzezinski, who served under Richard Nixon and Jimmy Carter respectively, openly usurped the powers of, and were constantly in conflict with, the secretaries of defense and (especially) state; they embraced the advisor's policy-making role while abusing its gatekeeping function. Sometimes the advisor has practiced what J. D. Crouch artfully refers to as the "policy entrepreneurship" typical during Ronald Reagan's presidency.[10] But while the NSC staff's entrepreneurship may have helped craft Reagan's Strategic Defense Initiative in 1983 (Crouch's example), it also created disorder and dysfunction that allowed more harebrained schemes to take shape. In the Reagan administration, the NSC process broke down completely as advisors and their staff freelanced covert efforts to sell arms to Iran and funnel the proceeds to the Contras in Nicaragua, in direct violation of the law. As a result, President Reagan faced possible impeachment, and several of his aides were criminally indicted.

Since then, the national security advisor has managed the NSC process more successfully, with the honest broker ideal emphasized and the policy-making function held more in check. Some advisors have been more effective than others—by virtually unanimous consent, none has been as effective as Brent Scowcroft when he was advisor to George H. W. Bush[11]—but after the excesses and abuses of the 1970s and '80s the position has been one of stability rather than dysfunction. Scowcroft was the ultimate honest broker, and the NSC process functioned smoothly. As Dick Cheney, reflecting about the surge decision-making process, puts it, "I always felt that in the first Bush administration, that was very well managed in the sense that you had a unique set of relationships among the principals, and we generally avoided" problems of turf wars, personality clashes, and power grabs.[12] Ever since, the conventional wisdom has been that Bush's triumph in the Gulf War owed much to his administration's seamless policy coordination.[13]

Seamless policy coordination, however, doesn't necessarily lead to the adoption of successful policy. Procedural seamlessness, after all, occurred during Johnson's Vietnam deliberations in 1965, and so a successful outcome does a lot to legitimize whatever process leads up to it rather than the other way around. As Leslie Gelb and Richard Betts once argued, "the irony of Vietnam" was that "the system worked"—the national security bureaucracy functioned more or less as it was supposed to, from the principals on down.[14] Despite the disastrous policy outcome he helped produce, it is remarkable how few policy-making principals complained afterward that Bundy had frozen them out. While it is true that Johnson and McNamara had a strained relationship with the Joint Chiefs of Staff,[15] this had a relatively marginal impact on the final decision to deploy troops. To be sure, the JCS withheld their reservations from Johnson and McNamara, but every civilian policy maker—including Johnson and McNamara—was well aware of the military's doubts. There was no blind march to war, and certainly no unreflective, uncritical "groupthink."[16] The Vietnam policy makers were not the "sleepwalkers" of 1914 who stumbled unwittingly and unintentionally into war.[17] Instead, as historian Fredrik Logevall has decisively shown, they chose war against an alternative (withdrawal) in the full knowledge that war carried significant risks and that the alternative was viable. They also knew that going to war had serious opposition in Congress and the media.[18]

It is clear, from the historical record on Johnson and the Collective Memory Project oral histories on George W. Bush, that both presidents were predisposed to favor the deployment of troops to solve a foreign problem that was equal parts military and political. Some historians have even speculated that LBJ's July 1965 decision had already been made months before, and that the internal debate and consultations with congressional leaders and journalists like Walter Lippmann were all for show, designed to prove that Johnson wasn't rushing into war.[19] While that accusation is almost surely an overreach, it's true that Johnson created his own momentum for escalation by launching Rolling Thunder and deploying the Marines to Danang in March. By July, when it was clear that the security situation in South Vietnam hadn't improved, and that political instability couldn't be quelled, not surging troops would have been politically risky, at home and around the world. By July, then, not enlarging the war effort was highly unlikely.

Bush's behavior in 2006 was different, but so was the situation he confronted. For one thing, it is evident from the oral histories that he was determined, from an early point, to make a decisive move in Iraq, and that his decisiveness would come in the form of escalation, not withdrawal. "I said if you're in, you're in. You don't tiptoe," Bush explains of his mind-set when the possibility of the surge was first raised. "At this point, I'm not interested in tiptoeing."[20] By contrast, LBJ would have loved simply to continue tiptoeing through Vietnam. By early December 2006, Robert Gates recalls, Bush had "already answered in his own mind" the question of whether to go ahead with the surge. "Then he was talking about . . . how do we do it, politically how do we handle it, how do I get the chiefs on board? . . . This is a point at which the president of the United States is basically taking this whole thing onto his shoulders."[21] Condoleezza Rice has a similar recollection, even though she was on the opposite side of the debate on the surge. "I could sense that the president wanted to surge forces," she says in an exchange with Meghan O'Sullivan. "I could sense it. He didn't say it, but I think he was becoming attached to the idea that he was going to make one last play."[22]

That level of presidential authority was particularly crucial for National Security Advisor Hadley. Without it, he couldn't have done his job in coordinating the policy process and moving from formulation to consensus to implementation, particularly with the Pentagon also running several other policy reviews of its own.[23] Rice, Hadley's predecessor before she became secretary of state, discovered this to her cost during the initial decision to go to war in Iraq in 2003. There is something of a myth that the national security advisor's job is to impose harmony on an administration. Only the president can do that. Bush succinctly identifies the tension at the heart of the national security advisor's role: "If Hadley had his mind made up," he asks rhetorically, "how can he be an honest broker?" The release for that tension, and the solution to Bush's riddle, are found in the skill of the advisor and the confidence the president has in him or her. The advisor can favor a certain policy (as Hadley did in promoting the surge), but he or she will command respect and foster consensus if others in the administration believe the advisor's power isn't being abused. Bush certainly had no doubt that Hadley was indeed an honest broker. "Hadley's a fair player, [a] fair guy. He's not a political guy. Very fair and he wanted to make sure everybody, and that's what made him a really good national security advisor, wanted to make sure everybody's opinion was known."[24] Hadley could feel free to be both a policy advocate and an honest broker because he respected the policy-making process while simultaneously knowing that he had the president's complete confidence.

The national security advisor is therefore only as effective as his or her president. If other officials, especially cabinet secretaries, think that the advisor speaks for the president, he or she will have every chance of being effective. But if cabinet secretaries believe they can act autonomously, without consequence, then the advisor, on his or her own, is unlikely to bring them into line, particularly if those cabinet secretaries have stature of their own and experience with the executive and legislative bureaucracies in Washington. "A lot of people wonder, how will Hadley stand up to Cheney or Rumsfeld or Rice," Hadley told the *New York Times* not long after his appointment. "The answer is: you don't have to. They are 600-pound gorillas, but I work for the 1,500-pound gorilla."[25]

Hadley's theory is entirely correct, but it works only if the biggest gorilla is willing to flex his muscles. The reason the Reagan NSC's policy entrepreneurship ran into trouble was that there was little presidential guidance: Reagan left the NSC staff to its own devices, almost completely unmonitored, while he allowed the secretaries of state and defense to wage open bureaucratic warfare against each other. Sometimes this kind of internal chaos is deliberate, and sometimes it's even successful. Franklin Roosevelt's presidency is a prime example, but it is also a unique case and an impossible model to emulate.[26]

The clarity of presidential wishes, then, is vital; this must be actual power, not latent. An episode Hadley recounts in his oral history is seemingly minor but highly instructive. In the summer of 2006, Hadley posed fifty questions to the Pentagon (including General Casey in Baghdad). This was unusual—the military, especially commanders in the field, didn't normally expect to be second-guessed by the national security advisor. "I think they were surprised by them," Hadley says of his fifty questions. "I think they were more pointed than they expected. I think they were surprised to hear them from me. . . . It was unusual, and I think it was noticed. We were pushing them, and we needed to." But the military responded, initiating a productive series of reviews that helped plan for the surge and fulfill Hadley's mandate of forging harmony and consensus behind a common policy. The key, Hadley explains, was that "we were pushing them with the president's blessing. And they knew that." As he observes later in his oral history, "the president basically by his conviction and confidence holds the whole team together."[27]

This does not mean that Bush had predetermined the outcome and that the deliberations in the fall of 2006 were merely for show. He instead wanted to arrive at a consensus that most if not all of his advisors could support, and that required effort. For just as Lyndon Johnson faced a deeply divided administration, between hawks and doves and a great deal more people trapped somewhere in the middle, Bush had to deal with a large number of officials who wanted to ease US forces out of the conflict and turn it over to the Iraqi army and government. J. D. Crouch, the deputy assistant for national security affairs, jokes of the administration's pre-surge document, titled "Iraq: The Emerging Consensus," that "no greater oxymoron had ever been created in government."[28] In 1965, those who doubted that US troops could solve the problem of Vietnam included Secretary of State Rusk (who favored the existing policy of supporting Saigon but without US troops; this isolated Rusk as the straw man in Bundy's more hawkish "fork-in-the-road" memo), members of the JCS, members of the congressional leadership (especially LBJ's fellow Democrats), and influential voices in the press. In 2006, those who were wary of or even flat-out opposed to the surge were just as widespread, and one senses from the oral histories that if few of his advisors had been open to the surge, and if they had stood their ground, Bush would not have approved it.

Secretary of State Rice was one of the most important skeptics of the surge, and her war weariness is palpable in her interview. "I think everybody was distressed. The president was distressed," she says when asked about the mood in Washington in the spring of 2006. By September, "I was pretty worried . . . I thought we were losing, flat out thought we were losing." Doing more of the same—the advice Rusk had once given on Vietnam—was untenable in Iraq, Rice explains, because "the option of continuing to do what you're doing . . . means you're essentially going to lose." But instead of the surge, she thought US forces should stand back and let the civil strife in Iraq take its course. In her interview, Rice admits that Bush was "really furious" with this advice, which would concede defeat and probably lead to even greater bloodshed in Iraq. "I think it was the only time he was really angry at me."[29] In his oral history, Bush concurs: "I could not stand the thought of allowing somebody who sacrificed to just wither on the battlefield. . . . And I couldn't stand the thought of making decisions that enabled defeat." Nor could he stomach a plan to "withdraw to the periphery and watch them kill each other."[30]

In addition to Rice, the other key figures who were initially uncomfortable with the surge were the uniformed military and, less clearly, the civilians in the Office of the Secretary of Defense, including Donald Rumsfeld himself. "I couldn't read Don," Rice reveals. "Don kept expressing confidence that what we were doing was working," as did General George Casey, the commander in Iraq.[31] That policy was designed to secure existing US strongpoints in Iraq and turn the war over to the Iraqis themselves. Given the pressures the military faced in Iraq, particularly the damage the war had already inflicted on its personnel, combined with its worldwide commitments, this is perhaps unsurprising. It is also unsurprising given that the surge represented a significant change in tactics in Iraq, and any change would be interpreted as an admission that the existing tactics weren't working and were unlikely to work. Asking military officials to support the surge was tantamount to asking them for an admission of failure. This had been a reason why McNamara and Bundy pushed for ground troops in Vietnam in 1965: the credibility of gradual escalation, a policy that they had crafted in the teeth of fierce internal opposition, was on the line. Accepting withdrawal would have meant turning their backs on their own advice of the previous four years. A similar dynamic threatened to undermine planning for the surge. Bush's chief of staff Joshua Bolten recalls that "the process we had in place" between the 2003 invasion and the spring of 2006 "wasn't serving the president particularly well, because it was set up in a way in which his instinct to defer to the people in uniform was encouraged, rather than discouraged." This became a problem when the reality on the ground didn't corroborate the optimism expressed by General Casey. Overriding such optimism, Bolten explains, was "hard to do" and "quite delicate."[32] Bringing the military on board would be Bush's greatest challenge.

Ultimately, though, after months of internal debate, the surge was backed by a broad consensus within the Bush administration. In the end, Rice supported the surge, including endorsing it before a hostile congressional committee, because she had faith in the process and in Bush's judgment.[33] So too did the Pentagon, both civilians and uniformed personnel. This success in reaching a consensual outcome behind a common policy owed much to process, but the process itself was based on a solid foundation. If the deliberative process that resulted in the surge was "nearly textbook," as Gates concludes, the oral histories are in almost unanimous agreement that it was due to presidential leadership. "You had a lot of interagency discussion," Gates explains, but there was also "a lot of presidential interaction."[34] Bush knew what he wanted, but he didn't force it against anyone's will. "One of the things about the process," Hadley explains, was that "we did not try to discourage or funnel or control the flow of information to the president. Because part of his getting comfortable with his decision is we wanted him to have information from as many different folks as he could." Of the policy-making process, Hadley stresses the importance of striking a balance between interagency deliberation and presidential authority: "I thought that it had to be done within the system and had to be done in a way with all agencies participating. But I thought that . . . the strategy review process had to be presidentially led."[35] Bolten praises Hadley's "adroitness" in being simultaneously "perceived as honest broker while pushing the most radical option [the surge] that nobody else supported." But the key to Hadley's success, Bolten concludes, was that "he was doing that on behalf of the president."[36]

And yet, according to the oral histories, Bush was also adept at quietly steering his administration toward his preferred decision without making officials feel as though they were being forced into doing so against their better judgment. Bush, often through Hadley and Bolten but sometimes on his own, persuaded rather than coerced. Hadley, possibly the most important nodal point in the entire surge planning process, operated "on the theory that we're all one team," a simple but powerful concept that several previous administrations—including George W. Bush's first term—didn't even acknowledge, let alone fulfill.[37] This meant working with opponents of the surge, not isolating them. Before his December meeting in "the tank" with the Joint Chiefs, Bush knew that one of their main concerns with the surge was the effect it would have on end strength in the Army and Marines, thereby placing additional strain on those front-line forces in other hot spots such as Afghanistan and Korea. Thanks to General Pace, among others, Bush not only anticipated this and other objections, but was able to lay the logistical groundwork for meeting them ahead of time—for example, knowing that he would raise the total end strength before the request had even been put to him. The meeting in the tank could have been a showdown between the president and the military reminiscent of the Vietnam era; instead, it affirmed the outcome Bush sought and shored up the consensus in his administration.[38] This was because Bush, Hadley, and others wanted to bring the military along. Bush "very much wanted his decision" on the surge by the time he went to the tank, says Bolten, "but he wanted very much to avoid any impression that he was just overruling them and disregarding them. He wanted them very much to be bought into it, which is why he went to the tank in the first place."[39] When asked about Pentagon involvement in the surge deliberations, Crouch responds, "we had to get the [Defense] Department involved." When asked why the White House "didn't . . . just task DoD to answer that question, or task the JCS to tell us that answer," Crouch responds that a more "cooperative" way would build internal support for the surge and reduce the risk of leaks to the media that could have killed the surge before it had been given a chance to form.[40] Rice agrees: "The president can always just order, but it's not always the prudent thing to do or the right thing to do." As Bush himself puts it, "cramming down an idea as big as this one down the throats of reluctant people is not good for team morale."[41]

Vietnam II, 1967–1968: Tet and Vietnamization

The summer of 1965 was not the only time Lyndon Johnson faced a crisis moment when he was forced to choose between a troop surge and withdrawal. Three years later, in the winter of 1968, he was right back to where he started—despite the deployment of over a half million US soldiers to Vietnam and despite launching the largest bombing campaign in aviation history. The Tet Offensive of January–February 1968, when Vietcong insurgents capped off the roughly three-year period since LBJ's initial surge with a widespread attack designed to topple the government in Saigon and force an American withdrawal, sparked a two-month debate in Washington that bears striking resemblance to the deliberations following the February 2006 bombing of the al-Askari mosque in Samarra. Crouch understatedly describes the Samarra attack as "a huge wake-up call," but it was a shock to the system not unlike Tet.[42] In both cases, a stunning attack led to a policy review in Washington that eventually resulted in a reversal of direction. The main difference between the effects of Tet and Samarra, however, is substantial: whereas Tet was the turning point for a de-escalation of America's military role, Samarra led to the surge.

The Tet Offensive shattered the Johnson administration's attempts to instill optimism in the face of a difficult war. The conflict had stalemated by the middle of 1966. As casualties mounted, and with no victory in sight, public support for the war slowly began to soften. The 1966 midterms, in which Vietnam was the major issue and the Republicans made huge gains, delivered a severe blow to Johnson. Paradoxically, while conservatives were in the ascent, the antiwar movement exploded in size, voice, and radical sentiment. The year 1967 saw a significant increase in antiwar protest, capped in October by the March on the Pentagon. With doubts growing about Johnson's competence in handling the war, General William Westmoreland, the theater commander in Vietnam, returned to the United States to mount a public relations campaign. Westmoreland spoke frequently about an imminent victory, including before a special joint session of Congress, and Johnson administration officials provided him with a vocal supporting cast. Thus when Tet hit without warning on January 30, 1968, it came as a complete shock to the American people as well as to Westmoreland and Johnson.

The sense of shock in the United States was pivotal, for its scale was great enough to transform what could have been an American and South Vietnamese victory into a catastrophic defeat. After initially making dramatic gains, Vietcong fighters were halted and then pushed back everywhere within a week or two. The old imperial capital of Hue, which had been overrun by North Vietnamese and Vietcong forces, was their longest-held prize, but the city was retaken in March. The fighting was intense, even by the standards of the war's previous two years, but by early February it was clear that Tet would not deliver a knockout blow to South Vietnam. Westmoreland then requested more troops in order to retake the initiative. This in turn set off a month of deliberations in Washington: should LBJ deploy yet more US soldiers, should he begin a process of withdrawal, or should he do nothing? His dilemma, which he already faced in the spring and summer of 1965, would have been painfully familiar.

By coincidence, McNamara left the Pentagon at the same time Tet unfolded, and on February 29 Clark Clifford succeeded him as secretary of defense. Clifford initiated his own review and, despite his staunch support for the war—one of the main reasons why Johnson chose him to succeed McNamara, who had become thoroughly disillusioned with the commitment to Vietnam—Clifford recommended that LBJ reject Westmoreland's request to send more troops to Vietnam and instead begin looking for a way out. Clifford was bolstered by other defections from hawks, including a group of former officials, dubbed the Wise Men, who periodically met at Johnson's request to advise him on Vietnam policy. Until Tet, the Wise Men had been steadfastly supportive of the war. Many of them, such as McGeorge Bundy, had themselves been responsible for the Americanization of the war, yet in the wake of Tet they now recommended that LBJ cease further escalation and begin withdrawal. Stunned by what he considered the Wise Men's betrayal, Johnson reluctantly followed Clifford's advice, and on March 31 used a prime-time television address from the Oval Office to announce that he would halt Rolling Thunder, open negotiations, and, most shockingly, not run for reelection in November.

Once again, the similarities to the surge decision of 2006–2007 are compelling. Many of the dynamics analyzed above, in relation to LBJ in 1964–1965, recurred in 1968. There were different similarities as well—that is, conditions that were similar between 1967–1968 and 2006–2007 but were largely absent in 1964–1965. One is the role of personnel change, where the replacements of one or two individuals can unclog a serious blockage to change. In both 1968 and 2007, the decision to change was facilitated by the departure of an unpopular secretary of defense who had become closely associated with the strategic failures that had got the United States mired in the jungles of Vietnam and deserts of Iraq. But the resignations/firings of McNamara and Rumsfeld were coincidental, not causal; neither departure was intended to lead to a policy change. In 1968, Clifford was brought in to shore up the existing policy; McNamara had increasingly turned against the war, marked by dramatic congressional testimony in 1967 when he seemed to question the effectiveness, even the very purpose, of US strategy. Yet once Clifford was in office, and he began reviewing all the information he hadn't seen before, his views quickly turned. Johnson hadn't intended this; indeed, Clifford's defection all but sealed Johnson's own political fate. The circumstances surrounding Rumsfeld's departure were slightly different. Bush was already thinking about replacing Rumsfeld but wouldn't do so before the midterm elections. When Bush announced Rumsfeld's resignation right afterward, his replacement, Robert Gates, was already lined up. Gates already favored the idea of the surge and quickly came to play an instrumental role in its implementation. Thus while Rumsfeld's leaving the Bush administration wasn't a catalyst for the surge, it did smooth the path toward a consensual policy. As Bolten puts it, "it all dovetailed pretty well."[43]

Yet there were also key differences between the circumstances surrounding Tet and the surge. In 1968, it was clear that domestic politics was one of Johnson's most important considerations. To be sure, he didn't play politics with the Tet decisions—he was simply aware that the country had had enough of Vietnam and that the American people no longer trusted his judgment on the war. Even his own party turned against him in the wake of Tet, with primary challenges from Eugene McCarthy and, more seriously, Robert F. Kennedy. Uncertain he could carry the country or his party with him any longer, Johnson rejected Westmoreland's request for a surge of troops and decided to look for a way out of Indochina.

This was somewhat true of the situation Bush faced over Iraq. The war was the main issue in the 2006 congressional elections, which saw the Democrats take control of both houses, and as Bolten points out, Republicans felt angry with the Bush administration for not doing more to calibrate war strategy with public opinion.[44] But this was deliberate, a point on which the oral histories are virtually unanimous. The "president didn't want to play politics" with the war, says Hadley. Rice remembers that Bush "was never really influenced by politics on things like this." General Pace agrees: "I think one of the beauties of the way that the Bush administration operated was that everybody went out of their way to keep politics and military separate." Bush himself is emphatic on this point: "I couldn't imagine making decisions on national security based upon politics."[45] With the situation in Iraq deteriorating on a daily basis, he was desperate for a solution. Advisors whose function was purely political, such as Karl Rove, were barred from national security meetings, including those to discuss the surge.[46] In fact, if domestic politics had any influence, it was in making Bush not do things, especially policy or personnel changes, that could be construed as pandering to public opinion. Cheney says as much in citing Kissinger's dictum about troop withdrawals being like "salted peanuts" because the public can't get enough of them.[47] The timing of Rumsfeld's departure was another prime example, for the "Revolt of the Generals" in April 2006 led Bush to shelve the idea of replacing him lest he be seen to be bowing to pressure: "If their intent was to get rid of the secretary," Pace points out, "they actually added, at a minimum, six months to his tour." As Bush declaims, "It pissed me off. I'm not going to have the generals force my hand. I thought it was a PR stunt, and it made me very sympathetic to Don Rumsfeld."[48]

It's difficult to know what to make of these assertions that Bush's foreign policy—or at least his decisions on the surge—were apolitical. A president is, by definition, someone who has mastered the art of American politics; this is doubly true of a president who wins reelection, something only fifteen other people had achieved in American history up to that point.[49] An apolitical president is thus something of an oxymoron. And of course, George W. Bush ruthlessly "played politics" with national security in his first term, particularly during the 2002 midterms and the 2004 general election. But every president to some extent "plays politics" with every issue, if this means that he pays attention to public and congressional sentiment and uses it to calculate the feasibility of what he wants to do in foreign policy. That is, after all, an inherent part of the job. National security has always been political; it would be impossible to divorce the two, and it has been a long time since politics stopped at the water's edge (if it ever did).[50]

It is probably more accurate to say that Bush and his advisors sensed an opportunity in 2006, despite the Republican setback in the midterms; politics and policy fell into a strange and temporary alignment. Bush was not facing reelection, and he believed the surge was the right thing to do—and if it worked, the domestic-political ramifications would take care of themselves. For Bush, it was politically a low-risk, high-reward gamble (in military terms, of course, the risks were much greater). Even the Democrats taking control of Congress didn't pose much of a problem, despite the fact that, as Bolten points out, the administration was "always at risk of having the money just cut off and having the Congress step in and make it impossible for the president to actually execute in a way. This is the way in which politics was important."[51] But Gates sensed this wouldn't be much of an actual problem. "At that juncture," when he would have to request appropriations for an increase in end strength, "the thought of not succeeding never occurred to me. It never occurred to me that I might not be able to get those additional troops," because "there is no way the Congress is going to vote no. Especially if you're in the middle of a war." So confident was Gates that he confesses, "I had no plan B."[52] The confidence Gates expresses in his oral history is probably stronger than it would have been at the time—congressional anger over Iraq was running high, and political advisors such as Rove thought the funding votes would be close—but it was well placed. The case of Vietnam, when legislators were much more antiwar, is instructive: Johnson never faced a funding cut for war operations, and while Congress passed several resolutions designed to curtail the fighting during Richard Nixon's presidency, none was effective, and funding wasn't cut off until 1975, two years after the last US troops had departed South Vietnam.

Another similarity between the policy process surrounding Tet and the surge is the role of outside advice, which was prominent on both occasions. In 1968, the Wise Men were assembled by the Johnson administration for their advice. In 2006, the role of outsiders differed in that they were not so much sought out as discovered. The advice of some—for example, the political scientist Eliot Cohen or the columnist William Kristol—was in fact actively solicited; Bolten refers to this outreach as an attempt to "educate" the principals and "ventilate" the process.[53] But for the most part, influential outsiders were already running their own reviews of Iraq policy and making their own recommendations, which just so happened to coincide with the surge. The most notable was the team of retired general Jack Keane and American Enterprise Institute fellow Frederick Kagan, who drafted a report, released in early January 2007, that called for Bush to authorize a fresh deployment of troops to Iraq. Somewhat less welcome was the Iraq

Study Group, an esteemed, bipartisan panel created by an act of Congress and chaired by James Baker and Lee Hamilton. While the ISG report, published in December 2006, didn't rule out the possibility of a troop surge, its emphasis was on the need to find a way to withdraw US forces, potentially via diplomacy with Iran and Syria.

None of the oral histories dismisses these outside voices, but almost none gives them credit for the surge. Instead, they come across as distractions that had little or no actual impact. "For me," Hadley recalls, "when I finally meet with Jack Keane, the decision has largely been made." According to Hadley, the Keane-Kagan effort did not generate any fresh ideas; instead, "it validates what we have come up with. It's not that it's the author of the surge; we've already developed the surge option at that point. But it's very much along the same line. So that's good. It's a validator." Crouch's characterization is nearly identical: "Kagan's argument that the forces were there was a validation, but it wasn't a surprise to us. . . . But it was a good validation." So too is Karl Rove's. Of Keane and Kagan, he observes, "the president was well along this path, so they were helping burnish it, rather than develop it."[54] As is that of Bush himself. Keane and Kagan helped in that they "confirmed the eventual decision," Bush recalls. "They weren't the originator of the idea." The Keane-Kagan initiative "probably boosted my sense of confidence that had we decided to do something, there's a voice that basically said it would succeed."[55] At least the Keane-Kagan report validated the administration's plan. The ISG, a much more elaborate effort, was deemed irrelevant and, despite Congress's intentions, was ignored. "I know in the histories, it will sort of play large," Bolten says. But it "did not have much influence . . . on the president's thinking."[56]

Instead, one is left with the impression that the idea for the surge was internal to the Bush administration, and that it was concentrated particularly in the White House, and even more particularly within the NSC staff. Support for the surge then spread outward, from the White House through the rest of the top echelons of the administration, until even the holdouts—the State Department and the Pentagon—were fully on board. Given the history of discord between these two institutions, it's remarkable that they were initially united against the surge, only to be later united in favor of it. That's testament to the effectiveness of the policy process that led to the surge. But the entire process was dispersed widely through the administration. As Meghan O'Sullivan, in this instance acting as interviewer rather than interviewee, says to Cheney, "in the early fall of 2006, there are a number of initiatives: JCS, State, we at the NSC start thinking more seriously about what a review might look like, what an alternative strategy might look like. These are uncoordinated events," and that doesn't even include the various outside consultants. Later in the same interview, when Peter Feaver asks Cheney whether such a "compartmentalized" approach was warranted, Cheney replies, "I thought it was OK. . . . I think that there was a lot of good work being done out there, but imposing your will at that point and saying, 'This is what it's going to be' would have probably discouraged some of the diversity of thought. . . . It's OK if there's some ferment out there."[57]

Vietnam, Iraq, and the Meaning of Victory

It is important to recall that these oral histories are part of an ambitious project titled "The Surge—Collective Memory Project." But while collective memory is a powerful concept, it's also problematic, because collectivities don't have memory. They just don't possess the physiological capacity to produce memories and store them—only an individual's brain can do that. Collective memories exist, of course, but they are not organic, natural, or inevitable. They are instead cultural and social constructions.[58] Sometimes they're incidental, accrete haphazardly, and gain legitimacy with the passage of time. Still, this kind of collective memory—say, how bell-bottoms and disco epitomized the fashion of the 1970s—represents an almost accidental array of reference points that allows people to acquire their cultural bearings. It isn't so much collective memory as nostalgia.

True collective memory, by which a nation or other large grouping of people shares a common understanding of their history, seeks to ascribe social or political meaning to the past. Remembrance, in this sense, isn't incidental or frivolous, but serves a purpose as a political endeavor designed with a specific political end in mind. This kind of collective memory is often (but not always) constructed in tandem with the state and the various means the state has for fostering a collective memory (through museums, art galleries, commemorative stamps and currency, national holidays, and so forth).[59]

Nothing is more elemental or fundamental to human societies than war, and no other phenomenon has the power of war to alter and shape everything else, at the time and especially for generations to come. For this reason, wars instigate fiercely contested battles over collective memory.[60] The Iraq War will surely not be an exception. In turn, the ultimate interpretation of the surge will play a large role in determining what shape the overall collective memory of the Iraq War takes. One can sense that the participants in the SMU project feel this heavy weight of history. For that reason, it's uncertain how much we should accept these oral histories as a collective memory. The participants simply have too much of a direct personal stake in the outcome to forge a memory for the rest of us.

Where does all this leave us as we wrestle with the meaning of the surge, and through it the meaning of America's intervention in Iraq? A lot depends on how one perceives the surge and its effects. And perhaps it's no surprise that those interviewed for SMU's oral history project all assume that the surge was an unqualified success. If there is a collective memory trying to be forged from these oral histories, it is this: the surge worked.

Bush receives praise for his surge decision because it ran against the flow of expectations about an American war gone disastrously wrong. "I think he felt his greatest obligation was not to create Vietnam, not to lose," says Rice. She could "sense" that Bush was "going to make one last play, and he was not going to lose this war, and this was his best option."[61] Crouch recounts "the president saying to me, 'If we can win, I want to win.'"[62] Virtually everyone interviewed for this project agrees, but perhaps none puts it better than Cheney: "It was very important for us to win in Iraq, that we were capable of winning in Iraq." And according to Cheney, the surge accomplished just that. "I go back now and read my book," he says of his memoir at the end of his interview. "You know at the end of that chapter we win. The end of the president's chapter on the surge, we win."[63]

This is certainly Bush's view. He recalls the impact of the daily barrage of bad news from Iraq; by the spring of 2006, the cumulative effect was devastating. Until then, he admits, "we were hoping things would get better, and they weren't." Instead of transforming Iraq, the United States was "losing this battle." But instead of cutting his losses and withdrawing from Iraq, he sought victory. Bush asks his interviewers, "What caused me to want to win?" The answer was obvious: he had never stopped wanting to win, and the surge offered a new and different way to do so. "I understood the stakes," he explains. "I believed we could win. I believed we could win because we're a superior military, but I also believed we could win because we have a superior philosophy to those we're fighting." Just as important, "I couldn't stand the thought of making decisions that enabled defeat."[64]

It's not within the remit of this chapter to assess the effectiveness of the surge. Scholars have already begun to pass judgment, and while most of them rate the surge as a success, they disagree as to whether that success was due to the deployment of more US troops, the change in tactics based on a savvier counterinsurgency approach, or a change in conditions within Iraq over which the United States had limited or no control.[65]

Whatever the reasons, it is undeniable that violence in Iraq, either directed at US forces or Iraqis, declined dramatically after the summer of 2007. And if that is the metric to be used, then the surge was a success. But that is not what Rice, Cheney, and others mean, in their oral histories, when they talk about victory in the war. Whether the surge was a strategic success in that it secured victory for America in Iraq is much too soon to tell. But the odds are not good.

Karl Rove states that the "problem is in this kind of situation it's hard to define what victory is,"[66] but that's not really the case. The terms of victory were laid out clearly in 2003 when the United States invaded Iraq. That's the standard by which the surge must be judged, for the surge wasn't the objective but a means by which to achieve the objective. The surge was an important tactical success, but it wasn't the end in itself; by its very nature, it was a small part of a much larger and more complicated story. Hadley insists that "the situations of the decision to go to war in 2003 and the need to review and get a different strategy [in 2006–2007] were completely different."[67] That is true in terms of the facts on the ground that confronted the policy makers, but it is not the case at all when it comes to assessing the success of the surge for a simple reason: the surge was a servant to the original war aims expressed in 2003. So while the surge might have been a tactical success, we have to place it within the objectives expressed in 2003 to determine whether it secured a strategic victory. The battle may have been won, but what of the war?

Remarkably, Bush's essential objectives in Iraq changed little between 2003 and 2007. On March 19, 2003, he gave a brief address that outlined three basic war aims: "to disarm Iraq, to free its people, and to defend the world from grave danger." Doing so would result in the United States "helping Iraqis achieve a united, stable, and free country." The first step in securing any of these goals was the removal of Saddam Hussein's regime.[68] Nearly four years later, on January 10, 2007, Bush laid out strikingly similar objectives when announcing the surge. He essentially reiterated his original war aims. "The most urgent priority for success in Iraq is security," he explained, but this was just a precondition for the attainment of more important goals. The change in policy that the surge embodied "aimed at ensuring the survival of a young democracy that is fighting for its life in a part of the world of enormous importance to American security." This was of paramount importance because "victory in Iraq will bring something new in the Arab world: a functioning democracy that polices its territory, upholds the rule of law, respects fundamental human liberties, and answers to its people."[69] By these standards, victory in Iraq is still a long, long way off.

Similarly, US war aims in Vietnam changed little during Lyndon Johnson's presidency. In fact, they changed little from the time Dwight Eisenhower committed the United States to the defense of South Vietnam in 1954 to the signing of the Paris Peace Accords in 1973. As LBJ explained at Johns Hopkins University in April 1965, in a speech that was probably the closest thing we have to a war address on Vietnam, "Our objective is the independence of South Viet-Nam, and its freedom from attack. We want nothing for ourselves—only that the people of South Viet-Nam be allowed to guide their own country in their own way." Ensuring South Vietnamese independence was not only the right thing to do; it would also protect American security from distant threats in an interconnected Cold War world.[70] Three years later, Johnson reiterated this goal even as he announced his own retirement: "Our objective in South Vietnam has never been the annihilation of the enemy. It has been to bring about a recognition in Hanoi that its objective—taking over the South by force—could not be achieved."[71] Yet no amount of US military firepower could achieve that goal. In April 1975—almost exactly ten years after Johnson outlined America's purpose—Saigon fell to DRV troops, and South Vietnam fell out of existence.

Iraq's trajectory may prove to be different, and veer away from the pattern established by Vietnam, even if the Iraqi conflict has followed the same path so far. At this moment it seems unlikely, but only time will tell. The final verdict on the surge, then, is yet to be delivered.

Chapter 11

Decisions and Politics

Robert Jervis

The oral histories of the surge are so rich
that it may seem ungenerous to start with methodological doubts. We all
know that memories are fallible even when they are not self-serving. More
intriguingly, memories may not reveal the way people actually reached
judgments. Modern psychological research has confirmed one aspect of
psychoanalytic thinking: most of our cognitive processes are unconscious
and inaccessible to us, which means that our attempts to reconstruct why
we believed or acted as we did may fail. We are, in the words of a study
that summarizes this research, "strangers to ourselves"[1]—only it is worse
than that, because while we realize that we cannot be certain of the reasons why others acted as they did, we think we know ourselves quite well.
Scholars often can draw on the contemporary records and meeting notes,
but these too are frequently less sturdy than they seem. Papers are written
to persuade, and they may tell us more about the author's views of the
audience than they do about the author's own views. They also are incomplete: as Condoleezza Rice notes, she conveyed her skepticism about the
surge to the president in private: "You won't see that in the State Department papers, and you won't see that in the NSC notes."[2] We should not
be paralyzed by the limits on our ability to understand past decisions, but
neither should we fool ourselves into thinking that we can drill down into
bedrock.

Beginnings, Endings, and Politics

Telling the story of the surge is also hard because it is part of a larger story. This is always true, but here there are particular intellectual and political complications. Obviously, this is a fragment of the Iraq War, which I and most international relations scholars opposed, and it was widely believed that the processes for making foreign policy under George W. Bush were even more dysfunctional than usual. This means that most international relations scholars are prone to be skeptical of the more favorable judgments offered by the participants. Further skepticism, combined ironically with a touch of condescension, stems from what I will assert as the facts that most academics believed: that if the US was going to invade Iraq, it had to be prepared for an occupation, and that by the fall of 2003 it should have been clear that the American forces were not being greeted as liberators and that a fundamental review of the strategy was needed. The US was faced with an insurgency, and our standard generalizations told us that this required a larger force and one that was deployed for counterinsurgency (COIN). In other words, within a year of the invasion, outside the government it was almost conventional wisdom that the US had to either withdraw or do something like what it actually did with the surge. This leads to a perspective of asking not "how and why did the US reach this decision and what does it tell us about policy making?" but "why did it take so long to abandon an unsuccessful strategy and adopt one of the only two possible alternatives?"

The question of when we end this story also raises both intellectual and political complications. It is not inappropriate to stop when the oral histories do, with the launching of the surge, but try as we might to avoid doing so, the understanding and, even more, evaluation, of a decision is likely to be influenced by how we believe it worked out.[3] Indeed, the inquiries into how a decision was reached are often triggered by the outcome. If it turned out that Saddam Hussein did have active WMD programs, I doubt whether anyone would have gone back over the intelligence to see that the judgments outran the evidence and that they were based more on the implicit sense of the plausibility of the claim than on hard evidence.[4] If the accepted view had been that the surge did not make much difference one way or the other, I am not sure we would have this project. Although it would be perverse to argue that there is no connection between the quality of the decision-making process and the quality of the output, we should not exaggerate the strength of the connection. In fact, the processes leading up to the decision to invade Iraq were not so different from those involved in the surge. Both were made over the hesitations if not the objections of the State and Defense Departments;

both were personal decisions by the president; both processes involved less than complete information-sharing within the government.

Because of the links between process and outcome, I want to note two important questions about the effect of the surge that lurk in the background, both of which I will touch on later. The first is whether the surge actually involved population-centric COIN and played a large role in the subsequent decline in violence.[5] The second, which is more politically charged, is the broader one of whether the surge and associated policies put Iraq on a relatively peaceful and stable path, and whether the later ills, most obviously the rise of ISIS, are to be attributed to subsequent events in Iraq, especially the unwillingness or inability of President Obama to leave a residual force in the country. Proponents of Bush and critics of Obama (in principle, these can be different, but there is a heavy overlap) want to believe that the surge's momentum could have been maintained had Obama not been set on a complete withdrawal. Critics of Bush and defenders of Obama are prone to see things in a different light, and to stress not only that the Status of Forces Agreement (SOFA) signed by Bush committed the US to withdraw by the end of 2011, but also that subsequent events showed that the surge was largely a Band-Aid and revealed the falsity of the underlying assumptions that Prime Minister Nouri al-Maliki was not a narrow sectarian and that a temporary respite to the violence would permit the emergence of a viable polity. To put it more broadly, Bush's nation-building goal was beyond reach, and overthrowing Saddam (almost) inevitably set in train destabilizing dynamics that brought us to the current unfortunate situation. This second question will be debated for years to come and has major implications for future American foreign policy, because it reflects the broader question of whether US-imposed regime change can lead to a stable democracy. Was the hope to transform Iraq false from the start, or might it have succeeded if done better? Should the US pursue such goals in the future?[6]

Although this debate about whether the Iraq project was doomed from the start may seem irrelevant to the topic of how the decision to surge was reached, I raise it for three reasons. First, I think that politics and psychology being what they are, our views on them cannot but color (although not determine) how we analyze the surge decision. Second, although these broader questions were not explicitly discussed during the decision-making process, it is possible that implicit views about them lurked in the background and affected the participants' views. Third and perhaps most important, they can lead to us to ask whether the creative compromises needed to make the surge possible may have contained the seeds of its own destruction.

Talking about Iraq, but Thinking about Vietnam

The participants of course looked forward, but they were influenced by much in the past, especially Vietnam. Most obviously, this contributed to Bush's commitment not to be defeated; as Rice put it, "I think he felt his greatest obligation was not create Vietnam, not to lose."[7] The participants could not avoid remembering the conventional wisdom that the American defeat in Vietnam emboldened adversaries, sowed disunity at home, and crippled the military for years to come. Whether this is an accurate picture can be debated, but not the pervasiveness and power of this narrative within Bush's policy-making team. While there certainly were grounds for believing that for the US to withdraw without having established at least a modicum of order would have had unfortunate consequences for the region, America's reputation, and its self-image, Vietnam may have made it harder to make an unbiased estimate of the likely magnitude of these effects.

Vietnam also influenced the way the military fought: the reaction to the war was that it was the kind of conflict the US should never fight again. The counterinsurgency lessons from the war, contestable as they were, were consequently forgotten. The relevant manual was not updated, counterinsurgency training vanished, and the high-energy conflicts of the Gulf War and the initial phases of the fighting in Afghanistan and Iraq led to a deepening of the concept of using advanced technology to fight other armies. This mind-set contributed to the failure to recognize the situation in the first two and a half years of the Iraq War. In parallel, Secretary of Defense Donald Rumsfeld was bent on reforming the army in the widely touted "Revolution in Military Affairs," which substituted technology for manpower and did not have a place for nation building and pacification. So he tried to banish the term "insurgency" and insisted that those killing American troops were only the "bitter-enders" left over from the old regime (as though this mattered, if there were a sufficient number of them).

The other side of this coin is that memories of Vietnam appear to have inhibited Bush from pressing the military as hard as he should have for information and options. Although the participants explain that he grew more assertive as he gained experience, the image of Johnson picking targets from the Oval Office (much exaggerated) may have made it more difficult for Bush and his colleagues to realize that the White House had the responsibility to set the basic strategy and that even tactics like how often to stage night raids had important political implications.

The NSC System

A final legacy, more recent than Vietnam, was the redesign of the NSC by Brent Scowcroft when he was national security advisor to George H. W. Bush. Scowcroft felt that the NSC had grown to have too many operational responsibilities and too often cut out the expertise and skills of the departments, leading in the most extreme case to the Iran-Contra scandal under President Ronald Reagan. Many of the participants in the surge decision (Stephen Hadley, Condoleezza Rice, Philip Zelikow, and others) began their careers working for Scowcroft, and they point out that this model involved the NSC staff as being "honest brokers" rather than the implementers or the developers of policy.

The changes developed by Scowcroft and continued after him, for all their merits, limited the staff's ability to reach out and take the initiative in requesting, let alone demanding, information or options. This does not mean that the staff was passive; and Rumsfeld for one felt that it often overreached, and his reaction may have policed the boundaries to their activities. As he put it in a breathtaking memo to Rice three months before the start of the war: "You and the NSC staff need to understand that you are not in the chain of command. Since you cannot seem to accept that fact, my only choices are to go to the president and ask him to tell you to stop or to tell anyone in DoD not to respond to the NSC staff. I have decided to take the latter course."[8] This system might have worked well, but only if Rumsfeld himself had been more concerned about how the war was going or responded more positively to the urgings of others to consider alternatives.

Related was the shared belief that those on the spot in the Baghdad embassy and the military command should initiate information and requests for reviews and that their analyses of progress should be treated with some deference (although according to one of her top Iraq advisors, Rice came to have little faith in these reports).[9] Even when Bush came to probe more aggressively, as in the fifty questions posed to General George Casey in July 2006, the staff itself could not readily query the departments. Most obviously, when Meghan O'Sullivan, Peter Feaver, and others came to believe that a surge might be the best way of dealing with the deteriorating situation, they could not directly dispute the military's assertion that even if the deployment of more troops was advisable, they were simply not available ("we're out of Schlitz" was the common phrase, taken from the old advertisement declaring that "if you're out of Schlitz, you're out of beer"). Instead of asking the military to look harder or to explain how they could respond if the president were to order more troops, they had to act surreptitiously.

It was a lucky accident that a member of Feaver's staff had come from the Pentagon, where she was an expert in force-generation models. When Feaver asked her to work on the problem, he cautioned that it had to be done "very, very quietly" so that high-ranking Pentagon officials would not learn about this.[10]

Most importantly, the histories make clear that National Security Advisor Hadley felt that options could be fleshed out and presented to the principals only if they emanated from the field or one of the departments.[11] Although there had been quite public discussion about a surge, a great deal of energy if not scheming had to go into getting the State or Defense Department to put forth a paper that could be interpreted as putting the surge on the table. As the participants note, the NSC staff could have interpreted an honest-broker function as including bringing forth options additional to those supplied by the departments on the grounds that its job was to present the president with all reasonable ideas and to stimulate discussion. Indeed, Deputy National Security Advisor J. D. Crouch did not see this as much of a problem, arguing that the honest-broker role did not preclude the NSC staff from being the president's "policy entrepreneur."[12] My own sense is that this would have been seen as compatible with the Scowcroft model by a different national security advisor, including Scowcroft himself, but that there were also grounds for believing that this more assertive stance was not in keeping with Bush's views of how things should be run.

The restrictions imposed by the Scowcroft model made the role of outsiders more important. General Jack Keane, Fred Kagan and the American Enterprise Institute report he headed, and to a lesser extent the Baker-Hamilton Commission all helped put the surge on the agenda. The fact that the existence of this possible course of action was widely known made it easier for its proponents within the government to see that it was presented to the president, even though neither the secretary of defense nor the secretary of state nor the authorities in Bagdad wanted it. In parallel, the difficulties of using the formal interagency procedures in the face of this opposition led to intense and productive, if convoluted, informal discussions within and between agencies. Although the degree of compartmentalization required by the resistance of the highest-level officials, the fear of leaks, and the understandable if debatable belief that knowledge of a reevaluation would demoralize the soldiers on the front line made for a strange scene, there were advantages to this procedure. Although even in retrospect it seems odd that even Hadley and Crouch did not know of everything that was going on, the fact that several lines of investigation converged bolstered confidence in the analysis, and the multiple studies provided not only information but the development of networks that would ease the path of the formal review once it was instituted.[13] People and organizations are adaptable, and so were able to cope with what may have been the unfortunate rigidities of the Scowcroft model as it was interpreted by the participants.

None of this is to say that memories of Vietnam determined what Bush and his colleagues would do in Iraq. But for them it produced lessons—mostly negative lessons—that marked off paths to be avoided as well as shaping civil-military relations and national security institutions. In a counterfactual world in which Vietnam had never happened, the Bush administration might have entertained different options for coping with the deteriorating situation in Iraq, ranging from early withdrawal to waging a longer counterinsurgency. History makes an impact even on those who know that its lessons are not simple or beyond dispute.

Time

Looming behind many of the arguments was the question of how much time the US had to make its efforts bear fruit. One aspect of this is captured by the apocryphal saying attributed to an insurgent in Afghanistan: "They have all the clocks, but we have all the time." The problem embedded within the quip was not lack of will and patience at the highest levels of the government, but public opinion. Thus the notion of "Baghdad time and Washington time," and the race between them. If the standard counterinsurgency argument that the population is the center of gravity in Iraq came to be accepted by leaders in Washington, throughout they were aware that the basic center of gravity for them had to be the American people. The question then was not so much whether any particular strategy in Iraq would eventually work, but whether it would do so before public opinion in the US decisively turned against the war. Stephen Cambone zeroed in on this when he said that in 2006 "the president had a strategic problem of the first order. He wasn't losing the war in Iraq. He was losing the war here at home." Crouch agrees: "The strategy that [Rumsfeld and General Casey] were executing might have worked, but . . . the timeline on which it would have taken to work was politically not viable."[14] The parallel here to Vietnam was striking. Nixon felt that it was vital to win, and if it had been politically possible, he would have kept a large force in the country rather than opting for "Vietnamization," which he knew might fail. Perhaps Bush would have opted to keep a large force in Iraq for years if he thought this would have been feasible. Senator John McCain talked of this in his 2008 presidential campaign, comparing it to American indefinite deployments in South Korea and West Europe, and the public response showed that Bush had judged public opinion correctly.

The Nature of the War

> The first, the supreme, the most far-reaching act of judgment that the statesman and the commander have to make is to establish . . . the kind of war on which they are embarking.
>
> —Carl von Clausewitz, *On War*

From the beginning the US was confused and divided about the nature of the adversary (or adversaries) it was confronting. As I noted, Rumsfeld character-ized them as "bitter-enders," a descriptor chosen to convince others—and himself—that the violence was only scattered and short-lived, and also to deflect criticism from the decisions to disband the Iraqi army and carry out deep "de-Baathification." It was not all politics and theater, however. Even leaving aside the pernicious role of Syria and, after a certain point, Iran, the situation remained extraordinarily complicated. The simple division among Sunni, Shia, and Kurds hardly scratched the surface. As Zelikow notes, the war was different in each region, and even in retrospect clarity is lacking.

This matters because Clausewitz is correct: as Crouch said, "Understand-ing the character of the conflict was necessary to figuring out whether the strategy would work or not."[15] As in medicine, diagnosis has to precede pre-scription.[16] To say the insurgents were remnants of the old regime implied not only that they lacked legitimate grievances, but that they could not be brought back into the political process and that their numbers were limited and could be reduced by standard military operations, tactics that would not generate new fighters.[17] In other words, since this was not an insurgency, the military did not need to relearn counterinsurgency and focus on protecting the population, a task that was not only extremely difficult, but uncongenial to both the army and to Rumsfeld. Furthermore, in the early years of the war the strategy of the insurgents was hard to discern. Presumably they sought to drive the Americans out; but the only reason the Americans were staying was that the level of violence was unacceptably high. This presented the odd situation in which we and our adversary shared the goal of our leaving as soon as possible.[18]

In fact, it was much more complicated than this, and even now our under-standing of the nature of the war in its early years is far from complete. It is telling that when a British provincial political officer returned to his district some months after the end of his yearlong term there, he found that his picture of the scene had been completely wrong.[19] Local alignments were obscure to even relatively well-informed observers, and of course few of the American or British occupiers had any knowledge of Iraq or spoke Arabic. Alignments also shifted in ways that were hard to predict, the crucial example being the "Sunni Awakening" in Anbar, which although facilitated by American improvisation on the scene, was based on the mistreatment of the local population by al-Qaeda in Iraq (AQI) and, perhaps even more, on AQI's usurping of the smuggling routes to Syria.[20]

I think it is fair to say that the American attempts to come to grips with understanding the conflict were slow and fitful, in part because the question was so difficult and in part because to probe the question would have been to draw Rumsfeld's ire. This may explain an otherwise puzzling deficiency. A part of the way countries coped with insurgencies during the Cold War was to undertake "motivation and morale" studies. Pioneered by the British in Malaya and used extensively by the US in Vietnam, this entailed interrogations of captured insurgents not only for tactical information, but to understand their motives and what might influence them. The US started such an investigation only in the summer of 2007, and it was never pursued with vigor. One important diagnostic probe was made, however. General Casey believed that the American presence was an important source of the conflict. To return to the medical analogy, we were the foreign body that was causing the inflammation. If this was correct, then adding more troops and sending them out among the population, as was called for by standard counterinsurgency doctrine, would only make things worse. So the proponents of the surge sought to test this argument by asking local commanders how they were greeted when they entered the neighborhood and whether their departures were welcomed or deplored, and they also ran statistical analyses to see whether the correlation between American presence and local violence was positive or negative.[21] Although the findings were hardly definitive (even if violence went down when the Americans moved in, the longer-run effects could have been bad), they were not consistent with Casey's diagnosis and strengthened the argument for a surge.[22]

Another aspect of the nature of the war had a direct bearing on the distribution of effort between security and political reconciliation. The military argued that while it was handling its tasks quite well, the source of the difficulty was elsewhere. As James Jeffery channels to this position, "There were failures in the political-economic-social order. Well, who's in charge of that? Not Donald Rumsfeld, Condoleezza Rice."[23] The civilians, it was claimed, were failing to push Iraqi leaders in Baghdad and provide local reconstruction and services. From this diagnosis it followed that the State Department and other parts of the US government should be making a much greater effort. (There is also much truth to the argument that it was the desired prescription that drove the diagnosis rather than, or at least in addition to, the other way around.) The common saying was that the Pentagon and the CIA had gone to war, but the rest of the government hadn't. Concretely, this came down to a call for more and stronger provincial reconstruction teams.[24] There were major squabbles over who was going to provide the protection that these people needed, but the main point here is that views on whether this effort should be a high priority turned in part on how one understood the war.

The other side of the coin was that those in charge of political questions believed that their progress was being held back by lack of security. Ambassador Zalmay Khalilzad testified that when Hadley pressed him on "how the politics is going," and "how am I doing on the constitution, why [do] you need two more days to get this thing agreed to," in addition to explaining the situation, he told Hadley that "when it came to security, you should be asking questions, which area are you going to secure next and what is your strategy for securing Baghdad to the airport road? Because why is Zal taking helicopters when he goes to the airport constantly?"[25]

A further complication, one crucial to the surge, was that the war not only varied from one part of Iraq to another, but changed over time. Ironically, it can be argued that it did so in part because of the significant if still limited American success in containing the insurgency. Although the line between an insurgency and a civil war is blurred, the balance shifted from the former to the latter with the AQI bombing of the "Golden Dome" al-Askari Shia shrine in Samarra in February 2006. Before then, Shia violence against Sunnis or the American occupiers had been limited; after this provocation it greatly increased. Indeed this is the response that AQI wanted, presumably to solidify its influence in the Sunni community that would now be endangered by the Shia, and to accelerate the American withdrawal.[26]

The problem was first in recognizing that the violence between Shia and Sunni was coming to rival the attacks on American forces, and then in seeing that this was becoming a civil war that was tearing the country apart.[27] This diagnosis undermined the military's preferred policy of concentrating on training Iraqi forces so that they could provide security and allow the Americans to leave ("as they stand up, we will stand down") because the Iraqi army, even if it could enroll Sunnis, would be split the same way the society was.[28] How could the army and police be deployed to protect the population when the army and the police were part of the group that was, if not killing civilians themselves, then at least linked to the militias that were doing the dirty work? As some of us on the outside put it, it was easier to create an Iraqi *army* than to create an *Iraqi* army. Hadley explains that being convinced of this by O'Sullivan was a turning point in his thinking.[29]

If the changing nature of the war discredited the ideas developed to deal with its previous incarnation, the diagnosis did not have a clear prescription, and so it is not surprising that opinions within the government were split. Of course the US could take one side in Iraq or the other, and John Hannah, the vice president's national security advisor, urged that we "bet on the Shia." But understandably, few government officials found this attractive, because without massive and American-backed violence this did not seem to provide a route to stability and the withdrawal of American forces. One possibility, in fact I think the most obvious one, was to say that, in Rice's words, "we can't referee someone else's civil war"[30] and to let it "burn itself out," to use a phrase of some of the other participants, and then presumably try to pick up the pieces. Interestingly enough, this appears to have been rejected by Bush and the military largely on moral and morale grounds. As Rice recounts it, "I think it was the only time [Bush] was really angry at me. And he said, . . . 'So your view is you're just going to let them go at each other, and they're just going to kill each other and we're just going to stand by and watch?'"[31] For General Peter Pace, chairman of the Joint Chiefs of Staff, it was even more personal. As O'Sullivan explains, "This is totally intolerable from a US military perspective, because US forces are not going to sit by and watch hundreds of thousands of people being killed and just say that's not our mission. . . . This was going to be incredibly demoralizing for our forces, and it was not a position that he [Pace] or any other military person would put our forces in."[32] Realists may not be happy with this, but it appears that a consequentialist analysis of the national interest was not the center of attention.[33]

The Decision for the Surge

With staying on the sidelines being ruled out, continuing with training and transition no longer viable, and an unwillingness to concede defeat, the surge was the only possible option. "We're out of Schlitz" now applied, not to troops, but to viable alternatives. As I read the participants' accounts, there remained a great deal of (justified) skepticism, and very little hard analysis pointing to how and why the surge would work. As Cambone said, "It can't solve the sectarian violence. It's not going to solve the differences politically."[34] Even if the surge was a possible road to victory, its proponents could not be sure that is where it would lead. Although by late 2006 more officials had been converted to the ideas of COIN as articulated by General David Petraeus, who was selected to replace Casey and lead the effort, how this would work in a context of civil war remained unexplained. The idea that more forces were needed and had to be deployed differently was developed both inside and outside the government in the pre-Samarra context when the diagnoses were different. This may in part be an example of the "garbage can model" developed by James March and Johan Olsen in which solutions for new problems are not crafted for the circumstances but rather are selected from ideas that have been developed previously.[35] The prescription did not closely fit the current diagnosis.

The surge was then something of a "Hail Mary," or in the words of David Satterfield, "a final role of the dice."[36] I do not think that seeing the surge decision as born of desperation is to denigrate it, however. The fact that something needed to be done does not mean that this decision would emerge, even less did it mean that the government would come to this policy in a united way, a major achievement to which I will return. Peter Feaver draws on the academic argument that it is rational for leaders who see that they will suffer grave loses if they continue on their current course to put more chips in the pot and "gamble for resurrection."[37] But, as Feaver knows, there is a twist to this argument. Downs and Rocke say that while this behavior can be rational in terms of the interests of the decision maker because increasing the effort is the only course of action that holds out any hope of political survival, it may not be so for the nation as a whole that is paying the price.

The decision to surge is also consistent with the less rational (and also less cynical) argument of Prospect Theory. A now fairly widely accepted generalization is that while people are generally risk-averse when dealing with the possibility of making gains, they are risk-acceptant when seeing the possibility of recouping recent losses or avoiding losses in the future.[38] This is not to argue that the decision was irrational, but that the belief that a sure loss would follow if nothing else were done makes the risky decision less of an anomaly than it would otherwise be.

From this perspective it is not surprising that the conventional story that the surge "worked" may not be correct. For one thing, detailed military reports cast doubt on whether the troops in Baghdad actually carried out population-centric COIN operations with much frequency.[39] Second, the respite that was gained may have been only temporary (the counterargument is that if the US had kept a residual force in place, the later disintegration and the rise of the Islamic State would not have occurred). Third and more relevant to the story at the time, the surge was not the only new development taking place, as the participants make clear. By the time the troops arrived, not only was the Sunni Awakening well under way, but for reasons that remain less than completely clear Muqtada al-Sadr had decided to greatly reduce his attacks on the Americans and Sunnis, General Stanley McChrystal had greatly improved the ability of special operations forces to find and stage raids against militants (although these operations may also have inflamed the political environment), and Baghdad had experienced a great deal of "sectarian cleansing," which, in combination with the American erection of walls around neighborhoods, greatly reduced the violence. It would be an exaggeration to say that the civil war had burned itself out, but I believe there is a good case to be made for the claim that many of the Sunni leaders had come to realize that they were not a majority of the population and that they were losing the civil war. This is not to say that the surge had no impact; without it the other factors might not have been so powerful. But perhaps the surge's most important contribution was to buy time by convincing Congress and the American people that there was a reasonable chance of a decent outcome. (Of course this did not happen on its own and required a massive and skillful effort by the administration.)

How are we then to judge the decision to undertake the surge? John Hannah concludes that the surge was "a genuine testament to presidential leadership and courage"; Feaver agrees: "it was a remarkably courageous decision," although he adds that it "played out in a much slower way than I would have liked."[40] Feaver is clearly right that it took a long time to reach this decision, and Bush moved well after many people had concluded that the current policy was failing, that the US needed to shift to COIN, and that this required additional troops. Both cognitive and political factors contributed to the inertia, and those who strove to overcome it deserve great praise. But if the surge's success depended in large part on the developments that I noted above, a quicker deployment would not have had the same effect.

In one way, Bush's decision certainly was courageous. I think Hannah's elaboration is accurate: Bush made the decision "against the inclinations of a lot of his top advisers, indeed some of his closest advisers . . . [and] against the inclinations of a lot of the US military, certainly against public opinion in the United States, certainly against the majority of people in the Congress, against the feelings of the international community." As I discussed earlier, however, any other course of action seemed almost inevitably to lead to defeat, and once Bush decided that was simply intolerable, he had little choice but to try something else, with the surge being the last real alternative at his disposal.[41]

Bringing the Government Around

This is not to demean what Bush did. To the contrary, I am struck by his extraordinary skill, but this came not in his making the decision, but in his ability to craft what he was doing so that it would minimize the opposition and allow him to proceed with a united government. As Hannah says, this was extraordinarily difficult; until very late in the process the surge had no powerful proponents and was opposed not only by public opinion and Congress, but by the two main departments responsible for security policy. Had Bush moved quickly and decisively in line with the image he projects in his memoirs, he would have failed. The departments would have obeyed a direct presidential order, of course, but their opposition to the policy would have immediately leaked, making it impossible to overcome the resistance in the public and Congress. What we see in the record confirms Richard Neustadt's classic analysis of presidential power: the power of the president is the power to persuade. Part of the persuasion came by the delay that so frustrated many observers. Bush's top advisors and the members of the departments that would have to carry out the policy saw that this was not a snap decision, but an agonizing one that the president came to only after overcoming his own doubts. As Rice said, "The president can always just order, but it's not always the prudent thing to do or the right thing to do. You want your military really on board with something,"[42] to which I would add he wants the State Department to be on board as well. Important here also was the change in Bush's stance toward the military from the run-up and early stages of the war. He maintained a great "respect, affection, and deference for the people in the military" but now combined it with greater assertiveness and a willingness to "really push and press and prod."[43] This was an appropriate and effective combination.

Even more remarkable was Bush's skill in bringing the diverse fractions together. O'Sullivan recounts that in the late fall of 2006 when Hadley tasked her with writing a paper on the emerging consensus for an important meeting in the White House solarium, she replied, "Look, there is no emerging consensus. This is an impossible paper to write, because the interesting thing is that actually nobody agrees with anybody about even fundamental issues."[44] She was correct, and the meeting neither revealed nor produced a consensus. The only person who could do this was the president: "This is a point at which the president of the United States is basically taking this whole thing onto his shoulders," as the incoming secretary of defense Robert Gates correctly put it.[45] What Bush needed to do was to craft and frame the policy so that it was at least minimally acceptable to his advisors and could be credibly explained to Congress and the public. He was helped in this by the fact that he had fired Rumsfeld and that Gates had become persuaded of the virtues of the surge. But this was still insufficient, because there was a widespread opposition in the Pentagon and the field. Indeed, he had to replace the commanders in Iraq with ones who believed in the policy, but this also posed problems, since firing commanders had not been done since President Truman removed Douglas MacArthur in the middle of the Korean War, and that caused a political firestorm. So Bush did not fire Casey; he promoted him to chief of staff of the Army.[46] Although he did so partly because he thought Casey was a good man and had served his country well, undoubtedly he also realized that this move was politically helpful. But had this been only a political move, it would have been seen as such and would have failed to have the desired effect. It had to rest on honest and widely held evaluations of Casey, and in fact there seems to be little doubt that he did well in his new position.

A related skillful move was Bush's meeting with all chiefs of staff together rather than just going through the chairman, who by law was the president's designated military adviser. Although the other chiefs were not in the chain of command, they were responsible for assuring that the forces were properly sized and maintained and for looking after their well-being. Much of their opposition to the surge stemmed from their well-grounded belief that the repeated and lengthy tours in Iraq and Afghanistan had left the forces overstretched and fragile. Additional deployments could "break the force." Bush realized that this judgment was a serious one and that his telling the chiefs that losing the war would be even worse for morale than the extraordinary sacrifices that would be required by the surge, while useful in showing his commitment, would not be sufficient. So he did two things, one entirely symbolic and the other partly so. First, he not only met with the chiefs and let them air their concerns, but he did so in the tank, their own meeting room. When Bush's chief of staff told Rumsfeld this is what he wanted, he met resistance. As Joshua Bolten recounts it, "I think Rumsfeld said, 'But the protocol is that the secretary of defense sits between the president and the chiefs, and those meetings are held in the secretary's office,' and I said, 'He wants to send a message that he's hearing directly from the chiefs, and he's going to their turf to hear from them.'"[47] More substantively, Bush approved an increase in the size of the Army and Marines. As the participants note, this would not meet the immediate problem because it would take years for this to take effect. So the move was, as several of them said, a "sweetener." But again it could not have had the desired effect if the chiefs (or Congress) had seen this as a bribe. Rather it was a sign that the president understood that the chiefs had legitimate concerns, that the well-being of the military was a part of the national interest, and that he was not being reckless.

The military had another concern as well: much of the problem was with the politics of reconciliation and reconstruction in Iraq, and this required greater effort from the rest of the government. As Hadley recalls, when he talked to Chairman Pace about additional troop deployments, the latter replied, "Well, first of all, it can't just be a surge in the military. Where is— the civilians?" Pace also said "It can't be just the American forces. The Iraqis have to do it, and the Iraqis have to be willing to cooperate with the surge."[48] Bush was able to meet both these requirements, and, again, doing so was not merely providing side payments to the military, but meeting legitimate requirements. The effort to increase the provincial reconstruction teams has been discussed earlier, and Pace was clearly right that without Prime Minister Maliki's cooperation and willingness to clamp down on Shia militias the surge could not work. So Bush went to the region several times and met with Maliki in order to overcome his resistance to additional American troops and to persuade him that he had to be less sectarian. He also had to be convinced that Maliki was a reliable partner, because even though he did not adopt Hannah's plan, to a significant extent he was betting on Maliki.[49] This was a considerable feat of personal diplomacy, but part of the effort to sustain Maliki's backing (and perhaps American support as well) was to commit to withdrawing all American troops by the end of 2011. A surge without Maliki's strong support was impossible, so this bargain was a necessary and perhaps a creative act, one that only the president could strike. But it may have doomed the effort in the long run.

Rice remained skeptical if not opposed until close to the end. Having grave doubts that the US could effectively intervene in a civil war and believing that the previous military efforts had failed, she explained that "the one thing that I'd really become convinced of was more troops doing the same thing was just going to get more Americans killed, and that that was one thing I couldn't support."[50] This was certainly a legitimate concern, which is why Bush and the proponents stressed that the surge was not only additional troops, but a new and promising approach. Whether she was actually persuaded or took this as a graceful way to support the president to whom she was deeply loyal is not clear, but at minimum she felt the president had listened to her and responded.

Although I doubt that Neustadt would have approved of many of Bush's policies, he would have admired the dedication, skill, and creativity the president employed to bring the resisting members of his government around to the position he had come to see as necessary. Early in his presidency, Bush had told Bob Woodward that "I'm the commander—see, I don't need to explain . . . why I say things. That's the interesting thing about being the President. Maybe somebody needs to explain to me why they say something, but I don't feel like I owe anybody an explanation."[51] Perhaps this was just foolish posturing, but if not, the intervening years had taught him how wrong he was. And he learned well. It is hard to think of other cases in which a president was able to overcome such deep and widespread opposition. He realized that making the decision was not enough and that he had to do so in a way that would enable his administration to muster the congressional and public support that would be required to implement the policy. I think it is fair to say that the odds were against his being able to do this. What is perhaps even more praiseworthy is that he did so not through a series of side payments and compromises, but by coming to grips with legitimate objections and reshaping the policy so that it had a better chance of surviving not only politically, but in terms of the national interest. Mary Parker Follett, an important scholar of public administration, argued that the most skillful leaders seek not compromise, but to upgrade the common interest through integration.[52] By strengthening the civilian component, pushing Maliki hard and keeping in close touch with him, and bolstering the military, Bush did more than bring people on board—he increased the chance that the surge would have the desired effect. Even if skeptics like me are correct that temporarily sending more troops with a (slightly) different mission accomplished less than its proponents expected, especially over the long run, this still was a major accomplishment of presidential leadership.

CHAPTER 12

Blood, Treasure, and Time

Strategy-Making for the Surge

RICHARD K. BETTS

> I would like to know, did we win the war?
>
> —General John Abizaid

Why should anyone but historians care especially about pinning down the record of one strategic decision about one important campaign in a long war? As Bernard Brodie asked at the beginning of his magnum opus, *War and Politics*, invoking Field Marshal Foch's famous frequent question: De quoi s'agit il? What is it all about?[1] If the focus is on the surge per se, one might pose an interesting but narrow question: How did top national security policy makers decide that the strategy being executed was a failure and engineer change in that strategy against the combined weight of professional soldiers, diplomats, and public opinion? On this the history revealed in the interviews behind this book provides a fascinating but straightforward story.

The surge is only important, however, in how it affected the overall project of the American war in Iraq. The significant question is whether the history of the surge offers lessons beyond itself, or at least whether the surge was decisive for achieving US objectives. As with any belief in what experience teaches, this depends on counterfactual history: What would have happened if something different had been done? Such speculation is inevitably contentious and inconclusive, yet it is the only meaningful basis for evaluating the surge. In this larger ambit, the surge story is above all about the interdependence of objectives, strategy, costs, and time: What strategy could produce success in Iraq? How much time would such strategy require?

Would that time be available? Would whatever ultimate success persistence could achieve be worth the cumulative price?

What would constitute success or failure in Iraq as of the parlous days of 2006? Ideally the answer would be an American withdrawal leaving in place a country at least peaceful and stable and at best democratic and prosperous. Failure would mean accepting defeat—a withdrawal leaving chaos and catastrophe unresolved. Between these stark alternatives would be indefinite American involvement that kept conflict in the country limited but ongoing, in hope of eventual resolution. This intermediate range is where things stood as Washington came to the surge issue.

Suppressing the violence could not be the only aim; US withdrawal had to be part of the objective. This assumption is not accepted by all. Some who managed the war came to the view that a permanent American presence could be a reasonable result. A situation of indefinite American rule, however, would be a quaint throwback to the era of forthright imperialism a century ago, and Washington had forsworn direct rule anyway by rushing to democratize Iraq. American military intervention without end, but also without clear control, in a situation where the locals had the final say on political developments, would be the worst of both worlds. In that case the surge would have to be counted an ultimate failure despite its immediate success.

By 2006 the question was whether strategy could move events toward success (including US withdrawal) or would leave the situation mired in indefinite stalemate, as American forces inflicted steady attrition on rebels without reaching the crossover point of marginalizing them. The inconclusive strategy then unfolding had degenerated in effect into a program of *war maintenance*: more than three years after invasion, military leaders had become consumed by the demands of implementing standardized operations, executing difficult but routinized combat tasks, clearing the in-box of attrition each day, rather than reassessing strategy to devise a route to leaving in good order.

The surge decision evoked the basic division over strategic alternatives that applies in most foreign military interventions: the choice between a big footprint, which would apply maximum American combat power and political influence directly, and a small footprint, which would reduce popular resentment of foreign occupation and make it easier for the client government to mobilize support. Either footprint could make sense, depending on the diagnosis of the main source of political violence, but implications for the time necessary diverged. The small-footprint strategy aimed to hand over responsibility to the local clients as soon as possible—to take daddy's hands off the bicycle seat, in the metaphor made prominent by Secretary of Defense Donald Rumsfeld. This also comported with the policy objective of

democratizing the country. If the clients were not politically capable of rally-
ing the population, however, more time would be needed to apply American
aid and tutelage to good effect. *How much* time would be necessary to repair
Iraq's politics, if indeed it was within American power to do so? How much
time would a surge provide for either route to success, for attrition of the
enemy, or reform of the polity?

As it turned out, tactical success and positive short-term results of the surge
are indisputable. Predictable as a matter of arithmetic, more forces enabled
more forcible pacification. Less predictable as a matter of politics, additional
US forces increased cooperation from the population.[2] Longer-term results
are more ambiguous. In fact all strategic options were shaky because American aims in Iraq—democratization, pacification, and withdrawal—worked at
cross-purposes. Untangling the contradictions would require more time, perhaps more than American domestic politics would afford.

This reserved view of the surge decision highlights the importance of not
contaminating analysis with predispositions, vested interests in vindication,
and confirmation bias in assessment of evidence. As someone who believed
adamantly in 2003 that launching the war was a terrible mistake strategically,
politically, and morally, and whose anger over the hubris that prompted it
has simmered since, I risk this potential error. Supporters of the war might
understandably suspect that critics are fixated on the beginning and insensitive to the practical imperative of how to cope with it once committed.

For those justifying persistence in the war there is a different risk: the sunk-
costs fallacy—an assumption that the original decision is irrelevant because
in the face of huge investment the venture *had* to be salvaged, that cutting
losses and accepting defeat was not an option. For all but the most cold-
blooded strategists, there is a powerful emotional imperative: not to lose a
war. Economists tell us why sunk costs logically should not affect a decision
about whether to go on spending, but psychologists tell us why they nevertheless do. For what must be powerful psychological reasons, statesmen
rarely follow Clausewitz's logic that as soon as "the expenditure of effort
exceeds the value of the political object, the object must be renounced."[3]

The drama of the surge decision was that it was seen to be "the last card in
the deck," that if it did not work, defeat was the alternative. This implied that
if the surge was not the right choice, accepting defeat and cutting losses was
the alternative. The president seemed seized by this notion at some points.
Reflecting back, he recalled telling Meghan O'Sullivan, a central staff figure
in engineering the strategy review, "I'm looking to you to advise me on how
we can fix this, but I'm also looking to you . . . to tell me if we can't." This
stance in principle, however, was overwhelmed by Bush's contemplation of

sunk costs: "I could not stand the thought of allowing somebody who sacrificed to just wither on the battlefield. . . . I couldn't stand the thought of making decisions that enabled defeat." He focused on the conviction that "failure was not an option to me."[4]

The power of the loss-aversion instinct is reflected in President Bush's emotional 2005 statement to the wife of one casualty, Alan Rowe: "I made her a promise: Alan's sacrifice would not be in vain."[5] The chief operations officer on the Joint Staff at the time later reflected, "We essentially held constant our ends, and we adjusted our ways and means. . . . Another way to approach from the outset would've been to say, do we have the right ends? Or should we adjust our ambitions, our goals?"[6] The surge would make sense if, but only if, its cost produced long-term success rather than just postponing a reckoning.

If the best result of the time bought by the surge is postponement of defeat, or if no amount of time could enable strategy that ends in success, the surge story is less edifying. This possibility goes with the dark version of the American experience in Iraq that State Department counselor Philip Zelikow saw long after the surge: "a cyclical pattern now of what I would call catastrophes and rescues." Reflecting in 2015, he said, "I believe we are now in the third such cycle."[7] This cyclical view suggests that no decisive combination of strategy and time came out of the surge. The wisdom or folly of the surge decision, however, must be judged without benefit of hindsight, but according to the plausible options that existed at the time.

Context: Diagnoses and Divisions

> So Don Rumsfeld for a long time has been saying, "You know, we're teaching the Iraqis to ride a bicycle, and at some point, you have to take your hands off the bicycle seat." . . . The president says, "Yeah, but Don, we can't afford to have the bicycle turn over. We can't start again.". . . So that was the kind of the pushing back he's doing on terms of the military. The pushing back on Condi is very much [that] you can't simply let Baghdad melt down.
>
> —Stephen Hadley

Consideration of a surge arose because military operations had failed. More than two years after US forces invaded the country, the situation was so bad that the American ambassador had to admit, "we couldn't secure the road from the airport to the center of the city, where we had to go by helicopter."[8] The strategy that produced this failure—or what Zelikow called the strategy void—was "rooted in dysfunctions. . . . that date mainly from the spring and summer of 2003. . . . [It is] essential to understand the Rumsfeld approach to Iraq as the context for everything." That approach was deliberate and energetic opposition to the occupation mission, to controlling Iraq after conquering it.[9]

Prolonged unwillingness to acknowledge the nature and severity of the conflict flowed from that root. First, after being dragged into occupation by the chaos that followed conquest, Secretary of Defense Rumsfeld led the administration in refusing to admit that mounting violence was an insurgency. Then, after two years, the administration had to be dragged into recognizing that the insurgency against foreign occupation was now a civil war—as the US commander General George Casey said, "that it wasn't any longer totally about us, it was about them."[10] The conceptual debate over whether the violence was insurgency or civil war in itself reflected confusion over the American purpose in Iraq. It is hard to think of cases of internal wars in which the two terms are not practically synonymous.[11]

Yet there was sharp controversy within Washington over which words should be applied to Iraq in 2006, the concern apparently being that civil war made American policy choices more complicated. For example, as General Michael Hayden notes, "In fighting an insurgency it was axiomatic that you would want to strengthen the Iraqi police. But if they were but one predatory element in a complex civil war, strengthening them might actually make things worse."[12] Preferring insurgency, however, implied that it was the very US role in the country, the big footprint, that was the problem—Arabic-speaking General John Abizaid's "antibody theory" of insurgency, that "foreign forces are always rejected."[13] If so, why should increasing that role be the solution? If it was all-out civil war, on the other hand, effective US action to stop it would depend on a choice between supporting one side to tilt the balance over the other, if US force was to be limited, or, if the aim was to force *both* sides to stand down, the US combat role would have to be much larger.[14]

The American government split in initial views of what to do. As President Bush was coming to the conviction that a dramatic change was necessary, his military leadership wanted to continue the "train and transfer" strategy and move toward withdrawal of US troops rather than reinforcement.[15] The military preference comported with the view that American presence aggravated the situation, but not with the emerging view that civil war made resentment of the occupiers less salient. Until Casey and the Joint Chiefs of Staff (JCS) began to come around in late 2006, the most significant difference in reading the situation was about the effect US troops would have on the violence. Whether because they were closer to action on the ground, or just looking for an excuse to disengage, some of the military leaders believed American forces were aggravating the violence. Abizaid's "antibody" theory was consistent with Prime Minister Nouri al-Maliki's resistance to the idea of a surge because any troop increase would dash the Iraqi population's expectation of receding US presence.[16]

The State Department leaned toward leaning back, letting the locals fight it out. Vice President Dick Cheney pushed to side with the majority Shia because "You can't ride all three horses."[17] This would have been consistent with a limited American combat role but contradicted Stephen Hadley's view in the White House that "an inclusive process" was necessary, that the solution had to be a "neutral law-enforcer, a neutral provider of security" to control sectarian violence. With the Iraqi army incapable of that function, "the only force that was going to be accepted by the communities was actually an American force."[18] This view within the White House circle comported with the president's conviction that persisting in devolution meant defeat, and the United States had to take back the reins.[19] This is remarkable for its firm rejection of the antibody theory and conviction that that foreign forces would be more trusted than locals by the majority of the population—thus a big-footprint strategy.

A different judgment, that Iraqi politicians would never agree peacefully to do what Americans thought was in their country's interest, would have required forgetting sunk costs and accepting defeat, an unpalatable choice as long as defeat could not be shown to be inevitable. The rationale for reversing the pace of devolution was to buy time in which Iraqi politics could settle down and sober up. To skeptics, that rationale is never-ending. It was the same for those who criticized the Obama administration's fulfillment of the Bush-mandated withdrawal schedule in 2011 as precipitous—the charge that a residual American force could have kept a lid on internal conflict to buy more time yet again for the Iraqis to get their act together, by then more than eight years after "liberation."

Overcoming War Maintenance

> I had never seen a president defy so much of the institutional establishment in his own government.
>
> —Philip Zelikow

> There was no senior advocate for the surge inside the interagency.
>
> —Peter Feaver

In his swaggering way, Bush had always prided himself on being "the decider," and on the surge he most certainly was. As White House chief of staff Joshua

Bolten put it, Bush's decision was "ahead of the process." The National Security Council staff worked "to lead the rest of the government . . . toward a conclusion that the president had already reached on his own."[20] The most obvious political challenge he had in selling the surge was the strong domestic political opposition to upping the ante in Iraq. Less publicly obvious was the need to unite the institutions of the American government outside the White House in support of a course that none favored initially. Foremost in this task was gaining approval from the military in charge of fighting the war, a prerequisite for the sale to the public outside.

Bush has to answer to all concerned for willfully starting the war in the first place—the biggest and least forgivable disaster in US foreign policy since the Vietnam War. But in the surge decision, his engineering of the shift in military preferences—with and through adept NSC staff—was a delicate and skillful exercise in leadership. Some worried that the pushy role of the NSC staff contravened its proper function as neutral or honest broker among the departmental views, substituting the Kissinger model, as it were, for the Scowcroft model. When a vital point of view is unrepresented at high levels, however, someone has to carry the water, even if it is the national security advisor by default.[21] The exercise was especially impressive in imposing the judgment of White House civilians on the professionals engaged on the spot and at the top of the Pentagon, as well as on the rest of the executive branch at home. Hadley wheedled Casey, the US ambassador in Baghdad Zalmay Khalilzad, and the Pentagon to get interested in revision of strategy "so it would not have the 'not invented here' reaction that Meghan and I got when we brought some constructive ideas over about Afghanistan." Constrained from asking the JCS how many troops could be available, he used staffer Lisa Disbrow to generate an estimate covertly, and had William Luti, who had Rumsfeld's confidence, "use his informal contacts at the Pentagon to design a surge."[22]

In any policy-making controversy, the president can simply order bureaucrats and soldiers to do what he says, but then only at the price of being attacked in Congress and the press for disregarding expert professional advice. As Bush's national security advisor said, "Divisions within the military would be used by critics of any engagement of Iraq to undermine the strategy and to force us out"—and more dramatically, "If not handled right, a case where the president and his military are at odds in the middle of a war is a constitutional crisis."[23] So Bush handled civil-military relations with manipulation of the most subtle sort. As JCS chairman General Peter Pace noted, "Not once did I ever hear the president say do not do this, this way, or say do it that way. The president always asked questions . . . until he was satisfied. . . . The president was not directive when he was talking with his senior military."[24]

The White House had to tiptoe with the Pentagon at two levels. An activist president who wants to push the military would normally use his political lieutenants in the bureaucracy, the agencies in the Office of the Secretary of Defense and the secretary himself, as arms of the president, enforcing White House will or running interference. In Donald Rumsfeld, however, Bush faced as much recalcitrance as from any of the uniformed professionals. Well before the surge debate, Rumsfeld had coldly rebuffed even mild White House meddling when the NSC staff offered polite suggestions of potential initiatives to consider. He told Hadley, "If you and the president have lost confidence in the ability of this building to do military planning, then you should get yourself a new secretary of defense."[25]

Rumsfeld fully backed military resistance to any responsibility for political, economic, and social functions of counterinsurgency, for example opposing provincial reconstruction teams because they "would become another charge on the military."[26] He had no interest in shaking the soldiers out of professional fixation on combat operations and tactics and into wider strategic considerations of the social chaos and political developments that undercut the effectiveness of those operations.[27] Bush felt constrained from replacing Rumsfeld, in part because of the antagonism to the secretary outside the government. The so-called Revolt of the Generals—an incident of grossly exaggerated significance in which several retired two- and three-stars publicly called for Rumsfeld to leave—had no effect but to make dumping him at that point impossible for Bush.[28]

It is not surprising that civilians and soldiers had different priorities and outlooks, but in this case it was surprising how those differences lined up. Bush faced an unusual situation in military attitudes toward strategy in wartime. Historically, professional soldiers are reluctant to initiate war but, once engaged, oppose limitations on action to win it.[29] They often confront civilian politicians whose instinct is to limit the scale of commitment in order to minimize domestic political opposition. In Kosovo and Iraq, however, this pattern shifted, and military leaders opposed ratcheting up forces when victory appeared in doubt. One reason in both cases was concern that diversion of more forces to the war in progress would put at risk capability to cope with other commitments around the globe, such as defense of South Korea, or, within CENTCOM (Abizaid's command, which included Iraq), deployments for Somalia and Afghanistan and contingency plans against Iran.[30] Most remarkable was how strongly constrained pro-surge policy makers felt to convince the field commander that his strategy was failing and to bring him to embrace change. The simple option of just relieving General Casey did not appear to be on the table.

These sensitivities coincided with stress over the basic viability of military institutions. The entire Army and Marine Corps were exhausted, owing to the combination of smaller numbers of personnel since the end of conscription and the condition of permanent war—repeated deployments in peace operations in the 1990s, followed by continuous combat in two separate wars for years after September 11, 2001. The rotation schedule these commitments required was straining families to the breaking point and wearing out the combatants. Sustaining the institution had quite starkly come to conflict with implementing foreign policy.

With the exception of General Jack Keane, the retired outsider, military leadership was desperate to start doing less, while the civilians felt driven to do more. The "train and transfer" strategy to enable the Iraqis as fast as possible to take over suppression of internal disorder themselves had a natural appeal to the American soldiers who had been told that they fought the war to liberate Iraq. That strategy faltered in several directions. Although the ostensible aim was to hand off to the natives and withdraw US personnel expeditiously, US combat forces still always had first call on resources, and the advisory mission's high priority in principle was slighted in practice. In the view of the J3 (chief of operations for the Joint Chiefs of Staff) and later NSC coordinator for Iraq the advisory effort was "ad hoc teams . . . slapped together. . . . In some cases they were advising the Iraqis on roles that they had never performed themselves. . . . It was years after the invasion of Iraq that we actually got serious in terms of resources for the advisory effort. . . . By '05 and '06 . . . we were beginning to understand the price we paid for taking that economy early on."[31]

Nor was the Iraqi raw material US advisors had to work with ideal, because of viceroy Jerry Bremer's dismantling of the old force. In Zelikow's view "the Iraqi army had no strategic capability. . . . We had amputated the higher-order functions."[32] General Douglas Lute too lamented that "they were not absorbing the training as they should've. . . . Much of the military culture, the institutional knowledge of how to be an army, had been legislated away by way of de-Baathification. . . . The vehicle which was supposed to take us from stand up [to] stand down was flawed at the core."[33]

The president himself saw the contradiction between the troop-intensive "clear, hold, and build" strategy and the generals' urge "to reduce our footprint."[34] The American command in the region resisted the newly articulated strategy because they were staunchly in winding-down mode—"we had this view from CENTCOM that our time was waning, and the clock was running, the window was closing"—and at least until late in 2006 they did not see this as defeatist.[35] They had also been directed to minimize American casualties, which would necessarily increase in the event of more aggressive combat action or more energetic counterinsurgency. At the same time, in a sobering example of the Rashomon effect, Abizaid said of his own view and that of the top generals in Baghdad, Casey, Peter Chiarelli, and Raymond Odierno, "none of us ever thought we were losing. But when I came back to Washington, everybody thought we were losing."[36]

This difference in perspective is striking. To critics from Washington the view in the field had a strong flavor of goal displacement and tunnel vision: instead of adapting promptly to strategic direction from home—the shift to clear, hold, and build—and in the face of worsening results in the local politico-military situation, the leadership in Baghdad remained wedded to the priority of disengaging and their preference for inappropriate conventional operations over genuine counterinsurgency, and had to be dragged to focusing on their political masters' commitment to victory. On one hand, Rumsfeld and Casey were upset when Rice promulgated the clear, hold, and build strategy because they wanted the Iraqis to do the building.[37] On the other hand, initially, forces in the field reacted as if the new strategy was not new—as if "that's what we are doing. . . . It's just some new word."[38] The Defense Department's tin ear contributed to State's initial opposition to a surge: Secretary Rice's line was "I'm opposed to sending a bunch of troops in there to do what we're already doing."[39]

Consistent with their exhaustion, both the political and military leadership succumbed to a very demanding but very un-Clausewitzian routine: war maintenance, straining to fulfill recurrent operational and tactical chores. As Zelikow recalls, "Meetings, by '05, had acquired a stylized, routine quality. . . . How can you meet on Iraq forty or fifty times and not discuss these basic issues. . . . You do the briefing on all the things we're doing, and all the little tactical things that go with that, which can easily burn up all your time."[40] JCS chairman Pace described this plodding and its results to the secretary of state: "I don't get it. We keep . . . these metrics that the Pentagon had. We keep blowing up caches, we keep capturing people, and the security situation just keeps getting worse. I don't understand what's going on here."[41] As he summed up the process that fed the maintenance frame of mind: "It was all day, every day, you know, get up at 4:30 in the morning, go to bed at ten, get up the next morning, do the same thing, for six years."[42]

Part of General Jack Keane's crucial intervention was to jolt the chairman out of this routine, when he told him that he would give him a grade of F for his performance. He recalled to Pace: "Your predecessors during the

Vietnam War—the same thing happened to them. The process of running these huge military bureaucracies eats you alive, and you can let the process pull you away every single day, sapping your energy if you let it, versus focusing your efforts on one thing and one thing only as a top priority: winning the war we're fighting."[43] Nor were civilians at the top immune to such routinization either, as the secretary of state admitted. That is why consultation not only with Keane but with civilian observers outside government was less superfluous in this period than it usually is.[44] Keane and Fred Kagan were used as independent "validators" of the surge decision.[45]

Policy vs. Strategy: The Paradox of Democratization

> The bloodbath in Baghdad was on, and what was the reason for that? . . . Because it was the year of the purple fingers, the elections, and the writing of the constitution. . . . But what the Sunni insurgency and the al-Qaeda are trying to do is undermine that government's effectiveness before it even gets connected to the people.
>
> —General Jack Keane

> We knew that politically, the sorts of things the Maliki government needed to do: de-Baathification, the oil law, the election law . . . reform of de-Baathification—that all these things were stillborn in the Iraqi political system.
>
> —Lieutenant General Douglas Lute

When weapons of mass destruction were not found after the American assault in 2003, the ostensible reason for invasion that was left was the liberation of the country. This then meant providing the blessings of democracy to the country as soon as possible. Occurring well after Iraq's first election and the move to train-and-transfer, the surge represented a recognition that democracy, too rough and unready, had failed. In effect the surge meant rolling back Iraqi self-determination—but as it turned out, ironically, not enough. The United States had to take back the reins, tighten its grip on the bicycle seat, and do what it wanted to do rather than what enough Iraqis wanted to do, at least as evidenced by the unfolding of their vicious political process. President Bush, admitting no option but American success, said, "If they can't do it, we will."[46] But reassertion of US control did not go as far as restoring predemocratization direct rule, which would have been necessary to prevent counterproductive actions by the Iraqi government. So the surge was a strategy to get out by jumping back in militarily and coaxing the Iraqis politically.

US military leadership had been arguing that political progress had to come before security; civilian critics believed the reverse.[47] If the latter view was correct, the surge could be the turning point in settling the Iraq War. If not, the surge was a temporary solution to the problem that the American project in Iraq could not be accomplished with the Iraqis and could not be accomplished without them.

The malign effects of democratization that must have surprised the architects of the war against Iraq were no surprise to academic analysts.[48] As democratization proceeded, it frustrated American purposes in three ways. First, it was gummed up, in a long-hung parliament after the 2005 elections. Second, when the democracy did get to functioning, it was not just rickety but illiberal, with mechanisms for majority rule but not for genuine protection of minority rights. Indeed, it facilitated inter-sect aggression, as Sunnis and al-Qaeda tried to prevent the Shia majority from governing, and the Shia tried to exploit their majority.[49] Third, it empowered Prime Minister Maliki, whose aims were not congruent with Washington's.

Some Americans believed it was the first problem—"the six months of drift," the "frozen piston," the delay in forming a government, in effect the incompleteness of democracy—that blocked reconciliation of Shia and Sunni.[50] Resolution of the first problem brought on the second, doing as much to facilitate sectarian aggression as to suppress it. The third problem was murky. Maliki's own agenda accommodated American wishes in some respects but undermined them in others, including the top-priority issue of sectarian reconciliation and another important American concern, containment of Iran.

Rumsfeld believed Maliki's predecessor Irbrahim al-Jaafari had to be replaced because he was too weak. Abizaid believed Jaafari was bad, but Maliki made sectarianism "twice as bad."[51] On the scene, the deputy commander in Iraq said Maliki "constantly impeded U.S. operations during the summer and fall of 2006."[52] The intelligence community assessment was that Maliki "was playing Shia politics . . . also playing a very complicated game between engagement with the United States . . . and engagement with the Iranians." Intelligence warned Bush that the United States could not decisively wean Maliki away from Tehran.[53]

The White House fully recognized that banking on Maliki was a risk. Hadley understood the open question of whether Maliki "was a nonsectarian at heart but didn't have the means to prevent the sectarianism," or was really promoting a Shia agenda himself. The White House maneuvered to box him in by pressing him to give a nonsectarian speech, which did not turn out right, and then insisted he give a second speech, which was satisfactory.[54] This sequence implies grudging lip service on Maliki's part.

NSC staff saw a necessary blending of two options for the surge: "Bet on Maliki and double down." The hope was that Maliki was problematic because he was "either poorly advised, or poorly informed, or poorly equipped. We're going to solve those other three problems for him."[55] Most pertinent, the president felt he had to support Maliki despite all the doubts because he could not succeed without Maliki's support.[56] This understandable reasoning implies the common optimist's error of assuming that because something is necessary it must be possible. As one of the chiefs in the intelligence community said, however, "The CIA view of Maliki was pretty dark. It proved correct."[57] While Maliki did prove tractable when he most needed American help, in 2007–2009, subsequently he went his own way.

Because of the Shia ambitions, Washington could not be politically consistent in counterinsurgency initiatives. Sunni resistance could not be eliminated just by force, but had to be countered by "some sort of incentives for the Sunnis to buy into the political future of the country." The skeptical view was that efforts to do that "worked almost not at all . . . because . . . we deferred to the Iraqis."[58] The principal great success in wooing the Sunnis—US support for tribes in the "Anbar Awakening"—undermined the central government.[59] So that success against al-Qaeda was achieved by means bound to collapse later when the Shia-dominated government took back the reins.

Democracy in the system that the United States imposed on Iraq left the Americans able to coax but not to control. To end the war, however, required controlling the vicious fragmentation of Iraqi society. Saddam Hussein's Baathist regime had done that quite effectively, by brutal use of an iron hand. When the United States unwittingly removed the lid on social conflict, it found itself stuck with the task of putting the lid back on militarily, without the political iron hand.

The Washington Clock

> The president had a strategic problem of the first order. He wasn't losing the war in Iraq. He was losing the war here at home. . . . So he had to make a change.
>
> —Stephen Cambone

The paradox of democratization was that achieving one half of the mission undermined the other half. Empowering unstable illiberal democracy undercut the neutralization of sectarian conflict needed for stable liberal democracy. Both the military's originally preferred train-and-transfer strategy and the civilian-driven surge strategy aimed to *buy time* for the Iraqis to get their act together, embrace western standards of political decency, and run a government acceptable by those standards. The difference was about how much time would be sufficient for such a cultural transformation. Train-and-transfer ran out of time as chaos burgeoned. The question then was how much time for any American role in the country would be possible in the face of public disenchantment on the home front. NSC special advisor Peter Feaver believes "the surge worked . . . because we were able to maintain the political support for the surge long enough."[60] But how long is long enough to count in the end?

If the two-part logic of the surge was that, first, outside forces had to do what needed to be done because the locals would not, and second, that the American surge could buy enough time for the Iraqis to come to their senses and compromise, doubling down with the surge made sense. As it was, the amount of time bought by the surge could hardly be considered paltry—four years, until implementation of the withdrawal deadline negotiated by Bush. If the first point in the logic implied that the second was wrong, however, and far more time would be needed before the Iraqis should take back the reins, the answer should have been not doubling down but tripling down—planning for a much longer and more direct phase of American control. That alternative, however, was not available in 2007. Domestic political tolerance depended on minimizing time for the strategy to work rather than increasing it.

Rumsfeld's successor Robert Gates recognized when he endorsed the surge that he had to sell it by how short it would be; it had to work within a window of one to two years, and was not a sustainable substitute for handover to the Iraqis. The surge did buy time to enable the status of forces agreement (SOFA), which permitted US forces to remain for several more years. If the violence had not been reduced in 2007, General Lute said, "we would never have been in a position to negotiate that in '08, and we probably would've been gone a lot earlier than December of '11."[61] But was it enough time, and would any amount of time be enough, to mold Iraq into something that would allow US withdrawal in good order? For those who believe that the country was on track to stability, and just needed a little more time with American forces around beyond the scheduled withdrawal date, the answer is yes. For those who believe the Iraqis were just waiting for the Americans to leave to get down to final business, or that a token American residual force after 2011 would have controlled little and been blamed for whatever went wrong, the answer is no.

Obama saw things the second way. He went ahead with the withdrawal deadline Bush had negotiated when the Iraqi government refused to grant a potential residual force legal immunity. Within a few years the Islamic State arose, and Obama re-intervened with American advisors on the terms rejected in 2011. If the Islamic State's emergence should have been foreseen, and if it could have been prevented by a small group of US military advisors—two huge ifs—critics may fairly judge Obama's choice a mistake. In that view the surge could be judged as enabling longer-term effort, a success then squandered by cutting that longer term short. But then the question remains: how much more time would have sufficed to enable Iraq to be independent? And exactly how would a small US military presence solve the fundamental problem—lack of internal political civility?

Modern precedents for foreign conquests that remolded non-Western societies were not as encouraging as some interventionists have thought. President Bush mistakenly looked to the experiences in Germany, Japan, and South Korea.[62] Even he recognized, "Each had required many years—and a US troop presence—to complete the transition."[63] But Germany (which was not non-Western) and Japan both had previous experience of democracy. The chastening they had experienced in 1945 was also not just defeat and damage. Rather they had been absolutely destroyed, their cities flattened in a manner far more brutal, stunning, and decisive than what happened to Iraq with the march to Baghdad in 2003. The condition of total destruction was a powerful disincentive to attempted resistance by their populations. In Korea the United States had supported the prewar government, not attacked it; there was no postwar insurgency, and democracy did not take root until more than three decades after the war. The Philippines might be considered a success, but the American experience there was a half-century project of tutelage under direct rule, followed after independence by democracy that has proved quite rocky over time. If control and tutelage by foreigners might succeed in reforming Iraq well enough for Washington to claim success within some acceptable time, there was not a good model by which to make that bet. Tutelage *without* control was even a longer shot.

Some deflect that conclusion by arguing for military presence unlimited in time, mistakenly invoking the generations-long stationing of US forces in Germany, Japan, and Korea and overlooking the crucial difference between stationing foreign military forces for the purpose of imposing internal stability by force and stationing them to defend against external national enemies. *In none of the cases cited have American troops remained for the purpose of indefinite combat against internal rebels*, counterinsurgency, or internal pacification operations. They have not functioned to regulate client-state politics since the 1940s. Rather their purpose has been solely external deterrence and defense against the outside Soviet, Chinese, and North Korean armies.

Whatever the potential for long-term success there might have been, the surge certainly worked in the short term. Getting the domestic political permission for it was an uphill battle. The secretary of state argued in an important November 11, 2006, meeting that "the public had just voted on this issue in the midterm elections, and it voted against" increased effort in Iraq.[64] The blue-ribbon Iraq Study Group report around the time did not help, since it was seen as a tacit plan for withdrawal[65] (even though a member of the group, Senator Charles Robb, supported a surge). Yet Bush more or less banked on acquiescence of all on the outside who were tired and skeptical about the war.

That was a bold gamble, but the surge provided a path from stalemate and, once it took effect, confirmed the limits of public concern. Despite much fulmination in public commentary, and the turn against the administration in the 2006 congressional elections, there was no antiwar movement of any consequence in the United States. Except for extreme partisans in the political class, public skepticism was detached more than angry. Apart from the small number of military families and the few whose relatives were casualties, Americans were untouched by the war, or the other one in Afghanistan. Not only was no one threatened with conscription, taxes were even cut rather than raised during the two wars. The wars were unpopular, but not a priority concern.

Iraq is not the only case of surging US military effort to buy time for a client's healthy political development. In Vietnam the United States fought for years while promoting elections and land reform. In Afghanistan Obama undertook a surge modeled on the one in Iraq, while pouring resources into building the Kabul regime's governing capacity. In both cases war maintenance took over much of the time, as routinized military operations substituted for strategy with an identifiable end point. South Vietnamese politicians filled roles designed by Americans but in a weak political culture that impeded popular mobilization.[66] In both cases administrative achievements were mistaken for political development, and the building of client government capacity was misunderstood as unalloyed progress rather than empowerment of local factions with interests that conflicted with Washington's. Stephen Biddle argued about Afghanistan in words as applicable to both Vietnam and Iraq:

> The underlying problem here is a tacit assumption . . . that U.S. political interests align with the host's. . . . This problem will not diminish merely by the West increasing Afghanistan's material capacity to govern. On

the contrary, poorly monitored "capacity building" often makes the problem worse by supplying patronage networks with the money and resources needed to reward their allies, punish their rivals, and extract resources from the public. . . . Local governments which actively promote a fair distribution of resources rarely face major insurgencies in the first place.[67]

Like the Iraq surge of 2007, the aftermath of the 1968 Tet Offensive in Vietnam, in which US and South Vietnamese Army operations weakened Communist forces, and Obama's 2009 Afghanistan surge both bought time militarily—several years—for political progress to unfold. The time bought did not prove long enough, and there is no way to know whether yet more time would have been enough. In Vietnam for sure, and yet to be seen in Iraq and Afghanistan, the internal political weakness of client governments left them vulnerable to their enemies despite years of American tutelage, gallons of American blood, and trillions of American treasure, which all outclassed the material resources of those enemies.

Costs, Benefits, and Alternatives

> In the long run, the Surge did not resolve Iraq's problems. . . . Maliki did not take the opportunity to unite Iraq. . . . The final cost in lives in Iraq operations between 2003 and 2011 was 4,486 Americans, 218 coalition partners, and at least 103,775 Iraqis.
>
> —Frank G. Hoffman and Alexander Crowther, "Strategic Assessment and Adaptation: The Surges in Iraq and Afghanistan"

My point has not been to drag assessment back to the original mistake of attacking Iraq in 2003. Nor is it to deny the impressive immediate results of the surge, which discredited the conventional wisdom of the time. Nor is it to bias assessment with facile analogies to Vietnam. To assess the interplay of personalities and ideas that led to the surge in isolation from its significance in the war as a whole, however, and to ignore problems that recur in US interventions in civil conflicts, would have little point.

As of 2017 the Iraq strategy for which the surge provided a lifeline has not ultimately failed as thoroughly as American support for the final Vietnamization strategy did, if only because there is no analogue for a powerful conqueror from outside Iraq to support internal rebels, like North Vietnam. Iran plays in Iraq, but on the side of the government the United States supports. (One sardonic characterization of the surge's success is Charles Freeman's, that it enabled temporary control of Iraq by a pro-Iranian regime.)

The situation a decade later, in any case, was nothing to celebrate: continued internal war, by then against the Islamic State, a more frightening enemy than any of the contestants in the war in 2006. If that was the fault of Obama's consummation of the Bush disengagement agreement, as critics claim, that fault neither affirms nor invalidates the success of the surge, because a surge is by definition temporary. The surge did buy time for the political contestants in Iraq to find a modus vivendi, but if they did not, the relevant issues are whether and how the United States could have controlled political developments after the surge, and what would have happened without a surge.

Considering the situation in 2017, how much worse should we think it would have been without a surge ten years earlier? Remember that at that time most outside the White House—the leadership of the State Department, Defense Department and military, Congress, and press—wanted to let events in Iraq take their course. Some were ready to withdraw. Some believed that the trends in Iraq were not catastrophic. Ambassador Khalilzad believed there was political progress and Sunnis had become more receptive to accommodation already. General Lute believed ethnic cleansing was burning itself out and the peak of conflict had passed.[68] The last point is crucial. If the cause of the violence had been eroded by the violence—that is, the ethnic unmixing of neighborhoods in Baghdad—the benefits of the surge loom lower.

Things did improve tremendously as the surge unfolded. It also facilitated US support of the Sunni tribes in the Anbar Awakening. But that experiment was more or less direct control by Americans in the area, not support of the Baghdad government's initiatives there. Indefinitely continuing the American subsidies to those Sunnis who had turned to our side might have made the situation today better. But that would then amount to indefinite American direct rule, not what anyone ever had in mind. It can be no surprise that the Maliki government subverted the arrangement when it came into control of it.

An alternative modus vivendi would be to give the Sunnis a genuine stake in the government, an incentive to stand with it more than under it. That would require meaningful autonomy—not de jure partition, roundly criticized as impractical, but de facto partition similar to the Dayton settlement in nominally unitary Bosnia, or to the status carved out by Iraqi Kurdistan. Granted, this option was blocked by the Sunnis' ambitions to regain control of the whole country and opposition to federal-type arrangements. As the Shia government "liberates" Sunnis from the area ruled for several years by the Islamic State, however, some guarantee of autonomy should seem more attractive to them, as well as a necessary incentive for the government to rally them to Baghdad rather than renewed resistance. (The reintroduction of American military assistance in the war against the Islamic State in Iraq without demanding as a condition such a solid concession to the Sunni population was a dubious abstention from leverage.)

What about the argument that somehow arranging a small American residual force in the country beyond the planned withdrawal deadline would have averted Iraqi government misbehavior after 2011? If true, the wisdom of the surge can be celebrated as a solution and mourned as a victory thrown away. But why is it realistic to believe that a token force, with scant capacity to act decisively against bad developments at various distances within the country, would control Maliki any better than he was controlled before? Positive effects were certainly plausible.[69] Lack of direct rule, however, would still leave those possibilities hostage to the ambitions of Baghdad's politicians.

The short-term benefits of the surge exceed the costs only if they are large in scope or do not prove short in time. The relative peace for a few years after the high rate of carnage in 2006 qualifies for clear short-term benefit. The long-term balance of costs and benefits depends on whether the country overcomes recurrent threats such as recent challenges from the Islamic State and achieves some stability or is caught in a permanent cycle of catastrophes and rescues. If the latter happens, the surge will look like an expensive surrender to the sunk-costs fallacy.

President Bush is well known to have agonized over the human cost of the war he elected to start. Each day he read the "blue sheets" that reported both American military and Iraqi civilian casualties. The relevance of the sunk-costs fallacy lies not in the question of whether American honor was redeemed, or whether the costs in the years since the surge have been less than in the first four years of the war. Rather it is in three questions: whether the totals in the accumulated blue sheets in the years since the surge have been lower than they would have been without it, or are worth the marginal difference in stability of the situation since then over what it would have been, or are a reliable cause of a better peace in the future.

If the surge provided only a respite in an otherwise intractable conflict, the answer is harder to take. If the answers to those three questions is no, the spirit rebels, but the mind compels us to consider that accepting defeat earlier might have been a more moral course, just as hindsight suggests that accepting defeat in Vietnam in 1965 would have been better than paying much more for nothing over the years of costly and failed persistence that followed in fact. Given all the uncertainties in counterfactual history, and the grimness of the economist's standard, one might fairly get away with hoping the answers are yes, but without enough confidence to take them as a guide to future cases.

Chapter 13

Strategy and the Surge

Joshua Rovner

Strategy is the bridge that links military operations and political objectives in war. A practical strategy describes those objectives and explains how military action will achieve them. Strategies that focus on operational matters without reference to politics are likely to fail, as are those that focus on politics while ignoring operational realities. A strategy considers what targets to strike, what kind of forces to commit to battle, and how to use organized violence to signal resolve and restraint in order to compel the enemy to back down. It is a theory of victory.

This chapter asks what the oral histories and declassified documents reveal about US strategy in the months leading up to the surge announcement. Iraq's deteriorating security led to multiple and largely independent reviews in 2006, culminating in an interagency review that generated a range of competing proposals. This burst of creativity was born of desperation, as officials in Baghdad and Washington came to grips with the possibility of failure. It also reflected growing confusion about the nature of the war. What officials in Washington previously saw as a Sunni insurgency against the government in Baghdad had morphed into a series of overlapping ethnic and sectarian conflicts, punctuated by the emergence of radical Islamist terror and organized crime. This chaotic environment created a serious control problem for military planners, who struggled to respond against a growing number of threats.

The surge deployed five combat brigades to Iraq, and it rested on two new arguments. The first was that security must come before political progress. Prior political accomplishments, like nationwide elections and a new constitution, were close to meaningless as the country spiraled into civil war. Subsequent efforts must therefore begin with efforts to restore security, which, it was hoped, would spur Iraqi leaders into forging a more durable political settlement. The second argument was that Iraqi forces were incapable of restoring security, so the United States must take the lead. Before the surge, the administration was urging a quick handoff to Iraqis. While training and equipping Iraqi forces would continue during the surge, the balance of effort would shift toward US-led operations. In sum, the new priority was reducing violence, and US forces would bear the main responsibility for stopping the killing.

These changes allowed the Bush administration to simplify its approach to the war. The administration did not reduce its ambitious objectives, despite pressure from critics. Nor did it withdraw support from the Iraqi prime minister, Nouri al-Maliki, despite fears about his sectarian motives. Holding the political goals steady and prioritizing security allowed the administration to focus on operational questions. Solving the military problem—how to use the new US forces to reduce violence—would buy time for Iraqi moderates to rebuild their institutions. The administration also hoped that a period of relative peace would encourage more responsible behavior among Iraq's political and military elite. But the decision to rely on US forces to make peace risked delegitimizing Iraq's government and its army, thus complicating any future efforts to transform Iraq into a competent and self-reliant state. It also allowed Maliki to offload security responsibilities to the United States and indulge his worst instincts. Finally, it aggravated the breakdown in Iraq's civil-military relations and worked against efforts to improve the Iraqi army's battlefield performance. These problems would contribute to the Iraqi government's disastrous failure against the Islamic State several years later.

The oral histories focus more on the process of decision making than the substance of strategy. This is not surprising, given the structure of the project. Nonetheless, the interviews and documents include details about the different options under debate in late 2006, and they suggest a few important conclusions.

One has to do with how political and military organizations grapple with strategic ambiguity. Leaders face a basic trade-off between centralized and decentralized solutions to security challenges. Centralization enables efficiency and reduces bureaucratic friction, but it discourages creativity and flexibility. Decentralization enables innovation by creating space for new and novel ideas, but it works against institutional coordination. In general, centralization makes sense in cases in which the structure of the problem is relatively clear. In cases when the nature of the threat and the basic response are uncontroversial, then the imperative for leaders is fostering a unity of effort. Innovation and new thinking can be counterproductive if they undermine the processes that are needed to execute complex plans within large organizations and across multiple agencies. In the Battle of Britain, for example, the air defense problem was straightforward in principle: locating approaching German bombers and vectoring British fighters to intercept them before they reached their targets. Defenders faced one enemy using a specific weapons platform to attack a set of known targets over a constrained geographic space. But while the structure of the problem was clear, solving it required an elaborate command and control scheme, along with disciplined execution of standard operating procedures at all levels.

Centralization is less appropriate in cases of strategic ambiguity. Relatively unstructured problems involve multiple actors using several tools for various purposes. The nature of the enemy or enemies is uncertain in these cases; so too is the nature of the war itself. For instance, strategists grappling with a case like Iraq might view the problem in terms of counterinsurgency, counterterrorism, civil war, or some combination of all three. They may view armed groups as deadly rivals or as necessary partners in any political settlement. Local allies may appear dubious, depending on their short- and long-term interests. In these cases the logic connecting military operations and political results is likely to be unclear and the subject of intense disagreement. Efforts to enforce top-down solutions in the name of coordination and efficiency may prematurely close off important efforts to reconsider the nature of the problem and find the right response.

The benefits of centralization and decentralization thus depend on strategic context. Highly structured problems demand institutionalized solutions; ambiguous and unstructured problems demand the opposite. The problem, of course, is that organizations must at some point switch from decentralized search to centralized implementation. Knowing how and when to make this switch is an enduring challenge for strategists. A related problem is making the switch without inadvertently locking in the wrong fix.[1]

The situation in Iraq in 2006 was ambiguous in the extreme. A bewildering array of armed groups operated against US and coalition forces, and each other. A vicious war pitted al-Qaeda in Iraq (AQI) against powerful tribes in Anbar Province and other Sunni areas. The south was characterized by a war of ethnic consolidation, as Shia factions squared off in Basra and the surrounding areas. Violence in Baghdad was quickly spiraling into reciprocal street-to-street fighting, where the fighters were the process of separation via ethnic and sectarian cleansing. Regional powers were intervening in support of different proxies, and US officials struggled to assess which Iraqi leaders were more or less beholden to outsiders. Some also suspected that Iraqi security institutions, especially the police, were deeply penetrated by sectarian militia. This compounded the problem of widespread and growing organized crime, which led to further insecurity and instability. The earlier characterization of the problem as a straightforward exercise in postwar reconstruction was overwhelmed by events. The earlier belief that Iraq would unify through a technocratic process, in which political institutions would be systematically rebuilt in a post-Saddam grace period, was bankrupt.

The growing complexity of the problems faced by US forces, charged at once with stabilizing the country and with preparing for its handover to local forces, led to the emergence of multiple strategy reviews in 2006. These included public inquiries like the Baker-Hamilton commission, as well as separate in-house efforts in the Pentagon and the National Security Council. Separate proposals also emerged from the Office of the Vice President and the Department of State. An interagency strategy review led by J. D. Crouch included representatives from across government. Meanwhile, academics and think tank analysts contributed their own reports on the nature of the problem and the best way forward. Some of these analysts gained access to the White House and participated in the discussions that led to the surge.

Strategy reviews proliferated as the violence in Iraq intensified. As the chairman of the Joint Chiefs of Staff Peter Pace recalls, "we had four separate things going on—three military and one at the White House. Plus, you had the vice president getting views from other people as well. So there were lots of people looking at this."[2] Participants tried to look at all aspects of the campaign, and considered a variety of different solutions to bring order to a chaotic environment. "When you look at a military operation," Pace continued, "you look at everything from surrender to nuke 'em, OK? And during this process, we looked at all that."[3] There was little doubt about the need to look at the situation anew, given broad agreement about the direction of the war. As Pace concluded, "It was a consensus between the folks in theater, the folks in the Pentagon, and the folks across the river at the White House. In my mind, there was consensus that this is not going right, we need to rethink it."[4] Rethinking the war meant examining all options, even some that were hard to accept. One was "hunkering down" and focusing on force protection while the Iraqis sorted out their differences. But Pace and other generals rejected this option because of their legal and moral responsibility to act if they witnessed atrocities.[5]

Vice President Cheney had no problem with the parallel reviews in the summer and fall of 2006. "I thought it was OK," he said. "I was aware that there were different operations in different places, but under the circumstances and given the complexity of the problem, the history that was involved and so forth to try to drive one central view this way and no other way, that this is going to be the only study or the only analysis, would have been a problem."[6] Attempts to consolidate reviews during a period of high ambiguity might have discouraged creativity and candor at a time it was needed most. This would change at the end of the year, when the president had made a decision requiring a unity of purpose, but not before that time.

Secretary of State Condoleezza Rice agreed. "I didn't think there was any harm in having everybody look at this separately for a little while. You didn't want to come to a too soon conclusion about what was possible or what you ought to do."[7] Informal outside reviews, such as those conducted at the American Enterprise Institute, were also useful. According to Eric Edelman, the undersecretary of defense for policy, it would have been "foolish" for the president to seek advice only from within the chain of command.[8]

Some participants preferred the compartmentalized approach, fearing a formal integrated review might have been demoralizing to deployed personnel by signaling that the administration had lost faith in the current effort. Not everyone agreed with this argument. CENTCOM's General John Abizaid argued that morale had never been a problem, and that soldiers were willing to adapt as necessary.[9] More broadly, Abizaid suggests that while there was nothing wrong with conducting multiple reviews, one consequence was a lack of communication between key figures in Iraq and Washington. He was particularly critical of General David Petraeus and General Jack Keane (retired) for failing to reach out to him directly.[10]

The only clear dissenter was Secretary of Defense Donald Rumsfeld, who according to a close aide did not "find the subject or the process congenial."[11] Rumsfeld had consistently supported efforts to hand off responsibilities to Iraqi security forces. His long-standing hopes for military transformation, which envisioned rapid interventions without requiring a large and prolonged military presence, were threatened by an indefinite commitment of additional troops. Rumsfeld also worried that the outcome would be more responsibilities for the services to transport and protect civilians at a time in which the military was already overstretched.[12] His concerns led to hesitation among some officials, who worried about the internal politics of force generation. At one point, National Security Council special advisor Peter

Feaver asked Lisa Disbrow from the Joint Staff to figure out whether there were available troops for a surge. As Feaver recalls, her analysis was done discreetly because "we had no authorization from the suite . . . this was certainly not where Secretary Rumsfeld and the Joint Staff were. But we just wanted to get an independent assessment."[13]

The midterm election and the change in leadership in the Pentagon cleared the way for integrating the parallel reviews.[14] Rumsfeld was soon out; Robert Gates took his place. Reaching a consensus proved difficult, given the various options favored by the Joint Chiefs of Staff, the National Security Council, the Department of Defense, and the State Department, whose positions were informed by their own independent strategy reviews. These differences did not disappear even after the president reached the decision to surge troops. For instance, there was some pressure to achieve a compromise by sending a "mini-surge" rather than the full five brigades, with the option of sending additional troops as needed. While some officials believed this maximized operational flexibility, others argued that it would be politically counterproductive, because subsequent requests for more personnel would look like admissions that the new strategy was failing.[15]

The surge debate was not simply about sending more troops, but about how to reduce uncertainty in a complex and deteriorating conflict. Surge advocates sought to simplify the problem in two ways. First, they concluded that security must precede political progress. While all those involved sought improved security and stronger political institutions, they argued about the appropriate sequence.[16] The previous approach was based on the notion that reaching important political milestones—transferring sovereignty, holding free elections, and so on—would allow US forces to hand off responsibility to their Iraqi counterparts. Establishing the institutional foundations for the new Iraqi state was important for reducing the US military footprint. As those institutions grew in strength, they would set the bounds of legitimate political contests and provide a space for various parties to compete for power and influence. They would also provide an outlet for Iraqis to air legitimate grievances. As a result, they would take the air out of postwar ethnic and sectarian rivalries by channeling very dangerous disputes into the political arena. In the absence of political progress, Iraq would remain dependent on the United States, and US forces would remain tied down indefinitely.

Rapidly escalating violence called this argument into question. US officials were excited about political progress in 2005–2006, and some military officers believed that they were making important progress in Anbar against al-Qaeda in Iraq.[17] Others argued that superficial reforms were not enough to alleviate Sunni fears that they were being marginalized and persecuted in the post-Saddam Iraq. As Abizaid put it, "We weren't doing enough to ensure that the Sunnis understood that we were going to try to elevate their status from being an unhappy minority to a minority that could participate in the future of the country. And I think all of us did that very poorly." This problem became worse as Shia militia increasingly penetrated the Iraqi police.[18]

Political progress did nothing to stop the sectarian fighting.[19] Meghan O'Sullivan, who then served as deputy national security advisor for Iraq and Afghanistan, noted that the core assumptions underlying the pre-surge strategy—that political milestones would lay the groundwork for security, that anti-Americanism was fueling the violence, and that Iraqi forces must therefore take the lead—were in tatters by the time the surge debate began.[20] Feaver recalled that at meetings in August and September 2006, "we listed all of the assumptions of the strategy and then assessed, do we still believe them? One by one it was clear that none of us in this little group . . . believed those assumptions anymore. We couldn't credibly defend those assumptions. That suggested that . . . on our own terms, we must not believe that the existing strategy is going to work, because they're the premises for the strategy. That was a very clarifying moment."[21]

Petraeus, who would later become the public face of the surge, was active behind the scenes. According to the incoming secretary of defense, Robert Gates, Petraeus made a persuasive case that security must come first.[22] This logic increasingly dominated US conceptions about how and when Iraq would achieve a semblance of political stability. Some of the earlier skeptics came around to this position, though they still emphasized the importance of political deals that were necessary to enable the renewed security effort. Rice, for instance, argued that the crucial moment was the president's success in winning support from Maliki in late 2006. A virtuous circle followed in which military operations build trust, enabling more and better efforts against insurgents and militia, culminating in real political results. As Rice put it, "You get the surge, and the surge starts to have an effect, it empowers the Anbari tribes, who now don't have to worry that their heads are going to be cut off, because you're not actually leaving at night, and then you create an environment into which the politics can actually start to work."[23]

The notion of using military operations to foster micro-level political deals, which would then create space for national political growth, required visible evidence of US commitment to all of Iraq. Petraeus succeeded, according to his aide, by showing that US forces were "even-handed in dealing with Shiite extremists as well as Sunni extremists. The people on the ground—the Iraqis saw that—and is part of what eventually brought the

Sunnis back into the political framework, at least for a time."[24] Conspicuous efforts to protect civilians on all sides would facilitate long-term political reconciliation, which would enable the emergence of a true unity government and strengthen political institutions.[25]

Since the beginning of the insurgency, US officials expressed concern that Iraq's Sunni minority was disillusioned and vulnerable to persecution from the US-backed government in Baghdad. While these concerns remained, some participants in the surge debate emphasized the importance of Shia security because violence in Baghdad and to the south was pulling the government apart. Increasing security would strengthen the hand of the government and facilitate a badly needed intra-sectarian housecleaning. John Hannah, who spoke for the Office of the Vice President in the Crouch-led interagency review, argued that "getting control of the security situation, through reestablishing that kind of confidence with the Shiite government in Baghdad . . . [would] empower them not only to be more confident in taking necessary steps on reconciliation toward the Sunnis, but also eventually, in getting after their own problem inside of their own camp, in terms of those Iranian-backed militias, and actually confronting the Iranians, fighting the Jaysh al-Mahdi and [Muqtada al-]Sadr and really beginning to take those people down a peg."[26]

Such optimism was tempered by the belief that a significant number of Iraq's security forces were incompetent and corrupt. Improved security would encourage intra- and inter-sectarian reconciliation, which was necessary for genuine political progress. But the dismal performance of Iraq's army and police made even a temporary reduction in violence seem unlikely, and its long-term sustenance even less so.

The bedrock of the US approach to Iraq before the surge was to train Iraqi security forces quickly. General Abizaid gave clear orders to General Casey upon taking command of Multi-National Force–Iraq (MNF-I): "I gave General Casey the instructions, both verbally and in writing, that he was to put his main effort in developing Iraqi security capacity, in order to enable our eventual drawdown and departure from the country." This was consistent with the belief that the main source of violence was the rejection of foreign occupying troops.[27] It was also consistent with guidance from Secretary Rumsfeld, who wanted badly to avoid open-ended occupations. More broadly it followed the Bush administration's desire to quickly transfer sovereignty to the new Iraqi government. Training a modern professional fighting force would strengthen Iraq's sense of national identity, promote postwar stability, and strengthen deterrence against Iran.

But the expanding insurgency called these hopes into question, especially given the disastrous response of the Iraqi security forces. Operation Together Forward II in the summer of 2006 was especially disheartening. Rice was dismayed by the idea that the Iraqi army's poor performance revealed underlying weaknesses in the Iraqi state. The problem, she thought, was both a matter of skill and will. Iraqi nationalism was a prerequisite to a committed and effective Iraqi army, but it was not clear there was enough nationalism to do the job. "I had started to wonder if there really was an Iraqi unifying spirit, or were we really in the middle of something that couldn't be unified."[28] In addition, Rice viewed the Iraqi army as bloated and incompetent. "The numbers of Iraqi security forces just kept growing and growing and growing, but weirdly, they would never actually seem to be there, because they'd forget to come back after going home on leave or whatever, but the numbers were just—the numbers were almost as if they were being created out of thin air."[29]

Because Iraqi security personnel appeared ineffective, unmotivated, and corrupt, some US officials began to advocate that US forces take more responsibility for providing security. Such a move would reduce the effects of ambiguity and restore a semblance of order and control to the war.

Throughout much of 2006, commanders in Iraq and officials in Washington debated the issue of handing off responsibility to Iraqi forces. The crux of the debate between MNF-I and the NSC staff was whether US forces should focus on training in preparation for a US withdrawal, or whether they should provide population security directly. "We had this debate," recalls Feaver. "Do we provide population security? Is that the mission, or is the mission train and transition?" If Iraqi security forces were ready to act independently, then the United States could "let go of the bicycle seat." If not, then US forces would have to at least temporarily put training aside and take responsibility for Iraqi security. The argument was not settled until the president sided with the NSC in late November or early December.[30]

The decision rested on the belief that the main sources of violence were internecine rather than anti-American. This was a critical premise for surge advocates, because the prevailing wisdom to that point had been that a long-term occupation would cause lasting hostility. Indeed, the train-and-transition approach was based on the idea that a visible and enduring US presence would lead to self-perpetuating violence. Angry Iraqis would target US forces and their Iraqi allies, causing the United States to send more forces, leading to ever-increasing attacks. Breaking the vicious cycle required reducing the US presence, even if Iraqi forces were somewhat less capable in the short term.

The intelligence community was aware of the intensification of the sectarian civil war in late 2005, though administration officials were somewhat slower to recognize this dynamic.[31] The leadership of Multi-National Force–Iraq concurred, with Casey reporting on the roots of violence during the June 2016 meeting at Camp David. Far from being motivated by hatred of US troops, the civil war was the culmination of AQI efforts to provoke a sectarian bloodletting.[32] The bombing of symbolic sites like the al-Askari mosque revealed the depth of the conflict. It also revealed the weakness of the Iraqi security forces (ISF) and impelled Iraqis to rally around militia for self-preservation.[33]

The recognition that the US was stuck in the middle of a brutal sectarian fight did not suggest an obvious strategic response. To some observers, it meant that the United States had little impact on the course of events and thus should begin extricating itself from Iraq. Rice recalled thinking, "We can't referee someone else's civil war."[34] To others it suggested that the United States needed to take sides. Rather than trying to pacify everyone, which was impractical given the depth of hostility, the surest route to stability was to back the Shia-led government in Baghdad. In time this became known as the "bet on Maliki" approach and was strongly associated with John Hannah and Vice President Cheney.

Advocates of the surge, however, believed that US forces would have a calming effect on all sides. Rather than inspiring more attacks, they would be seen as a moderating force who could protect civilians on all sides by targeting sectarian extremists.[35] This was especially likely if the US acted aggressively against extremists from all sects while simultaneously promising political inclusion to moderates.[36] The depth of sectarian animosity meant that the Iraqi army was going to be suspect, regardless of its actions. On the other hand, "the only force that was going to be accepted by the communities was actually an American force. And that's why the surge in the end of the day had such a strong American component. . . . US military needed to inter-position itself and of course provide security to all three communities."[37] Surge advocates also refused to bet on Maliki, because even though they recognized the need to reassure the Shia, they already had suspicions of the prime minister's intentions.[38] Others doubted that the United States could pursue this line without inadvertently aiding Iran.[39]

In December, weeks before Bush went public with the surge decision, administration officials remained divided on basic issues.[40] Rice told the president that the sectarian violence was ultimately not a US problem to solve. Pace argued that progress was possible but would badly stretch an already overburdened force. And despite the disappointing results of Together

Forward II, the president still wondered whether Iraqi forces could reduce the violence. He settled on the surge only after he was finally convinced they could not. With Bush having accepted that the United States would take responsibility, strategic planning began in earnest. As O'Sullivan recalls, his comments "shifted the conversation. If you decide that we're actually going to take on the mission of quelling sectarian violence because we see it as being fundamental to the larger mission of stabilizing Iraq, then you get into this category, OK, how can you achieve that? What kind of mission should our forces have? And that's how we got into the counterinsurgency option."[41] Other prominent voices weighed in, bolstering the president's decision and setting the stage for the debate over operationalizing the surge. General Petraeus made this argument convincingly to the incoming secretary of defense, Gates.[42] The decentralized search for solutions was giving way to centralization, as the relevant departments and agencies went about institutionalizing the surge. In the process, however, the administration locked in an operational commitment that risked unexpected strategic results.

The decision to commit additional US forces led to a renewed focus on operational questions. The reason for this was that the surge retained the ambitious goals that had defined the administration's prior approach: "a unified democratic federal Iraq that can govern itself, defend itself, and sustain itself, and is an ally in the War on Terror."[43] These were extraordinary goals, given the ferocity of the Iraqi civil war and the breakdown of political and social cohesion. What changed was the commitment to improve security with additional US forces; nothing good could happen without it. The overarching need was figuring out what to do with those new forces in order to quell the violence. Later, with some stability restored, policy makers could return to the details of translating security gains into political progress.[44]

Several interviewees suggest that the surge amounted to a strategic pause. The goal was to stanch the bleeding. Accomplishing that would provide breathing space for efforts to reconcile competing factions and strengthen Iraqi institutions. As described above, the most persuasive surge advocates recognized that political milestones were hollow in the absence of security, and that genuine progress required a decent stretch of peace.[45] Abizaid believed the five additional surge brigades would provide one or two years of improved security. While this would give the Iraqis a "psychological opportunity to do more," however, it was not clear they would take the opportunity. Nor was it clear how a brief respite would change the underlying political dynamics driving the violence. Abizaid also recalls there was a great deal of tactical thinking, but little to no strategy, no commitment to accept the costs and time required to reach a durable peace, and no real appreciation for the depth of Islamic extremism.[46]

Pace agrees that the pressure to increase US numbers preceded a common understanding of how to use them. Commanders indicated the need for more forces as early as August, months before the surge debate concluded. Pace saw that his role as JCS chairman was to coordinate planning based on input from observers in Iraq and analysts in Washington.[47] Another participant suggests that Army and Marine leaders were not interested in a serious strategy revision until the president committed to increasing end strength. This is further evidence that strategy was lagging behind operations, given that Bush didn't make this commitment until settling on the surge.[48] Critics of the military leadership may argue that this reflects misplaced priorities. The fact that military leaders were waiting on promises about the total size of the force implies that they didn't believe that near-term strategic adjustments would have any lasting impact on the war.

Pace suggested that the surge relied on the wrong personnel, with little hope of relief. Creating security would buy time, but the surge of civilians who would do jobs like civil affairs was not forthcoming. Implicitly, the surge rested on hopes not just of reducing violence, but that something good might come later. "So from the military standpoint, we were doing not only the job we were supposed to do, but we were holding on as best we could, in the jobs for which we'd never been trained, and if we were going to surge with the military, then we were going to buy time, but buying time for other military officers to do what they don't know how to do made no sense."[49]

State Department officials viewed these planning issues as relatively unimportant. Decisions about the number of new brigade combat teams in theater, for instance, would not affect the underlying causes of violence in Iraq. Better, they argued, to focus on "containment and mitigation" of the violence in Iraq, coupled with efforts to pressure Saudi Arabia and the Gulf states to rein in al-Qaeda in Iraq. Secretary Rice sympathized with this argument, though she kept her own position close to the vest. In other words, because State Department officials had little faith in the ability of US forces to effect lasting political change, they had no reason to focus on strategy in the war itself. Better to mitigate the regional consequences.[50]

Rice also worried that additional forces would arrive without a new strategy. Her "biggest concern was that the president would double down with the same strategy, and I thought that would be a disaster."[51] The president assured her that he would not, though he was vague about precisely what the new strategy entailed.[52]

Some Department of Defense officials expressed similar sentiments. They questioned the strategic value of the surge and simultaneously worried about what strain it would place on existing forces. As Undersecretary of Defense Stephen Cambone explained, "The department can't be pressed to do things that are beyond its remit. So it can't solve the sectarian violence. It's not going to solve the differences politically. It hasn't the wherewithal to do that, and if that kind of burden is going to be put on the department, it has to be politely said that that's not what we're capable of doing."[53] Cambone also gives the impression that the Department of Defense had little influence on the surge decision, though his view may reflect the fact that he was preparing to exit the Pentagon with Secretary Rumsfeld. While the strategy review meetings in November and December included Department of Defense personnel, for Cambone the decision ultimately came down to a binary choice of escalation or withdrawal. The president would not tolerate the notion of losing, meaning that the surge became the "default" option. After that was settled, "then the question was how big, how long, to what end, and those kinds of things."[54]

Even advocates of the surge concede that strategy took a backseat to immediate operational demands. The interviews suggest that conversations about how to use additional forces were simplistic and did not tie new operations to clear political objectives. O'Sullivan describes the basic debate, for instance, as being one among groups who felt that Iraqi violence was "primordial" and insensitive to US influence, versus those who believed that US forces could still shape the result of the war.[55] Feaver argues that the surge was born out of the recognition that US forces had a rapidly closing window of opportunity to rescue the war. It was, as he put it, a "gamble for resurrection."[56] Nothing was possible unless US forces arrested the deteriorating security situation. This is made clear in the first line of the NSC's documentary history of the surge, written a year later: "Although security and politics are intertwined, a certain level of security must be achieved before Iraqis can be expected to do the tough political work necessary to resolve sectarian violence."[57] How they would do so remained uncertain, especially because the United States would have to work through a prime minister who some suspected was more interested in settling sectarian grievances than building a unified Iraq.

Administration officials were aware of this problem, but were also confident that General Petraeus could fill in the strategic gap. His effort to rewrite counterinsurgency doctrine impressed key officials. He had assembled a striking team of military officers and academics to sort through the practical problems of "population-centric" counterinsurgency, which required protecting civilians while working to increase the legitimacy of the government and the armed forces. The resulting document convinced surge advocates that they had the right leader in place when it came time to implement the president's decision. Said Edelman, "If you were going to move toward a more population-centric counterinsurgency strategy it made a lot of sense that the guy who wrote the manual would be there to execute the strategy."[58]

However appealing, Petraeus did not actually produce a strategy. FM 3–24, *Counterinsurgency*, was an operational doctrine, not a plan for connecting operations with policy objectives. Moreover, the doctrine potentially worked at cross-purposes with the surge. On the one hand, the surge proponents argued that Iraq had descended into a sectarian civil war, and that it had become much more than an insurgency against occupying US forces and the government they protected. But the strategic review led by J. D. Crouch seemed uncomfortable with the strategic implications that followed. Acknowledging that Iraq was in the midst of civil war suggested that the United States ought to either take sides or back out and seek to contain the regional consequences. This, of course, was not the preference of surge proponents. They wanted to intervene without picking favorites, to reduce the threat to civilians and buy time for Iraq to resolve its political problems. In other words, they favored the kind of counterinsurgency that Petraeus was advocating, despite the fact that the war did not fit the classical insurgency model.[59]

Classical counterinsurgency as expressed in the field manual required building a competent local force, which would in time gain the confidence and support of the population. Counterinsurgency without such efforts was self-defeating. If the host-state military remained incapable, then foreign forces would have to choose between open-ended occupation and ignominious withdrawal. But the surge came about only because US officials determined that a large number of Iraqi forces were incompetent and that years of training and investment had proven futile. The whole point of the surge was to replace them, and the signal to Iraqi civilians was that their armed forces were not to be trusted. Perhaps that trust could be won later, but it was not clear why the United States would help them improve later after such a dismal show, especially after having publicly repudiated their performance and loyalty. At best, the surge would buy time to train a more reliable Iraqi security force, and MNF-I planned to continue efforts to train and equip Iraqi forces.

FM 3–24 also emphasized the importance of government legitimacy. Unless the population recognize their government as legitimate, they will continue to turn to other groups for security. The surge, however, required investing in a government that some US officials believed was sectarian and corrupt. Somewhat ironically, the "bet on Maliki" approach made up part of the surge strategy. As Feaver puts it, of "two of the options that had been presented as alternatives, 'Bet on Maliki,' and 'Double down' . . . the actual surge strategy ends up being the blending of those two. The elements that were bet on Maliki, empower Maliki, and also we're going to send the surge. You need to do both." Some officials rationalized their decision by arguing that Maliki was not the sectarian leader they had feared. Instead, they hoped, he was "either poorly advised, or poorly informed, or poorly equipped."[60] While some were suspicious of Maliki, it was impossible to ignore the prime minister, and the administration hoped that improved security would lead Maliki to improve his behavior. Bush and Maliki met in Jordan in December 2006, and the prime minister outlined his own new strategy for bringing the war under control. Bush apparently went along, but with the proviso that the Iraqi army could not be in the lead. As Hadley paraphrased Bush, "I agree with your strategy. Let us work with you on the fine points. But you don't have the troops to do it. Let me lend you my troops."[61]

Some in the administration believed that part of the surge was a political test for Maliki, and the administration attached strings to its new commitment of resources. According to David Satterfield, coordinator for Iraq for the State Department, Maliki had to agree that US and Iraqi forces would target any violent actor, including armed Shia groups, and that US officers would be in command. Moreover, the president wanted to see demonstrations of good faith before new US forces arrived: "No more Iraqi units being pulled out of the fight when the targets were Shia figures that couldn't be touched."[62] Bush's own comments about his December meeting with Maliki are somewhat different, at least in tone. Making unswerving demands, he thought, would come across as "hectoring and lecturing." Instead, he sought to commiserate as a fellow leader who understood the demands of domestic politics. Bush's transcript does not provide any specific details of his conversations, however, so it is unclear if his recollection differs from Satterfield's.[63] But his judgment of Maliki at the end of November 2006—that he had the will to succeed, but not the capacity—suggests that Bush was less concerned about the need to test the prime minister.[64]

This oral history project does not include perspectives from Iraqi officials, so it is hard to know the effect of US-Iraq negotiations in 2006–2007, but the problem of inadvertently encouraging self-serving behavior from proxy states is familiar to students of counterinsurgency. Efforts to retain leverage require putting tight conditions on aid, but public promises of support take the air out of threats to enforce those conditions.[65] Moreover, Bush's softer private tone with Maliki may have reinforced the belief that the United States would back him, even if his subsequent actions departed from the kind of reconciliation needed to achieve a "unified federal democratic Iraq."

If some thought the surge was a political test for Maliki, the prime minister's subsequent actions would test Washington. President Bush had urged Maliki to give a public speech promising to target all militias, regardless of sect. The administration was pleased when he did so in a televised address from the Iraqi legislature on January 25, 2007. This was an act of political courage, as the speech threatened to alienate some elements of his base in the Shia community, and surge advocates saw it as a sign that Maliki could be an effective and unifying leader. But there were already signs that this was wishful thinking. Shortly after his speech, Maliki fell into a particularly nasty sectarian spat with a member of parliament, Abdul Nasser al-Janabi, which was broadcast live. According to one account, Maliki's behavior during the angry exchange "was the polar opposite of the inclusiveness he had been advocating just minutes earlier."[66]

The following spring, Maliki took the administration by surprise by launching a military push into Basra. After some initial hesitation, US forces supported his action, and generally backed his effort to strengthen the central government. This was understandable, and doing otherwise risked fomenting political chaos at a time in which the country was already suffering terrible violence. But US military assistance was a clear signal of political support. And while he marginalized his Shia rivals in the south, Maliki continued to consolidate his power in Baghdad.

By doing so, he risked further harm to Iraqi civil-military relations and military effectiveness. Regimes that fear internal enemies take efforts to protect themselves against coups. Such efforts include promoting officers based on loyalty rather than competence, and discouraging realistic training. These actions are the opposite of what is required to build an effective fighting force, of course, but they also increase officers' ability to choreograph a government takeover.[67] Because the Bush administration signaled its willingness to take responsibility for Iraq's security, Maliki had no incentive to encourage military professionalism. Instead, he could build the kind of security services that were good at protecting the regime but ineffective in battle.

Maliki used his position to control military appointments and promote loyalists in regional operations centers.[68] Following his lead, the ISF responded ferociously to attacks in central Baghdad that threatened to make the government look impotent, but it paid scant attention to rural violence. Corruption in the ranks remained endemic, and the ISF continued to rely on heavy-handed tactics, despite US exhortations to emulate FM 3–24. According to one close observer, the military was "part of the problem" and "an irritant along ethnic and sectarian fault lines."[69] Some worried that the situation would worsen if US forces left the country, as there would be little to stop the worst units from the kind of actions likely to provoke an angry response and rekindle sectarian bloodshed. These concerns were warranted. Maliki's officer corps lived down to expectations, and political leaders ignored various forms of harassment and abuse of the population in Sunni areas.[70] This was the worst of both worlds: ISF units were simultaneously provocative and incompetent. All of this contributed to its dismal performance against the Islamic State (ISIS) in 2014, when ISF units melted under the pressure of the group's eastward advance. The surge is sometimes portrayed as a triumph of US civil-military relations. For Iraq, it was a civil-military disaster.

The administration was apparently satisfied that it had guarded against this risk during the surge deliberations in 2006–2007. As described above, Satterfield reports that Bush extracted a promise from Maliki that ISF would not pull back from the fight, even if Shia militants with connections to the government ended up on the target list.[71] Maliki's public pledge to attack all militias was a hopeful sign that the ISF would become more professional and that it would work to improve security across the board. Rice reports that ISF performance improved: "When they were all running for their lives and dealing with suicide bombings every day, that was not the environment in which you could—but we had doubled down. They now had a lot of confidence in us. Their security forces started to perform better. They started to see themselves a real country, with real leadership and real problems that any of us who have been in government could understand."[72] Real improvement was illusory, however, and Iraqi forces reverted to form after the departure of US troops in late 2011.

The surge decision was an understandable response to a badly deteriorating security environment. Administration officials plausibly argued that no political good could come without reversing Iraq's descent into civil war. Nonetheless, what began as an operational stopgap created a host of new strategic problems. Most importantly, it reinforced the political and institutional pathologies in Iraq that were partly responsible for the civil war in the first place.

Nonetheless, it is hard to argue against the decision to restore security as a necessary precondition to political progress. Continuing to work on political and institutional development in the midst of ethnic violence and sectarian cleansing would have been absurd and tragic. In places with weak or nonexistent regimes, civil wars are bloody and ruthless competitions for power.

Making genuine political progress requires establishing a new hierarchy, which itself requires putting down violence and enforcing control. Efforts to win over "hearts and minds" and earn legitimacy by accommodating reasonable political grievances must wait.[73] The Bush administration failed to heed this lesson from 2003–2006, preferring to view the conflict first as the result of sporadic fighting by Saddam regime dead-enders, and later viewing it as a kind of violent protest against the government that could be resolved by political accommodation and legislative change. In a sense the surge debate was an important recognition of the depth of the conflict, and the decision reflected a clear-eyed conclusion that only US forces could restore order and control.

In addition, none of the alternatives were particularly attractive. The train-and-transition model seemed to have failed utterly, given the Iraqi army's poor performance. A rolling surge would have created new domestic political problems for the administration, which surely recalled Vietnam-era controversies that erupted each time President Johnson went to Congress to ask for more troops. A pure bet-on-Maliki strategy was impossible because the prime minister did not have sufficiently capable military forces to consolidate his rule without US assistance.

The only option left was withdrawal. It may have been that the value of victory was less than the costs of sustained fighting in a war where there was no clear path to enduring stability and peace. President Bush disagreed, arguing that leaving Iraq would have terrible consequences for the region, the broader US counterterrorism campaign, and ultimately for US national security. But assessing those claims requires examining how strategy in Iraq fit in with grand strategy writ large, which is beyond the scope of this chapter.

CHAPTER 14

Civil-Military Relations and the 2006 Iraq Surge

KORI SCHAKE

The United States lost the Iraq War from 2003 to 2006; it set the conditions for winning the Iraq War from 2006–2008. President Bush's replacing of his defense secretary with Robert Gates, and Bush's refashioning of the way he carried out his own responsibilities were the true and essential catalysts for change. In that regard, the story of the 2006 Iraq surge is primarily a story of civil-civil, not civil-military, relations. The failures were failures of civilian leadership, not primarily those of the military or its relationship to its civilian masters. What military failures there were were largely derivative of the political choices, including support for making the selected strategy work and the selection of senior officers congenial to the elected leaders' views.

Still, the transition from a failing to a succeeding strategy for the war reveals some striking civil-military misconceptions on the part of the civilian leadership in the Bush administration. Most importantly—and worryingly for the conventions of civil-military relations in the United States—the president, the White House chief of staff, and the national security advisor allowed the political cost of veterans' opposition to be treated as though it were indistinguishable from insubordination by active-duty military.[1] In order not to be seen as giving in to veterans' calls for the resignation of the secretary of defense, the White House (with the collusion of the chairman of the Joint Chiefs of Staff) retained Defense Secretary Donald Rumsfeld in office for six additional months after they had concluded a change of strategy was essential to win the Iraq War and that change could not be carried out with Rumsfeld as secretary. As a result, they paid a very high price in blood, treasure, and continued failure of the war effort in order to uphold a spurious principle of civil-military relations.[2]

In doing so, those good men were not invidiously cloaking political cowardice as principle. They genuinely believed that the public makes no distinction between the American military and its veterans, and therefore the president could not, either.[3] And they were not wrong to be concerned about the political resonance of veterans' voices: forty-five years into an all-volunteer military force, small relative to our population, the American public has largely outsourced its judgment on the wars to the military and to veterans.[4] But by not defending the distinction between dangerous insubordination of serving military and the civil liberty of veterans participating in political debate, the White House failed in its responsibility of strengthening and upholding an important civil-military norm. Civil-military norms that treat as military insurrection any veteran contribution to public discourse will very quickly impoverish our public understanding of warfare. And that will ultimately make more difficult the work of our elected political leaders to successfully prosecute wars.

Process Perceived and Real

The 2006 Iraq surge is sometimes characterized in terms of civil-military divide: the refusal of political leaders to listen to the generals, resulting in a disastrous and inconclusive war; a costly "generals' revolt" against their civilian masters, forcing the Bush administration to sacrifice its defense secretary; a humbling of the civilian masters in the 2006 midterm elections; a reconsideration of the war effort based on the new congressional realities; the appearance of a military genius riding in on a white horse to provide the ideas and leadership needed to resuscitate the war effort.[5] Almost none of these elements accord with the information now available about Bush administration decision making during 2006 as the Iraq War became untenable.

The humbling of the political masters in the 2006 election is objectively true. Almost everything else needs reconsideration based on the extensive interviews conducted for the Iraq Surge project. While criticisms are certainly valid of the lateness in coming to realize a different approach was necessary and the inchoate process of early reviews, the Bush administration review of the Iraq War in 2006 is still a remarkable example of US government policy making. The Samarra mosque bombing in February caused both the civilian and military leadership to reconsider the nature of the conflict that the US was engaged in fighting in Iraq. National Security Council staffers initiated processes to widen the aperture of information and ideas reaching the president. The vice president began independently engaging civilian and military thinkers for the same purpose. The military leadership conveyed through the chain of command to the secretary and the president that existing plans could not be carried out. The chairman of the Joint Chiefs of Staff initiated reviews in theater, at the combatant command headquarters, and within the Joint Staff to provide the president fresh military advice about alternatives. Civilian leadership in the Pentagon and White House were informed of the reviews, and supported them without interference. Simultaneously, the National Security Council staff initiated an interagency review process to reconsider the strategy and its underlying assumptions. The White House chief of staff and the national security advisor privately initiated discussions with the president (in April) about replacing the defense secretary. The president rightly challenged them to identify a successor, which they commenced to do. The national security advisor and the chief of staff married processes of consultation and decision to their careful understanding of the president's management style. When the president reached a decision, his cabinet, the White House staff, and military leadership were brought in to his thinking, and he encouraged the airing of their concerns and provided policy remediation for them (the increase in military end strength). Despite the 2006 election losses producing a Congress opposed in both principle and practice to sustained—much less increased—commitment to the war, President Bush chose the course of action he believed would win the war. He made the choice cognizant of the political compromises and opportunity costs he would pay to achieve it. The president, with the help of advisors both inside and outside the administration, found a military commander whose thinking was congenial to what the president wanted to achieve and whose experience suggested he could operationalize the strategy. The new secretary of defense provided top cover with the Congress, identified and provided casualty-reducing equipment and other support that rallied the troops, and shook up the Department of Defense to make the war effort its top priority. The secretary of state created melded civil-military teams, subordinating diplomats to the military in provincial reconstruction teams to bring more nonmilitary heft to the war effort.

All of which was achieved despite highly unpropitious circumstances: a president politically damaged by the decision to go to war and its conduct across three years, central figures on the policy-making team circling each other warily, an overburdened military worried about its ability to hold together and divided over whether to persevere in the existing approach, policy processes five years in place and therefore difficult to amend, restive allies and emboldened adversaries among both the defense community and in the Congress. And, importantly, no obvious alternatives at any level of effort likelier to lead to a better outcome in the war.

The process story of orchestrating the strategy review, though, is only part of the success of the 2006 surge, and perhaps not even the most important part. The way Secretary Rumsfeld did his job, and the way the president did his, from 2003 to 2006, were the root causes of flagging prospects in Iraq. Both challenges are often characterized in civil-military terms, but the failures of the Iraq War that necessitated the surge were less civil-military problems than civil-civil problems.

There were military problems, as well, in the failure of the war effort between 2003 and 2006,[6] in particular the inability of the American military to anticipate and prepare for the kind of war our enemies could impose on us to fight.[7] Some military leaders genuinely believed that the presence of US troops in Iraq fomented the insurgency; the ambition or cowardice of others prevented advocacy of approaches they knew to be superior; and still others understood the unequal dialogue of civil-military relations in the United States to require them to effectuate any legal and moral approach elected civilian leaders chose. So there was not a unified military position, and much military complicity in the failure of the war from 2003 to 2006. But the principal causes of failure were above the military's pay grade.

Perhaps policy making should be graded like Olympic diving, with a degree of difficulty factored in to the score. Because if the process that produced the surge does not quite merit the effusion of praise its participants lavish on it (even the famously taciturn Robert Gates characterizes it as "textbook" good policy making), it succeeded in delivering a substantially improved outcome against long odds that positive change was possible. In the end, it provided an alternative that could succeed and that unified the executive branch around the alternative, which was essential to regaining public and congressional support for the war effort.[8]

Personnel Decisions *Are* Policy Decisions

The fundamental responsibility of the secretary of defense is to ensure that the president's political objectives are translated into military plans and resourcing adequate to achieve them. This Secretary Rumsfeld did not do, either in the run-up to the 2003 Iraq War, or in reconsideration of existing plans as the nature of the Iraq War changed.

For all the secretary's peripatetic activism with the Iraq War plans, he expended his energies doing things the military already does well, such as determining the number of port handlers in deployment orders or which specific units need to flow into theater on what timelines for the gears to mesh. He was policing the military's tendency to want a wide margin of error, seeking instead to usher in a transformation in military affairs.[9] What he did not seem to do was the work only the secretary of defense can: ensure that war plans designed for speed in overcoming enemy resistance and rapid subsequent repatriation of forces achieved the president's political objective of successful regime change in Iraq.

This incongruity of political objective and military operations was most in evidence with the initial "three brigade rolling start" plans in 2003 that alarmed so many in the military, but also provided the frame of intellectual reference that guided Secretary Rumsfeld's management of the war throughout.[10] Former national security advisor Condoleezza Rice flatly states that the Pentagon in 2003 inadequately resourced the invasion and that Secretary Rumsfeld was evasive on important elements of the plans, such as how order among a vanquished but fractious opponent would be maintained.[11]

The original conception driving force levels for stabilization in Iraq was predicated on the view of General Abizaid that US forces would, by their very presence, generate Iraqi opposition.[12] Whether Secretary Rumsfeld agreed with that assessment, it dovetailed with his belief that military involvements were "sticky," difficult to unwind even when military forces were no longer needed. The idea was eventually proven wrong by Iraqi support for US forces during the surge; but until that point, it served to justify a rapid drawing down of forces after the invasion. Defense Department flow charts for years represented the blocks of units rapidly descending, always just beyond the immediate time frame when positive political developments like the transition of sovereignty, elections, or government formation took place.

Vice President Cheney acknowledges that "there was sort of a disconnect between our execution of a strategy that's going to lead to stability in Iraq on the one hand, and on the other hand, this planning to begin withdrawing forces or bringing forces home relatively soon."[13] Condoleezza Rice, secretary of state at the time, also concedes the disconnect, acknowledging, "I'd not really done the kind of red-teaming that we perhaps should have done."[14] Jack Keane describes concluding in June 2003, while still on active duty as the vice chief of staff of the Army, that the US was facing an Iraqi insurgency and that "our strategy was incapable of dealing with this reality," but failing to get traction with either civilian or military leaders for a changed approach.[15]

The February 22, 2006, bombing of the al-Askari mosque in Samarra and resultant frenzy of sectarian violence in Iraq seems to have shocked nearly all administration policy makers out of the belief that Iraq was making progress toward the kind of national reconciliation on which US withdrawal timelines depended. After the bombing, the White House chief of staff described Iraq as "problem one, two, and three for the administration."[16] He describes President Bush's attitude as "he could see the results of the strategy were not working, and he had, I think, an evolving view, that maybe the reason it's not working is that, in fact, we are not successfully preventing these people from killing each other while we're withdrawing as rapidly as we can."[17] After the bombing, the commander in Iraq told his superiors the violence in Iraq would prevent withdrawal of US forces on the scheduled timeline. After the bombing, the chairman of the Joint Chiefs of Staff initiated strategy reviews at all three headquarters (Multi-National Force–Iraq, US Central Command, and the Joint Staff). After the bombing, the vice president began taking soundings from experts outside the government.

Seemingly the only place not to reconsider its approach to the conflict in the wake of the Samarra bombing was in the Office of the Secretary of Defense.[18] Secretary Rumsfeld considered Samarra "an affirmation of the nature of the struggle you're in, rather than a sign that you're losing."[19] As informal reviews got under way, the Department of Defense was "not in that flow of conversation. This conversation about the surge was taking place between the State Department, the White House, and people on the outside."[20] When the formal interagency review commenced, Secretary Rumsfeld "did not find the subject or the process congenial, and was making plain that he was not going to be an active participant in that undertaking."[21]

The secretary's office also seemed oddly detached from what was occurring in the military staffs. According to the chairman of the Joint Chiefs, the secretary knew of the military reviews under way, and participated in the meeting with the president informing him of the concern of General George Casey, the top Army commander in Iraq, about existing plans and forces; yet the Office of the Secretary of Defense believed the numbers of forces for the surge "did not come out of the military side of the house."[22]

According to the under secretary of defense for intelligence, Stephen Cambone, as late as the autumn of 2006 Secretary Rumsfeld's view was "that it wasn't going as badly as it was said."[23] He didn't think more forces to Iraq "was going to make a difference," was concerned that once there, they would be stuck because political leaders would always find reasons (as in Kosovo and Korea) not to draw down, and meanwhile the Department of Defense had other contingencies to worry about.[24] When departments were proffering alternatives for consideration in the interagency review, Defense's proposal was to accelerate disengagement from Iraq, essentially ceding the president's political objectives.[25] That is, losing the war.

In light of Secretary Rumsfeld's views, his outsize influence in the cabinet after Colin Powell's departure, and the weight he carried as defense secretary in any question of the use of military force, a structured and transparent process would have quickly produced an interagency stalemate—incurring to the president all the political costs of showing his doubt about the existing course of action without producing a different one. It would almost certainly have rallied opponents in the Congress during an election year (the campaign ads write themselves: even the president doesn't believe in his approach, he needlessly puts troops in harm's way, hit the pause button until the Congress can provide oversight) and exacerbated criticism from retired military leaders that constrained the president's choices.

General Peter Pace, who headed the Joint Chiefs of Staff, gamely defends his boss, saying "I never felt that Secretary Rumsfeld was opposed. . . . Once you show me the plan, I, as secretary, will approve or disapprove, and we'll take it to the president."[26] But by all other accounts, including Cambone's, Secretary Rumsfeld was out of step with the rest of the administration about the war. Secretary Rice delicately says that although Iraq strategy reviews were ongoing, they weren't talked about in the cabinet because those in the know didn't want to "provoke," but that after "the change as SecDef, it was entirely possible for the Pentagon to be a full partner."[27]

The Generals

The White House chief of staff and the national security advisor had both initiated conversations with the president about replacing Secretary Rumsfeld in early 2006. President Bush was willing, provided a suitable alternative was found.[28] Some of the most influential voices calling for Rumsfeld's replacement were retired senior military officers. Retired Marine lieutenant general Greg Newbold and many others publicly made the case.[29]

President Bush describes his reaction to the veterans' pressure as "I'm not going to have the generals force my hand."[30] The White House chief of staff, the national security advisor, and the chairman of the Joint Chiefs of Staff were also in agreement that it would be damaging to civil-military relations for the president to be seen responsive to that pressure.[31] General Pace advised against any moves for six months—a shockingly high price to pay in lives lost, war effort, and political consequence in order to reinforce the principle.

In defense of the administration, developing options, reaching consensus, and addressing second-order effects of adopting a new strategy might have taken just as long, had the White House not taken issue with the veterans' criticism. Secretary Rice believes the strategy process alone dictated the timeline across 2006–2007.[32] President Bush is insistent the veterans' criticism had no effect on his thinking.[33] But Bush and his national security advisor Stephen Hadley continue to believe it was important not to concede to the recommendations of retired military officers criticizing the conduct of the war.[34] That almost surely was sound political judgment in 2006; but it ought to be justified on a political rather than civil-military basis.

In fact, the sense of urgency felt by so many in the military and veterans about the costs of American strategy in Iraq was never felt in the same way by the civilian leadership—as the time elapsed in coalescing around a new strategy and the willingness to delay replacing Secretary Rumsfeld demonstrate. Four hundred seventy-nine American service men and women were killed in Iraq during those months between acknowledgment that the war effort was failing and adoption of the surge strategy.[35] President Bush, especially, felt the moral weight of those losses. But he allowed the process of course correction to evolve slowly while Iraq descended further into violence and political recrimination. The White House considered the military leadership united in support of existing strategy, when plenty of critical military voices existed (and were ultimately harnessed). Republican congressional candidates pleaded for a White House signal the administration was changing direction in advance of the 2006 election; loss of Republican majorities in both houses of Congress is widely attributed to the president's unpopularity because of the war.[36]

Vice President Cheney believes the president had basically decided on the surge when he decided to replace Rumsfeld: "It was pretty clear the road he was headed down."[37] President Bush's own testimony supports that.[38] The process of reviewing Iraq strategy could proceed in the open once Rumsfeld had tendered his resignation. By removing the only senior policy maker hostile to attempts to reconsider the approach, the administration opened up space for consideration of policy options that would otherwise have been unavailable.

And with the replacement of the secretary, what were thought to be problems in civil-military relations were revealed not to be,[39] because both the active duty and retired military were largely supportive of a new approach.[40] What concern existed about the new strategy was not (as was the case for Secretary Rice) questioning whether a counterinsurgency surge could succeed, but about the force management consequences of surging troops in Iraq.

The civil-military issue that arose in the course of the 2006 surge strategy development was building support for a different approach by the active duty leadership so that the administration proceeded unified into public and congressional debates. This President Bush and his national security team did with real skill in the 2006 strategy review. The American military has an independent voice in policy formulation, and its public stature is such that any president proceeds cautiously in winning its support. The president can force his war strategy on the military, but it is seldom politic for him to do so, especially if that president is in a weak position domestically because of his conduct of the war.

The White House choice to defend at such a price the principle of civilian leadership uninfluenced by veteran criticism is interesting on two counts. That the White House was sincere about doing so is not in question; the administration's frustration with public criticism by retired military officers in 2006 remains vivid.[41] But two aspects of the administration's own behavior suggest that White House officials were less adherent to the orthodoxy of civil-military relations than they profess: their own use of retired military officers as both private counselors and public defenders of the strategy, and their conflating of criticism from both active duty and retired officers.

In criticizing the existing strategy, advocating relief of military officers in command positions, determining whether to remove the civilian Department of Defense leadership of the war effort, developing alternatives to existing strategy, identifying active duty military officers better suited to conduct the new strategy (in addition to its civilian strategy team), the Bush White House also relied on retired military officers, including Jack Keane, Barry McCaffrey, and Wayne Downing. According to Keane, he "operationalized it" (the strategy) down to the platoon level, and the president even asked them who should replace General Casey.[42]

Steve Hadley defends the administration conflating active and retired military opposition on the grounds that the public makes no distinction.[43] And he is right: surveys conducted by YouGov for the Hoover Institution's project on civil-military gaps in 2013–2014 indicate that forty five years into an all-volunteer military, the American public has outsourced its judgment on the conduct of wars to the military.[44] Less than one-half of 1 percent of the American public now serves in the military, so it is perhaps natural that civilians look to those with military experience to voice approval or concern over the conduct of wars. If we are to have informed judgment on the war effort, much of that judgment will be provided by retired military personnel.

Perhaps instead of reinforcing the conflation of active and retired military in the public consciousness, the administration could have reinforced the distinction by emphasizing the rights of retired military to contribute to public discourse in contrast to the obedience demonstrated by the active duty military. It could also have defanged the public opposition by Newbold and others by bringing them into the consultations already ongoing with Keane, McCaffrey, and others. Newbold and others were unaware of the reconsideration within the administration but were, after all, arguing for similar lines of exploration. Several civilian participants in the surge debate argue it needed to be held closely in order not to discourage the military personnel fighting in Iraq; Keane and other participants with military expertise dispute the notion that reconsideration of a failing strategy would have been disheartening to the Americans most exposed to the futility of continuing on the stated course.

It is also an important civil-military distinction whether retired military officers opine on the subject on which they are trained and knowledgeable, or more broadly on politics for which they have no especial claim to expertise. Endorsements by retired military officers of political candidates, while worrisome in an American civil-military context, have become standard practice. Research by Peter Feaver and James Golby suggests such endorsements do not sway voters, instead serving to diminish public support for the military as an institution. Two successive chairmen of the Joint Chiefs of Staff have now expressed concern that retired military endorsements make more difficult the job of active duty military leaders to work with their elected civilian masters.[45] Yet President Bush himself released lists of retired military endorsements in the 2000 and 2004 elections.[46] Bewail it as we might, the Bush White House exceeded the doctrinal boundaries of civil-military relations when it provided political benefit.

Not only did retired military officers provide private counsel formally and informally to the president, the vice president, and the national security advisor, but McCaffrey wrote reports that were widely distributed in defense circles, Keane provided congressional testimony, and McCaffrey and Downing emerged from meeting with the president to give television interviews recounting their advice. So the administration made both public and private use of retired military officers in support of changing its policy—the same activities for which it criticized retired military officers who argued for changing such policy. The distinction seems only to be that some retired military officers were sanctioned by the administration to do so, while others were not. It is hardly a bright, impermeable line in the civil-military sands.

Hadley's Dictum

Stephen Hadley has (elsewhere) argued that presidents get the interagency processes they deserve: "Presidents can either pick the one they want, or if they ignore it, they are going to get a dysfunctional system, which they deserve because they have not taken ownership of the system to fix it."[47] What the evolution of the surge demonstrates is that by 2006, President Bush finally took ownership of his administration.

Academic evaluations of strategy very often underestimate the practical difficulties associated with governance. This is especially true of those (like my own) infatuated with the structured transparency of the Eisenhower administration.[48] But as Lawrence Freedman argues so forcefully in *Strategy: A History*, the politics neither can nor should be leached out of the process. The chief executive may be supreme in US government policy making, but that does not insulate him from either the political laws of gravity or the ways his own management style complicates or prevents the outcomes his policies are designed to achieve.

President Bush could not have instituted Eisenhower's choices because he wasn't Eisenhower—he didn't have the record of wartime achievement that underwrote Eisenhower's ability to discipline the process. What he had instead was the legacy from his first term of a national security team riven by disagreement and resentment, a welter of justified criticism for the choice and conduct of the Iraq War, and the necessity of choosing a different course in the teeth of a midterm congressional election. President Bush probably could not have forced a change over sustained Defense Department objections to his policy in 2006; he was simply in too weak a position. That is the fundamental fact for evaluating the process of policy making that produced the 2006 surge: President Bush had to achieve his objective by political persuasion. And his staff had to find a process that matched the president's need for a different policy without ignoring the practical reality of governing.

At the commencement of the process, President Bush was receiving very positive accounts of progress in the war. As the White House chief of staff describes it, "what he was getting from the military commanders was a realistic view, from their standpoint, but their standpoint is very much colored by the imperative to make the strategy that they were in succeed."[49] Secretary Rice was less diplomatic: "The metrics were surreal. . . . I no longer had any confidence in the numbers the Pentagon was putting out."[50] Having put the military in an untenable position of carrying out plans badly matched to the objectives and forces sized to availability rather than need, the president seemed to compensate by trying to give them as much latitude as possible in the conduct of the operations.

Joshua Bolten, coming into the chief of staff's job in 2006, noticed that "the president I saw at those war meetings was, to me, noticeably different from the one I saw in every other context, where he was in charge, he was challenging everything."[51] The chairman of the Joint Chiefs of Staff gently reinforced the point, saying "the president was not directive when he was talking with his senior military. He was always solicitous of opinions."[52] Bolten concluded, "The process we had in place wasn't serving the president particularly well, because it was set up in a way in which his instinct to defer to the people in uniform was encouraged, rather than discouraged."[53]

That deference clearly changed during deliberations over the surge. Secretary Rice agrees that "President Bush was different. He'd been reluctant early on to direct his secretaries in quite the same way, was more solicitous of the military, less questioning of what he was getting from them. It put him in a position where he wasn't very demanding of the military. By 2006 he was confident enough to push for different options than he was getting."[54] Both Bolten and Hadley were clearly essential in helping the president reconfigure the way he received information, preserved the space to develop and evaluate potential courses of action, engaged with senior policy makers—including the military—to build support for his policy preferences and ensure unity of effort in carrying out the policy. Bolten credits Hadley with "trying to ventilate the process, trying to give the president more avenues of information, trying to make sure that he was hearing more directly, and with more force, the bad news that everybody who was watching TV and reading the newspaper was seeing, rather than doing everything he could to support the commanders who were saying, 'We're not doing great, but we're just about to turn the corner; we think we've got the right strategy here.'"[55]

So many elements of the problem needed to be untangled: personnel issues (a new secretary of defense; nonpunitive moves for the military leadership in Iraq; identification of a military leader capable of conceptualizing, explaining, and enacting a different approach), rigorous reevaluation of the assumptions on which current strategy was based, cajoling the Pentagon to understand its activity was inadequate to the political need, determining whether resources were even available to enact a different approach.

The most important element of the process was changing the president's dynamic interacting with the military. As with planning for the surge, the problem was not civil-military in nature. It was instead a problem of misalignment of the processes the president had in place. The interviews don't make clear what the chief of staff and the national security advisor did differently to better match processes to the president's management style. That something important changed is evident in the accounts of President Bush's meeting with the service chiefs after deciding to change course in Iraq. The president's top advisors didn't seek to change his management style, to make him confrontational or compel the military's compliance. But they created circumstances in which the chiefs' concerns were respectfully heard by the commander in chief and policy solutions offered as part of the strategy he adopted.

As President Bush stated it, "The military's job is to figure out how to win. The president's job is to decide if we want to win or not, and if the strategy is not winning, then the president's job is to demand another strategy."[56] The American military understands it doesn't get to choose whether or even how to go to war; that is the prerogative of the civilian leadership in our system. Nor does the military get to determine the resources—the level of national effort—to put to the task. But our military has an outsize role in the formation of war policy because it is so crucial to the success of such policy. What the military expects from its civilian leaders isn't deference, but the opportunity to be heard and, where possible, have its concerns addressed.[57] All these things President Bush did when charting a new course in Iraq in 2006. The national security advisor's close work with the chairman of the Joint Chiefs removed the chiefs' potential opposition to the strategy by offering relief for their larger concern about strain on the force.

As similarly described by Secretary Gates, Chief of Staff Bolten, and General Pace, "the president was there to try and bring these guys on board."[58] Flanked by the outgoing and incoming secretaries of defense, President Bush engaged confidently with the chiefs, drawing out their concerns and making clear his determination to proceed in full knowledge of the risks he was incurring. When the chief of staff of the Army expressed his worry the surge of forces was too much for the force to bear, that it would break the military, President Bush replied, "Let me tell you what I think is going to break the military: a defeat like we had in Vietnam that broke the military for a generation, will break the military. We've got to do everything we can to prevent that."[59] He forcefully made the argument on terms the chiefs respected and earned their support, rather than giving them his support for whatever they believed was needed.

It is a hugely consequential difference. As Chief of Staff Bolten concluded, "I think he had seen that there's only one president and there's only one person that can step in and really redirect. And he had a higher comfort level doing that at the beginning of '07 than I think he did at the beginning of '06.[60] Condoleezza Rice agrees, poignantly saying, "George W. Bush was a different president in 2006 than he was in 2003."[61]

The process of reviews displayed a messy virtuosity. It was begun by the national security advisor pressing the Defense Department on a series of fifty questions, developing into a set of initially independent reviews throughout the administration, loosely orchestrated into a series of conversations for the president and his cabinet to evaluate three potential courses of action. Related resource evaluations occurred both inside and outside the military, providing the president with both the information and the time needed to make what would be the most consequential decision of his second term, and then shaping how the decision would be received by essential stakeholders in the military and Congress.

The president and his closest advisors acknowledged from the outset that removing the bureaucratic impediment of an opposing secretary of defense would be essential and worked that problem in parallel. They allowed misplaced concern about veteran criticism to delay the process, but developing and reaching consensus on the new strategy might have taken as long even without that concern. The president's closest advisors also understood that the president needed a different approach himself to engaging on the issues; he had to become a different kind of commander in chief for the strategy reviews to produce a better outcome in the war. The very different civil-military relationship that produced the 2006 surge was entirely a function of changes on the civilian side of the equation.

CHAPTER 15

The Bush Administration's Decision to Surge in Iraq

A Long and Winding Road

Richard H. Immerman

The process was "nearly textbook," remarks former secretary of defense Robert Gates, whose replacement of Donald Rumsfeld was pivotal to President George W. Bush's decision to "surge" five brigades of US troops in Iraq.[1] Gates's assessment accords with that of virtually all the twenty-plus officials interviewed for this project. Stephen Hadley, for example, who managed the process as national security advisor in Bush's second term, is more understated. He calls it simply "good."[2] Secretary of State Condoleezza Rice opposed the surge until the last minute. She nevertheless is "proud" of "the way the surge decision unfolded."[3]

Appraisals of the process do not depend on where one stood during the debate. Only three officials interviewed for this project did not use words equivalent to "textbook," "model," "proud," or "good" to describe the process. Meghan O'Sullivan, Hadley's deputy for Iraq and Afghanistan, orchestrated the internal National Security Council (NSC) review and was among the early proponents of a change in strategy that evolved into the surge. She describes the process as "not perfect" because it took longer than she would have liked. But had it moved more rapidly, she interjects, conditions in Iraq would have been less conducive to success.[4] General John Abizaid is more disapproving, but from a narrower vantage point. To Abizaid, who headed US Central Command (CENTCOM) from 2003 to 2007, the "process was not healthy, because the process did not use the whole-of-government approach to include the chain of command."[5]

Philip Zelikow, the counselor to the Department State whom Rice deputized to represent her on Iraq, is more expansive and critical. In his judgment, "the surge episode itself is an extremely strange policy-making episode." Zelikow identifies flaws from its beginning to end, flaws that are offset only at the eleventh hour by the "extraordinary act" of President Bush to "defy so much of the institutional establishment in his own government to promulgate what I thought was a courageous and instinctually correct strategy."[6]

But Zelikow's assessment is sui generis. Even David Satterfield, who joined with Zelikow in late 2006 to draft the State Department paper that recommended against augmenting US forces and does not attribute the achievements at the end of the administration primarily to the surge, disagrees with his colleague. He asserts that the "process of discussion" should be a "model for the future." Hadley managed a "highly successful structure," Satterfield continues. It generated "one of the last truly effective meta-policy debates and resolutions certainly that I've participated in or been part of."[7] Even Stephen Cambone, the loyal and trusted advisor to Secretary of Defense Rumsfeld, the chief obstacle to both the surge and its connected strategic review, praises the process because it was George Bush's. "He, the president, knew that *he* had to make this decision, and *he* took it and put in place a process to bring him what he needed to make that decision, and then *he* made it," explains Cambone. "I think it is one of the model instances of presidential leadership in wartime."[8]

The justifications collectively offered by the officials involved for lauding the process fit the conventional criteria for effective decision making. They include engaging the right people at the right level at the right time; providing an environment that is conducive to expressing views and building relationships required for evoking constructive debate that cuts across agencies and departments; and articulating those options in a manner that enables the president to reach an informed decision.

As should be expected from any difficult decision, some participants were disappointed in the outcome, and perhaps even unconvinced that the surge decision was the optimum one. But because they participated in a process that they respected, even those who were disappointed, the oral histories claim, could be entrusted with carrying out the decision. "You don't want any passive-aggressive behavior by some who might feel defeated," explains Rice. Peter Feaver, who as the NSC's special advisor for strategic planning and institutional reform teamed with O'Sullivan to push first for a review of strategy and then for the surge, suggests that the benefit of avoiding any "real losers" compensated for the cost of the process's length. Hadley, Feaver's boss, concurs. The "story of the surge," he summarizes, "is a president who decides he needs a new strategy, a process which gradually brings people along both to the reality that we need a new strategy and a series of options, and finally a preferred option which is going to work. And then putting together the elements that are required to both bring people along and to ensure its success."[9]

It comes as no surprise that participants in the process applaud the process. What is a surprise is that the evidence provided by their testimony calls into question so many of their assessments. The transcripts depict a decision-making process that was idiosyncratic and rife with shortcomings. In his interview Hadley remarks that he drew on no historical precedent as a guide.[10] I will. In particular, I will draw on the advisory structure established by President Dwight D. Eisenhower in the 1950s. I do not claim that the Eisenhower system is the equivalent of a "textbook" approach. There is no single textbook approach. Yet his decades of experience in government and the military and intimate observations of the growing pains of the advisory architecture established by the National Security Act of 1947 drove Eisenhower to institute a wide range of "best practices" that I maintain should be integral to any effective decision-making process. Many were largely absent from George W. Bush's approach in the lead-up to the surge decision.[11]

My argument is not that the Bush process should have mirrored Eisenhower's from a half century before. The context, conditions, and objectives are not parallel, and foreign and national security policy making embraces many more dimensions and much greater complexity in the contemporary environment than it did in the 1950s. Moreover, a vital feature of the Eisenhower system was that Eisenhower sat at the head of the table. No subsequent US president had his experience, political capital, reputation, credibility, and qualifications. No one since George Washington was better suited to serve as his own secretary of defense, a position that did not exist in Washington's day.

Yet at same time, no modern president, including Eisenhower with his five-star military résumé, has confronted the challenge of deciding on national security strategy with a secretary of defense as toxic to the process as was Donald Rumsfeld when George W. Bush had to reckon with the escalating violence in Iraq. Rumsfeld's influence pervades every oral history conducted for this study of the surge process, and by most accounts, not to his credit.

Nevertheless, as Fred Greenstein and I prescribed for Bill Clinton's successor in an article written during the 2000 campaign, the advisory system that Eisenhower put into place featured a range of best practices with broad applicability. These elements include a "custodian-manager"(Eisenhower's special assistant for national security affairs) responsible for ensuring that the president is exposed to advocates for a spectrum of options;[12] an advisory team whose only expectation is that each member will have his or her "day in court"; an advisory organ (Planning Board) composed of senior representatives from all pivotal components of the national security community who collaborate systematically for the purpose of framing the debates by explicitly identifying policy objectives and delineating the contrasting strategies proposed to achieve those objectives; regularly scheduled NSC meetings that begin with an intelligence briefing after which the principals debate the contrasting strategies in the presence of the president; and another organ (Operations Coordinating Board) charged with reviewing and evaluating the implementation of the decision.[13]

One size does not fit all. No president since Eisenhower has fully adopted his model, and each has tailored procedures appropriate for his needs. The Bush process had to take into account his lack of expertise in military affairs, an increasingly polarized political climate, the legacy of the Vietnam War, the proliferation of leaks of sensitive information in the new media age, the resistance of the uniformed military leadership, and most important, Rumsfeld. Administration insiders argue that for these reasons Bush jettisoned fundamental tenets of Eisenhower's system in an effort to make a virtue out of necessity.[14] Yet the evidence suggests that Eisenhower's best practices are just that—best practices. It further suggests that their rigorous application would have benefited Bush's process by expediting the instigation of a comprehensive review, co-opting opponents of a change in strategy, mitigating politicization, facilitating the exchange of information and advice, and accelerating implementation.

My critique begins with the struggle to initiate a coordinated review of the military strategy in the first place. The extant strategy, associated with Rumsfeld and pursued since 2005 under the direction of General George Casey, the commander of the Multi-National Force–Iraq (MNF-I), and CENTCOM commander John Abizaid, was to train and then turn over responsibility for combat operations to the Iraqi forces: "As they [the Iraqi security forces] stood up, we [United States and coalition forces] would stand down."[15]

The strategy placed a premium on transferring this responsibility as rapidly as possible. Its premise was that the presence of US troops generated antibodies—indigenous forces that would attack them as alien pathogens. Put differently, occupying forces generate nationalist resistance. The longer US forces remained, moreover, the more the Iraqi military would become dependent on them. In this context, multiple oral histories cite Rumsfeld's analogy to a parent teaching a child to ride a bicycle: only by the parent taking his or her hand off the bicycle seat can the child learn to ride without assistance. The Iraqi forces had to learn to ride and become confident in that capability. Self-assured in their assumptions, military strategists resisted talk about retaining, let alone augmenting, US forces in Iraq.[16]

Virtually all the interviewees testified to their discomfort with this strategy by early 2006—if not earlier. Within the NSC staff a consensus developed over the need for a change, or at a minimum the need to examine whether there was a need for a change. During this period "I became increasingly convinced that our strategy was failing," commented O'Sullivan. Feaver, who in 2005 thought that the problem lay with the inability of the administration effectively to explain its strategy, had by 2006 come to agree with O'Sullivan that the problem was the strategy itself.[17]

There was much the same disquietude over at Foggy Bottom—perhaps more. Ambassador to Iraq Zalmay Khalilzad stated that he "had been unhappy with the military strategy" from his arrival in Baghdad in the summer of 2005. He thus took the initiative to establish a "red cell" to challenge that strategy and identify alternatives to it. That exercise resulted by the end of the year in a recommendation to shift to a more population-centric approach.[18]

Secretary of State Rice's concern with the Rumsfeld/Casey strategy dates to 2004, when as national security advisor she established the Iraq Strategy Group to provide the NSC with "better insight" on the evolving situation. Then during her first year as secretary of state, she had Zelikow, who was reaching the conclusion that the current strategy was no strategy at all, draft talking points for her October 2005 testimony to the Senate Committee on Foreign Relations. Drawn from various sources, including Khalilzad's red cell report, among the talking points was the formulation "clear, hold, and build." That formulation provoked what Zelikow labeled a "violent reaction" in the Pentagon. Rumsfeld went so far as to publicly disavow it. "Clear, hold, and build" was off the table.[19]

While reflecting the widespread concern of senior members of Bush's national security team, these mini-reviews were ineffectual. An interagency organ similar to Eisenhower's Operations Coordinating Board responsible for systematically monitoring and assessing the strategy would have identified such concerns as cause for an "all of government" review. But there was no such organ, and Rice's successor Hadley insisted that only the military could initiate a review.[20] Because the military, satisfied with the current strategy, opposed a review outside the Pentagon or MNF-I, instead of conducting one the NSC constructed a white paper titled the "National Strategy for Victory in Iraq." Released on November 30, 2005, NSVI left the strategy intact, claiming that the war itself would be won if the administration could win the public debate over the war.[21]

Although conditions in Iraq continued to deteriorate in the new year even as domestic opposition to the war mounted, there was no comprehensive review of strategy, The reason was in part that the Bush national security machinery lacked a trigger for one and in part because not until spring 2006 did the president begin to appreciate the need to approve one.[22] Early that year Hadley tasked O'Sullivan with providing Bush with a steady stream of notes each night on that day's developments in Iraq. They drew on Pentagon reports, intelligence briefings, State Department cables, and parallel sources; Bush would read them intently. Concerned that reports from the field were overly optimistic, O'Sullivan bent over backward not to "sugarcoat" anything. She characterizes the notes as "portraying a very dark situation" and concedes that her reservations about the strategy unavoidably seeped into her reporting.[23]

Still there was no review. Zelikow emphasizes that Bush was "passionately interested in" and "intensely curious about" what was happening in Iraq. After reading the NSC's notes at night he would in the morning read the blue sheet, casualty reports he received from Baghdad. Often he marked them up.[24]

But the president's consumption of information did not translate into his interrogating the war's conduct, at least not formally. Of the 366 NSC meetings during Eisenhower's two terms, he chaired 339. His national security advisor would prepare an agenda that included the most salient questions of policy and strategy and distribute position papers in advance that identified different points of view. Thereby informed, the principals would debate the issues in Eisenhower's presence, exposing him to the diverse opinions and the reasoning behind them. If in Eisenhower's view a consensus was reached prematurely, he assumed the role of devil's advocate. In his oral history President Bush stresses he did not normally attend the NSC meetings. Whereas Eisenhower believed it vital to learn from and if necessary provoke debates, in Bush's judgment his presence would suppress or distort debates.[25]

On Iraq, Bush did meet with his military advisors. But as Chief of Staff Josh Bolten remarks and Bush concedes, he deferred to the military. More consequential were his meetings with Hadley, O'Sullivan, and/or counselor to the president Dan Bartlett. Doubtless these were constructive, and ultimately they influenced Bush to accept the need to change course.[26] Yet history suggests that had Bush's thinking evolved organically from successive meetings with his range of advisors, he would have approved a formal review earlier both to evaluate the current strategy and identify possible alternatives, his advisors would have better understood the rationale for the review even if they disagreed with conducting it, and thus he would have more readily galvanized support for whatever decision that review produced.[27]

Neither Bush's attending an NSC meeting nor the monitoring of policy by an Operations Coordinating Board should have been necessary for the February 22, 2006, bombing of the al-Askari shrine (Golden Mosque) in Samarra to ignite a comprehensive review. This destruction of one of Shia Islam's holiest sites by Sunni Muslims, for which US intelligence sources attributed responsibility to al-Qaeda in Iraq, underscored that despite Rumsfeld's consistent denials, the United States confronted a virulent insurgency.[28] (The absence of references to intelligence is striking throughout the transcripts, another stark contrast with Eisenhower's best practices.) Particularly because this tipping point in the escalating violence occurred at a time when it became apparent that Iraq's December 2005 parliamentary election was not going to produce a government capable of creating the requisite political space for a Sunni-Shia reconciliation, the need for the administration to revisit the assumptions that underlay the current strategy—as expressed in NSVI—was compelling. One of these was that by ameliorating the contamination of US military antibodies, Iraq's political environment would improve. The security environment would then follow suit. The combination of the Samarra bombing and the stalemated effort to form a government upended that assumption.

The NSC staff in their oral histories identify the Golden Mosque bombing as the "seminal moment" in their determining that the assumptions driving the current strategy were no longer valid and a "radical new look" at it was imperative.[29] But for the Bush's NSC, concluding that a new look was needed and initiating one were not complementary. There were two sides to Eisenhower's policy hill, to use Anna Nelson's metaphor for the relationship between the Planning and Operations Coordinating Boards. Eisenhower occupied the summit. When it came to Bush's Iraq strategy, Rumsfeld and the Pentagon substituted for the policy hill.[30]

This phenomenon produced stasis if not paralysis. In the spring of 2006 a half dozen retired US generals criticized the administration's management of the war and demanded Rumsfeld's resignation. Not only did this "Revolt of the Generals" fail to spark the strategy review that they sought, but also the oral histories suggest that it retarded progress toward one. Because the revolt was made public, administration officials predicted that within and beyond the Beltway various communities would perceive any ensuing replacement of Rumsfeld or revision of strategy as politically motivated.

Bush had to avoid the slightest appearance of caving to public pressure lest he further fuel the growing antiwar movement and alienate supporters of the war, including those in Congress on whom he depended to fund it. Yet Bush's national security architecture and protocols made Rumsfeld's replacement a requisite for revisiting let alone changing strategy. The Revolt of the Generals therefore "bought Rumsfeld another six months or so of tenure," estimates the NSC's Feaver. "Had we brought in a new SecDef, that might have been a time [spring 2006] for a fresh look at the strategy."[31]

That one cabinet officer, even one protected by his intimate relationship with Vice President Dick Cheney, could hold hostage the review of the strategy for an increasingly unpopular and expensive war reflects poorly on the advisory process. Ironically, however, or perhaps for this very reason, in April 2006, just as Bush's expression of confidence in Rumsfeld doomed the Revolt of the Generals' effort to provoke a relook of the strategy, the NSC staff began informally, or more accurately covertly, to establish the preconditions for a review. The catalyst was O'Sullivan's trip to Iraq that month, which reinforced her reservations about the extant approach. When she returned she wrote a memorandum to Hadley "just laying out my sense that our strategy is at fundamental odds with the realities on the ground." She judged that the military's current mission was "exacerbating a failing situation rather than contributing to its improvement."[32]

At this juncture in the journey to the decision to surge, the degree to which the Bush process departs from Eisenhower's best practices could not be more dramatic. With Hadley's approval but without the military's sanction or necessary resources, O'Sullivan conspired with Feaver and the NSC staff to "really force a strategy review, rather than from the top down, from the bottom up." They had interagency representatives prepare briefs evaluating a range of political, strategic, economic, and other considerations. The State Department even strayed well outside of its lane to submit a paper, cowritten by Zelikow and Rice's special representative for Iraq, James Jeffrey, which recommended a counterinsurgency strategy that would require the deployment of additional troops.[33]

In conjunction with these briefs, O'Sullivan and her colleagues formulated a list of pointed questions about the current strategy for Bush's senior national security officials to wrestle with at a meeting that the president would attend. In order to assure that the meeting did not appear to "ambush" Rumsfeld, the planners arranged for outside experts on record for favoring different prescriptions for Iraq—Eliot Cohen, Frederick Kagan, Robert Kaplan, and Michael Vickers—to attend as well. The meeting, characterized by Hadley's deputy, J. D. Crouch, as "a symbol that the seniors in the administration did not believe the strategy was working," was scheduled for June at Camp David.[34]

The results of the meeting were worse than what one might have expected from the most imperfect process. The NSC staff hoped that after the president and his senior advisors read the briefs, addressed the questions, spoke with the outside experts, and debated the issues, they would reach a consensus on the necessity of launching a comprehensive review. O'Sullivan's office even "teed-up full terms of reference for the follow-on review and developed plans for how it would proceed." The meeting could of course produce a decision that a review was unnecessary, or that it could lead to a review that reinforced the status quo. But from the perspective of senior officials in both the White House and Foggy Bottom, these outcomes were remote. The NSC staff structured the meeting "as a way to begin to kick off the discussion between the president and his principals about what were the assumptions of our existing strategy," remarked Hadley. "We were really trying to kick off a presidential-led strategy review at that point."[35]

Yet because the discussion was aborted, there was no decision about a review—one way or the other. The reason was partly due to the slight uptick in assessments of conditions in Iraq. After months of struggling to stand up a government following the elections at the end of 2005, in late May the Iraqi parliament agreed to seat Nouri al-Maliki as prime minister. Senior political and military officials in the administration welcomed this development because of their premise that a stable political environment was a precondition for tamping down the violence. Only days before the Camp David meeting convened on June 12, moreover, a US airstrike killed Abu Musab al-Zarqawi, al-Qaeda's leader in Iraq. For some "war council" attendees, the combination of Maliki's selection as prime minister and Zarqawi's death "reduced the intellectual valiance of it a little bit." Because the assumptions underlying the strategy remained no less problematic, it is highly unlikely that the custodian of Eisenhower's NSC process would have allowed such tactical successes to interfere with a strategic review. But as Vice President Cheney explains, "for those who were worried about the strategy or trying to organize debate and discussion about the strategy [at Camp David], their efforts were, to some extent, pushed aside."[36]

One might argue that a double dose of good news coming after an unending stream of bad news produced an irresistible turn toward optimism that no manager of the process could have curbed. I do not find that argument persuasive, but it is defensible. The fundamental reason that the Camp David meeting was a bust, however, is not. Bush "quietly slipped out" after the first day.[37] He flew to Baghdad for a surprise meeting with Maliki. There is value to the president assessing, building rapport with, and publicly showcasing his support for the new prime minister. But only a flawed process would permit such aims to conflict with let alone take precedence over a meeting scheduled for the purpose of triggering a review of strategy.

This begs the question: Did Hadley explain to Bush the purpose of the meeting? The testimony of senior officials suggests he did not. They were surprised and disappointed. Cheney's national security advisor, John Hannah, characterized the meeting as a "lost opportunity." Secretary Rice's assessment was more negative. It "seemed to me," she lamented, that Camp David "rather kind of affirmed that we were probably going to stay the course."[38]

The Camp David meeting ended, and President Bush visited Maliki in Baghdad on June 13. That same day Maliki announced MNF-I was launching Operation Together Forward, confirming Rice's judgment. With the stakes as high as they were, a frustrated O'Sullivan engineered an end run around the system in order to "force" a review despite the setback. In July she requested Hadley's authorization to undertake what she calls a "mock" review so that she could show him what the results might look like. O'Sullivan was explicit about what she expected those results, and by implication those of a "real" review, would be: a recommendation for more troops—a "double-down" or "additive strategy."[39]

Although the White House worried that the closer the timing of a review to the midterm elections, the more politicized it—and the strategy—could become, Hadley, in O'Sullivan's words "feeling really uncomfortable with where things are going," approved the "second best alternative" to a formal review. As a first step she and her staff used the briefs prepared for the Camp David meeting and further analysis to formulate fifty hard questions that she, Hadley, and others on July 22 posed in a secure video teleconference with Rumsfeld, Generals Abizaid and Casey, and Ambassador Khalilzad. Their objective was to acquire information on present conditions that exposed the shortcomings of the existing strategy and contributed to exploring alternatives to it. Feaver vested a more Machiavellian quality to this questioning: to invite "Casey to think that the president's doubting whether this strategy is going to work." While not explaining the purpose quite so baldly, Hadley seconded Feaver. The aim, he explained, was to "provoke Khalilzad and Casey working with, of course, Secretary Rumsfeld, to initiate their own relook at the strategy." If this gambit succeeded, it would satisfy Hadley's insistence that the impetus originate in "the field" rather than Washington.[40]

At the same time and continuing through August, with Hadley's "top cover authorization," O'Sullivan's interagency committee on Iraq, now augmented by the addition of the State Department's Satterfield, picked apart the NSVI white paper. By vigorously probing its assumptions, the committee determined that none remained valid. Hence the strategy needed a radical revision. O'Sullivan confronted Hadley with that conclusion and persuaded him to support it.[41]

This clandestine review by fall 2006 had produced a consensus among the NSC staff that the current strategy was failing. Furthermore, led by O'Sullivan and Feaver with Hadley's endorsement, most members of the interagency group, with the State Department representatives the notable exceptions, had embraced the "double down" strategy. It was a precursor to the surge. At this point what Bush knew and when he knew it are not evident from the interviews. What is evident from them is that he knew nothing about O'Sullivan's maneuvering, but from his trusted advisors he had learned that the prospects of the present strategy succeeding were bleak.[42]

What is likewise evident is that Hadley purposely left the Pentagon in the dark. To mitigate the resistance by Rumsfeld, Casey, and much of the uniformed military leadership, the threat of congressional opponents to the war exploiting leaks to the media to curtail appropriations, and the potential erosion of morale among theater forces produced by rumors of second-guessing, Hadley orchestrated a review process that placed a premium on compartments and silos at the expense of the free exchange of views and sharing of information. For the next four months what James Jeffrey labels "insurgencies"—ad hoc deliberative structures that operated in isolation from one another on the periphery of the NSC structure—characterized the processes, both formal and informal.[43]

Reflecting the insurgencies' invisibility to each other, O'Sullivan calls September–November 2006 the "you never know what you don't know" period.[44] This characterization would never be found in a textbook on policy making. Yet supporting Eisenhower's principle that at the end of the day the quality of the advisors is more important than the system, this was the most productive and constructive interval in the yearlong pathway to deciding on the surge. Most of those interviewed attribute this outcome largely to the compartmentalization of the process. They claim that it inhibited leaks and averted rifts among the individuals and agencies; it "was meant not to pollute the pool" and thereby allow small groups of advisors with similar expertise and portfolios to "percolate, formulate, articulate rather than immediately defending agency equities in an interagency kind of meeting"; and it concealed the discussions from Rumsfeld and thus prevented him from thwarting progress. All that may be true, and with the exception of

Rumsfeld's pernicious influence, these dynamics plague all administrations. But rather than seek to mitigate them, the Bush process bypassed them. That was costly.[45]

Zelikow identifies the cost. Euphemistically describing the process as "eccentric," in his oral history he expresses his regret that he, Rice, and others in the State Department "were out of the loop on so much of this, and therefore could not form a coalition to better help the president, because of the compartmented way" the decision unfolded. In "an ideal world," Zelikow explains, "we'd write a paper and the military people would sit with us, and they'd help edit it, and they'd mark it up, and we'd tear it up, and it'd go through five drafts, and get a lot better. But, see, that never—none of that ever happened." Bush's world was not ideal. But promoting collaboration and integration in policy making is a practice that should never be abandoned.[46]

Rather than textbook, then, it was an eccentric process that generated the decision to surge. That it did suggests that Hadley, with the encouragement of Bush at some point early during these four months, decided on the double-down strategy and used the system to produce that decision and galvanize support for it. This orchestration was in my judgment not deliberate in the sense that Hadley designed a process that would inexorably result in the surge. The process remained too decentralized to control with sufficient precision, and too many details remained to be worked out. Still, by the fall of 2006 Hadley had become convinced that a troop increase was the only antidote to conceding defeat in Iraq, which the president deemed intolerable. Hence, reversing a normative policy-making trajectory,[47] the process's challenge was not so much to weigh the options as to generate support across the administration for bolstering US forces and deploying those forces most effectively.

Behaving in a way that approximated the Operations Coordinating Board more than the Planning Board, O'Sullivan's NSC Iraq team focused its efforts on the requirements for an additive strategy, not the efficacy of such a strategy. The military's position was that this was a nonstarter because no troops were available—the old-time beer commercial tagline "We're out of Schlitz" became its mantra. At this juncture the parallels to the Operations Coordinating Board break down, because Rumsfeld's allegiance to "We're out of Schlitz" required hiding the review from him. For this purpose the addition to O'Sullivan's team of NSC senior director for defense policy William Luti was pivotal. Hadley, in conjunction with Bolten, "crossed all kinds of lines," to quote Rice, by approving Luti's circumventing Rumsfeld and his office and undertaking a force generation study. That study, run by Lisa Disbrow, a detailee to the White House from the JCS staff, revealed that five brigade combat teams could be mobilized and deployed to Iraq. This guerrilla operation satisfied the NSC staff that the Pentagon's claim that it lacked the necessary forces was specious. The study, Hadley explains, "really validated where Meghan and her team was [sic] going."[48]

The decision-making process quarantined this validation, however. Notably, because it "was generated from the White House from a JCS detailee that was basically going around what the JCS would have wanted a JCS detailee to do," JCS chairman Peter Pace was unaware of Disbrow's role.[49] But he was receiving an earful from retired general Jack Keane, a former JCS vice chair who was on the DoD's Defense Policy Board. By exploiting his personal contacts to skirt the chain of command to an extent that one participant judged "very unprofessional," Keane, a critic of the Rumsfeld/Casey strategy, claims credit for much of what would unfold over the following months.[50] That includes Pace's decision to convene an advisory group of military officers representing each service branch. Beginning at the end of September, this "Council of Colonels" met with the JCS outside normal channels and kept its proceedings invisible from other components of the government. Unlike the NSC staff, it did not express support for the surge. It did, however, develop three options for Pace and the JCS to consider: mobilize the reserves and significantly augment US forces, which the group labeled "go big"; "go long," by which it meant maintain the current force structure and a sizable advisory presence until the insurgency was under control, no matter long it took; or "go home"—a phased withdrawal. Because of its insulation from the process, the Council of Colonels' deliberations were not grist for the decision-making mill. Nevertheless, they may have mitigated the military's opposition to the decision once Bush reached it.[51]

With the NSC staff and the State Department independently concluding that *some* dramatic departure from the current strategy was necessary, the follow-on to Operation Together Forward—Together Forward II—likewise unsuccessful, and the convening of the Council of Colonels signaling some flexibility within the military, Hadley decided the time had arrived to formalize the review. The precipitant was his visit to Iraq to assess Maliki and the capabilities of his government. In the memorandum he wrote Bush upon his return, Hadley expressed doubts about both but emphasized that for Maliki to overcome the sectarian divisions and "build an Iraq for all Iraqis," he would require a secure environment. For this purpose, the United States might "need to fill the current four-brigade gap in Baghdad with coalition forces if reliable Iraqi forces are not identified."[52]

Hadley and his staff had already decided that the United States needed to fill the gap. As became evident at a Saturday meeting of senior officials on November 11, 2006, such a decision was beyond the reach of the process as it was structured. Hadley candidly explained, "At that point, we needed a formal review because the informal reviews were not going to take us to where we needed to go." Further, Hadley understood that with the Republicans' defeat in the midterm elections on November 7 and Rumsfeld's resignation the following day, the likelihood of the formal review recommending something along his preferred lines improved. Bush endorsed Hadley's approach. The president and I "were both moving toward the surge as the way to go," Hadley continued, "but wanting to reach that decision" through the process.[53]

But the process's flaws stood in the way. The multiple options on the table did not include the double-down strategy. State had raised something akin to it in the paper Zelikow coauthored with Jeffrey in the spring, but its contribution to the formal review was a different paper that Zelikow cowrote with Satterfield on October 31. It proposed allowing the sectarian violence to burn itself out while the United States, drawing down its forces, retained the capability only to contain the hostilities and prevent a Srebrenica-scale massacre.[54] Cheney's representative, John Hannah, proffered that the United States should abandon the goal of building an Iraq for all Iraqis and instead "bet on the Shia."[55] Deploying more US troops in an effort to squash the insurgency was among the options that the Council of Colonels had "teed up" for the JCS. But it did not have a voice in the review, and the position of the JCS, represented by Lieutenant General Douglas Lute, was Casey's strategy.[56] Hadley's deputy, J. D. Crouch, managed the formal review process, and the NSC staff participated in it. But its interpretation of what Feaver calls the "Brent Scowcroft rules," named for the widely respected national security advisor to Presidents Gerald Ford and George H. W. Bush, precluded its offering advice outside the privacy of the Oval Office. Its role within the interagency review was limited to that of an "honest broker": it could only broker options proposed by the NSC's components. None of them proposed a surge—it was "an orphan."[57]

George W. Bush's NSC staff misunderstood the guidelines that Scowcroft formulated in the wake of Henry Kissinger's and Zbigniew Brzezinski's stewardships of the NSC and the perversions that attended the Iran-Contra scandal. Scowcroft permitted the national security advisor to manifest policy entrepreneurship by expressing a point of view independently of the NSC principals so long as doing so did "not disadvantage" their positions. According to the formulation John Burke labels the "Honest Broker 'plus,'" Scowcroft "was not averse to bringing forth his own views if he felt the questions under discussion or the options before the principals were not adequate."[58]

His "rules" thus dovetailed with the missions of Eisenhower's special assistant for national security affairs and Planning Board. Their mandate was to ensure that all options were debated, regardless of origin. Hadley, however, sought a consensus, despite the review's excluding the surge from consideration. Rather than a consensus, Crouch's review predictably produced a stalemate between State's drawdown and retrenchment proposal and the Pentagon's advocacy of staying the course.[59]

The process was still deadlocked when the Senate confirmed Robert Gates as secretary of defense on December 5. When Gates agreed to replace Rumsfeld the month before, he expressed his support for a surge.[60] The Baker-Hamilton (Iraq Study Group) report released the day following Gates's confirmation did not advocate a surge but conceded that one might prove valuable in the short run to promote stability in Baghdad and accelerate the training of Iraqi forces.[61] And that weekend Fred Kagan led a wargaming exercise at the American Enterprise Institute that produced a report championing a surge option and providing extensive details on the requirements and mission. AEI's "Choosing Victory" report judged that the deployment of five additional US brigades to Iraq committed to counterinsurgency tactics would address the problem of sectarian violence sufficiently to allow the Maliki government the time and environment needed to "repair Iraq." By coincidence, five was the number of brigades the Luti-Disbrow force generation study had determined were available.[62]

Tom Ricks writes that the AEI's weekend of planning "change[d] the war."[63] He exaggerates. Hadley would not finally have launched the formal review, and Bush would not finally have replaced Rumsfeld, were a change in the strategy not a foregone conclusion. It was the nature of the change that remained in question. Bush, Hadley, and the NSC staff were predisposed to surge and had replaced Rumsfeld with a secretary of defense who supported it. "Choosing Victory" made that option available to them; it provided a rationale, details, and "credibility cover," and through Keane a "force multiplier" that generated wider support. Because AEI had an intimate relationship with the administration, General Keane had attended AEI's planning weekend, and the advisory system's structure was so protean, the following week he and Kagan briefed "Choosing Victory" to the NSC staff, the vice president, and the president. Concurrently, the NSC staff arranged for other outside experts, notably Eliot Cohen and Stephen Biddle, to meet with Bush and Cheney to discuss the value of and historical precedents for a president overruling his generals.[64]

Serendipitous as its contribution may have been, AEI "validated" the decision that Hadley and Bush had already reached and allowed them to claim that the option arose from the deliberative process.⁶⁵ What remained was for Bush to articulate his decision—especially to the generals. He laid the groundwork the next week. In an extraordinary gesture, on December 13 Bush and Cheney traveled to the Pentagon to meet with the service chiefs and both Rumsfeld and Gates in their conference room—"the tank." The chiefs had prepared their defense of the existing strategy: A surge would further erode public support and break the force. Coordinating with JCS chairman Pace in advance, Bush had prepared as well. He would manage the politics, he assured them, and the surest way to break the force was to lose the war. Bush then added that to allay their concerns he would increase the total end strength of the Army and Marine Corps. Eisenhower would have objected to Bush's process of decision making, but he would have been proud of how Bush ended it.⁶⁶

Bush waited until January 10, 2007, to make public his decision. By then Gates had taken the oath of office, Bush had met with Gates and Rice at his Crawford ranch, Gates had traveled to Iraq to meet with Casey and Abizaid, and Bush had decided to replace Casey with General David Petraeus. The president had also tied up a vital loose end by overruling Casey and accepting Petraeus's advice to deploy all five additional brigades (over twenty thousand troops, mostly Army) to Baghdad as rapidly as possible, as opposed to holding some in reserve until needed.⁶⁷ "The new strategy I outline tonight" was the product of a "comprehensive review" conducted by "my national security team, military commanders and diplomats," Bush assured the American people when announcing the change in strategy. He then added, "Our military commanders reviewed the new Iraqi plan" and "report that this plan can work."⁶⁸

Bush stretched the truth by choosing words like "comprehensive" and "team." Nevertheless, those interviewed unanimously praise Bush for his decision and credit it for turning the tide of the war. History will judge both assessments; it is too early. Historical perspective is not necessary, however, to conclude that the long and winding road to the surge was more idiosyncratic than textbook. If historians do one day commend Bush and his advisors for the surge, they will be paying tribute to the participants in the process, not to the process itself. There is an important lesson in that, one that Eisenhower learned and brought to his presidency: any process or system is only as good as the individuals on which it depends.⁶⁹

CHAPTER 16

The President as Policy Entrepreneur

George W. Bush and the 2006 Iraq Strategy Review

COLIN DUECK

The 2015 oral history interviews conducted by the Collective Memory Project allow for an unprecedented opportunity to explore the internal dynamics of the Bush administration's 2006 Iraq strategy review process—and to either verify, correct, or update existing accounts.[1] Taken as a whole, the interviews strongly suggest the president himself played the leading role in that process. I draw on John Kingdon's model of policy entrepreneurship, together with this new primary evidence, to analyze and describe Bush's role. First I define the concept of policy entrepreneurship, including the ability to connect three distinct streams: problems, policies, and politics. Then I analyze these three streams as they existed regarding US policy in Iraq by mid-2006. Next comes a description of how and why Bush was able to connect the three streams. Finally, I offer some concluding thoughts on retrospective judgments of George W. Bush, and the centrality of presidential leadership in US foreign policy.

Policy Entrepreneurship

In his influential work, *Agendas, Alternatives, and Public Policies*, John Kingdon wrote that within the US political system policies sometimes change quickly and unpredictably, through a process that joins three separate streams: problems, policy ideas, and politics.[2] Within the problem stream, issues are carried to the attention of leading officials and their advisors through systematic indicators, crises, negative feedback, and events that focus the mind. If top officials are not giving a problem adequate attention, or have not identified it as problematic, then the issue is not really even on the government's agenda, regardless of its severity. Within the policy stream, specific proposals pop up as experts push forward alternative ideas. It can take years before such alternatives are adopted, if they ever are. The substance of this stream is often shaped by low-visibility networks of policy specialists among government staff, think tanks, academia, and executive branch bureaucracy. In order to eventually survive in this stream, policy ideas must appear to be politically, financially, and technically feasible under the right conditions. Lastly, within the political stream, circumstances of administrative turnover, electoral outcomes, interest group pressure, and changing public opinion help push some ideas ahead of others. But in Kingdon's model, these multiple streams do not automatically join on their own. Their conjoining requires what he terms "policy entrepreneurs." These people play a vital role in connecting the various streams, by joining feasible solutions to pressing problems—and then connecting them to political conditions.[3]

The policy entrepreneurship model has had considerable influence in the field of domestic public policy, but is only rarely applied to the study of American foreign policy.[4] In part, this is because the process of making US foreign policy is frequently more hierarchical, closed, and counter-bureaucratic than the domestic issue arenas examined by Kingdon.[5] Consequently, alternative foreign policy ideas are sometimes assembled rapidly, in response to new international conditions, and without extensive prior lobbying by outside experts. To a striking extent, in this particular issue arena, presidents and their advisors can bypass existing bureaucracies if they so choose, and reach down into the policy stream directly—specifying those alternatives they wish to consider.[6] In other words, when it comes to foreign policy, the president can act as his own policy entrepreneur. In the following pages, I suggest that during the 2006 Iraq strategy review, this is precisely what George Bush did.

Three Streams: The Case of Iraq 2006

The Problem Stream

In February 2006, Sunni militants attacked the Shia al-Askari shrine at Samarra, deliberately triggering an increase in sectarian violence around Baghdad. Many US officials recognized this as a dangerous turning point at the time.

The problem by spring 2006—and much earlier—was not only the terrible carnage in Iraq, but the failure of US policy to stop it. President Bush was well aware of the continuing violence. Indeed the Iraq War was consistently his top policy priority. As early as that spring, he told his national security advisor Stephen Hadley "this strategy is not working . . . we need to find a new one."[7] But there was a serious challenge in terms of problem definition on the part of US military leadership. General George Casey—the American field commander in Iraq—believed that his leading mission was to gradually withdraw and transition US troops out of that country, so that trained Iraqi forces could take on the primary burden of the conflict themselves.[8] General John Abizaid of the US Central Command (CENTCOM) agreed with Casey's interpretation of the mission as "train and transition," and so did the US Joint Chiefs of Staff. Secretary of Defense Donald Rumsfeld was inclined to defer to US field commanders.[9] Altogether, well into 2006, neither Casey, nor Abizaid, nor Rumsfeld, nor the Joint Chiefs felt that existing US strategy was fundamentally flawed.[10] The result was that while President Bush and his foreign policy team were regularly presented by the military with impressive metrics to consider, these metrics started from the premise that the best indicator of success was the gradual removal of US troops from Iraq, rather than the defeat of insurgents per se. This made it extremely difficult at the highest level to even identify and assess the problem, much less formulate a viable solution. Consequently, American strategy in Iraq was stuck. Bush, for his part, had no desire to repeat what he viewed as mistakes of the US war effort in Vietnam, by meddling in or overruling his military advisors in military affairs.[11] The president's chief of staff, Joshua Bolten, described his own surprise when he first witnessed the way Bush handled meetings related to the Iraq War:

> The president that I saw in every other context, that is to say non-Iraq issues, was a different person than the one I saw in the Iraq meeting. . . . The president I saw at those war meetings was, to me, noticeably different from the one I saw in every other context, where he was in charge, he was challenging everything. . . . And in this meeting, I remember thinking he's in this meeting to encourage and satisfy them, that he's viewing his role as supporting the military, because they are the ones sacrificing. . . . I think he did not want to interpose his own judgment ahead of theirs nearly as aggressively as I saw him do in every other context.[12]

Stephen Hadley and his staff at the National Security Council (NSC)—including the deputy national security advisor for Iraq and Afghanistan Meghan O'Sullivan and the special advisor for strategic planning and institutional reform Peter Feaver—wanted the president to hear alternative views about US strategy in Iraq, and Bush had told O'Sullivan he expected as much.[13] The staff arranged for a June 12 meeting at Camp David between the president and several outside defense experts, including Frederick Kagan from the American Enterprise Institute (AEI), Eliot Cohen from the Johns Hopkins School of Advanced International Studies, journalist Robert Kaplan, and onetime CIA officer Michael Vickers. But Bush was about to make a surprise visit to see Iraq's new prime minister, Nouri al-Maliki, and so from the president's perspective the focus of the day became the upcoming trip to Baghdad. Furthermore, Bush and many of his leading advisors were once again hopeful that the existing approach might work.[14] US troops had just killed Abu Musab al-Zarqawi, the leader of al-Qaeda in Iraq; General Casey was undertaking a new campaign with allied forces, Operation Together Forward; and Bush was optimistic about the newly elected Iraqi government under Maliki. As a result, any searching presidential reassessment of US strategy coming out of Camp David was stillborn.[15] Hadley and his staff followed up with a July 22 teleconference between General Casey, General Abizaid, Secretary Rumsfeld, Chairman Peter Pace of the Joint Chiefs of Staff, and leading observers from throughout the interagency. In a series of questions from the national security advisor, the US field commander was pressed as to the validity of existing strategy. Casey did not appreciate the interrogation.[16] But the results allowed O'Sullivan to formulate a summary memo, sent to President Bush along with meeting participants, raising the question of whether major changes in US strategy were now warranted. As Hadley says, "we were pushing them."[17]

As the summer wore on, it became clear to Bush that Operation Together Forward had failed and that Iraqi forces were as yet incapable of standing on their own.[18] The president met with his war council on August 17 in a teleconference that included Generals Casey, Abizaid, and Pace, Secretary Rumsfeld, White House chief of staff Josh Bolten, and Vice President Cheney, with counselor Philip Zelikow representing the State Department. Bush asked the generals a series of tough questions, pressing them to explain how existing US strategy could work amid worsening conditions in Iraq.[19] The generals' answer was essentially to recommend staying on course with the existing approach of train and transition. In Rumsfeld's words, the United States needed to take its "hand off the bicycle seat," allowing Iraqi forces to operate on their own. The president's reply was, to the contrary, "If the bicycle teeters, we're going to put the hand back on." As he told the assembled generals, "We have to have enough military personnel. . . . If you can't answer the questions, that makes me nervous."[20] Bush left the meeting increasingly persuaded that his military commanders did not have a workable plan to arrest the deteriorating conditions inside Iraq. He told Hadley that a serious reassessment of US strategy would need to start from the White House, since the military appeared either unable or unwilling to launch such a review.[21] This was a clear assertion of presidential authority in the face of increasing dysfunction. Bush did not normally speak this way with his generals, and they were taken aback—but they got the message. Casey and Abizaid called Peter Pace to say that in the end, more US troops might be required on the ground in Iraq.[22] The August 2006 meeting was a key moment in Bush's evolution toward effectively addressing grinding frustrations in the American war effort. He had accurately identified important parts of the existing problem—both in Iraq, and within the US civil-military process—while furthermore indicating his preferred direction. Altogether, the president had begun to play the role of policy entrepreneur.

The Policy Stream

Throughout 2006, US military and foreign policy experts proposed a variety of alternatives for Iraq. Many called for the accelerated disengagement of American forces from the conflict. A persistent theme in such proposals was to argue that the US armed forces were largely incapable of stopping increased sectarian violence inside Iraq. Ironically, Secretary Rumsfeld, along with the most highly placed American military leaders, shared this desire to transition US forces out of Iraq, albeit at a gradual pace. A very different alternative, recommended by a smaller number of national security experts, was to put fresh emphasis on counterinsurgency techniques.[23] Some well-versed defense policy experts called for new counterinsurgency methods combined with fewer troops, and in the abstract it was possible to do so.[24] But since doctrines of counterinsurgency (COIN) typically emphasize securing the allegiance and safety of potentially sympathetic civilians—or population security—the case for counterinsurgency tended to dovetail with the case for more US troops. By comparison with dense policy networks on leading domestic issues, as of 2006 the COIN policy network was not especially influential, extensive, or coordinated. Yet there did exist a loose, thin network of credible and articulate experts inside the US government, the career military, and the DC think tank world—often in touch with one another—advocating the more assertive use of counterinsurgency in Iraq.[25] Their emphasis on COIN and population security also informed, and was in turn informed by, the practical experience of highly effective US field officers such as Colonel H. R. McMaster and General David Petraeus.[26]

President Bush was cognizant of and intrigued by the positive impact that the above officers were having using COIN techniques in Iraqi cities such as Mosul and Tal Afar.[27] So was Vice President Cheney.[28] In fact Petraeus returned stateside from Iraq to help write the Army's new counterinsurgency guide, US Army Field Manual 3–24. The argument for COIN was therefore bubbling up not only from think tanks inside Washington, but for the most practical of reasons, from the Iraqi battlefield itself. What this argument still lacked, as of the summer of 2006, was a detailed military proposal, and a decisive influence on US government officials at the highest level.

The Political Stream

The management of the 2006 Iraq strategy review cannot be fully understood in the absence of political conditions within the United States. This is not because Bush's final decision was made for domestic political reasons. As Josh Bolten suggests, the president was not especially interested in his own falling approval ratings, or whether the continuation of the war might damage Republican fortunes in Congress: "He was oblivious to concerns about how he might be seen, how his party might be seen."[29] Indeed the notion of a surge in US troop strength was very unpopular at the time.[30] The political challenge was precisely how to manage the process and build support for an unpopular concept amid a season of congressional midterm elections.[31]

American public support for the war in Iraq had of course declined dramatically by 2006. By the middle of that year, criticism of the president's Iraq policy was a major campaign theme for Democrats looking toward the November midterms. Bush officials were well aware the administration was in trouble politically because of the war. In Cheney's words, they were "feeling the heat."[32] Congressional Republicans were deeply concerned by the course of the Iraq War, as they were by the midterm losses they looked likely to suffer. Vulnerable GOP House members tried to distance themselves from the president and his handling of Iraq. Some prominent Republicans such as Senate Majority Whip Mitch McConnell of Kentucky suggested to Bush that a partial withdrawal of US troops might reduce Republican losses in Congress.[33] Only a handful of senators, including John McCain of Arizona, remained adamantly opposed to this sort of withdrawal. President Bush did not look to satisfy his critics, and he resented what from his perspective looked like a politicization of the US military effort.[34] The White House was therefore unlikely to admit to grave mistakes in Iraq, or to engage in any sweeping reassessment of basic US strategy, if news of such review could be leaked and used by critics as political ammunition heading into November. In the words of Meghan O'Sullivan, "It would have been potentially awkward for there to be a strategic review of our Iraq strategy publicly out there in the run-up to the elections."[35] Nor was this concern entirely partisan. Since Bush was increasingly interested in the option of a surge, against the clear preferences of the US Joint Chiefs of Staff, he risked open division with his own top military advisors if he pressed the issue too early or too quickly. Critics might then use the resulting schism to argue against the very idea of a US troop surge. This at least was Bush's concern.[36] As Stephen Hadley suggests,

> In order to get everyone to the point where they understood a change needed to be made, we needed to go through those individual, informal processes within the individual agencies. . . . It is not easy to change strategy in the middle of a war. . . . A situation where the military is split on the issue of conduct of a war is a kind of political crisis that will make it very difficult to move forward in any strategy. Because for something as controversial as Iraq, those divisions within the military would be used by critics of any engagement in Iraq to undermine the strategy and to force us out and to give up and basically come home.[37]

This in turn dictated an initially low-key, compartmentalized (less likely to leak) review process, not only to puzzle out some genuinely difficult strategic challenges, but to build support within both the administration and the national security bureaucracy for a potentially dramatic policy departure.[38]

Connecting the Streams: September 2006 to January 2007

By the end of the summer, the president had indicated to Stephen Hadley that any searching reassessment of US strategy in Iraq would have to come from the White House. Hadley authorized a team of NSC staffers, led by Meghan O'Sullivan, to probe existing assumptions and consider some alternative options. The team included Peter Feaver, Brigadier General Kevin Bergner, and Brett McGurk, with John Hannah representing the vice president's office. This group concluded that most existing assumptions animating US strategy in Iraq were simply not valid. Needless to say, many external observers and even some inside the administration—including, for example, O'Sullivan—had long since arrived at and voiced this conclusion.[39] Reassessments of America's Iraq strategy were of course under way within all the relevant government agencies and departments throughout 2006 and before, including at State and Defense, but without broad agreement on either the nature of the problem or the best solution. The key difference during September 2006 was in having a leading group of White House staff members formally determine and recommend not only that existing strategy was fundamentally flawed, but why—and what to do about it. For example, the group found that in those Iraqi provinces where the US retained a troop presence, violence went down, rather than up. This argued for a surge in the numbers of American troops. O'Sullivan's group outlined its findings and gave them to Hadley.[40] The national security advisor then asked NSC staff member William Luti to conduct his own study, asking whether it was practical or possible to envisage a surge in US troop presence. Luti determined that it was in fact possible to surge up to five additional brigades into Iraq, after checking with Army staff separately from either the Joint Chiefs of Staff or American commanders on the ground.[41] Hadley passed this information on to JCS chairman Pace, and began to merge the NSC Iraq team with that of Secretary of State Condoleezza Rice, looking toward a formal interagency review. Hadley then flew to Iraq late in October to inspect conditions firsthand. The resulting report he gave to the president recommended a systematic consideration by US military leaders of an American troop surge in Iraq, among other options. As Hadley says, referring to Bush: "He and I were both moving toward the surge as the way to go, but wanting to reach that decision through this process."[42]

The prospect of congressional midterm elections weighed on the administration up until November 7. Furthermore, the sheer severity of GOP losses on that day operated as a shock and a stimulant in relation to US Iraq strategy. Bush would not concede that wartime frustrations were pivotal in Republican losses, yet those midterm results amounted to a referendum on the president's handling of Iraq, and within the White House the message was heard very clearly.[43] A growing number of leading Republicans now called on Bush to change course in Iraq. The widespread expectation was that an incoming congressional Democratic majority in 2007 might act to force American military withdrawal from that country. The status quo was simply no longer viable, either on its own merits—or politically.[44] Still, there existed multiple alternatives in various directions. For example, Bush might have decided to seize upon the midterm results by announcing an accelerated withdrawal of US troops—essentially, the recommendation of the bipartisan Iraq Study Group report, released in early December. This would have been a popular choice, with broad support from the US foreign policy establishment. But Bush was already operating proactively in a very different direction. In a sense, while the midterm elections had complicated the president's strategy review process, the final results liberated him to act as he wished, through a formal interagency review with reduced fear of public leaks.[45] In Cheney's words, "we've lost the election. I think that clearly was a significant factor in terms of the president's thinking and willingness to consider a bold move."[46]

Within hours of the midterm results, Bush announced publicly that Secretary of Defense Rumsfeld would step down, to be replaced by former CIA director Robert Gates. The president had already decided, by early October, to replace Rumsfeld with Gates. Like Bush, Gates was by this time predisposed toward the surge.[47] Certainly many congressional Republicans would have appreciated an earlier public indication that the White House was about to shift US strategy in Iraq. But the president was not interested in appeasing his critics by announcing Rumsfeld's retirement before the midterm elections.[48] Nor did he want Gates subjected to the grilling of a congressional confirmation in the midst of a heated election season. In Karl Rove's words, the president's "feeling was if it happened after the election, Gates would have a less difficult time in the confirmation hearing, and as a result be able to be a more successful secretary of defense."[49]

At Bush's direction, the White House on November 10 now called upon representatives from all relevant government agencies and departments, including deputy secretaries, to meet for a formal review of existing strategy in Iraq. J. D. Crouch led the interagency task force, also known as the Iraq Strategy Review team. Hadley made clear this team needed to at least consider the option of a US troop surge, because he knew Bush wanted that option available.[50] But Bush also told Hadley and Crouch directly that he wanted an unvarnished analysis from this review: "If we can win, I want to win. If we can't, we have to find a way to get out."[51] A series of intense meetings over the rest of November helped to clarify some underlying differences in bureaucratic perspectives. Outgoing secretary of defense Rumsfeld remained quite skeptical of boosting US troop numbers in Iraq. He feared that the Army and Marines could hardly afford additional strain or overextension, and was not convinced that added troop numbers would solve the underlying problem of sectarian violence. Generals Abizaid and Casey and several of the Joint Chiefs of Staff shared these concerns. Consequently, representatives from the Department of Defense continued to stress the need for a gradual process of training and transition out of Iraq.[52] Secretary of State Rice was also a skeptic, having been told more than once by US military officials that any such surge was neither practical nor desirable. State Department representatives therefore proposed an alternate course by which the US would step back militarily, refocus on counterterrorism, emphasize local political reconciliation, and intervene only in the event of mass killings.[53] NSC staff, on the other hand, as well as the vice president's office, were supportive of a US troop surge.[54]

These interagency discussions helped to clarify the various departmental perspectives, producing some distinct options for the president's consideration. Yet as of the end of November, there was really no consensus on how to move ahead—only an agreement that the existing approach was not working. The issue therefore went up to the level of the president and his principal advisors.[55] Bush's National Security Council met from late November into early December to debate US strategy. During these meetings, culminating with the president in attendance on December 8 and 9, the position of Bush's leading advisors came into sharp relief. Cheney argued for the surge.[56] Rice questioned the idea, saying, "We just can't win by putting our forces in the middle of their blood feud. If they want to have a civil war, we're going to have to let them."[57] Bush replied that such disengagement was unacceptable: "You can't just step out on the perimeter and let it burn out, because it's not going to burn out; it's going to consume the whole country."[58] Again, through these meetings, the president made plain his unwillingness to withdraw from Iraq, along with his readiness to consider a surge. In his own words, "I was leaning that way pretty heavily."[59] The fact that he had openly prioritized Iraqi population security was especially significant in predisposing the process this way.[60] Hadley says of Bush during this period:

He wanted his decision to be something all his cabinet secretaries would support. . . . What's going on is the president is asking questions to get views and information to inform his decision. He's already pretty clearly leaning toward the surge, but he has not decided on the surge. But what's really going on underneath that, is he is asking a series of questions that are going to put facts on the table because he's also trying to bring his other national security principals to where he thinks he's going to come out. That's what's really going on. And it's been building over the two-month period.[61]

Bush next met with several outside defense experts on December 11, including the Council on Foreign Relations' Stephen Biddle, Eliot Cohen, and retired generals Wayne Downing, Barry McCaffrey, and Jack Keane. These experts all agreed the situation in Iraq was terrible, but they differed over what to do next. McCaffrey and Downing spoke in favor of accelerated withdrawal. Biddle disagreed. Cohen urged Bush to replace existing US field commanders in Iraq. Keane told the president very bluntly that existing strategy had failed and that the only hope was an American troop surge, together with proven counterinsurgency techniques. Vice President Cheney, also in attendance, was especially impressed with Keane's presentation, as was Bush. Indeed, Cheney had been in touch with Keane for some time. Keane followed up by briefing Cheney more fully later that same day, joined by the American Enterprise Institute's Frederick Kagan, who offered slides describing the basic outlines of a US troop surge. Coincidentally, the Iraq working group at AEI had just convened a few days earlier to flesh out a proposal for troop deployments, with Keane in observance, and the group had concluded that a five-brigade surge was possible and adequate to address population security concerns around Baghdad. Kagan and Keane were thereby ready with specifics when they met with Cheney, who passed them on to the president. The AEI surge proposal was not the first such study; William Luti had already done something similar in October. Still, it was added validation, and certainly Jack Keane's support lent the concept a certain weight that only a four-star general could bring. As Bush put it, outside experts "weren't the originators," but they "boosted my sense of confidence" and "confirmed the eventual decision."[62]

Two days later, on December 13, Bush met with the Joint Chiefs of Staff at the Pentagon, with Cheney, Rumsfeld, and incoming defense secretary Gates in attendance. The chiefs were still unenthusiastic about the prospect of sending additional US troops to Iraq, and in prior interagency meetings had been unwilling to even entertain it. By now, however, JCS chairman Pace had to a considerable extent smoothed the way by letting the chiefs know the president's perspective and vice versa. Their single greatest worry remained that US forces were already badly strained and overextended because of the war. In meeting with Bush, the chiefs reiterated long-standing concerns about insufficient support from civilian government agencies, along with the need to maintain overall readiness in case of other contingencies such as a new Korean conflict. General Peter Schoomaker, chief of staff for the Army, openly warned that an Iraq surge might break the US military and fail to win over the American public. Bush replied politely but firmly, "Let me tell you what's going to break the army. What's going to break the army is a defeat like we had in Vietnam that broke the army for a generation."[63] He added, in effect, that any domestic political challenges would be his concern, not that of the JCS. Bush was, however, very sympathetic to the chiefs' argument that civilian agencies, including the State Department, needed to do more in Iraq—and that the end strength of the US Army and Marines would have to be increased, to relieve any added strain.[64] Bush had made it very clear in front of the JCS that he was leaning in the direction of a US troop surge. The chiefs agreed to formulate detailed plans for such a surge. By listening to their concerns, addressing them seriously, and bringing them into the process, Bush had nudged the Joint Chiefs along. As Gates says, "The president was there to bring these guys on board, not to confront them or to sort of challenge them." This still left the question of exactly how many troops to send, along with where and how to deploy them.[65]

William Luti at the NSC and defense experts at the American Enterprise Institute had each recommended that the United States send at least five additional brigades (over twenty thousand more US troops) to Iraq. The JCS would only recommend "up to five."[66] General Casey continued to resist the idea of deploying so many added troops, recommending one or two brigades, with three more held in reserve. Lieutenant General David Petraeus—by this time, Casey's probable replacement—contacted Meghan O'Sullivan and recommended a full five brigades.[67] Others, including Jack Keane, urged the White House in the same direction.[68] Politically, some within the administration felt that a smaller number of brigades would help placate congressional Democrats. Bush viewed this as both militarily unwise and politically pointless. As he said: "I'm only going to make this decision once. . . . If the commander wants to decide at some point in the sequence he doesn't need the force, that's a different question. But I'm not going to make this decision five times."[69] With the president now indicating his readiness to adopt a new team, including Gates and Petraeus, and a new counterinsurgency strategy—rather than simply more troops—Condoleezza Rice was on board.[70] Karl Rove agreed, as did most congressional Republicans, that a full-blown US troop surge was politically difficult yet strategically necessary—and that if the Band-Aid had to be ripped off, better to do it all at once. In Rove's words, "The question is not, well, what's the political consequence of that going to be. The political question is how best can you sell this. . . . If it starts to work, and I start showing support for it, then the political system will accept it and applaud it. . . . If you change the policy, and the policy goal is victory, you will at least cause a pause in our decline, and then if the policy begins to work then the American people will respond to that. But it has to visibly work."[71]

At a National Security Council meeting on December 28, held in Crawford, Texas, the president settled on a US troop surge with a full five brigades. Bush announced his decision to the American public on January 10, 2007, committing himself to the success of a new strategy in Iraq based on improved counterinsurgency techniques and additional US troops. In that address, the president specified the precise number of five brigades to help overcome any remaining bureaucratic resistance. General William Fallon replaced General John Abizaid as CENTCOM commander, and Petraeus took over from Casey as commander of the Multi-National Force in Iraq (MNF-I). Altogether, Bush was determined to avoid any suggestion that he was blaming the US military or its commanders for previous policy failures.

He took full responsibility for any such mistakes, including in his January 2007 public address, and insisted—as did JCS chairman Pace—that Casey and Abizaid were blameless.[72]

Conclusion: Assessing Bush

It is clear from the evidence that multiple groups and individuals, beyond the scope of this chapter, played the role of policy entrepreneur in helping to nudge along the 2006 Iraq strategy review. Key NSC staff members helped the administration to identify the problem in Iraq and locate a possible policy alternative. "Dissident" US generals, both active (David Petraeus) and retired (Jack Keane) played their part in reassuring Bush that a troop surge involving bolstered counterinsurgency was a viable military option. The Iraq strategy working group at the American Enterprise Institute helped to validate and reinforce the concept. The vice president's office also argued for a US troop surge, acting as intermediary between several of the above actors. And National Security Advisor Stephen Hadley played a critical role in managing the entire review, as honest broker, policy entrepreneur, and presidential agent.[73] But as Hadley himself suggests, he was not an aggressive advocate for the surge, and the single most important player throughout the process was President Bush.[74]

At several crucial turning points in the 2006 Iraq strategy review, the president signaled to leading advisors where he wanted the process headed. During and after the August teleconference with General Casey, Bush indicated his waning confidence in the existing strategy, along with a readiness to consider increased troop numbers. It was then that the president let Hadley know any searching strategy review would have to emanate from the White House, rather than the Pentagon or US field commanders. At NSC meetings early in December, Bush again made plain his unwillingness to disengage from Iraq, along with his inclination toward a US troop surge. During his meeting with the Joint Chiefs of Staff on December 13, the president clarified not only these same predispositions, but an overarching determination to assert his role as commander in chief. In other words, it would be Bush and no one else who made the final decision, based on a full range of considerations available only to him. Later that month, he settled the question of how many new brigades would be deployed to Iraq, specifying the larger number of five. He brought in a new US field commander in Iraq, a new CENTCOM commander, and a new secretary of defense to implement the new strategy. Along the way, he reached down into the policy stream and searched for possible alternatives to the existing approach. He further managed the political and bureaucratic aspects of the decision-making process, postponing the announcement of a major overhaul until after the congressional midterm elections. He did this partly to avoid a civil-military rupture that might in turn undercut any prospects for the surge. Indeed, by the end of 2006, there were really only two options left: disengage or surge. Another president might easily have chosen to disengage.[75] But once that binary choice was clarified, given Bush's personality and beliefs, his final decision was a given. As he put it, "I was deeply influenced by meeting with our troops and with the [families of the] fallen. . . . I couldn't stand the thought of making decisions that enabled defeat. How could I look at a mother and say . . . what your son did ended up being useless. And so behind the thought was, failure was not an option to me."[76]

The only necessity then was for a specific plan—and the plan was provided. Once the president made clear his support for a surge, all the other bureaucratic players eventually came around. More than anyone else, it was Bush who connected the existing problem in Iraq with a feasible alternative, while linking both to domestic political conditions. As Peter Pace says, "The way he did it had everybody together."[77] In the end, the leading policy entrepreneur during the 2006 Iraq strategy review was really the president himself.

Richard Immerman is right to say, as he does in his chapter for this volume, that the 2006 Iraq surge review process departed significantly from the example set by President Eisenhower.[78] The real question, however, is whether that departure in process worked. The evidence from these oral history interviews suggests that it did. Only one US president ever liberated France from the Nazis. Others must develop decision-making procedures that work for them, and if these are initially informal and compartmentalized, yet successful and effective, then so be it. Moreover, NSC processes in the twenty-first century are unlikely to exactly replicate those from the 1950s. Over the past sixty years, for better or worse, there has been a long-term centralization of foreign policy decision-making influence toward the White House, and this will probably not be entirely rolled back regardless of who is president. The internal fear of leaks is also greater than it was in Eisenhower's time, and not without reason. This in turn complicates the ability of the president's leading foreign policy advisors to hold confidential yet comprehensive inside strategy reviews. If outside critics want both increased governmental transparency and increased US strategic coherence, they may have to sacrifice one or the other. Still, Immerman is certainly correct in noting that it was remarkably hard to get the 2006 strategy review started.

The question that obviously remains is: given severe US frustrations in Iraq from 2003 through 2006, why did Bush not initiate this sort of effective strategy review sooner? His own answer is that "a year earlier the circumstances were different. . . . I think we had to give the [existing] strategies a chance to work."[79] Whether or not this is persuasive depends on a judgment regarding the visible situation in Iraq between 2003 and 2005. Yet at least within the context of the autumn of 2006, most of the Collective Memory Project interviewees offer a consistent, granular, and plausible response. Bush needed to clarify the nature of the problem, work out a genuinely feasible alternative, build bureaucratic support for that alternative, and overcome resistance from the Pentagon while keeping everyone inside the administration on board.[80] The fact that he accomplished this successfully in the end suggests that he was capable of leadership qualities generally denied by his critics. It also points to the sheer centrality of the presidency in US strategic adjustment, for better or worse.

During the autumn 2006 strategy review, Bush revealed a leadership style quite different from his approach in 2003. His earlier inclination, during the original planning for the invasion and occupation of Iraq, was deferential toward his military advisors with regard to details, even when those details had broad strategic implications. As he says himself: "I tended to be deferential to our military."[81] It took considerable time and information for him to recognize that existing US strategy was not working, but he eventually did so. This was a form of learning.[82] Certainly, Bush's central foreign policy beliefs never altered in the way his critics might have preferred. He never concluded, for example, that the original decision to invade was a mistake. Yet the picture of the former president that emerges from this case is significantly different from the cartoon caricatures of the time. Bush really was at ease making difficult decisions, but he was surprisingly uncomfortable with inevitable policy frictions within his national security team. Instead of policing such frictions energetically, he tended to assume a collegiality among leading advisors that did not always exist.[83] In the case of Iraq, this encouraged a lengthy bureaucratic deadlock whereby American field commanders, the Joint Chiefs of Staff, and the Department of Defense were permitted by default to conduct the US war effort according to their own assumptions, even when evidence mounted that several of those assumptions were in error. Once the president became fully aware that this deadlock was ruining any prospects for success in Iraq, he broke it. In other words, he learned not only that a specific policy was failing, but that he needed to intervene as president in order to reverse that failure, despite a profound personal reluctance to overrule US military leaders. In the words of Josh Bolten,

As I perceived it, his mind-set changed in the year, beginning in early '06, to the end of '06 and early '07, to the point where he still had enormous respect, affection, and deference for the people in the military, but I think he had seen that there's only one president and there's only one person that can step in and really redirect. And he had a higher comfort level doing that at the beginning of '07 than I think he did at the beginning of '06. . . . That was his own evolution.[84]

Bush's final redirection included the appointment of a new and capable team, from secretary of defense to MNF-I commander. Only then, in 2007, did American strategy in Iraq operate with the kind of functional collegiality that Bush had earlier taken for granted. Not only did his combative tenacity, so irritating to his critics, turn out to be useful in this case. The management style and decision-making process demonstrated by the president clearly improved while he was in office, at least in the case of Iraq. As Condoleezza Rice says in her interview,

George W. Bush was a different president in 2006 than he was in 2003. In 2006, he had a lot more experience dealing with the military. He'd sat through those meetings . . . going through a lot of bad outcomes, a lot of false starts that those outcomes were about to turn around. . . . So we can talk about civil-military relations, we can talk about the role of the NSC, we can talk about the secretary of state or whatever, but it ultimately comes down to the president, and whether the president is willing to make tough choices.[85]

The conventional scholarly view of how Bush handled the initial 2003 invasion of course remains very harsh, and since that earlier case is not explored in these interviews or on these pages, its most common interpretations can neither be confirmed nor denied.[86] Certainly, one can only wish the president had overseen US planning for the initial invasion and occupation of Iraq with as much hands-on attention, prudence, and skill as he showed three years later. But at the very least, we can say that in the case of the autumn of 2006, Bush demonstrated impressive qualities of foreign policy leadership. If that amounts to a partially revisionist view of President Bush, then scholars should go where the evidence leads them.

Cast of Characters (and their titles and positions in 2006, and dates interviewed)

George W. Bush served as president of the United States from 2001 to 2009. Interviewed December 1, 2015.

Richard B. Cheney served as vice president of the United States from 2001 to 2009. Interviewed August 6, 2015.

Condoleezza Rice served as US secretary of state from 2005 to 2009. Interviewed July 20, 2015.

Robert Gates served as US secretary of defense from 2006 to 2011. Interviewed October 12, 2015.

Stephen Hadley served as assistant to the president for national security affairs from 2005 to 2009. Interviewed June 2, 2015.

General Peter Pace, US Marine Corps, served as chairman of the Joint Chiefs of Staff from 2005 to 2007. Interviewed January 20, 2016.

General John Abizaid, US Army, served as commander, United States Central Command, from 2003 to 2007. Interviewed April 13, 2016.

Joshua Bolten served as the White House chief of staff from 2006 to 2009. Interviewed May 15, 2015.

Stephen Cambone served as under secretary of defense for intelligence from 2003 until 2006. Interviewed May 15, 2015.

J. D. Crouch served as deputy assistant to the president for national security affairs from 2005 to 2007. Interviewed June 25, 2015.

Eric Edelman served as under secretary of defense for policy from 2006 to 2009. Interviewed March 24, 2015.

Peter Feaver served as the special advisor for strategic planning and institutional reform on the National Security Council from 2005 to 2007. Interviewed April 27, 2015.

David Gordon served as the vice chair of the National Intelligence Council from 2004 to 2007. Interviewed May 28, 2015.

John Hannah served as assistant for national security affairs to the vice president from 2005 to 2009. Interviewed April 27, 2015.

James Jeffrey served as coordinator for Iraq and senior adviser to the secretary of state from 2005 to 2006. Interviewed August 17, 2015.

Frederick Kagan was a resident scholar at the American Enterprise Institute. Interviewed May 7, 2015.

Kimberly Kagan was adjunct professor in the Security Studies Program, Georgetown University. Interviewed June 26, 2015.

General Jack Keane, US Army (retired), served on the Defense Policy Board. Interviewed August 18, 2015.

Zalmay Khalilzad served as the US ambassador to Iraq from 2005 to 2007. Interviewed June 25, 2015.

Lieutenant General Douglas Lute, US Army, served as director of operations, Joint Staff, from 2006 to 2007. Interviewed May 28, 2015.

Colonel Peter Mansoor, US Army, served on the Joint Chiefs of Staff Strategic Dialogue Group in 2006. Interviewed, June 12, 2015.

Meghan O'Sullivan served as the deputy assistant to the president and deputy national security advisor for Iraq and Afghanistan from 2005 to 2007. Interviewed May 12, 2016.

Karl Rove served as senior adviser to the president and White House deputy chief of staff from 2005 to 2007. Interviewed February 2, 2016.

David M. Satterfield served as coordinator for Iraq and senior adviser to the secretary of state from 2006 to 2009. Interviewed January 14, 2016.

Lieutenant General John F. Sattler, US Marine Corps, served as director of strategy and policy, Joint Staff, from 2006 to 2008. Interviewed September 28, 2016.

Daniel Serwer served as the executive director of the Iraq Study Group in 2006. Interviewed June 11, 2015.

Frank Wolf served as a member of the House of Representatives from Virginia's tenth district, from 1981 to 2015. Interviewed January 20, 2016.

Philip Zelikow served as counselor of the Department of State from 2005 to 2007. Interviewed March 24, 2015.

APPENDIX B

Time Line

2003

March 19	President George W. Bush orders commencement of Operation Iraqi Freedom, the American-led effort to oust Iraq's Saddam Hussein from power by military force. Following an initial air strike targeting Saddam, nearly 150,000 ground troops, the overwhelming majority from the United States and the United Kingdom, engaged Iraqi forces. General Tommy Franks, the commanding officer of US Central Command, described the invasion force's eight principal objectives to reporters on March 22, 2003:

"First, ending the regime of Saddam Hussein. Second, to identify, isolate, and eliminate Iraq's weapons of mass destruction. Third, to search for, to capture, and to drive out terrorists from that country. Fourth, to collect such intelligence as we can relate to terrorist networks. Fifth, to collect such intelligence as we can relate to the global network of illicit weapons of mass destruction. Sixth, to end sanctions and to immediately deliver humanitarian support to the displaced and to many needy Iraqi citizens. Seventh, to secure Iraq's oil fields and resources, which belong to the Iraqi people. And last, to help the Iraqi people create conditions for a transition to a representative self-government."[1]

April	Coalition forces enter Baghdad, Iraq's capital. Saddam Hussein's whereabouts remain unknown. By April's end the coalition will have suffered 162 fatalities. Estimates of Iraqi military and civilian losses vary widely.
May 23	Ambassador L. Paul "Jerry" Bremer, head of the Coalition Provisional Authority charged with ruling and reconstructing Iraq until the formation of an indigenous democratic government, issues Coalition Provisional Authority Order No. 2, disbanding the Iraqi army.
July 2	Facing increased attacks on coalition forces, Bush challenges their assailants to "bring 'em on."
July 3	The Iraqi Governing Council, the country's first post-Saddam provisional government, is established.
May 1	Bush declares an end to "major combat operations in Iraq," while noting "our mission continues . . . the war on terror continues, yet it is not endless. We do not know the day of final victory, but we have seen the turning of the tide."
August 19	An explosion destroys the United Nations headquarters in Baghdad, killing UN Special Representative Sérgio Vieira de Mello, the organization's top official in the country, and twenty-one others.
November 2	Coalition forces suffer their largest single loss to date, with sixteen soldiers killed and twenty more wounded, when an American helicopter crashes under enemy fire.
November 12	A bombing at the headquarters of Italian forces within the coalition claims thirty-three lives.
November 15	The Iraqi Governing Council announces an accelerated timetable for assuming national control.
November 27	President Bush celebrates Thanksgiving in Baghdad with American troops.
December 13	Saddam Hussein is captured by US forces.

2004

March 31	Amid increasing unrest and violence, four American contractors are killed in Fallujah.
April 4– May 1	The first battle of Fallujah (Operation Vigilant Resolve).
April	Images of prisoner abuse in the American-run Abu Ghraib prison emerge.
June 28	The Coalition Provisional Authority formally ends its occupying role, returning sovereignty to Iraq.
October 1	The battle of Samarra commences. American and Iraqi forces secure control of the city from insurgents after three days of fighting.
November 7– December 23	The second battle of Fallujah (Operation Phantom Fury).

2005

January 30	Iraqi parliamentary election seats 275 members of a National Assembly to draft a permanent constitution.
August 31	Fear of suicide bomber attacks spark a stampede of Shia pilgrims in Baghdad, resulting in an estimated one thousand civilian deaths.
September 1	Coalition forces commence Operation Restoring Rights, colloquially termed the battle of Tal Afar, to remove insurgents from the city, its success serving as a potential model for ensuing pacification efforts. Coalition forces control the city within three days and declare the operation over by mid-month.
September 14	Explosions in Baghdad kill 160, injuring more than 500 more.
November 17	Citing increasing instability in Iraq and rising American casualties, Representative John D. Murtha of Pennsylvania calls for an immediate withdrawal from Iraq: "It's time to bring them home."
November 30	The White House publishes an updated "National Strategy for Victory is Iraq" (NSVI), followed by significant public outreach to explain the US strategy in Iraq.
December 15	Iraqi parliamentary election, held under the rules of the new constitution, seats 275 members of the Iraqi Council of Representatives.

2006

February 22	The bombing of the al-Askari mosque in Samarra obliterates one of the holiest sites in Shia Islam.
March 15	The ten initial members of the Iraq Study Group (Baker-Hamilton commission) are appointed.
April	"Revolt of the Generals": several retired generals publicly call for the resignation of Secretary of Defense Donald Rumsfeld.
May 20	Nouri al-Maliki assumes office as Iraq's prime minister.
June 8	Abu Musab al-Zarqawi is killed by US forces in Iraq.
June 12	President Bush convenes a "war council" meeting at Camp David, including his top national security aides and outside experts.
June 13	Surprising most of the meeting's attendees, Bush leaves Camp David one day into the war council and secretly travels to Baghdad to meet Prime Minister Maliki and the new Iraqi cabinet.
June 14	Operation Together Forward begins in Baghdad.
July 22	Stephen Hadley poses "fifty questions" to the US Iraq country team, asking fundamental questions about strategy in an effort to trigger recognition in Baghdad that a new approach was needed.
August 3	In testimony to the Senate Armed Services Committee, General John Abizaid, commander of Central Command, says that if the country's violence is not curtailed, "Iraq could move toward civil war."
August 6/7	Operation Together Forward I ends and Operation Together Forward II begins in Baghdad.

August 31–September 3	The Iraq Study Group visits Baghdad.
Late August	The National Security Council launches an internal review of US strategy in Iraq.
September	NSC analysis determines that five brigade combat teams (the Army's basic unit of maneuver) are available for deployment to Iraq.
October 5	Secretary of State Condoleezza Rice visits Iraq.
October 17	End of Operation Together Forward II.
October 29	National Security Adviser Stephen Hadley visits Iraq.
November 5	Robert Gates visits President Bush at the ranch in Crawford, Texas, to discuss his replacing Secretary Rumsfeld.
November 7	In midterm elections in the United States, Republicans lose heavily, yielding control of both houses of Congress to the Democratic Party.
November 8	Bush announces Secretary of Defense Rumsfeld's resignation and says that Gates, a member of the Iraq Study Group and former director of central intelligence, will replace him.
November 10	President Bush publicly announces a formal review of Iraq strategy, to be led by Deputy National Security Advisor J. D. Crouch.
November 11	Secretary of State Rice, National Security Advisor Hadley, and senior officials meet for a wide-ranging discussion about US policy in Iraq.
November 15	First meeting of Crouch's strategic review team.
November 26	The results of the strategy review are presented to the president in a meeting in the White House solarium.
November 30	President Bush meets with Prime Minister Maliki in Amman, Jordan.
December 5	During his confirmation hearings to be secretary of defense, Gates is asked by Senator Carl Levin: "Do you believe that we are currently winning in Iraq?" He replies: "No, sir."
December 6	The Iraq Study Group presents its report to President Bush.
December 9–10	The American Enterprise Institute holds a crash workshop on Iraq to investigate possible new strategies and new resources to improve US fortunes in Iraq.
December 11	Bush and Vice President Richard Cheney meet in the Oval Office with retired generals and military experts to discuss possible options in Iraq; some favor an increase in troops, while others oppose the idea.
December 11	After the larger Oval Office session, Cheney meets with retired general Jack Keane and Frederick Kagan of the American Enterprise Institute, who brief him on an AEI plan to reestablish stability in Iraq by deploying more American troops and refocusing on population security.
December 13	Bush goes to the Pentagon for a meeting on Iraq strategy with the Joint Chiefs of Staff, in large measure to hear their concerns and offer an increase in overall Army and Marine Corps forces to help alleviate the long-term stress on the military that any surge in Iraq might cause.
December 18	Robert Gates is sworn in as secretary of defense.
December 21	Secretary of Defense Gates visits Baghdad.
December 28	President Bush holds a meeting in Crawford, Texas, to finalize the surge decision and determine how many brigades would deploy, and when, to Iraq.
December 30	Saddam Hussein is executed by the government of Iraq.

2007

January 4	President Bush and Prime Minister Maliki hold a one-on-one videoconference in which the president stresses the need for a public welcome for new US troops.
January 6	Maliki makes a strong, nonsectarian speech committing his government and Iraqi forces to "a new assault against insurgents and militias" and making clear that US support was both welcome and required.
January 10	Bush publicly announces a "surge" of American forces in Iraq.

NOTES

Introduction

1. George W. Bush, "Surge in Iraq," interview by Peter Feaver, Meghan O'Sullivan, and William Inboden, December 1, 2015, transcript, 25. Copies of the transcript are in the possession of the editors and the George W. Bush Presidential Center.

2. Although the president, in his January 2007 speech, described a commitment of "more than twenty thousand additional troops," the United States would deploy thirty-three thousand more soldiers to Iraq in 2007. Amy Belasco, *The Cost of Iraq, Afghanistan, and Other Global War on Terror Operations since 9/11*, Congressional Research Service Report RL33110, December 8, 2014, 9; Amy Belasco, *Troop Levels in the Afghan and Iraq Wars, FY2001–2012: Cost and Other Potential Issues*, Congressional Research Service Report R40682, July 2, 2009, 66.

3. Bush transcript, 4.

4. Bush transcript, 4–5.

5. Secretary of Defense Donald Rumsfeld and General George Casey declined invitations to participate.

6. Hal Brands, *What Good Is Grand Strategy? Power and Purpose in American Statecraft from Harry S. Truman to George W. Bush* (Ithaca, NY: Cornell University Press, 2014), 171 and 140ff.

7. Brands, *What Good Is Grand Strategy?*, 164.

8. Donald P. Wright and Timothy R. Reese, *On Point II: Transition to the New Campaign: The United States Army in Operation Iraqi Freedom, May 2003–January 2005* (Fort Leavenworth, KS: Combat Studies Institute, US Army Combined Arms Center, 2008), 19.

9. Half were eventually permitted to return to work. Sharon Otterman, "Iraq: Debaathification," February 22, 2005, Council on Foreign Relations, http://www.cfr.org/iraq/iraq-debaathification/p7853.

10. Wright and Reese, *On Point II*, 96.

11. Wright and Reese, 32.

12. Wright and Reese, 92.

13. Linda Robinson, *Tell Me How This Ends: General David Petraeus and the Search for a Way out of Iraq* (New York: PublicAffairs, 2008), 70.

14. Zarqawi's group would not take the name "al-Qaeda in Iraq" until 2004.

15. Wright and Reese, *On Point II*, 32–36.

16. Richard B. Cheney with Liz Cheney, *In My Time: A Personal and Political Memoir* (New York: Simon & Schuster, 2011), 434.

17. Wright and Reese, *On Point II*, 100; Derek J. Harvey, "A Red Team Perspective on the Insurgency in Iraq," in *An Army at War: Change in the Midst of Conflict*, ed. John J. McGrath, 193.

18. Dan Murphy, "Siege of Fallujah Polarizing Iraqis," *Christian Science Monitor*, April 15, 2004, http://www.csmonitor.com/2004/0415/p01s02-woiq.html.

19. Michael Gordon and Bernard Trainor, *The Endgame: The Inside Story of the Struggle for Iraq, from George W. Bush to Barack Obama* (New York: Pantheon Books, 2012), 114.

20. Wright and Reese, *On Point II*, 39.

21. George W. Casey, *Strategic Reflections: Operation Iraqi Freedom, July 2004–February 2007* (Washington, DC: National Defense University Press, 2012), 31, 52.

22. Wright and Reese, *On Point II*, 43.

23. Wright and Reese, 42.

24. Casey, *Strategic Reflections*, 28–29.

25. "The Surge—Collective Memory Project," Center for Presidential History, Southern Methodist University, John Abizaid transcript, 00:10:00, available via https://www.smu.edu/CPH/. Henceforth Collective Memory Project interviews are cited only by the interviewee's name followed by the word "transcript" and the last minute marker before the quotation or paraphrased remark.

26. Casey, *Strategic Reflections*, 46.

27. "Second Inaugural Address of George W. Bush; January 20, 2005," Avalon Project at Yale Law School, http://avalon.law.yale.edu/21st_century/gbush2.asp.

28. Peter Baker, *Days of Fire: Bush and Cheney in the White House* (New York: Doubleday, 2013), 361–75.

29. Casey, *Strategic Reflections*, 53.

30. Bob Woodward, *The War Within: A Secret White House History, 2006–2008* (New York: Simon & Schuster, 2008), 31.

31. The list is Sunni Arabs; secular ideologues; Sunni tribes; religious groups; ultra radical Salafis and Wahhabis; Shia groups; AQ and foreign fighters. See Wright and Reese, *On Point II*, 105–10.

32. Casey, *Strategic Reflections*, 79.

33. "Chronology," undated (probably May 2008). From a document collection titled "2008 Meeting with Bob Woodward—Transcripts & Documents—Volume 1," provided to the Collective Memory Project by the George W. Bush Presidential Library and Museum, Southern Methodist University, Dallas. Copies of the documents are in the editors' possession.

34. Casey, *Strategic Reflections*, 82.

35. Some former officials remain uncertain about who planted the explosives. See Stephen Cambone transcript, 00:18:00.

36. Peter Feaver transcript, 00:03:00.

37. David Gordon transcript, 00:13:00.

38. Peter Pace transcript, 00:21:00.

39. Feaver transcript, 00:35:00.

40. Peter Mansoor transcript, 00:12:00.

41. Cambone transcript, 00:59:00.

42. J. D. Crouch transcript, 00:48:00.

43. Stephen Hadley transcript, 01:34:00.

44. James Jeffrey transcript, 00:46:00.

45. David Satterfield transcript, 00:47:00.

46. Condoleezza Rice transcript, 01:38:00.

1. America's War in Iraq

1. "National Strategy for Victory in Iraq," November 30, 2005, *Washington Post*, http://www.washingtonpost.com/wp-dyn/content/article/2005/11/30/AR200511 3000376.html.

2. "Iraq and U.S. Policy," Secretary Condoleezza Rice, Opening Remarks before the Senate Foreign Relations Committee, Washington, DC, October 19, 2005, https://2001-2009.state.gov/secretary/rm/2005/55303.htm.

3. Casey was commander, Multi-National Force Iraq (or MNF-I).

4. David Stout, "Representative John P. Murtha Dies at 77; Ex-Marine Was Iraq War Critic," *New York Times*, February 8, 2010.

5. The transcript reads "2015," but Feaver clearly meant 2005.

6. A reference to two successive commanders of Military Assistance Command, Vietnam: General William W. Westmoreland and General Creighton W. Abrams Jr. Abrams, in contrast to Westmoreland, is usually characterized as favoring counterinsurgency methods.

2. This Strategy Is Not Working

1. Sidney Blumenthal, "Revolt of the Generals," *Guardian*, April 20, 2006. For the historical context see Jeffrey Barlow, *Revolt of the Admirals: The Fight for Naval Aviation, 1945–1950* (Washington, DC: Government Printing Office, 1995).

2. Vice President Cheney met with Colonel H. R. McMaster, recently ordered to Washington to participate in the Chairman of the Joint Chiefs of Staff Strategic Dialogue Group, known informally as the Council of Colonels. McMaster had previously served as commander of the Third Armored Cavalry Regiment in Iraq, where he had used counterinsurgency methods to secure Tal Afar. Colonel (retired) Derek Harvey, previously senior analyst for Iraq on the Joint Staff Directorate for Intelligence, was in 2006 a civilian analyst at the Defense Intelligence Agency. Colonel John Nagl served in Iraq in 2003 and in the Office of the Secretary of Defense until 2006, when he participated in the drafting of the US Army / Marine Corps Counterinsurgency Field Manual at Fort Leavenworth, Kansas.

3. General Stanley A. McChrystal (US Army, retired) served as commander, Joint Special Operations Command, and commander, Joint Special Operations Command Forward from February 2006 to August 2008. Kagan refers to *My Share of the Task: A Memoir* (New York: Portfolio/Penguin, 2013).

3. Together Forward?

1. "The President's News Conference," December 19, 2005, in *Public Papers of the Presidents of the United States: George W. Bush (2005: Book II)* (Washington, DC: Government Publishing Office, 2007), 1885. As one reporter noted during Bush's visit to Hanoi later that year, the parallel between Vietnam and Iraq was one the administration typically strove to avoid. Yet it nonetheless resonated. "Until now, when asked what he had learned from Vietnam, Mr. Bush has almost reflexively reached for the same line," David Sanger of the *New York Times* noted: "That he does not micromanage his generals the way Mr. Johnson did. It is a response drawn from conservative

orthodoxy about what went wrong in Vietnam, underlying an argument that had the generals been allowed to fight their way, the United States might have won." See David E. Sanger, "In Visit to Vietnam, Bush Cites Lessons for Iraq," *New York Times*, November 17, 2006.

4. Silos and Stovepipes

1. "The President's News Conference," December 19, 2005 in *Public Papers of the Presidents of the United States: George W. Bush (2005: Book II)* (Washington, DC: US Government Publishing Office, 2007), 1886.

2. Steve Coll, "The General's Dilemma," *New Yorker*, September 8, 2008.

5. Setting the Stage

1. Jeff Zeleny and Meghan Thee, "Exit Polls Show Voters, Citing War, Favored Democrats," *New York Times*, November 8, 2006.

2. Michael Gordon and David Cloud, "Rumsfeld Memo Proposed 'Major Adjustment' in Iraq," *New York Times*, December 3, 2006.

3. An Airstream trailer installed in the back of a military transport aircraft.

6. A Sweeping Internal Review

1. The Joint Chiefs of Staff conference room was unofficially known as "the tank" in reference to a meeting room used in the 1940s that required entrants to pass through an archway into a room with exposed wires and tubes. Entering the room was said to be like an entering a tank.

2. In 1995, the Bosnian Serb army massacred more than eight thousand civilians held in the town of Srebrenica, in Bosnia and Herzegovina.

3. Satterfield refers here to an infamous moment in late 1944 when nearby Soviet troops failed to aid the Polish resistance in the Warsaw Uprising against their joint Nazi foes.

7. Choosing to Surge

1. What would be published in mid-December 2006 as United States Army and Marine Corps Field Manual 3–24, *Counterinsurgency*.

8. What Kind of Surge?

1. Thomas E. Ricks, "Situation Called Dire in West Iraq," *Washington Post*, September 11, 2006.

10. Iraq, Vietnam, and the Meaning of Victory

1. Many studies of the Iraq War make at least passing reference to Vietnam, but beyond these relatively brief discussions there is a small cluster of work that examines such links at length. See Lloyd C. Gardner and Marilyn B. Young, eds., *Iraq and the*

Lessons of Vietnam: Or, How Not to Learn from the Past (New York: New Press, 2007); John Dumbrell and David Ryan, eds., *Vietnam in Iraq: Tactics, Lessons, Legacies and Ghosts* (New York: Routledge, 2007); and Robert K. Brigham, *Iraq, Vietnam, and the Limits of American Power* (New York: PublicAffairs, 2008).

2. Richard E. Neustadt and Ernest R. May, *Thinking in Time: The Uses of History for Decision Makers* (New York: Free Press, 1986); Francis J. Gavin, "History and Policy," *International Journal* 63 (December 2007): 162–77; William Inboden, "Statecraft, Decision-Making, and the Varieties of Historical Experience: A Taxonomy," *Journal of Strategic Studies* 36 (2014): 291–318; Hal Brands and Jeremi Suri, eds., *The Power of the Past: History and Statecraft* (Washington, DC: Brookings Institution Press, 2015). For the pitfalls as well as potential see Ernest R. May, *"Lessons" of the Past: The Use and Misuse of History in American Foreign Policy* (New York: Oxford University Press, 1973); and Margaret MacMillan, *Dangerous Games: The Uses and Abuses of History* (New York: Modern Library, 2009). Historical reasoning was especially prevalent among the Vietnam policy makers: see Yuen Foong Khong, *Analogies at War: Korea, Munich, Dien Bien Phu, and the Vietnam Decisions of 1965* (Princeton, NJ: Princeton University Press, 1992).

3. "Bush Compares Iraq to Vietnam," *Washington Post*, August 23, 2007. Bush's point was that a precipitous American withdrawal from Iraq could result in bloody reprisals akin to those in South Vietnam after its collapse in 1975. Bush was by no means unusual in referencing Vietnam. On the applications of Vietnam see Mark Atwood Lawrence, "Policymaking and the Uses of the Vietnam War," in Brands and Suri, *Power of the Past*, 49–72.

4. George W. Bush, "Surge in Iraq," interview by Peter Feaver, Meghan O'Sullivan, and William Inboden, December 1, 2015, transcript, 8, 22. Copies of the transcript are in the possession of the editors and the George W. Bush Presidential Center.

5. Peter Feaver and William Inboden, "Looking Forward through the Past: The Role of History in Bush White House National Security Policymaking," in Brands and Suri, *Power of the Past*, 253–79.

6. "The Surge—Collective Memory Project," Center for Presidential History, Southern Methodist University, Jack Keane transcript, 00:43:00, available at https://www.smu.edu/CPH/. Henceforth Collective Memory Project interviews are cited only by the interviewee's name followed by the word "transcript" and the last minute marker before the quotation or paraphrased remark; Peter Pace transcript, 00:51:00.

7. Steve Coll, "The General's Dilemma," *New Yorker*, September 8, 2008; Thomas E. Ricks, *The Gamble: General David Petraeus and the American Military Adventure in Iraq, 2006–2008* (New York: Penguin, 2009).

8. Andrew Preston, *The War Council: McGeorge Bundy, the NSC, and Vietnam* (Cambridge, MA: Harvard University Press, 2006), 164–67.

9. Andrew Preston, "The Little State Department: McGeorge Bundy and the National Security Council Staff, 1961–65," *Presidential Studies Quarterly* 31 (December 2001): 635–59.

10. J. D. Crouch transcript, 00:58:00.

11. For a good explanation why see Bartholomew Sparrow, *The Strategist: Brent Scowcroft and the Call of National Security* (New York: PublicAffairs, 2015).

12. Dick Cheney transcript, 01:45:00.

13. See Jeffrey A. Engel, *When the World Seemed New: George H. W. Bush and the End of the Cold War* (New York: Houghton Mifflin Harcourt, 2017).

14. Leslie H. Gelb, with Richard K. Betts, *The Irony of Vietnam: The System Worked* (Washington, DC: Brookings Institution Press, 1979).

15. The now-classic account is H. R. McMaster, *Dereliction of Duty: Lyndon Johnson, Robert McNamara, the Joint Chiefs of Staff, and the Lies That Led to Vietnam* (New York: HarperCollins, 1997). Interestingly, McMaster was involved as an Army officer in the planning for the surge in 2006–2007; later, in 2017, he became President Donald Trump's national security advisor before leaving the post in 2018.

16. Irving L. Janis, *Victims of Groupthink: A Psychological Study of Foreign-Policy Decisions and Fiascoes* (Boston: Houghton Mifflin, 1972).

17. Christopher Clark, *The Sleepwalkers: How Europe Went to War in 1914* (London: Allen Lane, 2012).

18. Fredrik Logevall, *Choosing War: The Lost Chance for Peace and the Escalation of War in Vietnam* (Berkeley: University of California Press, 1999).

19. See David Kaiser, *American Tragedy: Kennedy, Johnson, and the Origins of the Vietnam War* (Cambridge, MA: Belknap Press of Harvard University Press, 2000); and, more cautiously, Larry Berman, *Planning a Tragedy: The Americanization of the War in Vietnam* (New York: W. W. Norton, 1982).

20. Bush transcript, 16.

21. Robert Gates transcript, 00:20:00.

22. Condoleezza Rice transcript, 01:04:00.

23. Peter Pace transcript, 00:24:00.

24. Bush transcript, 17.

25. "Quiet Bush Aide Seeks Iraq Czar, Creating a Stir," *New York Times*, April 30, 2007. Hadley repeats this story in his oral history (Stephen Hadley transcript, 01:19:00).

26. Matthew J. Dickinson, *Bitter Harvest: FDR, Presidential Power and the Growth of the Presidential Branch* (New York: Cambridge University Press, 1996).

27. Hadley transcript, 00:17:00, 00:29:00.

28. Crouch transcript, 00:48:00.

29. Rice transcript, 00:11:00, 00:21:00, 1:06:00.

30. Bush transcript, 4–5, 7.

31. Rice transcript, 00:12:00.

32. Joshua Bolten transcript, 00:26:00.

33. Rice transcript, 01:32:00.

34. Gates transcript, 01:10:00.

35. Hadley transcript, 01:52:00. 00:07:00.

36. Bolten transcript, 01:13:00.

37. Hadley transcript, 00:10:00.

38. Pace transcript, 00:53:00.

39. Bolten transcript, 01:24:00.

40. Crouch transcript, 00:32:00.

41. Rice transcript, 01:12:00; Bush transcript, 13.

42. Crouch transcript, 00:04:00.

43. Gates transcript, 00:05:00; Bolten transcript, 01:03:00.

44. Bolten transcript, 01:42:00.

45. Hadley transcript, 00:58:00; Rice transcript, 00:37:00; Pace transcript, 01:08:00; Bush transcript, 18.

46. Bush transcript, 17; Karl Rove transcript, 00:02:00, 00:13:00; Hadley transcript, 01:50:00; Bolten transcript, 01:08:00.

47. Cheney transcript, 01:42:00. See "Special Forum: The Politics of Troop Withdrawal," *Diplomatic History* 34 (June 2010): 461–600, especially the articles by Robert Jervis, "The Politics of Troop Withdrawal: Salted Peanuts, the Commitment Trap, and Buying Time," 507–16, and Mark Atwood Lawrence, "Too Late or Too Soon? Debating the Withdrawal from Vietnam in the Age of Iraq," 589–600.

48. Pace transcript, 00:09:00; Bush transcript, 27.

49. This includes Grover Cleveland, who won two nonconsecutive terms, but doesn't include Theodore Roosevelt, Harry Truman, and LBJ, who served more than one term but won only one election of their own. Nor does it include Barack Obama, who of course served after Bush.

50. Julian E. Zelizer, *Arsenal of Democracy: The Politics of National Security—from World War II to the War on Terrorism* (New York: Basic Books, 2010); Andrew Preston, "Beyond the Water's Edge: Foreign Policy and Electoral Politics," in *America at the Ballot Box: Elections and Political History*, ed. Gareth Davies and Julian E. Zelizer (Philadelphia: University of Pennsylvania Press, 2015), 219–37.

51. Bolten transcript, 00:43:00.

52. Gates transcript, 00:36:00.

53. Bolten transcript, 00:29:00.

54. Hadley transcript, 01:37:00; Crouch transcript, 01:24:00; Karl Rove transcript, 00:43:00.

55. Bush transcript, 19.

56. Bolten transcript, 01:32:00.

57. Cheney transcript, 00:37:00, 00:56:00.

58. Susan A. Crane, "Writing the Individual Back into Collective Memory," *American Historical Review* 102 (December 1997): 1372–85; Anna Green, "Can Memory Be Collective?," in *The Oxford Handbook of Oral History*, ed. Donald A. Ritchie (Oxford: Oxford University Press, 2011), 96–111. This theory, now widely held, was first put forward by Maurice Halbwachs in two major works published in Paris in 1925 and 1950. For a condensed English-language version see Maurice Halbwachs, *On Collective Memory*, ed. Lewis A. Coser (Chicago: University of Chicago Press, 1992).

59. For insightful examinations see James Fentress and Chris Wickham, *Social Memory* (Oxford: Blackwell, 1992); and Richard Ned Lebow, "The Memory of Politics in Postwar Europe," in *The Politics of Memory in Postwar Europe*, ed. Richard Ned Lebow, Wulf Kansteiner, and Claudio Fogu (Durham, NC: Duke University Press, 2006), 8–16.

60. The historical memory of war has an incredibly rich historiography, but see especially Jay Winter, *Sites of Memory, Sites of Mourning: The Great War in European Cultural History* (Cambridge: Cambridge University Press, 1995); Jay Winter and Emmanuel Sivan, eds., *War and Remembrance in the Twentieth Century* (Cambridge: Cambridge University Press, 1999); and Jay Winter, *War beyond Words: Languages of Remembrance from the Great War to the Present* (Cambridge: Cambridge University Press, 2017).

61. Rice transcript, 01:00:00, 01:04:00.

62. Crouch transcript, 00:47:00.

63. Cheney transcript, 01:38:00, 02:01:00.

64. Bush transcript, 3, 4, 5.

65. See, for example, Peter D. Feaver, "The Right to Be Right: Civil-Military Relations and the Iraq Surge Decision," *International Security* 35 (Spring 2011): 87–125; Richard K. Betts, Michael C. Desch, and Peter D. Feaver, "Civilians, Soldiers, and the Iraq Surge Decision," *International Security* 35 (Winter 2011/12): 179–99; Peter L. Hahn, *Missions Accomplished? The United States and Iraq since World War I* (New York: Oxford University Press, 2012), 186–95; Stephen Biddle, Jeffrey Friedman, and Jacob Shapiro, "Testing the Surge: Why Did Violence Decline in Iraq in 2007?," *International Security* 37 (Summer 2012): 7–40; John Hagan et al., "Correspondence: Assessing the Synergy Thesis in Iraq," *International Security* 37 (Spring 2013): 173–98; and Andrew J. Bacevich, *America's War for the Greater Middle East: A Military History* (New York: Random House, 2016), 270–94.

66. Rove transcript, 00:18:00.

67. Hadley transcript, 01:17:00.

68. "Address to the Nation on Iraq," March 19, 2003, American Presidency Project, http://www.presidency.ucsb.edu/ws/?pid=63368.

69. "Address to the Nation on Military Operations in Iraq," January 10, 2007, American Presidency Project, http://www.presidency.ucsb.edu/ws/?pid=24432. Bush also refers to these parameters for victory in his oral history interview, conducted more than eight years after his 2007 address (see Bush transcript, 8).

70. "Address at Johns Hopkins University," April 7, 1965, American Presidency Project, http://www.presidency.ucsb.edu/ws/?pid=26877.

71. "The President's Address to the Nation Announcing Steps to Limit the War in Vietnam and Reporting His Decision Not to Seek Reelection," March 31, 1968, American Presidency Project, http://www.presidency.ucsb.edu/ws/?pid=28772.

11. Decisions and Politics

1. Timothy Wilson, *Strangers to Ourselves: Discovering the Adaptive Unconscious* (Cambridge, MA: Harvard University Press, 2004).

2. "The Surge—Collective Memory Project," Center for Presidential History, Southern Methodist University, Condoleezza Rice interview, transcript, 00:54:00, available at https://www.smu.edu/CPH/. Henceforth Collective Memory Project interviews are cited only by the interviewee's name followed by "transcript" and the last minute marker before the quotation or paraphrased remark.

3. Satterfield is correct that the retrospective judgment that the surge was effective inevitably colors the participants' views of how the decision was reached (David Satterfield transcript, 00:57:00; see also Zalmay Khalilzad transcript, 01:16:00, and Philip Zelikow transcript, 01:52:00).

4. In addition to my *Why Intelligence Fails: Lessons from the Iranian Revolution and the Iraq War* (Ithaca, NY: Cornell University Press, 2010), chap. 3, see the very insightful and correctly skeptical J-2 briefing "Iraq: Status of WMD Programs," September 5, 2002. As Rumsfeld said to the chairman of the Joint Chiefs of Staff Richard Myers in his covering memo of September 9, "It is big" (http://www.politico.com/magazine/story/2016/01/iraq-war-wmds-donald-rumsfeld-new-report-213530#ixzz3yI2vV0Pz).

5. See Stephen Biddle, Jeffrey Friedman, and Jacob Shapiro, "'Testing the Surge: Why Did Violence Decline in Iraq in 2007?," *International Security* 37 (Summer 2012): 7–40, and the subsequent debate between the authors and John Hagan, Joshua Kaiser, Anna Hanson, Jon Lindsay, and Austin Long, "Correspondence: Assessing the Synergy Thesis in Iraq, *International Security* 37 (Spring 2013): 173–98.

6. For contrasting views see Alexander Downes and Lindsay O'Rourke, "You Can't Always Get What You Want: Why Foreign-Imposed Regime Change Seldom Improved Interstate Relations," *International Security* 41 (Fall 2016): 43–89, and Paul D. Miller, *Armed State Building: Confronting State Failure, 1898–2012* (Ithaca, NY: Cornell University Press, 2013).

7. Rice transcript, 01:01:00.

8. Quoted in Stephen Dyson, *Leaders in Conflict: Bush and Rumsfeld in Iraq* (Manchester: Manchester University Press, 2014), 26. General John Abizaid's interview also presents a biting critique of what he sees as the meddling of the NSC staff in the surge decision. Rumsfeld's tone might be questioned, but this stance is not entirely unjustified. The chain of command is important to running any organization, and of course is particularly crucial for a military at war. Even when what is involved is not orders but information and options, lines of responsibility and accountability easily can become blurred.

9. Satterfield transcript, 01:21:00.

10. Peter Feaver transcript, 00:38:00; see also Dick Cheney transcript, 01:05:00.

11. Meghan O'Sullivan transcript, 00:29:00; see also John Hannah transcript, 00:14:00, and Stephen Hadley transcript, 00:15:00.

12. J. D. Crouch transcript, 00:58:00.

13. See, for example, O'Sullivan transcript, 01:11:00; Satterfield transcript, 00:51:00; for the frustrations felt by one of Rice's advisors who sympathized with this effort but felt excluded by the White House see Zelikow transcript, 01:44:00.

14. Stephen Cambone transcript, 00:59:00; Crouch transcript, 00:15:00.

15. Crouch transcript, 01:27:00; see also Jack Keane transcript, 00:02:00.

16. In fact, in medicine sometimes the reverse is true, and doctors come to understand the disease they are dealing with by seeing how it responds to various medications. I will note a parallel in Iraq below.

17. In fairness to Rumsfeld—difficult as this is—I should note that he did send a brief memo (one of his "snowflakes") to his subordinates asking if we were creating more enemies than we were killing, but apparently he did not follow up on this. See Dyson, *Leaders in Conflict*, for a sympathetic analysis of Rumsfeld.

18. An interesting counterfactual would be to ask what would have happened if the insurgents had lain low and the Americans withdrew within a year, as Rumsfeld had expected. They then could have tried to overthrow the largely Shia government, and no matter what happened I think it is unlikely that the US would have sent troops back in.

19. Rory Stewart, *The Prince of the Marshes: And Other Occupational Hazards of a Year in Iraq* (New York: Mariner Books, 2007).

20. Austin Long, "The Anbar Awakening, Survival," *Survival* 50 (March 2008): 67–94; see also John McCary, "The Anbar Awakening: An Alliance of Incentives," *Washington Quarterly* 32 (January 2009): 43–59.

21. O'Sullivan transcript, 00:18:00, 00:59:00; Feaver transcript, 00:19:00; see also Hadley transcript, 00:20:00, and David Gordon transcript, 00:35:00.

22. Casey's analysis may not have been wrong, but only outdated, as it could well have been correct in the earlier phase of the war. For interesting conflicting views on this question in Afghanistan see Astri Suhrke, *When Less Is More: The International Project in Afghanistan* (New York: Columbia University Press, 2011), and Paul Miller, "Graveyard of Analogies: The Use and Abuse of History for the War in Afghanistan," *Journal of Strategic Studies* 39 (June 2016): 466–71.

23. James Jeffrey transcript, 00:26:00.

24. There are significant parallels to the dispute between the Pentagon and the State Department over provincial reconstruction teams and the occupations after World War II. Indeed, the broader pattern of the Pentagon's planning for the post-hostilities phase in Iraq had its roots in the routines and organizational structures and cultures established in the earlier era, which in turn grew out of the Army's occupation of a sector of the Rhineland after World War I: Walter Hudson, *Army Diplomacy: American Military Occupation and Foreign Policy after World War II* (Lexington: University of Kentucky Press, 2015). For the resistance to the provincial reconstruction teams by the members of the Foreign Service see Mary Thompson-Jones, *To the Secretary: Leaked Embassy Cables and America's Foreign Policy Disconnect* (New York: W. W. Norton, 2016), 251–67.

25. Khalilzad transcript, 00:17:00.

26. For a good summary of the confused nature of the situation see the analysis of Eric Edelman, the undersecretary of defense for policy (Edelman transcript, 00:16:00). Indeed, Douglas Lute argues that the reason AQI bombed the shrine was that it realized that the insurgency was being defeated (Lute transcript, 00:38:00).

27. For a discussion of how framing violence as a civil war provided an excuse not to intervene see Michael Barnett, *Eyewitness to a Genocide: The United Nations and Rwanda* (Ithaca, NY: Cornell University Press, 2003).

28. There is an interesting parallel in the military's skepticism about helping rebuild the Lebanese army in 1982 because, in the words of General John Vessey, the chairman of the Joint Chiefs of Staff, it "is still beset with religious factionalism which makes their utility for governmental objectives doubtful in the absence of a political consensus": quoted in Gail Yoshitani, *Reagan on War: A Reappraisal of the Weinberger Doctrine, 1980–1984* (College Station: Texas A&M University Press, 2012), 77.

29. Hadley transcript, 00:21:00.

30. Rice transcript, 00:49:00.

31. Rice transcript, 01:06:00.

32. O'Sullivan transcript, 01:19:00.

33. This is not to say that there were no good arguments against the State Department option (see Feaver transcript, 01:12:00) but only that these do not seem to have weighed most heavily on the top decision makers. Interestingly enough, President Reagan's ill-fated decision to send Marines back to Lebanon in September 1982 was produced by his sense that he had "inherited a responsibility" because his earlier decision to withdraw the forces had made possible the massacres in the Palestinian refugee camps in Beirut: George Shultz, *Turmoil and Triumph: My Years as Secretary of State* (New York: Scribner's, 1993), 106. In the same way, President Obama's decision to intervene in Libya appears to have been strongly driven by his belief that forty thousand civilians would have been killed in Benghazi if he did not. For a treatment of American foreign policy in the first half of the twentieth century that stresses the importance of the feelings of the American elite and public opinion that the country

had a responsibility to use its power to help others see John Thompson, *A Sense of Power: The Roots of American Global Role* (Ithaca, NY: Cornell University Press, 2015).

34. Cambone transcript, 00:49:00.

35. Michael Cohen, James March, and Johan Olsen, "A Garbage Can Model of Organizational Choice," *Administrative Science Quarterly* 17 (March 1972): 1–25.

36. Satterfield transcript, 01:10:00; see also Feaver transcript, 00:52:00.

37. George Downs and David Rocke, "Conflict, Agency, and Gambling for Resurrection: The Principal-Agent Problem Goes to War," *American Journal of Political Science* 38 (May 1994): 362–80.

38. For elaboration and documentation see Robert Jervis, "The Implications of Loss Aversion for International Politics," in *How Statesmen Think: The Political Psychology of International Politics* (Princeton, NJ: Princeton University Press, 2017).

39. Lindsay and Long letter to the editor, in Hagan, Kaiser, Hanson, et al., "Correspondence," 181–89. In any case, one of the achievements of the surge was to capture approximately twenty-five thousand prisoners ("detainees," as they were called). These sweeps undoubtedly caught up many innocent people and by grouping many possible militants together may have produced many of the leaders and soldiers for the Islamic State (Abu Bakr al-Baghdadi was one of these), but the short-run effect was to take large numbers of actual and potential fighters off the battlefield. For discussion of the school for the younger detainees that the US established see Kathe Jervis, "A School under Fire: The Fog of Educational Practice in War," *Journal on Education in Emergencies* 2 (December 2016): 115–40, https://archive.nyu.edu/handle/2451/39658.

40. Hannah transcript, 01:26:00; Feaver transcript, 01:36:00.

41. Hannah transcript, 01:27:00; O'Sullivan transcript, 01:28:00.

42. Rice transcript, 01:12:00.

43. Joshua Bolten transcript, 01:31:00; Rice transcript, 01:38:00.

44. O'Sullivan transcript, 01:21:00.

45. Robert Gates transcript, 00:21:00.

46. Johnson had similarly made William Westmoreland Army chief of staff when he replaced him with Creighton Abrams during the Vietnam War.

47. Bolten transcript, 01:17:00.

48. Hadley transcript, 01:11:00.

49. Much of the debate about the trajectory of Iraq under Obama turns on one's evaluation of whether this bet paid off or not.

50. Rice transcript, 00:22:00.

51. Bob Woodward, *State of Denial* (New York: Simon & Schuster, 2002), 145–46.

52. Henry Metcalf and L. Urwick, eds., *Dynamic Administration: The Collected Papers of Mary Parker Follett* (New York: Harper & Bros., 1942); see also Harold Lasswell, "Compromise," in *Encyclopedia of the Social Sciences*, vol. 4 (New York: Macmillan, 1937), 147–49. For an excellent application see Richard Walton and Robert McKersie, *A Behavioral Theory of Labor Negotiations* (New York: McGraw Hill, 1965).

12. Blood, Treasure, and Time

1. Bernard Brodie, *War and Politics* (New York: Macmillan, 1973), 1.

2. Carter Malkasian, "Did the Coalition Need More Forces in Iraq? Evidence from Al Anbar," *Joint Force Quarterly*, no. 46 (3rd Quarter 2007): 120–26.

3. Carl von Clausewitz, *On War*, ed. and trans. Michael Howard and Peter Paret (Princeton, NJ: Princeton University Press, 1984), 92.

4. George W. Bush, "Surge in Iraq," interview by Peter Feaver, Meghan O'Sullivan, and William Inboden, December 1, 2015, transcript, 6, 4–5. Copies of the transcript are in the possession of the editors and the George W. Bush Presidential Center.

5. George W. Bush, *Decision Points* (New York: Crown, 2010), 357.

6. "The Surge—Collective Memory Project," Center for Presidential History, Southern Methodist University, Douglas Lute transcript, 01:17:00, available at https://www.smu.edu/CPH/. Henceforth Collective Memory Project interviews are cited only by the interviewee's name followed by the word "transcript" and the last minute marker before the quotation or paraphrased remark.

7. Philip Zelikow transcript, 00:10:00.

8. Zalmay Khalilzad transcript, 00:14:00.

9. Zelikow transcript, 00:31:00.

10. Jack Keane transcript, 00:02:00; Joshua Bolten transcript, 00:03:00; David Gordon transcript, 00:13:00. General George Casey quoted in Thomas E. Ricks, *The Gamble: General David Petraeus and the American Military Adventure in Iraq, 2006–2008* (New York: Penguin, 2009), 38.

11. Insurgencies are rebellions against governments; civil wars are conflicts between national groups to control the government; and foreign participation on behalf of one or both sides is common in many cases of either. For example, the Spanish Civil War was an insurgency against the republican government, in which Italian and German forces fought for the rebels, and Soviet aid (but not forces) went to the loyalists. Or the second Indochina War was an insurgency within South Vietnam against the Saigon government and a war between the Communist government in the North and the anti-Communist government in the South, in which US forces fought for the Saigon government, and Beijing and Moscow provided aid (but not forces) to the Communists. Anxiety over a difference between the concepts diverts attention from the simple point that in any war the issue is *which group will rule the country when the shooting stops.*

12. Michael V. Hayden, *Playing to the Edge* (New York: Penguin, 2016), 197.

13. John Abizaid transcript, 00:10:00.

14. For the full argument on these choices see Richard K. Betts, *American Force: Dangers, Delusions, and Dilemmas in National Security* (New York: Columbia University Press, 2012), chap. 3.

15. General Casey switched to asking for a slight increase in forces late in 2006. George W. Casey Jr., *Strategic Reflections: Operation Iraqi Freedom, July 2004–February 2007* (Washington, DC: National Defense University Press, 2012), 111.

16. Robert Gates transcript, 00:45:00.

17. Khalilzad transcript (citing Meghan O'Sullivan), 00:39:00; Stephen Hadley transcript, 00:19:00, 01:02:00.

18. Stephen Hadley transcript, 00:20:00.

19. Bush described the American stance as Iraqi control in principle and American control in practice: "You're in command but we really are ... and we'll have free movement with your troops in Baghdad even though it looked like you'll be in the lead." George W. Bush transcript, 14.

20. Joshua Bolten transcript, 00:58:00. Rumsfeld's successor Robert Gates was sure that Bush had decided for the surge before he offered the job to him and pretended to be uncertain, outside his inner circle, to prevent leaks. Robert Gates transcript, 00:13:00, 00:27:00.

21. The extreme example was in the Carter administration when neither State nor Defense had hawks in high positions, and Zbigniew Brzezinski was left to make the hard-line case on various issues, triggering strident criticism from Cyrus Vance and company for underhanded manipulation. Brzezinski also had to do this when half of his own staff was more or less on the other side.

22. Hadley transcript, 00:16:00, 00:34:00.

23. Gates transcript, 00:42:00; Hadley transcript, 00:25:00.

24. Peter Pace transcript, 00:19:00. Bush was understandably absorbed in his role as commander in chief, but to the point of obsession if his report that in the course of his presidency he read *fourteen* biographies of Abraham Lincoln is true. Bush, *Decision Points*, 368.

25. Hadley transcript, 00:10:00.

26. Eric Edelman transcript, 00:24:00. Rumsfeld's under secretary for intelligence similarly rejected the nonmilitary tasks implicit in counterinsurgency: The Defense Department "can't be pressed to do things that are beyond its remit. So it can't solve the sectarian violence. It's not going to solve the differences politically." Stephen Cambone transcript, 00:49:00.

27. The military was criticized by outsiders for paying attention only to what "affected American troops and the killing of Iraqis. Other actions affecting Iraqi civilians—kidnappings, rape, robberies, acts of extortion, and other forms of intimidation—didn't appear to be on the U.S. military's radar." Ricks, *Gamble*, 34.

28. Several civilians agreed the revolt delayed rather than provoked reexamination of strategy: Bolten transcript, 00:20:00; Hadley transcript, 00:07:00; Edelman transcript, 00:43:00; Peter Feaver transcript, 00:28:00. The president himself said the revolt "pissed me off . . . and it made me very sympathetic to Don Rumsfeld." Bush transcript, 27.

29. Richard K. Betts, *Soldiers, Statesmen, and Cold War Crises*, 2nd ed. (New York: Columbia University Press, 1991), 12–15 and passim.

30. Lute transcript, 00:20:00; Abizaid transcript, 00:30:00. Once the choice was made, however, the general weighed in for sending five brigades rather than the smaller number proposed by some: "I said once the decision was made that we're going to surge, I said we need to surge enough." Abizaid transcript, 01:14:00. On JCS limitation of action in actual war over Kosovo to husband forces for potential war in Korea or the Persian Gulf see General Wesley K. Clark, *Waging Modern War* (New York: PublicAffairs, 2001), 312–13.

31. Lute transcript, 00:42:00.

32. Zelikow transcript, 00:26:00.

33. Lute transcript, 00:44:00.

34. Bush, *Decision Points*, 367.

35. Douglas Lute, 00:17:00.

36. Abizaid transcript, 00:17:00, 00:39:00.

37. Edelman transcript, 00:31:00.

38. Khalilzad transcript, 00:27:00.

39. Cited in Gates transcript, 00:58:00. Zelikow complained that although the White House backed Rice on the move to clear, hold, and build, "It doesn't translate into action in the field. . . . Rumsfeld and Casey basically . . . ignore this and do nothing concrete about it." Zelikow transcript, 00:48:00.

40. Zelikow transcript, 00:41:00.

41. Pace quoted in Condoleezza Rice transcript, 00:23:00.

42. Pace transcript, 01:15:00.

43. Keane transcript, 00:42:00.

44. Outsiders like Eliot Cohen, the Kagans, and Michael Vickers "opened the aperture. It's very easy, when you're doing this every day, to get stuck in a particular place, and you're just trying to grind through and make it work. I don't know how many times I've said plan B is to make plan A work. You get into kind of that mind-set, and so opening the aperture was very important." Rice transcript, 00:17:00.

45. Hadley transcript, 01:34:00. In opposition to Army Chief of Staff Peter Schoomaker and Marine Commandant James Conway, Keane's special contribution, in the vice president's view, "was 'we can do this.' . . . That was very reassuring, coming from a guy who had been vice chief of the Army." Dick Cheney transcript, 01:10:00.

46. Bush, Decision Points, 371.

47. J. D. Crouch transcript, 00:50:00; Rice transcript, 00:09:00.

48. See Jack L. Snyder, From Voting to Violence: Democratization and Nationalist Conflict (New York: W. W. Norton, 2000); Edward D. Mansfield and Jack L. Snyder, Electing to Fight: Why Emerging Democracies Go to War (Cambridge, MA: MIT Press, 2004); and Fareed Zakaria, The Future of Freedom: Illiberal Democracy at Home and Abroad (New York: W. W. Norton, 2003), chaps. 3–4.

49. For example, in the CENTCOM commander's view the election enabled politicization of the Iraqi police, who "essentially became Shia militia." Abizaid transcript, 00:19:00.

50. General Peter Chiarelli quoted in Ricks, Gamble, 37; Feaver transcript, 00:08:00.

51. Edelman transcript, 00:15:00; Abizaid transcript, 00:35:00.

52. Ricks, Gamble, 51.

53. Gordon transcript, 00:17:00, 01:16:00.

54. Hadley transcript, 00:48:00, 01:14:00.

55. Feaver transcript, 01:32:00. Similar reasoning applied in the early 1960s when policy makers on Vietnam "saw greater American involvement as a way to overcome Diem's defects." Stephen Sestanovich, Maximalist (New York: Knopf, 2014), 104.

56. Bolten transcript, 01:36:00.

57. Hayden, Playing to the Edge. General Hayden was director of NSA, CIA, and deputy DNI.

58. Abizaid transcript, 00:33:00.

59. Austin Long, "The Anbar Awakening," Survival 50, no. 2 (May 2008).

60. Feaver transcript, 01:38:00.

61. Lute transcript, 01:11:00.

62. Bush transcript, 10.

63. Bush, Decision Points, 356.

64. Peter Feaver interjection in Crouch transcript, 01:02:00.

65. Hadley transcript, 01:42:00; Gates transcript, 01:02:00; Bolten transcript, 01:33:00.

66. See Allan E. Goodman, *Politics in War: The Bases of Political Community in South Vietnam* (Cambridge, MA: Harvard University Press, 1973); William R. Corson, *The Betrayal* (New York: W. W. Norton, 1968), chap. 4.

67. Stephen Biddle, "Afghanistan's Legacy: Emerging Lessons of an Ongoing War," *Washington Quarterly* 37, no. 2 (Summer 2014): 80.

68. Khalilzad transcript, 00:46:00; Lute transcript, 01:12:00.

69. Peter Feaver and Hal Brands suggest that a modest US contingent might have provided better intelligence on local developments, restraint on Maliki's politicization of Iraqi security forces, logistical assistance that might have prevented Iraqi army collapse, more robust training and professionalism for Iraqi forces, direct action in special operations against al-Qaeda and to forestall formation of the Islamic State, and other limited but helpful functions.

13. Strategy and the Surge

1. Jon R. Lindsay, "Shifting the Fog of War: Information Technology and the Politics of Control," unpublished manuscript. Copy in possession of the author.

2. "The Surge—Collective Memory Project," General Peter Pace interview, transcript, 00:30:00, https://www.smu.edu/CPH/. Henceforth Collective Memory Project interviews are cited only by the interviewee's name followed by "transcript" and the last minute marker before the quotation or paraphrased remark.

3. Pace transcript, 00:44:00.

4. Pace transcript, 00:35:00.

5. Pace transcript, 01:15:00.

6. Dick Cheney transcript, 00:57:00.

7. Condoleezza Rice transcript, 00:24:00.

8. Eric Edelman transcript, 01:11:00.

9. Compare Joshua Bolten transcript, 00:40:00, and John Abizaid transcript, 00:55:00.

10. Abizaid transcript, 00:48:00.

11. Stephen Cambone transcript, 00:56:00.

12. Edelman transcript, 00:24:00.

13. Peter Feaver transcript, 00:37:00.

14. Feaver transcript, 01:04:00.

15. Feaver transcript, 01:30:00.

16. J. D. Crouch transcript, 00:10:00.

17. Cambone transcript, 00:15:00, and Edelman transcript, 00:18:00.

18. Abizaid transcript, 00:14:00, 00:19:00. Abizaid argues that the core problem of Sunni disenfranchisement runs through the whole history of the war. "Today it's fairly clear that all of these things are successors, and when you look at ISIS today, ISIS is a successor of Baathist, al-Qaeda, Zarqawi, and if I had a dollar for every military commander or politician who said 'We've got them on the run,' I'd be a rich man today. Now, the truth of the matter is we never really did have it under control." Abizaid transcript, 00:24:00.

19. Crouch transcript, 00:03:00, and Edelman transcript, 00:10:00.

20. Meghan O'Sullivan transcript, 00:05:00.

21. Feaver transcript, 00:35:00.

22. Robert Gates transcript, 00:56:00.

23. Rice transcript, 01:24:00.

24. Peter Mansoor transcript, 00:27:00.

25. Mansoor transcript, 00:39:00.

26. John Hannah transcript, 01:34:00.

27. Abizaid called this the "antibody" theory of insurgency. Abizaid transcript, 00:06:00.

28. Rice transcript, 00:49:00.

29. Rice transcript, 00:46:00. See also O'Sullivan transcript, 00:37:00; Feaver transcript, 00:22:00; and Pace transcript, 00:21:00. Abizaid was also discouraged, though his main concern was with the Iraqi police. Abizaid transcript, 00:43:00.

30. Feaver transcript, 01:17:00. See also Edelman transcript, 00:21:00.

31. David Gordon transcript, 00:07:00.

32. Stephen Hadley transcript, 00:20:00.

33. Edelman transcript, 00:12:00.

34. Rice transcript, 00:49:00.

35. O'Sullivan transcript, 00:37:00.

36. Mansoor transcript, 00:39:00, and Hadley transcript, 01:02:00.

37. Hadley transcript, 00:21:00.

38. O'Sullivan transcript, 01:01:00; Gordon transcript, 00:50:00; Feaver transcript, 00:46:00. Maliki initially opposed the surge on the grounds that it would lead to more violence. See Gates transcript, 00:45:00. Eric Edelman recalls that he was "very opposed" to even two additional brigades. See Edelman transcript, 01:07:00. It is unclear why he changed his mind. The prevailing view among the interviewees is that Bush's commitment was the deciding factor. Ambassador Zalmay Khalilzad's more nuanced argument suggests that Maliki came to recognize the opportunity to act decisively to improve security in other parts of the country while US efforts were concentrated in Baghdad and Anbar Province. Specifically, Maliki used the surge as an opportunity to attack Shia rivals in greater Basra. This contributed to greater security. It also consolidated his position as prime minister and as political leader of the country's Shia, meaning he satisfied his sectarian and nationalist instincts. See Khalilzad transcript, 00:58:00.

39. Mansoor transcript, 00:37:00.

40. The president apparently cut off an earlier review that June by leaving a strategy conference at Camp David to fly to Baghdad. See Hadley transcript, 00:13:00.

41. O'Sullivan transcript, 01:28:00. This is consistent with other accounts of the surge that suggest the president had no clearly formed strategy until December 2006. See Thomas E. Ricks, *The Gamble: General David Petraeus and the American Military Adventure in Iraq, 2006–2008* (New York: Penguin, 2009).

42. Gates transcript, 00:56:00.

43. National Security Council, "Highlights of the Iraq Strategy Review," January 2007, p. 8.

44. Gates transcript, 00:08:00.

45. O'Sullivan transcript, 00:05:00; Crouch transcript, 00:09:00; Feaver transcript, 00:35:00.

46. Abizaid transcript, 01:05:00, 01:09:00, 01:19:00.

47. Pace transcript, 00:03:00, 00:23:00, 00:26:00. Pace claims that both Abizaid and Casey requested additional troops in August. This is at odds with other interviews. O'Sullivan claims that Casey opposed adding forces and requested that two brigades be sent home. O'Sullivan transcript, 00:58;00.

48. Mansoor transcript, 00:34:00. Indeed, the president's agreement to raise troop numbers made the surge "salable" to the JCS. Hadley transcript, 00:40:00.

49. Pace transcript, 01:22:00.

50. David Satterfield transcript, 00:41:00, and Rice transcript, 00:48:00.

51. Rice transcript, 00:51:00.

52. Rice transcript, 01:00:00, 01:11:00.

53. Cambone transcript, 00:48:00.

54. Cambone transcript, 00:55:00.

55. O'Sullivan transcript, 00:20:00.

56. See the discussion in Feaver transcript, 00:46:00.

57. "Iraq Strategic Review," February 28, 2008, 1, from a document collection titled "2008 Meeting with Bob Woodward—Transcripts & Documents—Volume 1," provided to the Collective Memory Project by the George W. Bush Presidential Library and Museum, Southern Methodist University, Dallas [hereafter GWBPLM]. Copies of the documents are in the editors' possession.

58. Edelman transcript, 01:02:00. See also Hannah transcript, 01:06:00, and Feaver transcript, 01:16:00. The faith in Petraeus is consistent with past cases of counterinsurgency. The historiography of the Huk Rebellion, the Malayan Emergency, and the Vietnam War are replete with stories of military officers and political officials arriving on the scene with new ideas about how to rescue failing efforts by increasing efforts to protect the population and win its support. According to familiar stories, Magsaysay in the Philippines and Templer in Malaya were able to turn around losing wars by changing the way their forces fought. Abrams made important progress in Vietnam, though he took command too late to change the outcome. This historiography is deeply flawed, however. See Joshua Rovner, "The Heroes of COIN," *Orbis* 56, no. 2 (Spring 2012): 215–32.

59. Crouch transcript, 00:50:00.

60. Feaver transcript, 01:32:00. See also Hadley transcript, 00:49:00.

61. Hadley transcript, 01:13:00. On US efforts to signal commitment see Crouch transcript, 01:15:00, and Hannah transcript, 01:29:00.

62. Satterfield transcript, 01:12:00, quoted at 01:13:00.

63. George W. Bush, "Surge in Iraq," interview by Peter Feaver, Meghan O'Sullivan, and William Inboden, December 1, 2015, transcript, 14. Copies of the transcript are in the possession of the editors and the George W. Bush Presidential Center.

64. Mike Scudder to Steve Hadley, "Bob Woodward's Interview of the President," May 16, 2008, 3, GWBPLM.

65. Walter C. Ladwig III, "Influencing Clients in Counterinsurgency: US Involvement in El Salvador's Civil War, 1979–92," *International Security* 41, no. 1 (Summer 2016).

66. Zaid al-Ali, *The Struggle for Iraq's Future: How Corruption, Incompetence, and Sectarianism Have Undermined Democracy* (New Haven, CT: Yale University Press, 2014), 115–18. See also Marc Santora, "Iraq Leader and Sunni Officials in Clash on Security," *New York Times,* January 26, 2007.

67. Caitlin Talmadge, *The Dictator's Army: Battlefield Effectiveness in Authoritarian Regimes* (Ithaca, NY: Cornell University Press, 2015).

68. For more on how Maliki solidified control of the security services see al-Ali, *Struggle for Iraq's Future*, 130–32. For more on how this affected their performance see Michael Knights, Lachlyn Soper, Andrew Lembke, and Barak Salmoni, "The Iraqi Security Forces: A Status Report," Washington Institute for Near East Policy, *Policy Watch* 1814, June 13, 2011, http://www.washingtoninstitute.org/policy-analysis/view/the-iraqi-security-forces-a-status-report.

69. Michael Knights, "The Iraqi Security Forces: Local Context and US Assistance," Washington Institute for Near East Policy, Policy Notes no. 4 (June 2011), 3.

70. Michael Knights, interview with Joel Wing, Washington Institute for Near East Policy, July 31, 2012, http://www.washingtoninstitute.org/uploads/Documents/opeds/KnightsInterview20120731.pdf.

71. Satterfield transcript, 01:12:00.

72. Rice transcript, 01:23:00.

73. Joshua Rovner, "Questions about COIN after Iraq and Afghanistan," in *The New Counter-Insurgency Era in Critical Perspective*, ed. Celeste Ward Gventner, David Martin Jones, and M. L. R. Smith (London: Palgrave Macmillan, 2014), 299–318.

14. Civil-Military Relations and the 2006 Iraq Surge

1. I can't emphasize enough just how much Stephen Hadley was a force for good in the story of the Iraq War surge, this criticism on narrow civil-military grounds notwithstanding. It was he who convinced President Bush the war effort was failing, he who orchestrated the masterly interagency process that produced a better alternative, he who understood that an alternative could not be effectuated with the sitting secretary of defense, and who found a sterling replacement whose addition to the cabinet fundamentally changed the dynamic of the Bush administration.

2. Peter Feaver, who nicely reviewed an early draft of this chapter, disagrees vehemently with this conclusion, and with many other elements of the analysis presented here.

3. Stephen Hadley, personal interview with the author, November 14, 2016.

4. For example, see the survey results in Kori Schake and Jim Mattis, eds., *Warriors and Citizens: American Views of Our Military* (Stanford, CA: Hoover Institution, 2016).

5. For a thorough review of the arguments see Peter D. Feaver, "The Right to Be Right: Civil-Military Relations and the Iraq Surge Decision," *International Security* 35, no. 4 (Spring 2011): 87–125.

6. The failures of imagination, operations, and accountability by the US military in Iraq are detailed by Thomas E. Ricks in *Fiasco: The American Military Adventure in Iraq* (New York: Penguin, 2006).

7. Eliot Cohen provides a thoughtful review of the failures and successes in *The Big Stick: The Limits of Soft Power and the Necessity of Military Force* (New York: Basic Books, 2017).

8. President Bush considered executive branch unity—and particularly military support—essential for garnering congressional support and funding for the approach. See George W. Bush, "Surge in Iraq," interview by Peter Feaver, Meghan O'Sullivan,

and William Inboden, December 1, 2015, transcript, 13. Copies of the transcript are in the possession of the editors and the George W. Bush Presidential Center.

9. Stephen Cambone objects to this characterization of Secretary Rumsfeld as "flat out untrue, not his management style." He puts an improbable gloss on the secretary's role in the planning process, though, describing it as "a secretary of defense leaning in and wanting to do this in a way that was actually designed to look after the troops": see "The Surge—Collective Memory Project," Stephen Cambone interview, transcript, 00:24:00, at https://www.smu.edu/CPH/. Henceforth Collective Memory Project interviews are cited only by the interviewee's name followed by "transcript" and the last minute marker before the quotation or paraphrased remark.

10. General Pace considers that all the chiefs supported the 2003 plan; my recollection (I was director for defense strategy and requirements on the NSC staff at that time) is that it was contested, particularly by the chief of staff of the Army and the Joint Staff directors of operations (J-3) and war plans (J-7), and widespread concern existed among commanders assigned to it, including the First Marine Division's General Jim Mattis.

11. Condoleezza Rice transcript, 00:53:00.

12. Dick Cheney transcript, 00:34:00. The contrasting approach to John Abizaid's concern about being an occupation force is Dwight Eisenhower in 1945 telling Germans "we come as occupiers, but not as oppressors."

13. Cheney transcript, 00:36:00.

14. Rice transcript, 00:08:00.

15. Jack Keane transcript, 00:00:00, 00:19:00.

16. Joshua Bolten transcript, 00:01:00.

17. Bolten transcript, 00:56:00.

18. It is disappointing that Secretary Rumsfeld declined to be interviewed for the project; his views throughout are imputed on the basis of Stephen Cambone's perspective as the aide most closely associated with Rumsfeld's thinking.

19. Cambone transcript, 00:19:00.

20. Cambone transcript, 00:53:00.

21. Cambone transcript, 00:56:00.

22. Cambone transcript, 01:08:00.

23. Cambone transcript, 00:37:00.

24. Cambone transcript, 00:28:00.

25. Cambone transcript, 1:08:00.

26. Peter Pace transcript, 00:33:00.

27. Rice transcript, 00:25:00, 00:39:00.

28. Bush transcript, 10.

29. Greg Newbold, "Why Iraq Was a Mistake," *Time*, April 9, 2006; David S. Cloud, Eric Schmitt, and David Sanger, "Rumsfeld Faces Revolt by Retired Generals," *New York Times*, April 13, 2006.

30. Bush transcript, 27.

31. Pace transcript, 00:10:00; Bolten transcript, 00:21:00.

32. Condoleezza Rice, personal interview with the author, January 26, 2017.

33. Bush transcript, 27.

34. Hadley interview; Bush transcript, 27.

35. Tabulated from "U.S. Casualties in Iraq," Global Security.org, http://www.globalsecurity.org/military/ops/iraq_casualties.htm.

36. "Democrats Retake Congress," November 9, 2006, CNN, http://www.cnn.com/ELECTION/2006/. President Bush disputes that explanation, considering congressional scandals as at least as important a factor (Bush transcript, 12).

37. Cheney transcript, 01:49:00.

38. Bush transcript, 18.

39. JCS chairman Peter Pace, a Rumsfeld defender in most instances, was adamant that "I don't see a civil-military relationship problem." Pace transcript, 00:11:00.

40. Secretary Rice describes the military in Iraq as coming earlier to the conclusion that the surge strategy could work. Rice interview.

41. President Bush succinctly describes his reaction as "pissed." Bush transcript, 27.

42. Keane transcript, 01:15:00, 01:11:00.

43. Hadley interview.

44. The YouGov data from Schake and Mattis, *Warriors and Citizens*, are publicly available at http://www.hoover.org/research/warriors-and-citizens (link at bottom right, under additional resources).

45. "Gen. Dempsey to Fellow Officers: Stay Off the Political Battlefield," National Public Radio, August 3, 2016; Tim Johnson, "Should Retired U.S. Military Leaders Be Sounding Off on Politics?," McClatchy, September 13, 2016.

46. Steve Corbett and Michael J. Davidson, "The Role of the Military in Presidential Politics," *Parameters*, Winter 2009, 58.

47. Stephen J. Hadley, quoted in Kori Schake and Will Wechsler, *Process Makes Perfect* (Washington, DC: Center for American Progress, November 2016), 20.

48. Kori Schake, "Security and Solvency," *Orbis*, July 2014.

49. Bolten transcript, 00:26:00.

50. Rice transcript, 00:45:00.

51. Bolten transcript, 00:12:00.

52. Pace transcript, 00:20:00.

53. Bolten transcript, 00:23:00.

54. Rice interview.

55. Bolten transcript, 00:14:00.

56. Bush transcript, 22.

57. For detailed discussions of the American civil-military bargain see Schake and Mattis, *Warriors and Citizens*.

58. Gates transcript, 00:27:00.

59. Bolten transcript, 01:19:00; Gates transcript, 00:27:00.

60. Bolten transcript, 01:31:00.

61. Her comments imply that the President Bush of 2006 might have pushed back harder on Department of Defense force levels for the invasion of Iraq in 2003. Rice transcript, 01:39:00.

15. The Bush Administration's Decision to Surge in Iraq

1. "The Surge—Collective Memory Project," Robert Gates interview, transcript, 01:10:00, at https://www.smu.edu/CPH/. Henceforth Collective Memory Project interviews are cited only by the interviewee's name followed by "transcript" and the last minute marker before the quotation or paraphrased remark.

2. Stephen Hadley transcript, 01:17:00.

3. Condoleezza Rice transcript, 01:37:00.

4. Meghan O'Sullivan transcript, 01:52:00.

5. John Abizaid transcript, 01:16:00.

6. Philip Zelikow transcript, 00:32:00, 01:50:00.

7. David Satterfield transcript, 01:23:00, 01:03:00.

8. Stephen Cambone transcript, 01:21:00 (author's emphases).

9. Rice transcript, 01:12:00; Peter Feaver transcript, 01:37:00; Hadley transcript, 01:14:00.

10. Hadley transcript, 01:18:00, 01:23:00.

11. On the National Security Act of 1947 and its evolution see Michael H. Hogan, *A Cross of Iron: Harry S. Truman and the Origins of the National Security State, 1945–1954* (New York: Cambridge University Press, 1998).

12. Alexander L. George, "The Case for Multiple Advocacy in Making Foreign Policy," *American Political Science Review* 66 (September 1972): 751–85.

13. Fred I. Greenstein and Richard H. Immerman, "Effective National Security Advising: Recovering the Eisenhower Legacy," *Political Science Quarterly* 115 (Fall 2000): 335–45.

14. In addition to the oral histories see the internally authored "Iraq Strategic Review," December 18, 2007, revised on January 3 and February 14, 2008. From a document collection titled "2008 Meeting with Bob Woodward—Transcripts & Documents—Volume 1," provided to the Collective Memory Project by the George W. Bush Presidential Library and Museum, Southern Methodist University, Dallas [hereafter GWBPLM]. Copies of the documents are in the editors' possession.

15. Kimberly Kagan transcript, 00:05:00. See also Thomas E. Ricks, *Fiasco: The American Military Adventure in Iraq* (New York: Penguin, 2006), 390–430; Ricks, *The Gamble: General David Petraeus and the American Military Adventure in Iraq, 2006–2008* (New York: Penguin, 2009), 3–15; and Bob Woodward, *The War Within: A Secret White House History, 2006–2008* (New York: Simon & Schuster, 2008), 119–30.

16. Abizaid transcript, 00:10:00; Eric Edelman transcript, 00:17:00; Dick Cheney transcript, 00:43:00; Hadley transcript, 01:07:00.

17. O'Sullivan transcript, 00:03:00; Feaver transcript, 00:03:00.

18. Zalmay Khalilzad transcript, 00:14:00.

19. Rice transcript, 00:00:00; Zelikow transcript, 00:14:00; Steven R. Weisman, "Rice in Testy Hearing Cites Progress in Iraq," *New York Times*, October 20, 2005, http://query.nytimes.com/gst/fullpage.html?res=9B01EEDC123FF933A15753C1A 9639C8B63.

20. Khalilzad transcript, 00:18:00.

21. National Security Council, "National Strategy for Victory in Iraq, November 2005, https://www.hsdl.org/?view&did=457955.

22. George W. Bush, "Surge in Iraq," interview by Peter Feaver, Meghan O'Sullivan, and William Inboden, December 1, 2015, transcript, 3. Copies of the transcript are in the possession of the editors and the George W. Bush Presidential Center.

23. O'Sullivan transcript, 00:12:00.

24. Zelikow transcript, 00:41:00; Joshua Bolten transcript, 00:50:00.

25. Fred I. Greenstein, *The Hidden-Hand Presidency: Eisenhower as Leader* (New York: Basic Books, 1982), 124–29; Robert R. Bowie and Richard H. Immerman, *Waging Peace: How Eisenhower Shaped an Enduring Cold War Strategy* (New York: Oxford

University Press, 1998), 88–90; Bush transcript, 17. Bush does not mention a single meeting of the NSC in his memoir's thirty-nine-page chapter on the surge. George W. Bush, *Decision Points* (New York: Crown, 2010), 355–94.

26. Bolten transcript, 00:13:00; Bush transcript, 3, 10, 16–17.

27. John Burke, Fred Greenstein, Larry Berman, and Richard Immerman, *How Presidents Test Reality: Decisions on Vietnam, 1954 and 1965* (New York: Russell Sage, 1991).

28. Abizaid transcript, 00:08:00.

29. O'Sullivan transcript, 00:09:00; Feaver transcript, 00:09:00; Hadley transcript, 00:03:00.

30. Anna Kasten Nelson, "The 'Top of the Policy Hill': President Eisenhower and the National Security Council," *Diplomatic History* 7 (Fall 1983): 307–26.

31. Peter Pace transcript, 00:07:00; Feaver transcript, 00:28:00.

32. O'Sullivan transcript, 00:10:00.

33. O'Sullivan transcript, 00:12:00; James Jeffrey transcript, 00:23:00, 00:38:00.

34. J. D. Crouch transcript, 00:07:00; Feaver transcript, 00:14:00; Fred Kagan transcript, 00:21:00.

35. Feaver transcript, 00:16:00; Hadley transcript, 00:13:00.

36. F. Kagan transcript, 00:16:00; Cheney transcript, 00:29:00.

37. Bush, *Decision Points*, 366.

38. Pace transcript, 00:16:00; Feaver transcript, 00:18:00; John Hannah transcript, 00:08:00; and Rice transcript, 00:17:00.

39. O'Sullivan transcript, 00:13:00, 00:42:00. See also O'Sullivan memorandum for Hadley and J. D. Crouch, n.d. [July 2006], "2008 Meeting with Bob Woodward—Transcripts & Documents—Volume 1," GWBPLM.

40. O'Sullivan transcript, 00:30:00; Hadley transcript, 00:15:00; Feaver transcript, 00:15:00.

41. Feaver transcript, 00:34:00.

42. Bush transcript, 3, 25.

43. Crouch transcript, 00:27:00; Jeffrey transcript, 01:30:00.

44. O'Sullivan transcript, 00:45:00.

45. Bolten transcript, 00:39:00; Pace transcript, 00:30:00; O'Sullivan transcript, 00:54:00.

46. Zelikow transcript, 01:53:00.

47. Alexander L. George, *Presidential Decisionmaking in Foreign Policy: The Effective Use of Information and Advice* (Boulder, CO: Westview, 1980).

48. Feaver transcript, 00:35:00; Rice transcript, 00:08:00; Hadley transcript, 00:35:00.

49. Feaver transcript, 00:52:00; Pace transcript, 00:24:00, 01:04:00.

50. Abizaid transcript, 00:48:00. Abizaid judges General David Petraeus's behavior the same way. Petraeus also expressed his criticisms outside the chain of command.

51. Jack Keane transcript, 00:45:00; Peter Mansoor transcript, 00:22:00; Douglas Lute transcript, 00:55:00; Edelman transcript, 00:32:00, 00:49:00.

52. "Text of U.S. Security Adviser's Iraq Memo," November 8, 2006, *New York Times*, November 29, 2006, http://www.nytimes.com/2006/11/29/world/middleeast/29mtext.html.

53. O'Sullivan transcript, 01:02:00; Rice transcript, 00:40:00; Feaver transcript, 00:62:00; Hadley transcript, 00:44:00, 00:51:00.

54. Satterfield transcript, 00:43:00, 00:55:00.

55. Hannah transcript, 00:42:00.

56. Mansoor transcript, 00:28:00; Feaver transcript, 01:14:00.

57. Bolten transcript, 00:39:00; O'Sullivan transcript, 01:15:00; Feaver transcript, 00:21:00. See also Stephen J. Hadley, "The Role and Importance of the National Security Advisor," address presented at the Scowcroft Legacy Conference sponsored by the Scowcroft Institute of International Affairs at the Bush School of Government and Public Service, Texas A&M University, College Station, on April 26, 2016, http://bush.tamu.edu/scowcroft/papers/hadley/.

58. John P. Burke, *Honest Broker? The National Security Advisor and Presidential Decision Making* (College Station: Texas A&M University Press, 161–67. The seminal work on policy entrepreneurship is John W. Kingdon, *Agendas, Alternatives, and Public Policies* (New York: Longman, 1995).

59. O'Sullivan transcript, 00:57:00, 01:20:00.

60. Robert M. Gates, *Duty: Memoirs of a Secretary at War* (New York: Knopf, 2014), 5.

61. *The Iraq Study Group Report* (New York: Vintage Books, 2006), 70–73.

62. Fred Kagan transcript, 00:41:00; Kimberly Kagan transcript, 00:34:00.

63. Ricks, *Gamble*, 94.

64. O'Sullivan transcript, 01:40:00; Karl Rove transcript, 00:43:00; Fred Kagan transcript, 00:57:00; Keane transcript, 01:06:00; Gates transcript, 01:00:00; Feaver transcript, 01:23:00.

65. Hadley transcript, 01:34:00; Hannah transcript, 01:04:00; Edelman transcript, 01:12:00.

66. Edelman transcript, 00:52:00; Gates transcript, 00:26:00; Pace transcript, 00:52:00; Hadley transcript, 00:40:00, 01:31:00.

67. Gates transcript, 00:12:00; Edelman transcript, 00:58:00; Hannah transcript, 01:15:00. Rather than augment the units already in Anbar Province, which totaled about four thousand troops, Bush extended their deployments.

68. President Bush Addresses Nation on Iraq War, January 10, 2007, http://www.washingtonpost.com/wp-dyn/content/article/2007/01/10/AR2007011002208.html.

69. Greenstein, *Hidden-Hand Presidency*, 103.

16. The President as Policy Entrepreneur

1. Useful accounts of the 2006 Iraq review can be found in Peter Baker, *Days of Fire: Bush and Cheney in the White House* (New York: Doubleday, 2013); Michael Gordon and Bernard Trainor, *The Endgame: The Inside Story of the Struggle for Iraq, from George W. Bush to Barack Obama* (New York: Pantheon, 2012); Peter Mansoor, *Surge: My Journey with General David Petraeus and the Remaking of the Iraq War* (New Haven, CT: Yale University Press, 2013); Stephen Metz, *Decisionmaking in Operation Iraq Freedom: The Strategic Shift of 2007* (Carlisle, PA: US Army War College, 2010); Thomas Ricks, *The Gamble: General David Petraeus and the American Military Adventure in Iraq* (New York: Penguin, 2009); Linda Robinson, *Tell Me How This Ends: General David Petraeus and the Search for a Way out of Iraq* (New York: PublicAffairs, 2008); and Bob Woodward, *The*

War Within: A Secret White House History, 2006–2008 (New York: Simon & Schuster, 2008). Memoirs from some of the leading figures include George W. Bush, *Decision Points* (New York: Crown, 2010); Dick Cheney, *In My Time: A Personal and Political Memoir* (New York: Threshold, 2011); Robert Gates, *Duty: Memoirs of a Secretary at War* (New York: Knopf, 2014); Condoleezza Rice, *No Higher Honor: A Memoir of My Years in Washington* (New York: Crown, 2011); Karl Rove, *Courage and Consequences* (New York: Threshold, 2010); and Donald Rumsfeld, *Known and Unknown: A Memoir* (New York: Sentinel, 2011).

2. John Kingdon, *Agendas, Alternatives, and Public Policies* (New York: Longman Classic, 2003).

3. Kingdon, 179–83.

4. One exception is Stephen Krasner, "The Garbage Can Model for Locating Policy Planning," in *Avoiding Trivia: The Role of Strategic Planning in American Foreign Policy*, ed. Daniel Drezner (Washington, DC: Brookings Institution Press, 2009), 159–70.

5. Robert Durant and Paul Diehl, "Agendas, Alternatives, and Public Policy: Lessons from the US Foreign Policy Arena," *Journal of Public Policy* 9, no. 2 (1989): 183.

6. Durant and Diehl, 189–91.

7. "The Surge—Collective Memory Project," Stephen Hadley interview, transcript, 00:04:00, 00:28:00, at https://www.smu.edu/CPH/. Henceforth Collective Memory Project interviews are cited only by the interviewee's name followed by "transcript" and the last minute marker before the quotation or paraphrased remark. See also George W. Bush, "Surge in Iraq," interview by Peter Feaver, Meghan O'Sullivan, and William Inboden, December 1, 2015, transcript, 3. Copies of the transcript are in the possession of the editors and the George W. Bush Presidential Center.

8. Bush, *Decision Points*, 364; Rumsfeld, *Known and Unknown*, 695, 702–3.

9. Rumsfeld, *Known and Unknown*, 696, 705, 708.

10. See Stephen Cambone transcript, 00:12:00, 00:38:00; Dick Cheney transcript, 00:10:00; Eric Edelman transcript, 00:05:00, 00:17:00; Meghan O'Sullivan transcript, 00:05:00, 00:15:00; Condoleezza Rice transcript, 00:10:00.

11. Bush transcript, 22.

12. Joshua Bolten transcript, 00:12:00.

13. Peter Feaver transcript, 00:10:00; O'Sullivan transcript, 00:12:00.

14. Bush, *Decision Points*, 364, 366.

15. Cheney transcript, 00:29:00; J. D. Crouch transcript, 00:12:00, 00:16:00; Feaver transcript, 00:11:00; Hadley transcript, 00:13:00; John Hannah transcript, 00:08:00; O'Sullivan transcript, 00:26:00; Rice transcript, 00:17:00.

16. Cambone transcript, 00:15:00.

17. Hadley transcript, 00:18:00; O'Sullivan transcript, 00:29:00.

18. Hadley transcript, 00:31:00.

19. Bush transcript, 10.

20. Bush, *Decision Points*, 370–71, Bob Woodward, *War Within*, 79, 88–99.

21. For background on this section see Bolten transcript, 00:37:00; Cheney transcript, 00:43:00; Edelman transcript, 00:18:00, 00:23:00; Robert Gates transcript, 00:10:00.

22. Peter Pace transcript, 00:03:00, 00:18:00.

23. See for example Stephen Biddle, "Seeing Baghdad, Thinking Saigon," *Foreign Affairs* 85, no. 2 (March/April 2006): 2–14; Frederick Kagan, "A Plan for Victory in

Iraq," *Weekly Standard*, May 29, 2006; and Andrew Krepinevich, "How to Win in Iraq," *Foreign Affairs* 84, no. 5 (September/October 2005): 87–104.

24. Metz, *Decisionmaking*, 36.

25. Ricks, *Gamble*, 15–31.

26. Frederick Kagan transcript, 00:04:00, 00:10:00.

27. Bush, *Decision Points*, 364–65.

28. Cheney transcript, 00:04:00, 00:38:00; Hannah transcript, 01:05:00. See also Cheney, *In My Time*, 441.

29. Bolten transcript, 00:43:00. As Bush put it, "I was through with politics." Bush transcript, 5. See also Karl Rove transcript, 00:07:00, 00:44:00.

30. William Schneider, "A Message about Priorities," *National Journal* 39, no. 1 (January 2007): 58.

31. As Bob Woodward's book has Stephen Hadley saying around October 2006, "We've got to do it under the radar screen because the electoral season is so hot, but we've got to pull this together now and start to give the president some options." Bob Woodward, *War Within*, 161.

32. Cheney transcript, 00:52:00. See also Rove transcript, 00:16:00.

33. Bush, *Decision Points*, 355; Rove, *Courage and Consequences*, 475.

34. Bolten transcript, 01:06:00.

35. O'Sullivan transcript, 00:30:00.

36. Bush, *Decision Points*, 375; Bush transcript, 13.

37. Hadley transcript, 00:12:00, 00:24:00, 00:25:00. See also Bolten transcript, 00:39:00.

38. Bush transcript, 13, 20; Cheney transcript, 00:56:00, 01:05:00; Feaver transcript, 00:54:00, 01:03:00; Hadley transcript, 00:10:00, 00:54:00; Rove transcript, 00:34:00.

39. Feaver transcript, 00:21:00, 00:32:00; Hannah transcript, 00:02:00, 00:15:00, 00:26:00; O'Sullivan transcript, 00:05:00, 00:40:00.

40. Feaver transcript, 00:38:00; Hadley transcript, 00:33:00; O'Sullivan transcript, 00:49:00.

41. Crouch transcript, 23; Hadley transcript, 00:29:00, 00:33:00.

42. Hadley transcript, 00:50:00.

43. Rove transcript, 00:38:00. For more on the role of Iraq in Republican midterm losses see Gary Jacobson, "Referendum: The 2006 Midterm Congressional Elections," *Political Science Quarterly* 122, no. 1 (Spring 2007)" 1–24.

44. Crouch transcript, 01:09:00; Frank Wolf transcript, 00:39:00.

45. Feaver transcript, 01:04:00; O'Sullivan transcript, 01:03:00; Rove transcript, 00:45:00.

46. Cheney transcript, 01:49:00.

47. Bush transcript, 18; Gates transcript, 00:04:00.

48. Bolten transcript, 01:03:00, 01:05:00; Cheney transcript, 01:17:00; Hadley transcript, 00:57:00; Rove transcript, 00:21:00, 00:24:00.

49. Rove transcript, 00:22:00.

50. Hadley transcript, 00:29:00, 00:52:00.

51. Bush transcript, 5–6; Crouch transcript, 00:24:00, 00:47:00; Hadley transcript, 01:57:00; O'Sullivan transcript, 01:08:00.

52. For the Pentagon's perspective see Cambone transcript, 00:37:00, 00:40:00, 00:46:00, 00:54:00, 001:14:00; Edelman transcript, 00:27:00, 00:32:00, 00:47:00; Pace transcript, 01:12:00, 01:20:00; and Rumsfeld, *Known and Unknown*, 702–3, 714.

53. Rice transcript, 00:22:00, 00:50:00, 00:54:00; Rice, *No Higher Honor*, 539–40; Philip Zelikow transcript, 01:10:00.

54. Cheney transcript, 01:36:00; Feaver transcript, 01:04:00; Hannah transcript, 00:39:00.

55. Crouch transcript, 00:50:00, 01:09:00; O'Sullivan transcript, 01:21:00; Rice transcript, 01:02:00. See also Bush, *Decision Points*, 372–73.

56. Although Bush does not recall Cheney pushing for the surge option in his presence. See Bush transcript, 19.

57. Cheney, *In My Time*, 447–49; Rice transcript, 00:49:00, 01:05:00; Rice, *No Higher Honor*, 542, 544.

58. Hadley transcript, 01:09:00; O'Sullivan transcript, 01:28:00.

59. Bush transcript, 23.

60. Feaver transcript, 01:17:00.

61. Hadley transcript, 01:02:00, 01:06:00.

62. Bolten transcript, 01:23:00; Bush transcript, 19; Cheney transcript, 01:03:00, 01:10:00; Cheney, *In My Time*, 449–51, 454; Crouch transcript, 01:25:00; Edelman transcript, 01:12:00; Feaver transcript, 01:22:00; Gates transcript, 01:02:00; Hadley transcript, 01:34:00, 01:56:00; Hannah transcript, 01:04:00; Frederick Kagan transcript, 00:32:00, 00:51:00, 01:07:00; Jack Keane transcript, 01:01:00; O'Sullivan transcript, 01:40:00.

63. Baker, *Days of Fire*, 520; Bush transcript, 21–22.

64. Bush transcript, 21.

65. On the preceding paragraph see Bolten transcript, 01:12:00; Bush, *Decision Points*, 376; Cheney transcript, 01:07:00; Cheney, *In My Time*, 451–53; Crouch transcript, 01:03:00; Edelman transcript, 00:52:00; Feaver transcript, 01:14:00, 01:25:00; Gates transcript, 00:20:00, 00:26:00; Hadley transcript, 00:41:00, 01:11:00, 01:31:00, 01:38:00; Hannah transcript, 01:00:00; O'Sullivan transcript, 01:11:00; Pace transcript, 00:51:00, 00:58:00, 01:11:00, 01:20:00, 58; Rice transcript, 00:45:00, 01:00:00, 01:08:00; Rumsfeld, *Known and Unknown*, 715.

66. Pace transcript, 01:27:00.

67. Hadley transcript, 01:46:00; Kagan transcript, 01:02:00; O'Sullivan transcript, 01:42:00, 01:49:00.

68. Keane had actually proposed as many as eight more brigades initially, but certainly preferred a five-brigade surge to none at all. See Hadley transcript, 01:37:00; Keane transcript, 00:36:00, 01:03:00, 01:27:00.

69. Or as he also put it, even more bluntly, "If you're in, you're in. You don't tiptoe." See Bush transcript, 16; Cheney transcript, 01:59:00; Crouch transcript, 01:14:00.

70. Bush transcript, 23; Rice transcript, 01:05:00; Zelikow transcript, 01:39:00.

71. Rove transcript, 00:46:00, 00:49:00, 00:59:00.

72. Bush, *Decision Points*, 377–78; Bush transcript, 18; Hadley transcript, 01:47:00; Pace transcript, 01:28:00; Rove transcript, 00:57:00.

73. Colin Dueck, "The Role of the National Security Advisor and the 2006 Iraq Strategy Review," *Orbis* 58, no. 1 (Winter 2014): 15–38.

74. Hadley transcript, 00:04:00, 01:16:00, 01:20:00, 01:29:00.

75. Stephen Benedict Dyson, "George W. Bush, the Surge, and Presidential Leadership," *Political Science Quarterly* 125, no. 4 (Winter 2010/11), 557–85.

76. Bush transcript, 5, 22.

77. Pace transcript, 01:37:00.

78. Immerman's own coauthored book on Eisenhower's national security deci-sion-making style is an excellent source on the subject. See Robert Bowie and Richard Immerman, *Waging Peace: How Eisenhower Shaped an Enduring Cold War Strategy* (New York: Oxford University Press, 1998).

79. Bush transcript, 26–27.

80. Bolten transcript, 00:39:00, 00:58:00, 01:23:00; Cheney transcript, 00:10:00, 00:57:00, 01:28:00, 01:45:00, 02:01:00; Crouch transcript, 01:13:00; Feaver transcript, 01:38:00; Gates transcript, 00:11:00, 00:27:00; Hadley transcript, 00:08:00, 00:25:00, 00:41:00, 01:01:00; Hannah transcript, 01:22:00; Frederick Kagan transcript, 00:18:00, 01:03:00; O'Sullivan transcript, 00:14:00, 01:33:00, 01:51:00; Pace transcript, 00:44:00, 01:34:00; Rice transcript, 00:37:00, 00:57:00; Rove transcript, 00:21:00, 00:24:00, 00:25:00, 00:45:00, 00:58:00.

81. Bush transcript, 10.

82. William Newmann, *Managing National Security: The President and the Process* (Pittsburgh: University of Pittsburgh Press, 2003), 41–42.

83. Peter Rodman, *Presidential Command: Power, Leadership, and the Making of Foreign Policy from Richard Nixon to George W. Bush* (New York: Vintage Books, 2010), 235–37, 247–49, 271, 277.

84. Bolten transcript, 01:31:00.

85. Rice transcript, 01:38:00.

86. My own view of Bush's decision to invade Iraq is laid out in *Hard Line: The Republican Party and US Foreign Policy since World War II* (Princeton, NJ: Princeton University Press, 2010), chap. 8.

Appendix B. Time Line

1. "Franks Holds Press Briefing," CNN, March 22, 2003, http://transcripts.cnn.com/TRANSCRIPTS/0303/22/se.22.html, accessed September 13, 2018.

Acknowledgments

A large project like this requires many hands—and for this its editors owe many thanks. This is not our story, but rather that of the interviewees who gave so generously of their time, memories, and thoughtful reflections. Interviewers gave precious time as well, including Aaron Crawford, Peter Feaver, Evan McCormick, Paul Miller, and Meghan O'Sullivan.

The team at Cornell University Press masterfully transformed our pages into a book. Michael McGandy has been a stalwart guide, and friend. Meagan Dermody perfected the data tables, while Jennifer Savran Kelly prepared our digital manuscript for publication. Thanks to Bill Nelson for redrafting key maps, to Glenn Novak for his diligent copyediting, and to Rachel Lyon for her indexing skills. Martyn Beeny, Adriana Ferreira Barboza, and Cheryl Quimba helped publicize and market the book for Cornell, aided by Cindy Birne in Dallas.

The project originated at the Southern Methodist University (SMU) Center for Presidential History, whose staff and fellows, including Evan McCormick, Sarah Coleman, and Paul Renfro, conceptualized, organized, recorded, and transcribed the interviews. Special thanks to Ronna Spitz and to Brian Franklin for organizing a sprawling multiyear effort, and to Aaron Crawford for thoughtfully setting an editorial approach to the spoken word. The John Goodwin Tower Center for Political Studies graciously orchestrated the book's launch, and we thank our cross-campus colleagues Jim Hollifield, Luisa del Rosal, Bora Laci, and Ray Rafidi. Provosts Paul Ludden and Steve Currell and SMU President Gerald R. Turner understood the political sensitivities at the core of the entire Collective Memory Project and ensured its academic independence.

This was never solely SMU's project, however. Colleagues from Duke University, the University of Texas at Austin, and Harvard University all generously lent their time. Duke University's Washington, DC, program hosted interview sessions, while its Program in American Grand Strategy hosted a workshop in which scholars, editors, and policy makers engaged in vigorous and sharpening debate. Our thanks to Melanie Benson, Aly Breuer, Colin Colter, Alyssa Dack, and Alex Pfadt, and particularly once more to Peter Feaver for his persistence, wisdom, and warm enthusiasm.

The George W. Bush Presidential Library and the George W. Bush Presidential Center assisted this project in several ways, including providing documents and records that aided the scholars in their analyses. In particular, we thank Alan Lowe and Patrick Mordente's staff at the former for their archival expertise, and Holly Kuzmich, Brendan Miniter, Catherine Jaynes, Fred Ford, and Michael Meese of the Bush Center who simultaneously facilitated access to former policy makers regardless of our editorial choices.

Finally, three of the editors wish in particular to thank the fourth, without whose diligence this book never would have seen the light of day. This was a group effort, but Tim Sayle's most of all.

Contributors

Richard K. Betts is director of the Saltzman Institute of War and Peace Studies at Columbia University. Among his books are *American Force, Enemies of Intelligence, Military Readiness, Surprise Attack,* and *Soldiers, Statesmen, and Cold War Crises.*

Hal Brands is the Henry Kissinger Distinguished Professor of Global Affairs at the Johns Hopkins School of Advanced International Studies, a senior fellow at the Center for Strategic and Budgetary Assessments, and a Bloomberg Opinion columnist. He is the author, most recently, of *American Grand Strategy in the Age of Trump* (2018) and coauthor of *The Lessons of Tragedy: Statecraft and World Order* (2019).

Colin Dueck is a professor in the Schar School of Policy and Government at George Mason University, and a Kirkpatrick visiting fellow at the American Enterprise Institute. He has published three books on American foreign and national security policies, *The Obama Doctrine: American Grand Strategy Today* (Oxford, 2015), *Hard Line: The Republican Party and U.S. Foreign Policy since World War II* (Princeton, 2010), and *Reluctant Crusaders: Power, Culture, and Change in American Grand Strategy* (Princeton, 2006). His current research focus is on the relationship between party politics, presidential leadership, American conservatism, and US foreign policy strategies.

Jeffrey A. Engel is founding director of the Center for Presidential History at Southern Methodist University. He has authored or edited twelve books on American foreign policy, including *When the World Seemed New: George H. W. Bush and the End of the Cold War* (Houghton Mifflin Harcourt, 2017) and *Impeachment: An American History*, with Peter Baker, Timothy Naftali, and Jon Meacham (Random House, 2018).

Peter Feaver is a professor of political science and public policy at Duke University, where he directs the Triangle Institute for Security Studies and the Duke Program in American Grand Strategy. His research focus is civil-military relations, grand strategy, and public opinion and the use of force. From 2005 to 2007 he served as special advisor for strategic planning and institutional reform on the NSC staff at the White House.

Stephen Hadley is a principal of RiceHadleyGates LLC, an international strategic consulting firm founded with Condoleezza Rice, Robert Gates, and Anja Manuel. Mr. Hadley is also board chair of the United States Institute of Peace (USIP) and an executive vice chair of the board of directors of the Atlantic Council. He served as Assistant to the President for National Security Affairs from 2005 to 2009.

Richard Immerman is emeritus professor and Buthusiem Distinguished Faculty Fellow in History at Temple University. The author of multiple books and recipient of multiple awards, he was assistant deputy director of national intelligence and held the Francis De Serio Chair at the US Army War College.

William Inboden is executive director and William Powers Jr. Chair of the Clements Center for National Security at the University of Texas at Austin. He also serves as associate professor at the LBJ School of Public Affairs, distinguished scholar at the Robert S. Strauss Center for International Security and Law, and editor-in-chief of the *Texas National Security Review*. Inboden is the author of *Religion and American Foreign Policy, 1945–1960: The Soul of Containment* (Cambridge, 2008) as well as numerous articles and book chapters on national security, American foreign policy, and American history.

Robert Jervis is Adlai E. Stevenson Professor of International Politics at Columbia University. His most recent book is *How Statesmen Think* (Princeton, 2017). He was president of the American Political Science Association in 2000–2001 and is the founding editor of the International Security Studies Forum and co-founding editor of Cornell University Press's Security Studies Series.

Meghan L. O'Sullivan is the Jeane Kirkpatrick Professor of the Practice of International Affairs at Harvard University's Kennedy School. She is also the North American Chair of the Trilateral Commission and an adjunct senior fellow at the Council on Foreign Relations. She served as Special Assistant to the President and Deputy National Security Advisor for Iraq and Afghanistan under President George W. Bush.

Andrew Preston is professor of American history and a fellow of Clare College at Cambridge University. He is the author or editor of several books, including *Sword of the Spirit, Shield of Faith: Religion in American War and Diplomacy* (Knopf, 2012). He is currently writing a book on the idea of national security in American history.

Joshua Rovner is associate professor in the School of International Service at American University. He is the author of *Fixing the Facts: National Security and the Politics of Intelligence* (Cornell, 2011) and coeditor of *Chaos in the Liberal Order: The Trump Presidency and International Politics in the Twenty-First Century* (Columbia, 2018). Rovner is currently scholar-in-residence at the National Security Agency and US Cyber Command.

Timothy Andrews Sayle is assistant professor of history at the University of Toronto and a senior fellow of the Bill Graham Centre for Contemporary International History. He is the author of *Enduring Alliance: A History of NATO and the Postwar Global Order* (Cornell, 2019).

Kori Schake is the deputy director-general of the International Institute for Strategic Studies. From 2002 to 2005 she was the director for defense strategy on the National Security Council staff. She is the author of *Safe Passage: The Transition from British to American Hegemony* (Harvard, 2017) and editor with Jim Mattis of *Warriors and Citizens: American Views of Our Military* (Hoover Institution, 2015).

INDEX

Abizaid, John
  antibody theory of, 8–9, 10, 43, 68, 281–82
  and decision on nature of surge, 184, 185, 186–87, 379n30
  on differing views of situation in Iraq, 76
  on effectiveness of Camp David meeting, 71
  on effectiveness of surge, 306–7
  on emergence of insurgency, 26, 29
  expertise of, 28
  extends rotation dates, 225
  on intelligence and regional politics in official strategy review, 141–42
  on meeting with Joint Chiefs, 173
  on National Strategy for Victory in Iraq, 41
  on November 11 meeting, 128
  on NSC and surge decision, 375n8
  on Operations Together Forward I and II, 81
  opposes surge, 352
  on original strategy, 346
  replaced by Fallon, 355
  on sectarian fighting, 302
  on strategy in Iraq, 42–43, 286
  on Sunni disenfranchisement, 381n18
  on surge announcement, 193–94, 195
  on surge process, 201, 328–29
  tenure of, 361
  on training Iraqi security forces, 303
  on troop increase, 87
  on troop morale, 110, 300
Abrams, Creighton W. Jr., 369n6, 383n58
Afghanistan, 191f, 214, 292–93
al-Qaeda in Iraq
  and al-Askari mosque bombing, 12, 45, 46, 47, 49, 51, 250, 269, 319, 334, 346
  as cause of violence in Iraq, 212
  emergence of, 8
  plans for civil war, 9, 210
  and Sunni Awakening, 185, 203, 223–24, 229, 234, 236, 268, 289, 294
  and timing of surge, 234

and undermining of Iraqi government, 76
  (See also al-Zarqawi, Abu Musab)
al-Qaeda in the Islamic Maghreb, 123
American Enterprise Institute (AEI), 153–54, 166–70, 217, 255–56, 342–43, 354
Anbar Province, 185, 193, 203, 223–24, 268, 289, 294
antibody theory, 8–9, 10, 43, 68, 268, 281–82
al-Askari mosque bombing, 12, 45, 46, 47, 49, 51, 250, 269, 319, 334, 346
Aspen Strategy Group, 33

Baath Party, removed from power, 7, 8, 27, 80
Baghdad
  Bush's trip to, 70, 72
  Gates's trip to, 182, 183, 220
  O'Sullivan's trip to, 230–31
  sectarian violence in, 219, 287
  securing, 197
  surge in, 193
Baker, James, 42, 165, 183, 207
Bartlett, Dan, 120, 150
Bergner, Kevin, 100, 214
Betts, Richard, 244
Biddle, Stephen, 292–93, 353
Blackwill, Robert, 30
Bolten, Joshua
  on announcement of formal review, 128
  on Bush as commander in chief, 326–27, 346, 358–59
  on Bush's political concerns, 349
  on decision to surge, 282–83
  on dynamic between Bush and senior military, 325
  on effectiveness of Camp David meeting, 71
  on fifty questions exercise, 86
  on meeting with Joint Chiefs, 170–71, 172–73, 250, 274
  on need for strategy change, 57–58
  on NSC and official strategy review, 146
  on original strategy, 248
  on politics, 254

Bolten, Joshua (*continued*)
  position on strategy change, 219
  on probable need for surge, 111–12
  on purpose of official strategy review, 133
  on "Revolt of the Generals," 52–53
  on Rumsfeld's resignation, 119–20
  on secrecy in strategy review, 108–9
  on solarium meeting, 152
  on support for strategy change, 75
  on surge announcement, 195
  on surge process, 199
  tenure of, 361
Bremer, L. Paul III, 7, 9–10
Brzezinski, Zbigniew, 379n21
Bundy, McGeorge, 241, 242–43
Bush, George W.
  on American control of Iraq, 378n19
  announces strategy change, 1–2, 182–83,
    192–98, 207, 224, 343, 355–56
  and authenticity of official strategy review
    results, 148, 149
  authorizes strategy review, 214–15
  and beginning of Iraq War, 6
  as commander in chief, 57–58, 275–76,
    283–84, 326, 346, 379n24
  commitment to armed forces, 200–201,
    225, 248, 273, 280, 321, 357, 358
  concern over insurgency, 27–28, 29
  on Crawford ranch meeting, 190–92
  and December NSC meetings, 156–57,
    159
  and decision on nature of surge, 280, 355
  and decision to surge, 154, 158, 282–87,
    305–6, 321, 329, 379n20
  decisiveness of, 245–46
  defends surge against Congress, 226–27
  as delegator, 116
  and development of surge, 213–28
  on differences between Vietnam and Iraq,
    369–70n1
  dynamic between senior military and,
    325–26
  early reports given to, 324, 333
  on effectiveness of Camp David meeting,
    72–73
  essential objectives for Iraq, 258
  and events leading to strategy change, 2–3
  and garnering support for surge, 273–76
  on Hadley as national security advisor, 246
  on impact of Keane and Kagan, 255
  and Iraq Study Group, 42
  on lead up to Camp David, 64
  meets with advisors, 333–34, 353–54

  meets with Joint Chiefs, 15, 154, 170–81,
    221–22, 249–50, 274–75, 326, 340, 343,
    354–55
  meets with Maliki, 161, 162, 220, 336–37
  meets with National Security Council,
    182, 217–19, 353
  on national security advisor's role, 246
  on National Security Council review, 100
  and need for strategy change, 53–54,
    57–58, 319, 346, 347–48
  on NSC and official strategy review, 147
  officially launches strategy review, 130–31,
    215, 341
  persuasion tactics of, 249
  politics as irrelevant to, 108–9
  presidency of, 361
  on radical strategy change, 89
  reasons for ordering surge, 3–4
  reelection of, 11, 30
  replaces Rumsfeld with Gates, 119–21,
    252, 316, 352
  and "Revolt of the Generals," 51–52, 53,
    320–21, 322, 335
  Rice's relationship with, 124
  on secrecy in strategy review, 107
  and SOFA and SFA, 232
  and solarium meeting, 151–52
  and success of surge, 201–2, 279–80
  on surge announcement, 195
  and surge process, 202–3
  takes responsibility for past failures,
    224–25
  trip to Baghdad, 70, 72
  on troop influence in Iraq, 154–55
  on turning control over to Iraqis, 159
  on Vietnam War, 240
  on withdrawing troops, 371n3
  (*See also* policy entrepreneurship)

Cambone, Stephen
  on DoD's position on strategy change,
    137, 308, 319, 379n26
  on intelligence and regional politics in
    official strategy review, 140–41
  on midterm elections, 118
  on National Security Council review, 101
  on public opinion, 14, 266, 289
  on results of strategy review as
    precooked, 147–48, 149–50
  on Rumsfeld, 385n9
  on success of surge, 201, 270
  on surge process, 329
  tenure of, 361

Camp David meeting, 67–69, 214, 335–36, 347
  effectiveness of, 70–73, 336–37
  lead up to, 62–67
Casey, George
  as commander of MNF-I, 10
  and decision on nature of surge, 184, 185, 186–87
  extends rotation dates, 225
  and fifty questions exercise, 83–84
  on increasing troops, 87
  on insurgency, 281
  on Iraqi security forces, 11
  and meeting with Joint Chiefs, 173
  and National Security Council review, 92
  and Operations Together Forward I and II, 81
  opposes surge, 64–65, 248, 352, 355
  on original strategy, 59, 346
  promotion of, 274
  reaction to Rice's statement on strategy, 40
  requests new strategic review, 74
  supports old strategy, 214
Center for Presidential History's "Collective Memory Project," 4
centralized solutions to security challenges, 297–98
Cheney, Richard
  on Bush's decision to surge, 321
  on compartmentalized approach to surge, 256
  on disconnect between strategy and execution, 318
  on effectiveness of Camp David meeting, 70–71, 72, 336
  on elections in Iraq, 31
  on emergence of insurgency, 27
  on Keane, 380n45
  and lead up to Camp David, 66, 67
  meets with McMaster, 369n2
  on midterm elections and decision to surge, 351–52
  and official strategy review, 217, 353–54
  on sectarian fighting, 282
  on solarium meeting, 151
  on strategy change, 15, 219
  on strategy reviews, 300
  on success of surge, 257
  supports surge, 353
  on surge decision-making process, 244
  on transition from insurgency to sectarian struggle, 46–47
  vice-presidency of, 361

civil-military relations, 314–15
  and perceived and real process of surge, 315–17
  and "Revolt of the Generals," 13, 51–53, 64, 227, 253, 284, 314–15, 320–23, 334–35
  Rumsfeld and, 317–20
  and strategy review process, 324–27
Clausewitz, Carl von, 267
clear, hold, and build strategy, 25, 37–41, 44, 60–61, 125, 285, 286, 332, 380n39
Clifford, Clark, 251–52
Coalition Provisional Authority (CPA), 7–9
Cohen, Eliot, 63, 64, 69, 347, 353
COIN techniques, 261, 262, 271–72, 348–49
collective memory, 256–57
Congress, Bush defends surge against, 226–27
Conway, Jim, 177
Council of Colonels, 14, 89–90, 102–4, 134, 135, 174, 340, 347, 369n2
CPA Order 1, 7, 8
CPA Order 2, 7, 8
Crocker, Ryan, 225, 226
Crouch, J. D.
  on American Enterprise Institute report, 170
  on al-Askari mosque bombing, 250
  on Bush's desire to win, 257
  on DoD's position on strategy change, 139
  on effectiveness of Camp David meeting, 72
  on impact of Keane and Kagan, 255
  on internal support for surge, 250
  on Iraq Study Group report, 165–66
  on "Iraq: The Emerging Consensus," 15, 247
  on lead up to Camp David, 65–66, 335–36
  on movement toward strategy change, 117
  on National Security Council, 265
  and National Security Council review, 215
  on National Strategy for Victory in Iraq, 40
  on NSC and official strategy review, 145
  and official strategy review, 130–33, 217, 341, 352
  on optimism regarding Iraq, 30–31
  on solarium meeting, 150
  on surge announcement, 192–93
  tenure of, 361
  on timing of surge, 266
  travels to Anbar Province, 223
  on troop availability, 96, 99
  on understanding nature of Iraq War, 267
Crowther, Alexander, 293

de-Baathification, 7, 8, 27, 80
  (*See also* CPA Order 1; CPA Order 2)
decentralized solutions to security
  challenges, 297–98
democratization, 7, 17, 210, 279, 287–89
DeMuth, Chris, 167
Department of Defense
  position on strategy change, 134–39, 217,
    308, 319–20
  response to insurgency, 379n26
  (*See also* Cambone, Stephen; Edelman,
    Eric; Gates, Robert; Rumsfeld, Donald)
Diem, Ngo Dinh, 241–42
Disbrow, Lisa, 96–97, 300–301, 339–40
Downing, Wayne, 323, 353

Edelman, Eric
  and decision on nature of surge, 185–86,
    309
  on DoD's position on strategy change,
    138–39
  on lead up to Camp David, 64–65
  on meeting with Joint Chiefs, 177
  on Rumsfeld's opposition to strategy
    review, 117
  on solarium meeting, 150
  on strategy review, 300
  tenure of, 361
Eisenhower, Dwight, 324, 330–31, 333, 334,
  357, 385n12
explosively formed projectiles / explosively
  formed penetrators (EFPs), 49, 141

Fallon, William, 225, 355
Fallujah
  first battle of, 9
  second battle of, 10–11
Feaver, Peter
  on analytic work, 112
  and decision on nature of surge, 308, 310
  on DoD's position on strategy change,
    134, 135–36
  on fifty questions exercise, 82
  on Iraqi security forces, 304
  on lead up to Camp David, 63–64
  on meeting with Joint Chiefs, 171, 178
  and National Security Council review, 91,
    92–93, 100, 157, 214
  on National Strategy for Victory in Iraq,
    14, 33–34, 36
  on need for strategy change, 55, 302, 332
  on November 11 meeting, 124, 125–26
  on Operations Together Forward I and
    II, 78, 80

on purpose of official strategy review, 131
on "Revolt of the Generals," 335
on secrecy in strategy review, 108
on strategy problem, 13
and strategy review trip to Iraq, 115, 116,
  219
of success of surge, 290
on surge announcement, 193
on surge process, 272, 329–30
tenure of, 361
and troop availability, 96–98, 264–65,
  300–301
fifty questions exercise, 82–86, 246–47, 327,
  337
FM 3–24, *Counterinsurgency*, 309–10
force generation studies, 96–100, 339–40
  (*See also* troop availability)
fork-in-the-road memo, 241, 242
Freedman, Lawrence, 324

Gates, Robert
  on Bush's decision to surge, 379n20
  on Bush's mindset regarding surge, 245
  and Crawford ranch meeting, 189
  and decision on nature of surge, 183–88
  and decision to surge, 158, 249
  Edelman on appointment of, 138
  on garnering support for surge, 273
  and meeting with Joint Chiefs, 171–72,
    176–77, 179, 354–55
  replaces Rumsfeld as Secretary of
    Defense, 32, 113, 119–21, 252, 316, 352
  supports surge, 254, 342
  on surge announcement, 195
  on surge process, 198, 202, 328
  tenure of, 361
  and timing of surge, 290
  trip to Iraq, 182, 183, 220
Gelb, Leslie, 244
Germany, 291–92, 385n12
Gordon, David, 13, 31, 47, 51, 132, 139–40,
  163, 361
Gordon, Michael, 116
Gunzinger, Mark (Gonzo), 97

Hadley, Stephen
  on American Enterprise Institute report,
    169
  on announcement of formal review,
    128–29
  on Bush and politics of war, 253
  on Bush and strategy review, 352
  on Bush's commitment to armed forces,
    200–201

on Bush's mindset regarding surge, 353
and Bush's presidential authority, 245–46
on compartmentalized approach to surge,
   350
on Crawford ranch meeting, 190
on December NSC meetings, 159–61
and decision on nature of surge, 184, 280,
   283
and decision to surge, 249
and dynamic between Bush and senior
   military, 325
on effectiveness of Camp David meeting,
   71–72, 336
and fifty questions exercise, 83–84, 246
on going to war versus surge, 258
on impact of Keane and Kagan, 255
on importance of Iraq, 30
on interagency processes, 324
on Iraqi forces in surge, 275
on Iraq Study Group, 42, 164
on lead up to Camp David, 65
on meeting with Joint Chiefs, 171, 175,
   179–80
and National Security Council review, 91,
   100, 215
on National Strategy for Victory in Iraq,
   34–36
on need for formal review, 112
on need for strategy change, 53–54
on November 11 meeting, 125
and official strategy review, 131, 146–47,
   217, 340–41, 342, 350, 351
on Operations Together Forward I and
   II, 81–82
and review process, 338
and "Revolt of the Generals," 52, 321,
   322
role in surge decision, 356, 384n1
on Rumsfeld's resignation, 119
on secrecy in strategy review, 108, 109,
   391n31
on sectarian fighting, 282
and solarium meeting, 150
on strategy change, 16
and strategy review process, 106, 107,
   337, 339
and strategy review trip to Iraq, 14,
   115–17, 219
on surge announcement, 166, 192, 193
on surge process, 198–99, 328, 330
on troop availability, 98, 340
on viability of surge, 225
al-Hakim, Ayatollah Mohammed Baqir, 26
Hamilton, Lee, 42, 183, 207

Hannah, John
   on American Enterprise Institute report,
      169–70
   on Bush and surge process, 202–3
   on Camp David war council, 68–69, 337
   and decision on nature of surge, 184, 185,
      186, 187
   on DoD's position on strategy change,
      137–38, 139
   on emergence of insurgency, 26–27, 28–29
   on fifty questions exercise, 83
   on Iraq Study Group report, 165
   on lead up to Camp David, 66–67
   and National Security Council review,
      101, 214
   and November 11 meeting, 125
   and official strategy review, 341
   on politics and security, 303
   on secrecy in strategy review, 107–8
   and State Department and official strategy
      review, 144
   on surge process, 272
   tenure of, 361
Harvey, Derek, 369n2
Hayden, Michael, 281
Hoffman, Frank G., 293
Hussein, Saddam, 1, 6–7, 8, 208–9

insurgency
   average number of daily, enemy-initiated
      attacks, May 2003–July 2007, 35f
   Camp David discussions regarding, 68–69
   as cause of violence in Iraq, 212
   COIN techniques for, 261, 262, 271–72,
      348–49
   Cold War coping mechanisms for, 268
   connection between CPA orders and, 8–9
   and Council of Colonels, 102–4
   cyclical nature of, 44
   defined, 378n11
   Department of Defense's response to,
      379n26
   emergence of, 26–29
   factors influencing, 11
   increasing violence in, 46, 281–82, 305–6,
      345–46
   Jeffrey on, 40
   and nature of Iraq War, 269
   and official strategy review, 131–32, 135, 334
   Rumsfeld's concern over, 29, 375n16
   and strategic ambiguity, 298–99
   transition to sectarian struggle from, 46–51
   in Vietnam, 241–42
   (See also sectarian struggle)

Iran, 49, 140–41, 158, 165
Iranian Revolutionary Guard Corps (IRGC),
    229–30
Iraq
    American control of, 378n19
    elections in, 11, 12, 31–32, 196
    essential objectives for, 258, 306
    fear and pessimism in, 214
    importance of, 30
    invasion of, 6, 261–62
    new dynamics at play in, 233–34
    original strategy in, 331–32
    outcome of invasion of, 209
    planning for post-hostilities phase in,
        376n24
    postwar plans for, 6–9
    provincial stability in 2006, 50f
    sovereignty given back to, 9–10, 230
    stabilization of, 209–10, 318
    status of forces agreement between US
        and, 231
    strategic ambiguity in, 298–99
    strategy review trips to, 113–17
    twin strategies for, 12
    undermining of government, 76
    United States as source of violence in, 115,
        155, 212, 268, 281–82, 304
    US "boots on the ground" in, 2003–2008,
        191f
    withdrawal of troops from, 235–36, 278,
        313, 346, 371n3
Iraqi National Assembly election, 11
Iraqi nationalism, 304
Iraqi security forces
    Maliki and, 311–12
    and official strategy review, 128, 135–36
    and Operations Together Forward I and
        II, 76–82
    strategy concerning, 42–45
    in surge, 161, 275
    training for, 303–4, 309
    transfer of power to, 67, 212–13, 285, 290,
        297, 304, 331–32, 347, 348
Iraq Strategy Group, 332
Iraq Strategy Review team, 352
Iraq Study Group, 41–42, 153, 164–66, 183,
    207, 255–56, 292, 342
"Iraq: The Emerging Consensus," 15, 150, 247
Iraq War
    beginning of, 6
    continuation of, 25
    failure of original strategy in, 280–81,
        314, 317

    and meaning of victory, 256–59
    nature of, 267–70
    original strategy in, 331–32
    and postwar plans for Iraq, 6–9
    public support for, 113, 117–18, 349
    similarities between Vietnam War and,
        239–41, 369–70n1, 371n3
    Vietnam War's influence on, 263, 266, 354
    voter dissatisfaction with, 113, 117–18
ISIS, 235, 262, 291, 294, 312, 377n39, 381n18

al-Jaafari, Ibrahim, 233, 288
al-Janabi, Abdul Nasser, 311
Japan, 190, 291–92
Jaysh al-Mahdi, 49, 203, 229
Jeffrey, James
    on articulating strategy change, 60–62
    on doubts at State Department, 122–23
    on effectiveness of Camp David meeting,
        72
    on National Strategy for Victory in Iraq,
        39–40
    on Operations Together Forward I and
        II, 77
    on political-economic-social order, 268
    on strategy in Iraq, 43–44
    on surge process, 18
    tenure of, 361
    on troop availability, 94
    on withdrawing troops, 59
Johnson, Lyndon, 94, 99, 154, 239–40, 241–
    45, 250–52, 258–59
Joint Chiefs of Staff
    conference room of, 370n1
    and Council of Colonels, 89–90, 103–4
    internal review of, 87, 214
    Johnson and McNamara's relationship
        with, 244
    meeting with, 15, 154, 170–81, 221–22,
        249–50, 274–75, 326, 340, 343, 354–55
    and official strategy review, 216, 316, 341
    position on strategy change, 135–36
    support for 2003 plan, 385n10
Jordanian embassy, attack on, 8

Kagan, Fred
    and American Enterprise Institute report,
        166–67, 169–70
    and Camp David war council, 68–69,
        70–73, 347
    and decision on nature of surge, 185
    impact of, 255
    and lead up to Camp David, 63, 64

and official strategy review, 217, 342, 354
on Operations Together Forward I and
II, 78–79
as outside influencer, 255
on possibility of surge, 153–54
on sectarian fighting, 75
tenure of, 361
Kagan, Kimberly, 78, 167, 168–69, 361
Kaplan, Robert, 64, 347
Keane, Jack
and American Enterprise Institute report,
167–68, 169–70
on Council of Colonels, 102
and decision on nature of surge, 185, 187,
188
on disconnect between strategy and
execution, 318
and force generation studies, 340
impact of, 255
on insurgency, 287
and official strategy review, 217, 342,
353–54
as outside influencer, 255
on possibility of surge, 153–54
and "Revolt of the Generals," 322
role in surge decision, 323, 380n45
tenure of, 362
on troop availability, 93–94
on troop morale, 110
on undermining of Iraqi government, 75
and war maintenance, 286–87
Kennedy, John F., 241–42
Khalilzad, Zalmay
on doubts at State Department, 124
and fifty questions exercise, 83–84
on impact of 2005 election, 12
on need for strategy change, 332
requests new strategic review, 74
on sectarian fighting, 114
on security, 269
and State Department and official strategy
review, 144–45
on success of original strategy, 59
supports old strategy, 214
tenure of, 362
Kingdon, John, 344
Koizumi, Junichiro, 190
Korea, 190, 291–92

Lebanon, 86, 376nn28,33
liberty, expansion of, 30
Libya, 376n33
long war, 29

Lute, Douglas
on Council of Colonels, 102–3
on December NSC meetings, 156
on DoD's position on strategy change, 136
on emergence of insurgency, 26
on intelligence and regional politics in
official strategy review, 141
on Iraqi security forces, 285
on meeting with Joint Chiefs, 179
and need for strategy change, 59–60
on objectives of Maliki government, 287
and official strategy review, 148
on Operations Together Forward I and II,
76–77, 80
on results of strategy review as
precooked, 148
on surge, 136–37, 139
tenure of, 362
on timing of surge, 290
on transition from insurgency to sectarian
struggle, 49–51
on troop availability, 93, 95
Luti, William, 97, 98, 215, 283, 339–40, 351,
354, 355

al-Maliki, Nouri
agrees to surge, 162–63
as barrier to surge, 116–17, 219–21, 287–
88, 382n38
Bush meets with, 161, 162, 220, 275,
336–37
and decision on nature of surge, 185–87
and effectiveness of Camp David meeting,
71–73
empowerment of, 236
Gates meets with, 185–86
and government legitimacy, 309–10
and Iraqi security, 311–12
and National Security Council review, 92
objectives of, 287
as political partner in Iraq, 233
and SOFA and SFA, 231–32
and strategy review trip to Iraq, 115–16
surge as political test for, 310–11
suspicions concerning, 305
takes on Shia militia, 229, 234
Mansoor, Peter, 90, 103–4, 110, 111, 134–35,
171, 174–75, 362
McCaffrey, Barry, 323, 353
McCain, John, 170, 266–67, 349
McChrystal, Stan, 68, 369n3
McConnell, Mitch, 349
McGurk, Brett, 92–93, 100, 126, 127, 214

McMaster, H. R., 103, 135, 369n2, 372n15
McNamara, Robert S., 202, 241, 244, 252
midterm elections, 90, 91, 113, 117–20, 126, 195, 227, 253, 349–52
Multi-National Force–Iraq (MNF-I), 10, 303, 305, 355
Murtha, John, 11, 33, 36

Nagl, John, 369n2
National Liberation Front (NLF, Vietcong), 241–42, 250, 251
national security advisor, 243–44, 246
National Security Council
    Abizaid on, 375n8
    and authenticity of official strategy review results, 149
    Bundy and, 243
    Bush meets with, 182, 217–19, 353
    December meetings of, 154–63
    internal review of, 89, 90–93, 100–102, 214–15, 334, 335, 337–38, 352
    and national security advisor, 243–44
    and National Strategy for Victory in Iraq, 332–33
    and need for strategy change, 332
    and November 11 meeting, 124–28
    and official strategy review, 145–47, 216, 217–18, 341–42
    position on strategy change, 340
    under Reagan, 246
    requests new strategic review, 74
    role in surge decision, 264–66, 283
    war council at Camp David, 335–36
National Security Council principals, 217–19
National Strategy for Victory in Iraq (NSVI), 12, 25, 32–41, 91, 332–33, 338
Negroponte, John, 11
Newbold, Gregory, 51, 320, 323
Nixon, Richard, 266
November 11 meeting, 124–28

Obama, Barack, 262, 291, 294, 376n33
Odierno, Ray, 36–37, 39, 138, 185, 189, 226
Operation Iraqi Freedom (OIF), 6
Operation Together Forward I and II, 13, 76–82, 92, 93, 214, 304, 337, 340, 347
O'Sullivan, Meghan
    on American Enterprise Institute report, 169
    on al-Askari mosque bombing, 47
    on December NSC meetings, 155–58
    and decision on nature of surge, 184, 187–88, 192, 306, 308
    on departmental positions on official strategy review, 133, 273
    on differing views of situation in Iraq, 75–76
    on fear and pessimism in Iraq, 214
    on fifty questions exercise, 82
    on Iraqi security forces, 13–14
    and lead up to Camp David, 62–63, 65, 335
    and National Security Council review, 90–92, 100, 214
    on National Strategy for Victory in Iraq, 32, 337–38
    on need for strategy change, 54–57, 58, 332
    on November 11 meeting, 126–27
    on NSC and official strategy review, 145–46
    and official strategy review, 350
    on Operations Together Forward I and II, 78
    and reports on Iraq, 27–28, 333
    on results of strategy review as precooked, 148
    on sectarian fighting, 270
    on September–November 2006, 338
    on solarium meeting, 150–51
    on strategy review and midterm elections, 350
    on strategy review process, 106–7, 255–56, 328
    and strategy review trip to Iraq, 115–16, 219, 230–31, 335
    tenure of, 362
    on troop availability, 99–100
    undertakes "mock" review, 337

Pace, Peter
    on Bush and politics of war, 253, 357
    on Bush's dealings with military, 283–84
    on civilians in surge, 160
    on Council of Colonels, 103, 104, 134
    and Crawford ranch meeting, 189
    on DoD's position on strategy change, 320
    on effectiveness of surge, 307
    and force generation studies, 340
    on increasing Iraqi security forces, 128
    on increasing troops, 87–88
    on Iraqi forces in surge, 161, 275
    and meeting with Joint Chiefs, 173–74, 175–76, 177–78, 179, 343
    and official strategy review, 139
    on Operations Together Forward I and II, 13, 76
    and "Revolt of the Generals," 53, 320

and strategy review process, 106, 107, 299
on surge announcement, 195
on surge process, 201–2
tenure of, 361
on troop availability, 95–96
on troop morale, 110
and Vietnam War, 240
and war maintenance, 286–87
Perry, Bill, 183
Petraeus, David
and Council of Colonels, 103
on de-Baathification, 8
and decision on nature of surge, 184, 187,
188, 192, 302–3, 308–9, 355
takes over command in Iraq, 225–26
and Vietnam War, 240
Pletka, Danielle, 166
policy entrepreneurship
assessment of Bush, 356–59
connection of policy, political, and
problem streams, 350–56
defined, 344–45
policy stream and Iraq 2006, 348–49
political stream and Iraq 2006, 349–50
problem stream and Iraq 2006, 345–48
political instability, security and, 30–32,
55–56, 223, 268–69, 301–3, 312–13
POTUS notes, 55, 56
Prospect Theory, 271

R4GEN model, 168–69
Reagan, Ronald, 243–44, 246, 376n33
"Revolt of the Generals," 13, 51–53, 64, 227,
253, 284, 314–15, 320–23, 334–35
Rice, Condoleezza
on al-Askari mosque bombing, 47
on being stuck, 380n44
on Bush and politics of war, 253
on Bush's mindset regarding surge, 245,
263, 359
Bush's relationship with, 124
on Camp David war council, 71, 337
on change in Bush, 327
and clear, hold, and build strategy, 39, 40,
44, 332
on Council of Colonels, 103
on Crawford ranch meeting, 189–90
on December NSC meetings, 158–59, 163
on disconnect between strategy and
execution, 318
on DoD's position on strategy change, 320
on doubts at State Department, 122, 124
on dynamic between Bush and senior
military, 325

on early progress reports, 324
endorses surge, 248–49
and fifty questions exercise, 84–85, 86
on finality of surge, 188–89
on garnering military support, 273
on increasing troops, 160
on internal support for surge, 250
on invasion of Iraq, 318
on Iraqi security forces, 304, 312
on Iraq strategy, 25
on Iraq Study Group, 42, 164
on meeting with Joint Chiefs, 172, 176,
179
on National Strategy for Victory in Iraq,
36–38
and need for strategy change, 59
on November 11 meeting, 124–25, 126,
127–28
on NSC and official strategy review, 147
and Operations Together Forward I and
II, 76
on politics and security, 302
position on strategy change, 219
on purpose of official strategy review,
131
reluctance to offer strategy, 38
and "Revolt of the Generals," 321
on sectarian fighting, 122, 159, 249, 270,
305, 352, 353
as skeptic of surge, 247–48, 260, 275, 286,
307, 352
on solarium meeting, 151–52
and State Department and official strategy
review, 144
and strategy review process, 214, 300
on success of surge, 257
on surge process, 199–200, 328, 329
tenure of, 361
on trip to Iraq, 114
on troop availability, 93, 99
Ricks, Tom, 134, 342
Robb, Chuck, 183
Rove, Karl
on American Enterprise Institute report,
170
on al-Askari mosque bombing, 47
and decision on nature of surge, 194, 355
on defining victory, 258
on discussing strategy review, 111
on impact of Keane and Kagan, 255
on midterm elections, 117–18
on National Strategy for Victory in Iraq,
36
on need for strategy change, 58

Rove, Karl (*continued*)
  on political stability and security, 32
  on purpose of official strategy review, 133
  on Rumsfeld's resignation, 119, 120–21, 352
  on surge announcement, 194
  on sustainability of surge, 126
  tenure of, 362
Rowe, Alan, 280
Rumsfeld, Donald
  Cambone on, 385n9
  and civil-military relations, 317–20
  on clear, hold, and build strategy, 332
  concern over insurgency, 29, 375n16
  and Council of Colonels, 102
  and decision on nature of surge, 280
  denounces NSVI, 39
  and fifty questions exercise, 84
  and force generation studies, 100
  on Iraqis, 267
  and lead up to Camp David, 65
  and meeting with Joint Chiefs, 172–73, 274
  on National Security Council, 264
  opposes strategy review, 117, 300
  opposes surge, 64–65, 248, 284, 330, 352
  resignation of, 13, 113, 119–21, 138, 139, 252, 352
  and "Revolt of the Generals," 13, 51–53, 64, 227, 253, 284, 314–15, 320–23, 334–35
  and "Revolution in Military Affairs," 263
  and strategy review process, 106, 107, 214
  on success of original strategy, 59
  and troop increase, 87–88
  on turning control over to Iraqis, 159, 347, 348
  and withdrawal of US forces, 45

al-Sadr, Muqtada, 9, 49, 220, 229
Sahwa, 223
Sanger, David, 369–70n1
Satterfield, David
  on assessment of situation in Iraq, 75
  on Crawford ranch meeting, 188–89
  on December NSC meetings, 162–63
  on departmental positions on official strategy review, 133–34
  on doubts at State Department, 123–24
  on effectiveness of Camp David meeting, 73
  on fifty questions exercise, 85–86
  on Operations Together Forward I and II, 77

on paper and digital records, 19
  on results of strategy review as precooked, 147, 149
  and State Department and official strategy review, 143–44, 145
  on strategy in Iraq, 44–45
  on strategy review process, 107
  on success of surge, 203
  on surge as political test for Maliki, 310
  on surge process, 329
  tenure of, 362
  on transition from insurgency to sectarian struggle, 48–49
Sattler, John, 93, 136–37, 144, 148–49, 175–76, 362
Schlitz
  (*See* troop availability)
Schoomaker, Peter, 177–78, 354
Scowcroft, Brent, 244, 264, 341–42
Second Indochina War, 378n11
secrecy, in strategy reviews, 107–9, 215–16, 391n31
secretary of defense, responsibilities of, 317
  (*See also* Gates, Robert; Rumsfeld, Donald)
sectarian struggle
  in Anbar Province, 223–24
  in Baghdad, 219
  and benefits of surge, 294
  Bush on, 159
  as cause of violence in Iraq, 212
  and debates on nature of surge, 301–2
  and December NSC meetings, 156
  and need for strategy change, 54–56, 210–11, 296, 319
  and Operations Together Forward I and II, 77–82
  reduction in, 228
  Rice on, 122, 159, 248, 270, 305, 352, 353
  and stabilization of Iraq, 210
  and State Department and official strategy review, 144–45
  and strategy review trip to Iraq, 114
  and strengthening of political institutions, 303
  in Syria, 49, 235
  and timing of surge, 233–34
  transition to, 46–51
  US actions against, 270
  US neutrality in, 212, 310
  (*See also* insurgency)
security
  decline in, 39–40
  emphasis on, in strategy change, 3

and political instability, 30–32, 55–56, 223, 268–69, 301–3, 312–13
strategy to increase, 42–45
(*See also* Iraqi security forces)
Serwer, Daniel, 165, 362
(*See also* Iraq Study Group)
Shia, 7, 9
(*See also* insurgency; sectarian struggle)
solarium meeting, 150–52
Spanish Civil War, 378n11
State Department
doubts in, 122–24
and need for strategy change, 59–62
and November 11 meeting, 124–28
and official strategy review, 142–45, 216, 339, 341
position on strategy change, 133, 217, 307, 340
status of forces agreement (SOFA), 231–32, 290
strategic ambiguity, 297–99
strategic framework agreement (SFA), 231–32
strategy change
calls for, 351
departmental positions on, 133–34
Department of Defense's position on, 134–39
development of, 213–28
and effectiveness of Camp David meeting, 70–73, 336–37
emphasis on security in, 3
events leading to, 2–3
as gamble, 2
impact of, 89
lead up to Camp David, 62–67
need for, 53–58, 208–11, 239
State Department and need for, 59–62, 122–24
support for, 75, 213
war council at Camp David, 67–69, 214, 335–36
(*See also* surge; surge, decision regarding; surge, type of)
strategy review
announcement of formal, 128–29
and Bush as policy entrepreneur, 356–59
Bush authorizes, 214–15
calls for renewed, 74–75
and civil-military relations, 322, 324–27
compartmentalized, 350
and Council of Colonels, 102–4
information sources in, 216–17

initiation of, 331–33
integration of, 301
intelligence and regional politics' impact on official, 139–42
of Joint Chiefs, 87, 214
of National Security Council, 89, 90–93, 100–102, 334, 335, 337–38, 352
National Security Council and official, 145–47, 216, 217
need for, 213–14, 296, 299
and November 11 meeting, 124–28
official, 113–14, 215–18, 316, 340–42, 350–53
process for, 105–7, 299–301, 315–17
purpose of official, 130–33
questions for, 82–86, 246–47, 327, 337
results of, as precooked, 147–50
secrecy in, 107–9, 215–16, 391n31
solarium meeting, 150–52
State Department and official, 142–45
trips to Iraq, 113–17
and troop availability, 93–100
and troop morale, 109–11
undertaken by O'Sullivan, 337
(*See also* surge; surge, decision regarding; surge, type of)
strategy void, 280–81
sunk-costs fallacy, 279–80, 295
Sunni Awakening, 185, 203, 223–24, 229, 234, 236, 268, 289, 294
Sunnis, 12, 76, 381n18
(*See also* insurgency; sectarian struggle)
surge
Bush announces, 1–2, 182–83, 192–98, 207, 224, 343, 355–56
Bush's reasons for ordering, 3–4, 297
Bush takes responsibility for, 224–25
context of, 261–62
costs and benefits of, 293–95, 377n39
development of, 213–28, 236–37
developments disrupting gains of, 234–36
effect of, 262, 312
need for, 53–58, 208–11, 239
objectives of, 306–7
overview of, 211–13
prerequisites for, 233–34
significance of, 277–78
success of, 201, 203, 227, 228–32, 257–58, 270–72, 279, 292
support for, 75, 213, 273–76
timeline for, 363–65
timing of, 232–34, 266–67, 280, 289–93
(*See also* strategy change; strategy review)

surge, decision regarding, 153–54, 270–72, 328–43
    American Enterprise Institute report, 166–70
    Cheney on, 244
    context of, 236–38, 280–82, 305–6
    December NSC meetings, 154–63
    and democratization of Iraq, 287–89
    division over strategic alternatives, 278–79
    impact of, 211–12
    Iraq Study Group report, 164–66
    meeting with Joint Chiefs, 170–81, 221–22, 249–50, 274–75, 326, 343
    and overcoming war maintenance, 282–87
    and Rumsfeld's resignation, 321
surge, type of
    Abizaid on, 184, 185, 186–87, 379n30
    Crawford ranch meeting regarding, 188–92
    debate concerning, 280, 301–2, 355
    Gates and, 183–88
    and government legitimacy, 309–11
Syria, 49, 141, 165, 235

Tet Offensive, 250–56
"three brigade rolling start" plans, 318
time
    buying, for political development, 289–93
    for success in Iraq, 266–67
train-and-transfer strategy, 287, 290, 313
    (See also Iraqi security forces)
Transitional Administrative Law, 9
troop availability, 93–100, 167–69, 179, 264–65, 339–40, 351
troop morale, 109–11, 179, 222, 285, 300
tyranny, ambitions to end, 11, 30

United Nations compound, attack on, 8

Vance, Cyrus, 379n21
Vessey, John, 376n28
Vickers, Mike, 63, 64, 69, 347
victory, meaning of, 256–59
Vietnam War
    and calls for withdrawal from Iraq, 33, 36
    escalation and Americanization, 241–50
    influence on Bush, 154
    influence on Iraq War, 263, 266, 354
    Jeffrey on withdrawal from Iraq and, 61
    lessons learned from, 74, 174
    and meaning of victory, 256–59
    similarities between Iraq War and, 239–41, 369–70n1, 371n3

Tet Offensive and Vietnamization, 250–56, 266
    troop increase during, 94
    and unfolding of political progress, 292, 293

war maintenance, 282–87
weapons of mass destruction (WMD), 208–9, 261
Westmoreland, William, 251, 369n6
Wise Men, 251–52, 254
Wolf, Frank, 41–42, 362
Wolf Brigade, 79
Woodward, Bob, 391n31
World War II, 376n24

al-Zarqawi, Abu Musab, 8, 9, 46–47, 70–71, 210, 336
    (See also al-Qaeda in Iraq)
al-Zawahiri, Ayman, 48
Zelikow, Philip
    on articulating strategy change, 60
    on clear, hold, and build strategy, 332, 380n39
    on cyclical pattern on intervention in Iraq, 280
    on December NSC meetings, 158
    on DoD's position on strategy change, 137
    on emergence of insurgency, 27–28
    on Iraqi security forces, 11, 285
    on lead up to Camp David, 66
    on National Security Council review, 101–2
    on National Strategy for Victory in Iraq, 38–39
    and need for strategy change, 59–60
    on November 11 meeting, 126
    on NSC and official strategy review, 145
    and official strategy review, 341
    on reports on Iraq, 333
    and State Department and official strategy review, 142–43
    on strategy in Iraq, 43
    on strategy review process, 339
    on strategy void, 280–81
    on surge process, 200, 329
    tenure of, 362
    on transition from insurgency to sectarian struggle, 47–48
    on troop availability, 93
    on war maintenance, 286
Zilmer, Richard, 185